The essays in *Fighting for Rome* confront the traumatic disjunction between the militarist culture of classical Rome, with its heavy investment in valour, conquest and triumph, and the domination of its history by civil war, where Roman soldiers killed so many Romans for control of Rome. The essays gathered and rewritten here range across the literary forms (history, satire, lyric and epic) and work closely with the ancient texts (Appian and Julius Caesar; Horace; Lucan and Statius; Tacitus and Livy). Close reading and powerful translation communicate the ancient writers' efforts to grasp and respond to the Roman civil wars, and to their product, Roman terror under the Caesars. The book aims to bring to life strong reactions to a world order run by civil war.

FIGHTING FOR ROME

FIGHTING FOR ROME

POETS AND CAESARS, HISTORY AND CIVIL WAR

John Henderson

Reader in Latin Literature,
University of Cambridge,
and Fellow of King's College

CAMBRIDGE
UNIVERSITY PRESS

PUBLISHED BY THE PRESS SYNDICATE OF THE UNIVERSITY OF CAMBRIDGE
The Pitt Building, Trumpington Street, Cambridge CB2 1RP, United Kingdom

CAMBRIDGE UNIVERSITY PRESS
The Edinburgh Building, Cambridge CB2 2RU, United Kingdom
40 West 20th Street, New York, NY 10011–4211, USA
10 Stamford Road, Oakleigh, Melbourne 3166, Australia

First published 1998

Printed in the United Kingdom at the University Press, Cambridge

Typeset in Plantin Medium and Greek New Hellenic

A catalogue record for this book is available from the British Library

Library of Congress cataloguing in publication data

Henderson, John Graham Wilmot.
Fighting for Rome : poets and Caesars, history and civil war / John Henderson.
    p.   cm.
Includes bibliographical references and index.
ISBN 0 521 58026 9 (hardback)
1. Latin literature – History and criticism. 2. Rome – History – Civil War,
49–48 BC – Literature and the war. 3. Rome – History – Civil War,
43–31 BC – Literature and the war. 4. Rome – History – Civil War,
49–48 BC – Historiography. 5. Rome – History – Civil War, 43–31 BC –
Historiography. 6. Epic poetry, Latin – History and criticism.
7. Horace – Political and social views. 8. Literature and
history – Rome. 9. War in literature. I. Title.
PA6019.H46 1998
870.9'359—dc21 97-6748 CIP

ISBN 0 521 58026 9 hardback

AO

Contents

Preface

Karen Henderson supported and endured the writing of these essays – and the re-writing. Mary Beard read through the whole typescript: she and Simon Goldhill have always been my first readers. Tony Boyle's belief allowed me to write free. My Faculty and my College constantly seethe with ideas. Cambridge Students make Classics a thrill. In particular, research with Joanne Brown on Statius, Emily Gowers on Satire and such, and Jamie Masters on Lucan is reflected in the relevant chapters. Shadi Bartsch on Lucan and Debra Hershkowitz on epic have also both made me think harder. Over the years Geoffrey Lloyd and Froma Zeitlin have helped me more than they know – but this list could easily get out of hand.

All the essays have been re-written for this book (but I retain the titles). Their inter-connection and length have extruded proper attention (e.g.) to Sallust, Virgil, and Tacitus' *Histories*, and all reference to Senecan drama (esp. *Thyestes*). I am indebted to the first editors for all their help, with wicked typescripts:

Chapter 1: John Moles, and *HISTOS* 1 (1996).

Chapter 2: Donald Mastronarde, and *CA* 15 (1996) 261–88 (by permission of the Regents of the University of California).

Chapter 3: Stephen Heyworth and Paul Millett, and *CQ* 44 (1994) 146–70 (by permission of Oxford University Press).

Chapter 4: Gian Biagio Conte and Alessandro Schiesaro, and *MD* (1997) (by permission of Giardini editori e stampatori in Pisa).

Chapter 5: Tony Boyle and John Penwill, and *Ramus* 16 (1987) = A. J. Boyle ed. (1988) *The imperial muse*, 1, Aureal Publications, Berwick, Vic.: 122–64.

Chapter 6: Philip Hardie, and *PCPhS* 37 (1991) 30–80, 'Form pre-made/Statius, *Thebaid*', combined with: Tony Boyle, and A. J. Boyle ed. (1993) *Roman epic*, London: 162–91, 'Statius, *Thebaid*/Form re-made' (by permission of Routledge).

Chapter 7: Tony Boyle and John Penwill, and *Ramus* 18 (1989) = A. J. Boyle ed. (1990) *The imperial muse*, II, Aureal Publications, Berwick, Vic.: 167–210.

Chapter 8: Averil Cameron, and A. Cameron ed. (1989) *History as text: the writing of ancient history*, London: 64–85 (by permission of Duckworth).

The book makes me a Hireling: my thanks to Pauline Hire for all her help. Susan Moore's editorial skills saved many a blush – and much more.

King's College, Cambridge and
Faculty of Classics, University of Cambridge

All dates are BCE except where indicated: *BC* means (Julius Caesar's, or Lucan's) *Bellum Ciuile*.

Maps are not provided – this is not that sort of book – but a date chart follows the text.

Introduction

Fighting for Rome means, as it meant for the Romans, fighting *over* Rome. The series of civil wars between Julius Caesar's crossing of the Rubicon in 49 and Octavian's victory at Actium in 31 overthrew the republican system of government and introduced the imperial régime of the Caesars. The dispute for control of the state revolutionized Roman experience thereafter. Classical Roman culture – between the mid first century BCE and the second century CE – invested heavily in the valour, conquest and triumph of ancestral militarism for its self-conception; yet a large proportion of the fighting and killing by Roman soldiers represented nothing but a conquest *of* Rome *by* Rome. This spectre amplified to become a total diagnosis of doom – the city built on Romulus' fratricide – and the story of Roman civil war retained a foundational role in political thought, for these events supplied terms for the re-negotiation of power-relations between each succeeding emperor and his subjects. The ascendancy, assassination and apotheosis of Julius Caesar, and the triumphant metamorphosis of his testamentary heir Octavian as the first Caesar Augustus, together provided paradigms and cautionary models from which the empire was *both* legitimized as a paternalist principate *and* reviled as tyrannical dictatorship. The politics of the Roman revolution have never lost their relevance to the princes and peoples of the West.

The essays in this collection, arranged in four pairs (Parts 1–4), explore how *fighting for Rome* coloured representations across the range of literary forms in Latin (but a Roman historian writing in Greek takes chapter 1). The strategy will be to focus on a series of particular texts. The object is to move between works that put the civil wars into writing, and writings that address their result, a dramatic shift in cultural mentality, sociolinguistics, and political reality. We begin by examining a pair of extended narratives of the civil wars, one in Greek prose and the other in Latin (part 1: chapters 1–2). Using the best contemporary accounts he could find and his own resources, Appian's dramatic and convincing version of the manhunt ordered by the second triumvirate of Antony, Lepidus and Octavian in 43 strives to deliver his readers to enormities of inhumanity across their distance from the events: writing up the despotic writing of death explosively impacts medium on message. Next, Julius Caesar, the Latin stylist. Caesar was, precisely, fighting for Rome in writing his version of his campaigns across the Roman world to hunt Pompey down in Egypt. The stylish effort to sanitize his invasion of Italy as simply a continuation of his campaigns in Gaul is a feat of manipulation that presents Caesar as simply a Roman commander, enormously successful in fighting and conquering for Rome, who had the misfortune to be prevented from a merited welcome home; steadfastly refusing to fight anything resembling a civil war, he pursued his muddled obstructors across the globe, as gently as he could, and then kept the peace for the Republic, as duly elected consul, all the way from outer Gaul to faraway Alexandria. Caesar the writer could not know that he was waging a campaign that inaugurated the invention of the emperor at Rome, but the power compacted into his (written) *Caesar* became the effective prototype for modelling autocratic rule.

The next pair of essays treat two short pieces of poetry by Horace, one a mischievous and unruly satire from between Octavian's wars against his father's tyrannicides, Caesar's assassins, and those against his former ally Antony; the other a sublime lyric looking back from the newly re-founded republic, the reign of Augustus, from a survivor who had lived through the turmoil (part II: chapters 3–4). The twenty-year interval, from the 40s to the 20s, has been remembered ever after as *the* Roman revolution: this first *Caesar Augustus* kept the role of model (or prototypical) monarch through the rest of Antiquity. The *satire* recounts an anecdote from the days when Horace had fought against Antony and Octavian, in the campaign of Philippi in 42 which cost Brutus and Cassius their cause and their lives. Through its re-told joke on Brutus' claim to live up to the example of the first Brutus, Brutus the Liberator who expelled the kings in Rome's first revolution and founded the Republic as its first magistrate, the tale pushes the politics of the Caesars before the readers. Horace writes with as *little* immediacy as he can of his own fighting for Rome as an intimate of Octavian. Horace's *ode*, too, reflects obliquely on his experience through the civil wars that had dominated his lifetime, and were ceremoniously closed in the celebrations in 23 for the restoration of consular elections, the permanent imposition of Augustus' powers. Horace uses his contemporary

Asinius Pollio as his intermediary figure, looking back from 23 over *his* shoulder. The poet empathizes with Pollio's experience – once a lieutenant of Julius Caesar by his side at the Rubicon; an active enthusiast of literature and the arts, and himself a celebrated tragedian; and the historian of the Caesarian and triumviral civil wars. Horace's retrospect impels the reader, too, to explore the shared and unshareable sense of tragedy at the cycles of civil carnage, and ask (over Pollio's and Horace's shoulders) what is history, to writer and reader, veteran and survivor? Who does it belong to? What are the politics of writing history? Where can a narrative of civil war(s) find or forge its necessary continuousness – without playing memories of turbulence and faction false? Fighting for Rome could be too hard to face. It could be more important to keep fighting over it, since the meaning of lives risked, staked and lost in the civil wars carried with it the legibility of the present and the chance to grasp where the world was going – fighting for the interpretation of Rome.

The second half of the book begins with a further pair of essays on poetry; but on the unHoratian grand scale of epic (part III: chapters 5–6). First, Lucan's *On the civil war* returns us to 49/8 and the war between Julius Caesar and Pompey already explored through Caesar's account (chapter 2). A century into the Julio-Claudian dynasty of *Caesares Augusti*, Nero's most explosive poet launches into a mighty campaign to fight Caesar off and stop history – head off emperors before they can arrive. In the process, he means to anticipate Virgil's *Aeneid*, permanently installed under Augustus as the national epic and colossal authority-text looming over all successors writing in Latin ever since.

For Virgil assumes – as he must – the perspective of post-Actium Rome of the 20s, and his project brings in the origins of Rome to sanction with divine unction the fateful destiny guiding the culture toward the ascendancy of Augustus as descendant of the *Iulii Caesares*, stemming from Aeneas through his son *Iulus*, and so ultimately re-motivating Homer's account of the Trojan war in the *Iliad* and *Odyssey* epics. Where Virgil's saga of Rome arising from the ashes of Troy turns the survivor refugees of Homer into the founders of the world state, Lucan moves in to try to forestall Julius Caesar's legacy of power to his adoptive heir Octavian through his fighting for Rome.

Virgil's moment to 'realize' (in both senses) the essential destiny of Caesarian primacy in Rome depended on a particular construction of the political stakes after Actium. Or, to put this the right way round,

the attempt to persuade the first 'Augustans' that the time was a funda-
mental moment of epistemic shift, which permitted the past up to
Actium to be seen, for the first time, as the strongly determined trajectory toward the present dispensation (chapter 8), depended not least
on the mythopoeic power and prestige of Virgil's writing. 'Virgil' was the
abiding 'Augustus' of literature – impressing a dominant view of Rome
on Romans that was renewed with each generation's reading, schooled
under each succeeding *Caesar Augustus*.

Lucan's poem of outrage regresses to *his* 'true beginning' of Rome –
as in the account written by Pollio, from much closer range: the First
Triumvirate (60/59) bearing poisonous fruit in 49/8 from the Rubicon
through the battle of Pharsalus. His writing shows in every line how the
materialization of Rome in Latin language and thought had been per-
vasively saturated with Caesarism. The future would forever be an
after-effect of the fighting for Rome. Lucan's own position as a precocious courtier in the precocious court of Nero abruptly ceased in 65 CE,
when this Caesar – '*Nero Claudius* Caesar Augustus *Germanicus pontifex
maximus tribunicia potestate pater patriae*' – liquidated him for con-
spiring his assassination. Lucan writes away the distance that separated
his world from Pharsalus, living in its wake under an emperor whose
great-grandfather was the Domitius Ahenobarbus we met being over-
run by Julius (in chapter 2): this same ancestor was the most notable
(or: only) casualty at Pharsalus among the great Republican aristocrats
who fought for Rome against Caesar. The fame-machine of Rome kept
fresh the story of the advent of the post-Augustan autocracy; revisionary interpretations extended their force into the formation of Roman
identities, careers and politics (chapter 7). Fighting for interpretation of
the fighting for Rome was an active front in the power-struggle in
Nero's Rome.

The story of Lucan's last words shows us how to read his work: he
died reciting some of his own verses on a soldier dying from wounds.
(Tac. *Ann.* 15.70.1: chapter 7). We shall find that *BC* blends life and
writing no less dramatically. Four years later, and Nero and the Julio-
Claudians were history. In 69 CE, civil wars tore through three emperors before Vespasian fastened control on Rome for himself and his
sons. The second dynasty decided, or else it was beyond negotiation,
to call its leader, still, *Imperator* Caesar *Vespasianus* Augustus *pontifex
maximus tribunicia potestate pater patriae*, legitimating their usurpation
at the price of blurring into their predecessors. The court of the

Flavians, as we call them, hosted its own epics, but none on the historical subject of their origins in fighting for Rome: Jason took another *Argo* to fleece fairytale Colchis of his heirloom, with witch-princess for bonus (Valerius Flaccus); Hannibal threatened to abort republican Rome all over again, as if the troubles had never brewed, and Lucan's Caesar, Virgil's Augustus, and Rome's emperors never been (Silius Italicus). A third – an extravaganza as pyrotechnical as Lucan – is explored in chapter 6: Statius' *Thebaid*.

To write his *maius opus*, the lyric and epic poet Statius moved no less far from Roman civil war, whether between 60/59 and 31, or in 68/9 CE. His *Thebaid*, however, does more than pre-fix itself to Homeric–Virgilian Troy by selecting the old saga of the *Seven against Thebes*. Throughout Antiquity 'Thebes' had *always* been the imploded city of suicidal fratricide – ruination in (worse than) civil war. Statius' atrocious poem inhabits a senseless universe of horrific cruelty, without the least sign of Rome, Julii, Flavians. But the free play of his imaginary world of histrionic diabolism is, inescapably, entirely made of Roman signs. Every word asks why Statius occupied a dozen years from the apotheosis of Vespasian composing his grotesque inferno. We have explored before why writers might write indirectly of Caesarian civil war (chapter 3 *versus* chapter 4). Statius does not *not* write of *bellum ciuile*, whether or not a Caesar, an adoptive-Caesar, or wannabe Caesar fights across his pages; whether the fighting is for Thebes, not Rome. The imperial cosmos of post-Augustan culture had long since fully incorporated Greek alongside Roman myth-making in its image-repertoire – whether Theban Polynices and Eteocles; Tarquin and Brutus; or Brutus and –

This book's half on poetry is spent. The final pair of essays (part IV: chapters 7–8) returns to historical narratives in prose. Tacitus' *Annales* and Livy's *Ab urbe condita* are in fact *the* great historical works in Latin. In neither can we read of the civil wars between Sulla, or the crossing of the Rubicon, and Octavian's Actium, or the invention of *Caesares Augusti*. As we shall see (chapter 8), Livy's manuscripts fail us and fade out – at only his forty-fifth book – back in the early second century, with the conquests of Macedon and Syria, less than a third of the way through his huge history of Rome 'From the foundation'. Written in the forty-odd years between the triumph of Octavian and his eventual apotheosis as Augustus, Livy's story originally put much of the time of its writing into words.

Tacitus (chapter 7) does narrate civil war fighting for Rome: he wrote his *Histories* as monument to Rome's second dynasty, the Flavians, starting from the beginning of 69 CE as a survivor of the assassination of Domitian in 96 CE. His eyewitness account of the declension of the dynasty which backed his own rise to prominence at court is lost to us, but Tacitus dwells for the four and a bit books we do have on the successive waves of conflict and massacre in Italy and Rome through this Year of the Four Emperors (uncomfortably like re-writing Caesar: chapter 3). On completion of this project, Tacitus turned, not to address the (need he say? 'felicitous': *sc.* 'present' – here, now, 'us') times of Nerva–Trajan–Hadrian's third dynasty, but back a century to the Julio-Claudians. For his start, he chooses to accept neither Julius Caesar's nor Octavian–Augustus' revolutions as determining the imperial era of power at Rome. Instead, he defines the world he lived in by introducing us to the ascension of Augustus and succession of Tiberius in 14 CE, *Ab excessu diui Augusti*. The success of succession is where the perpetuation of *Caesares Augusti* was decided – and modelled for the future. The goal of Tacitus' *Annals*, where he writes as secondary historian, about events before his experience, is pre-set as the demise of the first dynasty with Nero, in 68 CE, to link with the inception of the *Histories*. Clearly, Tacitus' overall project was to trace the stages in which autocratic government of Rome took shape as a 'system', not simply the apparatus of victors in fighting for Rome, but the replication of the first *Caesar Augustus* in the dozen known to Tacitus; and the replication of the first through the third dynasties he could review.

In this book, the reign of Nero, presented as an ultimate unhinging of despotism, is the chosen focus: with chilling irony, Tacitus' horrendous descent on the delirium of Nero's final phase, the end of the dynasty established by Augustus, is as lost as his narrative on Domitian's descent into the reign of terror that no doubt sparked his elimination. Leaving 69 CE to Statius' fighting for '*Thebes*' (chapter 6), we turn instead to the lifetime of Lucan and *his* Caesar (chapter 5). Tacitus' contribution will be to expose the impossibility of fighting against Caesars as the definition of imperial Rome. His return to the Julio-Claudians to expose the process by which autocracy came to be articulated shows how Empire consists in the subversion of Republican titles, concepts and discourses. Without needing to say so. The régime of terroristic civil oppression is manifested in sensational tales of distant crises, of psychosis and dementia. In Nero, the best- and worst-qualified Augustus to play emperor, the historian could portray a world that could make no sense. Was it his own world (and – all – successive worlds?) that was in pieces? Was it not?

The final chapter considers another survivor (like Horace and Pollio: chapter 4). Livy would not normally be treated alongside Caesar and Tacitus, let alone Lucan and Statius, but that is an accident of history. One which deserves to be set out, and (since history admits no accidents) scrutinized. As the writer of the definitive history of Rome '*From the Foundation*', Livy epitomizes the founding challenge to the classic historical narrative: to find a reason to begin. As we explore (in chapters 4, 7), the most important stake in beginning such a text is the presumption that the moment of writing may be posed as the end of the story; otherwise the claim of the account to be informed by a strong grip on its subject is radically undermined.

Traditionally, history-writing has been installed in the Western academy as an institution practising what we may dub willed/wilful imposition – the exegesis of authenticated events from an 'Olympian' perspective, guaranteed by the austere facticity and self-denying impersonality of its rhetoric. But to encompass this goal, the historian must be in control: the reason why a particular past may now be told, and told authoritatively, is because the nexus of the present permits it to be surveyed and grasped within this perspective – for the first time, or as never before. The inherent circularity which enables historians to turn their dependence on this epistemological teleology into the platform for dispensing a powerful interpretation of the present, in its construction, emergence, and trajectory towards the future, is the definitive mark of the prestige of historical writing. Writing history, culture explains itself to itself. Historians could address a less assertive topic than Tacitus or Livy: continuation of an existent narrative was perhaps the most common alternative. But once the text styles itself a 'total' account, it nails itself to the thesis that a major shift in perspective founds and shapes the project. Readers will need to read through the narrative if they are, eventually, to join the writer's understanding, when pen first hit paper.

In Livy's case, we face a voluminous writer – author of more words than any of the other writers explored in this book – who spent a lifetime on his monumental history of Rome. It is worth considering what we would be supposing if we attributed to him a robust intellection of his story as he began. The essay presses us to consider, further, what happens to the dynamic logic of his work when (as we remarked) he survives to write on, past the date when he first started to produce. Livy's was a vast exercise of applied will, which requires comprehension within the cultural politics of the emergence of Augustan from triumviral power-and-knowledge. The chapter is drastically cut short – like Livy. For his account of the fighting for Rome is entirely lost, and we need to ask why, and what it has done to our idea of his history *Ab urbe condita*.

We *cannot* do justice to Livy (let alone Pollio, whose writing is entirely lost); by the same token, this book can only betray Appian and Dio, whose accounts of the late Republic and early Empire (the only extended narratives extant) *can* be read, but whose MSS lapse before they can reach their own times, and show us where they have been coming from since they began: for us, Appian stops just when he touches base, ready to begin his Egyptian history; for the last quarter of Dio we have only epitomes, fragments, excerpts – after an abrupt halt in the middle of 46 CE. With Caesar, our only narrator of his own story, the position is the reverse: only the writer does not know where his 'notes' were going – and is caught trying to make sure his readers don't either. Horace is caught trying to make his readers *un*sure what he would say, had he to narrate. Lucan expects no justice; Statius knew to expect only the poetic kind. Tacitus speaks for his own times – up to a point: yesterday. Yet, if we can hear their say, these writers all along fight for Rome.

The essays in this book belong to their world, too. They try to think what and how Rome may have been; but thinking (with) Rome is also a way to relate, if not cope with, the one-world we live in and our representations of the unspeakable.[1]

---

[1] Not least, Northern Ireland, Romania, Iraq, Bosnia, Rwanda, Bosnia, Iraq, Romania, Ireland and [...] are here, you would find, between the lines I tried to write.

PART I

Histories of the civil wars

Three men in a vote: proscription
    (Appian, *Civil wars* 4.1–6)

List, sirs, and may this bloody record be a warning to future tyrants.[1]

This first chapter introduces a text written in gritty, no-nonsense *Greek* by a Hellenic Egyptian in the second century CE, as part of his comprehensive coverage of history seen as a series of Roman conquests that progressively interlinked regions of the known world, until Rome eventually incorporated Egypt into the world state of the Roman Empire. This was a by-product of the defeat of Antony and Cleopatra by Julius Caesar's heir Octavian. The battle of Actium in 31 ushered in his ascendancy as the first emperor, Caesar Augustus. Appian was a Roman citizen, but (clearly) with his own distinctive perspective. His work takes pains to find detailed and, where possible, contemporary Roman accounts of the eras he covers. As he treats the first century's agonies of civil war, his narrative seeks to combine circumstantially retailed precision with emotional investment in the traumas. But his project was to bring the narrative of *pax Romana* (global power) to debouch, finally, on his own Antonine times (with its Trajanic legacies of Dacia and Arabia).

As often with the history of Rome, as we shall reflect in chapters 4 and 8, the 'immediate' accounts have not survived. However, the throes of the Late Republic remained the foundational scene for the rest of imperial Antiquity. Just as the string of crises stayed with the participants through the rest of their lives (chapters 3–4), and affected their descendants' sense of their political identities and possibilities for generations (chapter 7), so for centuries the apparatus of imperial ideology kept present and dynamic the narration and revisionary renarration of the civil wars as the legitimation of the political order of the Caesars. As we shall consider, Augustus' metamorphosis from Octavian and his transcendence of Julius Caesar, his father by testamentary adoption, was the ever-fresh parable of autocratic power at Rome. It never became ancient history; it was always an operator of

[1] Walpole (1969) 109.

political contestation. In the effort to re-capture, to invent anew, this story, ancient Romans plunged their readers into engagement with the events. Whatever their tendency, the writers impel us to join the horror.

The focus of this chapter is on *proscription*, the writing of death in the form of public listing of heads wanted for a reward. We shall consider how this demonic invention of the civil wars was no momentary nightmare, but cast long shadows over the future. And we shall register how this writing used, and supplemented, murderous lists in an inescapably perverse ordering of society – and generated a killer of a subject for its historians. This is a specially reflexive case of the general challenge to communicate the scale and severity of suffering for all who would respond adequately to the fighting for Rome. You will soon see why this essay's sections are numbered as a count-down; and why the lists are counted out in Roman style ((i), (ii), (iii), *ad infinitum* ...).

5 WRITE EVERY WRONG

> You are a difficult case. But don't give up hope. Everyone is cured sooner or later. In the end we shall shoot you.[2]

We *write* history. Writing construes – imagines, crystallizes and analyses – history. Writing involves us in history mimetically, and in turn history is programmed in writing. Writing so pervaded and staked out the Hellenistic culture of Rome that it dictated the social formation and dominated the civic image-repertoire. Public figures wrote – politicians and orators, generals and poets, emperors and historians. Their texts – from military *communiqués* (chapter 2) to epic verses (chapters 5–6) – were important vectors of sense that arose from and fed back into the social 'text'. Public life was constructed and contested through the flood of writing that constantly monitored, shifted and revised the *status quo* of intelligibility. Continuity between primary official edict that delimited, mandated, sanctioned, terms and categories of behaviour, and reflective commentary on the significance of such peremptory formulae, was as obtrusive a fact of Roman existence as discourse contesting primacy between the many different institutions of writing – whether on paper, or bronze, or whatever.

The players in history already wrote their own narratives into the

---

[2] Orwell (1954) 220.

acts they authored; historicality was built right into the conceptualization of political action. When Roman statesmen glossed their decrees,
they knew they were writing themselves onto the pages of history.
Conversely, they knew, and so did Roman writers, that the narratives
to which the Roman world subscribed were never in the gift of the
players, but always beyond their command. The most absolute determination of a procedure, complete with bound-in prescription to
guarantee how it was to be thought, was already caught within the
contingencies of its sponsorship, and must take its turn in the stocks
of history, mocked by inclusion in the roll-call of attempts at self-
validation. The next such gesture of sovereign power would be no less
peremptorily imperative than its predecessor, but no more proof
against re-interpretation.

If history writing framed, shaped and controlled historical action,
nevertheless (Romans learned the lesson time and again) historical
action inevitably misread, eluded and thwarted the narrative scripts set
for it; but only as the replacement with another history, no less liable
to be displaced. Writing history could change anything, everything –
could (p)re-write history.

Historical narratives blur their stake in proposing terms for their own
interpretation with their interest in the legibility of the social text for
the actor-participants, who must read *events* as they occur. Historians
face a dilemma: are they power-merchants out to control and direct
reading of their stories, authorizing the apportionment of clarity and
intelligibility that their narrations dispense? Or, however masterful,
must they share, like it or not, in the aporias that engulf other social
actors, including the characters they write (with)? There is always a
self-reflexive dimension to the reading of historical narrative, and when
the narrative, in focussing on a critical written document, parades as
itself a relatively explicit instance of writing-as-'reading', this is to the
fore.

As narrative composition, history at such moments displays its own
status as part of, as well as apart from, the 'writing/reading' that constitutes its characters' experience: the participants live out their readings,
may die for and be nailed to them; historians, whether or not their
coevals, must model their own readings from, with and against, over and
above, these animated (mis)readings, committing themselves in their
own writing to a particular position before their readers' re-readings
in (both) their presents. On occasion, writing history proved suicidal.

Romans developed a keen regard for what kinds of appropriations of their own behaviour would commend themselves to contemporary historians and historians to come, and could model readings that would confute their host writings and might convict them of perhaps wilful, woeful, misreading of history. Roman writers knew that their characters lived, by their own lights, as *exempla* (paradigmatic figures) before the fact, meant themselves to become interpretants of the future. We shall see in the next chapter that some classical writings posed as speech-acts designed to deliver and impose monological messages; but the inclusivity of the major genres of narrative (epic in verse and history in prose) ensures that no item of writing was, or can be, out of the reach of dissent, dispute, displacement. Their resounding prestige should rather ensure polyphonous interpretation as the norm. These are multiple readings, and there to be read.

The text for this chapter résumés within its ambit the history of the implosion of the all-conquering Roman Republic; inaugurally emblematizes the transformation of the world into the monarchic autocracy of the *Caesares Augusti* which has remained the aetiological parable of power in Roman political thought to this day; indelibly baptizes the generation of Roman statesmen and writers who at once incarnated and figure the apogee of civilized sensibility at Rome, along with every word they or 'their' emperor Augustus ever penned or incised; and pressures its every writer/reader to stare into the viral horror of contagious writing programmed to enlist for legalized slaughter all who stand in its way, in infinite regression. Can you keep your head, your humanity, while all about you are losing theirs?

Appian's text writes around the text of an 'edict' (the *Appendix* translates his version). He reads the manhunt initiated by Lepidus, Antony and Octavian on entering Rome to be quasi-legally invested by the (mockery of the) *Lex Titia*, three men in one vote, with the task of restoring the state in late 43.[3] The approach will be to explore the logic of the death-list it prefaced, both within the episode in Appian that turns on it, and within the politics of the historical narrative. As we shall see, the 'edict' cannot be transcribed, only summarized away into normalcy: its point was to doom by naming, yet it was a vital part of the horror that the list was constantly open to re-writing and never fixed: Appian's text must elide precisely this – and repair the damage by

[3] Cf. App. *BC* 4.2.7.

narrating the *process* of writing-to-death. We open here the poisonous textuality of triumviral terrorism: *proscription*.[4]

4 THREE FOR THE PRICE OF ONE

proscriptionis miserrimum nomen illud[5]

The triumviral proscription is set in counterpoint to the civil war against the forces led by Julius Caesar's former lieutenants and now his assassins, Brutus and Cassius, gathering massive strength in the East (chapter 3). Despite mutual antipathy and distrust, the Caesarian leaders Antony, Lepidus and Octavian, have come together in a coalition brokered by their lesser brethren, especially Pollio and Plancus; they have united against the Pompeians grouped around Pompey's surviving son Sex. Pompeius; and the bulk of the body of senators now need to be deterred from further initiatives. They are taught a lesson in the elimination of their ring-leaders who had organized offensives against Antony, had had him declared a public enemy, and who then did the same for Lepidus when he joined Antony. Throwing in his lot with these outlaws carried the same implications for Octavian's position. Underlying the drama may have been the eruption of an explosion of 'latent forces' in what amounted to 'a social revolution',[6] but what captures the attention is the intromission of civil war within the walls of Rome.[7]

From the start, we need to check what kind of control this narrative claims: could this have been anywhere near so pre-planned, logical, calculated a sequence as my précis just intimated? Was proscription a routine?

Proscriptions were, particularly for (Greek and Roman) readers of Greek history, far from an unprecedented *genus* of atrocity. We might think, for example, of the Reign of Terror of The Thirty in Athens at the end of the Peloponnesian War, with their variously circumscribed

---

[4] On Appian's version of the προγραφή, see esp. Wallmann (1989) 43–51, 'Das Proskriptionsedikt', Bengtson (1972) 10–13, Hinard (1985) 227–30, 'L'edictum', Canfora (1980) 430–4, 'L'editto triumvirale (Appian. IV, 8–11)'.

[5] 'Proscription: the saddest word in Latin', Cic. *De dom.* 43.

[6] Canfora (1980) 435; Syme (1939) 194, finessed by Hinard (1985) 303–5, 'Terrorisme'.

[7] So App. *BC, Praef.* 1.2, 4.3.14. For powerful modern narrations-*cum*-commentaries of the events, cf. esp. Syme (1939) 187–201, 'The proscriptions', Bengtson (1972). For structural analysis, cf. Canfora (1980), Millar (1973), Bleicken (1990) 41–51.

lists of citizens, their legalized elimination even of close associates and intimates, the killings they ordered.[8] But the *species* 'proscription', marked out in Latin by its new (euphemistic, or menacingly mock-euphemistic) locution, and as such a problem for Greek, English, or whatever history narratives to register, was affixed to just two fateful moments of fatality. The Latin *proscribo* (+*aliquem*) was Sulla's contribution (in 82/81) to the European fund of barbarous terms for barbarity: 'Evil à la Sulla: proscription'.[9]

'*Sulla was first to proscribe* enemies to death ... Sulla proscribed killing on sight, for vast bounties and for ditto penalties for concealment.' Sulla 'proscribed them to death. For he it seems to be who *first proscribed* those inflicted with the death penalty, and inscribed bounties for killing, rewards for information leading to discovery, penalties for concealment.' Appian declares that 'the same sort of things happened under Sulla, and before him Marius', but, he writes, the triumviral proscriptions were 'all the more a living memory because they were *the last ones*'.[10]

At Rome, then, *proscription* was distinguished as a style of barbarity in a class of its own.[11] And proscription never lost its Sullan ring: thus, Cicero felt sure Pompey would emulate his teacher, 'for his mind is Sullavatin' 'n' proscripturatin' long since'.[12] And, as we shall consider in chapter 3, when the poet Horace turned *his* experience of 43 into a satirical parable for the 30s, the emblematic *proscriptus* that stepped into his lines, a certain Rupilius Rex, *had* to come from *Praeneste* because of what Sulla did when he stormed the Marians there, the moment before he invented proscription: 'he separated them from each other into three lots – Romans, Samnites, Praenestines; the Romans he

---

[8] Xen. *Mem.* 2. When Appian picks out the proscriptions as unparalleled among Hellenes in *stasis* or war (*BC* 4.1.1), he thinks especially of Thucydides on the Corcyraean *stasis* (3.82), signalling it by the Thucydidean editorial flourish, cf. Gowing (1992) 265f.

[9] *Sullani exempli malum: proscriptio*, Vell. 2.66.1.

[10] App. *BC* 4.1.1; 1.11.95: ἐπὶ θανάτῳ προγραφαί are also picked out as a particularly grim feature of the collapse of Rome in the *Preface*, 1.1.2, 1.5, cf. 4.1.1 (ἐπὶ θ. ... ἐς θ.); 4.3.16.

[11] Cf. Nippel (1995) 55f., 83f. for overlap and difference between proscription and its close kin; to an uncomfortable extent, Sulla's proscription must be imagined from its triumviral after-image, cf. Hinard (1985) 10.

[12] *ita sullaturit animus eius et proscripturit iam diu*, Cic. *Att.* 9.10.6; cf. Quintil. 8.6.32.

pardoned, ... all the rest he had used for target-practice ... The town he had them loot, top to tail.'[13]

When the triumviral proscription came in 43, it was christened a return, a 'son-of-Sulla' scenario, from what would one day be dubbed 'Sulla's student trio': 'those killings which once Sulla had used, from proscriptions, were repeated ... All the rest that had been done before in Sulla's day occurred at this time too.' It was worse, as rhetorical conceit has it, because Sulla's people had been 'improvising and experimentally innovating'; and because 'only Sulla's and his henchmen's enemies died, not his friends or other people ... apart from the odd multimillionaire'. Our other preserved narrative, from the third-century Greek of Dio Cassius, quotes the triumvirs as telling the People of Rome they 'hadn't emulated either the brutality of Marius and Sulla ... or the clemency of Caesar'.[14] After a decade of research (*c.* 201–211 CE), Dio wrote *Romaic History*, from the beginning to the death of Septimius Severus (211 CE), until 223 CE; then wrote on, *into* his own times, during lulls in his career at court, until retirement after the honour/frustration of his second consulship, with his emperor Severus Alexander for colleague, in 229 CE: writing his 80 books saw Septimius Severus, Geta, Caracalla, Macrinus, Elagabalus, come and go, and Severus Alexander arrive in the palace. The violence of Roman revolution, in any century, was not for him a theme from ancient history.

In Appian's version of the text of the triumviral *Proskriptionsedikt*,[15] they confess, in the full shame/shamelessness of denial:[16]

> We shall go hard on no swathe of people; we shall not regard as personal enemies all who opposed or schemed against us; nor for wealth on its own, or opulence, or status, or in the numbers that another supremo before us killed, when he too was ordering the state in a civil

---

[13] Hor. *Sat.* 1.7.1, 28, App. *BC* 1.10.94; Liv. *Per.* 88, *omnes Praenestinos inermes concidi iussit* ('he ordered all the disarmed Praenestines cut down').

[14] *Sullae ... discipuli tres*, Juv. 2.28; Dio 47.3.1, 2; 47.4.1, 5.1; 47.13.4, cf. Rich (1989) 96f., Gowing (1992) 251.

[15] Appian has re-touched a version of the edict, rather than dreamed it up, cf. Wallmann (1989) 43. As with the other 'document' of the proscription episode, the speech of Hortensia (4.5.32f.), Appian has originated little of the thought, or wording, but by the same token the actors in 43 originated precious little of it, too. Oddly enough, Appian's *uirago* Hortensia has aroused much less scepticism than the edict.

[16] Cf. Canfora (1980) 430.

war, the one you dubbed '*Felix*' for his success – though three must of necessity have more enemies than one.[17]

Within this tumbling sentence it is not clear how many of the denials relate to Sulla, as the euphemisms cling to 'us' and the 'killing' to Sulla, while 'our' rhetoric dashes on, through mild anacoluthon, to solicit felicitations and end in a 'witticism'.[18] So too the entire document, together with its surrounding narrational commentary and festoon of accompanying narratives, prods readers into comparison between the first and second proscriptions. Can we see how alike, how unlike they are – and how the comparisons are muddied, as they are forced upon us, by the triumviral denials? How the narrator plays false the thrust of the differences claimed in the edict?[19] How polluting the business of precisely calibrating the worst outrages perpetrated in the name of Roman law must be? Writing history, we are put in the same triumviral business of writing death. Everyone was, and is.

3 THREE'S A CROWD

Sulla potuit, ego non potero?[20]

The triumvirs of 43 let be the unshareable and abjured *dictatura* (dictatorship) favoured by Sulla and by Julius – however impressively it

---

[17] App. *BC* 4.2.10.

[18] The inconcinnity of the final arithmetic (cf. the same juggling in Dio 47.3.3) does not just betray hasty composition (Wallmann (1989) 49), or attribute it to the triumvirs, but projects the conceptual menace of the edict onto its tonality: this is the moment where the 'psychic terrorism', topically modulated as self-proclaimed *tutum, iustum, pium, modestum*, hits the rhetorical reef of brute 'necessity' in triplicate (the triumcolon of ἀνάγκης ... ἀνάγκη ... ἀνάγκη, *loc. cit.*; cf. the *color* that opens the προγραφή: ἠναγκαζόμεθα, 4.8); it is also the moment where the edict toys with the calculations it prompts in the minds of the audience: is anyone relieved that numbers will 'not exceed' (the several thousands of) Sulla's massacres? The throwaway clausula at once pushes expectations back up to hover *only just* below the Sullan figure – with the tease that *ceteris paribus* a 300% increase should be obligatory under a triple dictatorship.

[19] Cf. Gowing (1992) 251: 'As the surrounding narrative makes abundantly clear, where each of the pledges ... is methodically refuted, the edict was a masterpiece of sophistic propaganda. Appian's debunking began in ... a direct contradiction of the edict's terms. The intervening chapters ... further undercut the triumvirs' promises.'

[20] 'Nobody stopped Sulla – try stopping me', Cic. *Att.* 9.10.2.

may have served as model for the way to manufacture 'legality'[21] – and surprised Rome with proscriptions *before* their war.[22] Sulla's proscriptions had mopped up losers in the aftermath of battle: if Brutus and Cassius had prevailed at Philippi, they should have marched in his footsteps. Sullan proscription was *not* the way to vindicate filial piety toward Julius Caesar, whose background was with Sulla's enemy Marius. The publicly ceremonied and statutory triumvirate, if it did replay Caesarian politics, was bound to fissure into a re-run of the internecine progress of the first, private and unofficial, compact of 59. Who would be the Crassus? Who would play Pompey? *Not* Pompey's son? The bizarreries of historical precedent are a symptomatic facet of the unravelling of cultural poetics in crisis. Reading what was happening, what the triumvirs were doing and what was being done to Rome, could only operate in terms of the Sullan script of proscription. The connections could even seem to dictate, to prescribe, the *coup*. But were the similarities what would count, or the differences – or would it, for example, be the dissimulation of either of these?

A synopsis of ironic (p)re-writes would include the following brief but indicative tally:

(i) It was right, one and all could agree, that the *Labienus* 'who arrested and murdered many people in the Sullan proscriptions' should become a triumviral victim in 43; yet it was all wrong that he should 'feel dishonoured if he didn't take his medicine nobly, stepping out front of his home and taking a pew as he awaited his killers'.[23]

(ii) What should it mean that *Brutus' father* was a victim of Sulla's proscriptions?

(iii) That, limping *into* Rome on two good legs, *Q. Lucretius Vespillo* 'got to the city-gate where *his* father, proscribed by Sulla, had been captured, and saw a cohort of legionaries coming out at the double' – Vespillo's faithful slave support hid with him in a tomb, saved him from grave-robbers, and got him safely into

---

[21] Cic. *De leg.* 1.42 claims the interregnal *Lex Valeria Flacci* empowered Sulla as dictator 'to kill any citizen he pleased, even without a hearing for the charges', cf. App. *BC* 1.11.98. Augustus' 'life tribunate' could have been cloned from the Sullan dictatorship, voted 'not for a fixed term, but … at his pleasure' (ibid.). But *Sulla resigned* …

[22] Hinard (1985) 306.

[23] App. *BC* 4.4.26: Hinard (1985) 480f., no. 69.

his wife's false ceiling, stored till his pardon, and an eventual Augustan consulate (in 19)?

(iv)-(v)   Along with the *fathers of* the Antonian *L. Marcius Censorinus* (praetor 43), *and of* Antony's conqueror *C. Vibius Pansa* (the deceased consul of 43)?

(vi)-(vii)   The otherwise forgotten *L. Fidustius* and the dangerously well-connected tyrannicide sympathizer and husband of Pompeia, widow of Sulla's son and Pompey's daughter, *L. Cornelius Cinna*, both managed to get onto *both* the proscription lists, leaving the latter's sons, L. Cinna, Octavian's consul (in 32), and Cn. Cinna Magnus, Augustus' (5 CE), with a memorable family narrative to weave and bequeath.

(viii)   And a certain *Maecenas* was on the list in 82/81, too – some relation of Octavian's prime adviser.[24]

The symmetries and asymmetries in history shaped as repetition with(in) difference are precisely the ideal materials of paradoxography, and a drily sado-dispassionate eye reminds us, of Appian's and Dio's series of proscript anecdotes, that 'these stories went a long way towards compensating the lack of prose fiction among the Romans'.[25] But the fictionality, or otherwise, of the anecdotes plentifully supplied by Appian as the wake of proscription, is of far less moment than the effort which they represent, and pass on to us – the effort to encompass the senselessness, the destruction of sense, which the mapping of perverted human relations must pin to the triumvirate. Appian himself dubs these tales 'images', as replete with mimetic power as the ancestral Roman *imagines* such as Brutus', cherished by his old *quaestor*, the last proscript in the ledger – left with congratulations from Augustus for his fidelity.[26] These gripping images deliver their graphic messages.

We saw how the second junta was made from memories. To look back to the second triumvirate from the perspective of those who sur-

---

[24] Bruti: App. *BC* 2.16.111, Hinard (1985) 361–3, no. 35; Vespillones: App. *BC*. 4.6.44, Hinard (1985) 368f., no. 41; 491f., no. 84.; Censorini: 37, no. 46; Pansa: Dio 45.17.1, Hinard (1985) 408–10, no. 74; Fidustius: 353, no. 26, 468f., no. 56; Cinna: 343f., no. 17; 457f., no. 46; Maecenas: 369f., no. 42.

[25] Syme (1939) 190 n. 6, as ever giving an enhanced paraphrase in vindication of his beloved ancient sources, cf. App. *BC* 4.3.15, οὕτως ὁ καιρὸς ἦν ἐκεῖνος ἐπίδειξις παραδοξολογίας.

[26] εἰκόνες, App. *BC* 4.4.21, εἰκόνας, 6.51.

vived into post-Actian Rome, provokes similar thoughts (chapters 3–4). But first we need to consider briefly how historical narratives of the period are bound to echo and shadow the experience of these survivors. The project of 'tracking down the source(s)' (*Quellenforschung*) long tried to crack open 'secondary' narratives such as Appian's *Civil wars*, a segment of his lengthy *Romaika* (before he caught up with his own century in the last couple of books, 23–4 on the Dacian and Arabian Wars), along the seams of contrary attitudes expressed in particular passages towards particular figures or factions. These antinomies were huffed into contradictions which could then be puffed into diagnostic indications of shifts between subjection to one particular dominant source after another.[27] Did Suetonius *not* copy out the hype on Augustus from one narrative, the sleaze from another? Don't the former and the latter resemble respectively their equivalents in Appian and Dio? Can we *not* guess that (to pick out a triumvirate of historians) Pollio, who gave up his father-in-law to the blacklist,[28] Messalla, whose name glittered on it, and Livy, innocent of all this, took rather different lines on this issue? (Pollio: chapter 4; Livy: chapter 8). Of course, more recent efforts have productively concentrated on registering the devotions of monumental projects such as Appian's, or Dio's (who will also become a primary historian of his own lifetime, as he eventually reaches the 'point' of his project) – *in their own writes*.[29] Such revaluation has the potential to whittle down our notions of the distance between our activities *qua* narrative historians of Antiquity and those of our 'sources' – in particular, to jettison bogus superiority and scientistic *folies de grandeur*. But, more than this, the grist stripped out by *Quellenforschung* can feed straight into our mill, once it is re-assigned to contrary imaginings *within*, not between, individual reckonings of their subjects. Did not Suetonius firmly commit himself to an Augustus with two faces, duly fissured by contradiction?[30] Can anyone today entertain an integrated portrait of Augustus minus the ambivalence of fragmentation – without, that is, feeling their implication in the holistic

---

[27] Gabba (1956) urged a heavy and inert dependence on Pollio's *Histories* (225f. on the edict) on just these lines (cf. Zecchini (1982) 1290f.; *contra*: Canfora (1996)). The most sensitive modern investigation of the sort is Pelling (1979).

[28] App. *BC* 4.3.12: L. Quinctius, Hinard (1985) 511, no. 112, cf. Nisbet and Hubbard (1978) 168, on Hor. *Carm.* 2.11 (and chapter 4).

[29] See esp. Rich (1989) 91; Gowing (1992) 247–69, 'The proscriptions'.

[30] For a review, cf. Gabba (1984) 61–88.

politics of autocracy, as well (no doubt) as anarchy? So the narratives lived by those who survived to become Augustus and his imperial subjects must incorporate dissonance, cope with contrariety, and never, ever, obliviate barbarous uncreation.

2 WHOSE COUNTING?

Die Tage der Menschenjagd haben sich unauslöschlich in das Gedächtnis der Zeitgenossen eingegraben.[31]

Appian's narrative, where triumviral Octavian will be transfigured into the monarch Augustus who set the mould for the Antonine world inhabited by this Alexandrian *procurator Augusti*, is bound to the task of damning the barbarity of civil war (as interruption to the subsumption of other peoples' histories within that of conquest by Rome). History slows to a crawl, a near stand-still, between 44 and 42, from the Ides of March through Philippi (as in Dio, too, and in lost Livy: chapter 8), and the new Caesar's terrorist *entrée* is a phase of intense interpretivity. Adequate encounter with the period *demands* from a narrative the articulation of a breakdown in meaningfulness. Those who grew up with Octavian could scarcely talk the nightmares of their adolescence into anything less than tragic carnage (chapter 4). Efforts to exculpate Augustus' youth only attest and betray anew the permanent stain.[32] Or, in another transcription of history, the abominations of Octavian served an indispensable role in underpinning the narrative of Augustus, whose every blessing killed – with kindness. And so with all the line of *Augusti* to follow (chapter 5). In either case, the edict is designed to write into its reader an embryonic scheme for the impending imperial revolution: 'neither Sulla's ferocity nor Julius' insouciance' is to be the formula, a *via media* that denied the progression from Octavian's version of the former to Augustus' version of the latter, before the fact.[33]

---

[31] 'The day of the manhunt was indelibly engraved in the memory of contemporaries', Bengtson (1972) 19.

[32] E.g. Vell. 2.66.1, with Woodman (1983) 145, *ad loc.*; Dio 47.7, with Rich (1989) 97; cf. App. *BC* 4.3.16. The *Laudatio Turiae* parades prototype Augustan incrimination of Lepidus (*ILS* 8393, col. 2.11f., Wistrand (1976) 24f.). What might be the politics of the ruling, 'Condemnation and apology, however, are equally out of place' (Syme (1939) 191)?

[33] App. *BC* 4.2.8–10.

To run through the triumviral blacklist (after Hinard (1985), whose labours have proscribed 160 triumviral citizens, to join his 75 Sullan Romans)[34] is, intrinsically, to re-enact the ritual of proscription. Here, then, is one death-wridden story of survival into post-Actian Rome.

(i) For a start, to head the triumviral headhunters' list ('essentially a "media event" '?[35]) was Lepidus' brother, *L. Aemilius Lepidus Paullus*: first to vote Lepidus and Antony *hostes*; he contrived to join Brutus, then stayed at Miletus, for keeps; but his eponymous son became first a consul appointed by Octavian (in 34), then an Augustan censor (22): when he held this office with Plancus for colleague, who could not remember how Lepidus *IIIuir* had shared the consulate in 42 with Plancus, their names for ever dating the proscription campaign of terror?

(ii) What would his villa at Cumae, bought up from Cicero's confiscated estate, bring back to *C. Antistius Vetus*, once with the tyrannicides, later Octavian's appointee consul (in 30), and father of a consul of Augustus (6)?

(iii) *M. Appuleius* fought his way out to Brutus; to become another Augustan consul (in 20).

(iv) *L. Arruntius* fought his way out by Appuleius' side, to join Sex. Pompeius: with Octavian at Actium, he too became his consul (in 22). And a historian (of safely dead Punic Wars).

(v) *Brutus* lived the part of the *exemplum* his name programmed him for (chapter 3).

(vi) *Cn. Calpurnius Piso Frugi* served Brutus, later to have an Augustan consulate thrust upon him at the restoration of the Republic (in 23), his sons matching him in 7 and 1 CE.

(vii) *L. Cassius* fought to the death at Philippi for his uncle Cassius; his son was, eventually, Augustus' consul (*suff.* 11 CE).

(viii) *Cassius* is remembered (chapter 3).

---

[34] Hinard (1985) 13. The dynamics of listing – in particular, the stochastic strain for completeness (to *finish it off*) – are all about numbers, sheer, overwhelming, blank, or whatever: for example, Appian's countervailing catalogues of anecdotes accumulate a quite different sense of saturation than the roll-calls presented in this essay, precisely supplying the count Appian withholds. Schindler –

[35] Weigel (1992) 154 n. 34: but proscription was a volatile stunt to risk, cf. Hinard (1985) 313.

(ix) *Cassius Parmensis* the Caesaricide was a fellow officer with Horace, left in charge of Brutus' base in Asia during Philippi; he joined Sex. Pompeius, then Antony, and was hit on a contract from Octavian after Actium: he and his various writings didn't fade for Horace, who in the late 20s still finds Cassius leaping to mind when twitting Tibullus: 'you may be writing to outdo Cassius at his own game or refute his corpus of writings, or else creeping round the woods, head down and mouth shut, staying in one peace – it depends on whether it matters to you to ask what befits the *dignitas* of a *wise* man, and [is this the same thing or not?] the *dignitas* of a *good* man'. Pardoned Horace, 'now keeping *his* skin in tip-top condition', quizzes him on the vanity of human wishes: his advice is to put yourself in the shoes of ... the proscribed: 'reckon every dawn's your last, for every hour you don't count on will bring you happiness. As for me –'.

(x) *Ti. Claudius Nero*, praetor in 43, was not proscribed until the Perusine War, whence he rallied to Sex. Pompeius: what praises did his nine-year-old son, Rome's second Emperor Tiberius, memorialize in his *laudatio funebris* (in 33)?

(xi) *L. Cornelius Cinna* and his consular sons we have remembered already.

(xii) *L. Cornelius Lentulus Cruscellio* may have become an admiral with Sex. Pompeius: was his son the Augustan *cos.* 18?

(xiii) *Cn. Domitius Ahenobarbus*, great-great-grandfather of the Emperor Nero, survived Philippi and negotiated reconciliation with Antony, who sponsored his consulate in 32; he swung to Octavian on the eve of Actium, but died soon after: his son was Augustus' consul (16).

(xiv) The betrayed and slaughtered *Haterius* was likely father to the Augustan *cos. suff.* 5 CE: the *IIIuiri* re-enslaved the freed informer to Haterius' sons, for buying up their father's estates and insulting them grossly.

(xv) The freedman's son *Q. Horatius Flaccus* fell out from Philippi, and into a *scriptus quaestorius*. He writes, but does not narrate, the sublation of Augustus (chapters 3–4). Was he on the, or a, triumviral list? Even if we were in Rome in 43, no one could tell us (or him) for sure. Nor any post-crisis assurance or allegation: whose counting?

(xvi) *M. Iunius Silanus*, removed from the list by the Treaty of Misenum, was appointed consul by Augustus (in 25).

(xvii) *D. Laelius Balbus*, who killed himself in Cornificius' defeat in Africa (42), was (probably) father of Augustus' *cos.* 6 CE.

(xviii) *M. Licinius Crassus*: son of the *IIIuir*, left Sex. Pompeius for Antony, then Octavian and the consulate (in 30): his adoptive son was Augustan consul in 14.

(xix) *M. Lollius Paulinus* may have been the Marcus who played a slave after Philippi, was recognized by his purchaser, who won his pardon from Octavian; the situation was, believe it or not, replayed in reverse after Actium. The pair became Augustan consuls (in 21?).

(xx) *Q. Lucretius Vespillo* we have remembered already: Augustan *cos. ord.* 19.

(xxi) *A. Manlius Torquatus* survived Philippi to receive both an Epistle and an Ode from comrade Horace.

(xxii) A certain *Nonius* was grandfather of a triumviral consul (in 35 CE).

(xxiii) Horace whoops it up for a *Pompeius*, escapee from Philippi, then with Sex. Pompeius, until Octavian's post-Actium amnesty.

(xxiv) *T. Pomponius Atticus* was soon removed from the blacklist, by Antony. His biographer (who claims perfect instincts for Atticus: 'fearing a proscription' ...) makes a feature of memorializing his sheltering of other *proscripti*.

(xxv)– *Sex. Quinctilius Varus*, decapitated in Italy, and *Sex. Quinctilius*
(xxvi) *Varus*, suicide after Philippi, were grandfather and father of the Augustan consul of 13.

(xxvii) Horace's butt *Rupilius Rex* we have remarked upon.

(xxviii) *L. Saenius Balbinus* escaped to Sex. Pompeius, and became Octavian's consul (in 30).

(xxix) *L. Scribonius Libo* was Sex. Pompeius' aide, temporarily Octavian's father-in-law, joined Antony and held a triumviral consulate (in 34): his natural son held an Augustan consulate (15).

(xxx) *C. Sentius Saturninus Vetulo* was pardoned after serving Sex. Pompeius; his son was an Augustan consul (in 19).

(xxxi) *M. Seruilius*, who fought for Brutus and Cassius, was probably father of the Augustan consul of 3 CE and so grandfather of the historian Seruilius Nonianus.

(xxxii) *L. Sestius Quirinalis Albinianus* was Brutus' *proquaestor*, and his suffect consulate in 23 inaugurated Augustus' restored Republic – the new spring of Horace's fourth Ode (chapter 4).

(xxxiii) *Ser. Sulpicius Galba* had a historian for a son, an Augustan consul for a grandson (in 5 CE), and the emperor Galba for a great-grandson.

(xxxiv) The former Pompeian commander (chapter 2) and voluminous writer *M. Terentius Varro* was soon restored and lived to be a hundred.

(xxxv) It seems *L. Titius* took refuge with Sex. Pompeius and so saved his captured son M. Titius, Plancus' nephew; the latter joined Antony, then executed Sex. Pompeius, and crossed to become Octavian's consul for the vital year of Actium (in 31).

(xxxvi) *M. Tullius Cicero*, Junior, was an officer at Philippi, then for Sex. Pompeius, before becoming Octavian's *cos. suff.* (in 30).

(xxxvii) *M. Valerius Messalla Corvinus* followed Brutus, then joined Antony, before siding with Octavian (*cos. suff.* 31). One son was an Augustan consul (in 3), another a Tiberian (20 CE). Messalla's *Memoirs* preserved his own sense of the history he had suffered and made.

(xxxviii) *C. Velleius* worked with Brutus, committed suicide after the Perusine War; his grandson was Tiberius' senator historian.

(xxxix) *T. Vinius* was saved by his wife's intercession with Octavian; when the consul in the crisis Year of the Four Emperors died with the Emperor Galba, his epitaph tellingly placed him as 'the proscript's grandson'.

(xl) *M. Volusius* probably joined Sex. Pompeius. Was his nephew an Augustan *cos. suff.* (in 12)?[36]

---

[36] Lepidi: Hinard (1985) 418–21, nos. 4–5; Antistius: 422f., no. 8; Appuleius: 426–8, no. 12; Arruntius: 432f., no. 20; Brutus: 437f., no. 26; Piso: 442f., no. 30; L. Cassius: 447, no. 35; Cassius: 448, no. 36; Cassius Parmensis: Hor. *Epp.* 1.4.3, Hinard (1985) 449, no. 38; Nero: Suet. *Tib.* 6, Hinard, 451–3, no. 41; Lentulus: 459f., no. 47; Ahenobarbus: Suet. *Ner.* 3.3, Hinard (1985) 463f., no. 51; Haterius: App. *BC* 4.4.29, Hinard (1985) 471, no. 61; Horace: Acro *ad Epp.* 2.2.41, Suet. *Vit. Horat.*, Hinard (1985) 473–5, no. 63; Silanus: 479f., no. 68; Laelius: 482f., no. 71; Crassus: 483f., no. 73; Lollius: App. *BC* 4.6.49, Hinard (1985) 487f., no. 81; Torquatus: Hor. *Epp.* 1.5, *Carm.* 4.7, Hinard (1985) 492, no. 85; Nonius: 498, no. 93; Pompeius: Hor. *Carm.* 2.7, Hinard (1985) 506f., no. 106; Atticus: Nep. *Att.* 9–11, esp. 10.2, Hinard (1985) 508, no. 108; Quinctilii: 509–11, nos. 110–11; Rupilius: 512f., no. 114; Balbinus: 513f., no. 115; Scribonius: 516f., no. 118; Sentius: 518f., no. 120; Servilius: 521, no. 123;

Here, then, is a roll-call of forty, but not the best, of the proscribed who lived on, in person or as memories, to add their stories to the Augustan heap.[37] These proscribed were, as they were bound to be, from the ranks of the Roman aristocracy, old and new; the Augustan aristocracy was bound to include the survivors and the families of the victims, or at any rate to empathize with their predecessors as such, so the purge was necessarily inscribed on their lives.

The single most vocal legacy of the triumviral putsch was, however, the corpus of writings left by no. (xli), *M. Tullius Cicero*, its sole known consular victim, the *princeps senatus*, together with the reams of hagiographic commentary, biography and legend.[38] In Livy's history, the death of Cicero in book 120 has proved a convincing putative terminus for the work in its original conception (chapter 8). Likewise, in the declamatory world of the early empire, the slaughter of Cicero is both a favourite scenario for logorrhoea and the last moment in history the declaimers permitted themselves to colonize with their wild fancies and loose tongues: *tota tabula tuae morti proluditur ... Vt Cicero periret, tot parricidia facta sunt.*[39] The very dominance of the 'Augustan generation' over all ensuing conceptualizations of Rome has for foil the silencing of power as Cicero's Republican senatorial oratory. That is why the stories on this 'immortal theme' tell of his writing-hand severed and his tongue spiked in the mutilation of his corpse/*corpus*.[40] Not surprisingly, successive waves of Roman historians were induced to write up the lurid melodramas of these triumviral proscriptions to end proscription.[41]

Sestius: 523, no. 126, Will (1982); Galba: Suet. *Galb.* 3, Hinard (1985) 526f., no. 132; Varro: App. *BC* 4.6.47, Hinard (1985) 527, no. 133; Titius: 533f., no. 137; Cicero: 537, no. 140; Messalla: 540f., no. 145; Velleius: 541, no. 146; Vinius: Tac. *Hist.* 1.48.3f., Hinard (1985) 548f., no. 156; Volusius: 550f., no. 159.

[37] Appian's gallery of proscripted are given the twists to their fates, if any, beyond Actium (Gowing (1992) 263).

[38] Hinard (1985) 536, no. 139.

[39] 'The whole proscription list was a warm-up act for your death ... So Cicero might die, so many kin were murdered', Cornelius Hispanus *ap*. Sen. *Suas.* 6.7; *Contr.* 7.2, *Suas.* 6–7. For the copious materials on the death of Cicero, cf. esp. Homeyer (1977) 56–96.

[40] Syme (1939) 192; App. *BC* 4.4.19 (he even had to visit Caieta, to feel the scene: ibid.), Dio 47.8.4, etc.

[41] So Appian assures us, as he cries up his (considerably abridged) chapter of thrills and horror (*BC* 4.3.16).

I THINK OF A NUMBER, AND THEN . . .

L'ouverture des listes.[42]

Appian's plethora of proscription anecdotes composes a double series, with faintly etched chiasmus: first a trail of calamities, and last a stream of escapes, in a ring around a centrepiece which is prefaced by the mockery of Lepidus' triumph, with its enforced merriment on pain of proscription, and climaxed by the splendour of Hortensia's rebuke to the triumvirs at daring to rob the matrons.[43] Before he delivers these 'highlights of the irrational',[44] he has rapidly sketched an anonymous and general overview of the turmoil which the advent of proscriptions bestirred. The twin themes of the perversion of the social fabric and the tyranny of suspicion have been impressed on us;[45] discordance between narrative and cited document has shown up *proscriptio* as *Rechtswort* cloaking *Schreckenswort*,[46] yet we have faced the Sullan/ triumviral half-truth that proscription was a curb on indiscriminate massacre, if also a *carte blanche* for arbitrary butchery.[47] Parables attached to both proscriptions, pointing up the tease of circumscription as the play(th)ing of power:

> The young senator C. Metellus asked Sulla what would be the end of the troubles? Where was he going before they could expect what was happening to stop? 'We are not begging off from your vengeance those you have determined to eliminate, but we do beg you to relieve from ambiguity those you have decided to preserve.' To Sulla's reply, that he didn't yet know whom he was letting go, he put in with 'Then clarify whom you mean to punish.' And Sulla said he would do that . . . At once Sulla proscribed eighty, sharing this with none of those in power. When they all complained, he left a day, then proscribed two hundred and twenty, and on the third day at least as many again. Delivering a public speech on the subject, he said he was proscribing

---

[42] 'Opening the lists', Hinard (1985) 309: the armature of 'un procédé terroriste' (ibid. 305).

[43] See Gowing (1992) 259f.

[44] ὅσα παραλογώτατα ὄντα, App. *BC* 4.3.16.

[45] Ibid. 4.3.13f.: see esp. Canfora (1980) 435f.

[46] 'Legalism' for 'verbal trigger of panic', Fuhrmann (1959).

[47] App. *BC* 4.2.10, cf. Hinard (1985) 103, 139 (Sulla: damage limitation? Vengeance? Justice? . . . ?).

as many as he happened to call to mind, but those that slipped his memory he would proscribe another time.[48]

According to ?Julius/Junius? Saturninus, when the proscription was completed, M. Lepidus had deprecated the past in the senate, and given hope of forgiveness for the future, since enough punishment had been exacted. Octavian came right out with it, contrariwise: he had set a limit for proscription in such a way that he had left the world free – for him to do whatever he liked to it (... *ut omnia sibi reliquerit libera*).[49]

While the wording of Appian's edict is intimidatory not least through its 'vague and nebulous' lack of determinate programme, and is shown up by the narrative as a malevolently 'open text',[50] the theatre of proscription turned on the operational supplementarity of its writing.[51]

This textuality was sufficiently iterable for the blacklist to circulate across Rome, Italy and the world; yet it was metamorphic enough to operate a mutational instability (that we could think of as rhizomatic authorship, popping up arbitrarily, here and there, like mushrooms), resistant to documentary closure always deferred beyond progressive revision. The writing-space in proscription declared itself illimitably inclusive, programmed to draw in every name it could associate with another: there was room for all – whosoever aided or abetted the concealment or escape of a proscribed; anyone caught mourning a proscribed, or failing to celebrate a triumviral holiday; whomsoever the team of writers felt like adding, or substituting, or pretended had been included all along; anyone that ever crossed a proscriber, as events developed; anyone with the requisite cash; for however long the proscribers stayed in power, however long it might take to revoke, annul, cancel their edicts ...[52]

Thus Dio knows that counting will not account for the deaths: 'because many among those who were proscribed onto the blacklists first off were erased, many were later written up in their place, and while some of these people made it to safety, lots of others were done away with'. And he assures us that when Antony and Fulvia did take a

[48] Plut. *Sull.* 31.2–4, cf. Hinard (1985) 61.
[49] Suet. *Aug.* 27.2, cf. Hinard (1985) 232, 245f. The writer ?Julius/Junius? Saturninus is unknown, but perfectly named – named for perfect, carnivalized, ambivalence.
[50] Cf. Wallmann (1989) 51.
[51] Cf. Bleicken (1990) 46.
[52] App. *BC* 4.1.5, 2.7, Dio 47.13.1, Hinard (1985) 247.

bribe, 'so that the places of their names on the blacklists might not be empty, they wrote in some other people instead'.[53]

O REELING, WRITHING 'N' 'RITHMETIC (THE THREE 'R'S)

> La proscription a joué un rôle déterminant dans la définition de la nouvelle sagesse romaine.[54]

No wonder the portents that greeted the triumviral entry to Rome culminated in this: 'the senior *haruspex* summoned by the senate announced the return of kings to Rome and heralded a future of slavery for all, with the single exception of himself – whereupon he held his lip and his breath, until he was dead'.[55]

Full transcription of the narrative of proscription entangles the writing *of*, with the writing *in*, the account, particularly in Greek, where 'composition' (συγ-γράφω) delivers a sequence of 'public declarations' (προγραφαί).[56] For the spectrum of uses of προγράφω blurs between 'bill posting', 'public notification of auction', 'proclamation of edict', 'notice of confiscation', and the full, Sullan, 'proscription'.[57] In the abuse of law's scriptural formality, lives oriented around the production and consumption of manic writing attendant on the master-text of triumviral proscription: most explicitly in Dio's narration, Cicero's killer Popillius Laenas, 'so that he might not only get the credit for murdering him by occupying ears, but also eyes, set up a be-garlanded icon of himself beside Cicero's head, with his name and his deed *written up for the inscription*' (ἐπιγεγραμμένον); whereas a certain tribune

---

[53] 47.13.1, 8.5.

[54] 'Proscription played a determinative role in the definition of the new Roman wisdom', Hinard (1985) 326: *fin.*

[55] App. *BC* 4.1.4: cf. 4.17, where the dinner-guests of the first proscript victim – that symbolic figure of Roman *libertas*, including freedom of speech: a *tribunus plebis* – 'reclined paralysed into deepest night, next his beheaded torso' (τεθηπότες ἄναυδοι), Dio 47.10.7, where his son hid Q. Cicero and under torture 'kept his mouth shut' – until father took pity, 'came out and gave himself up to the hitmen'.

[56] So in Dio 47.10.1, συγγράφῃ 13.1, ... προγραφέντων ... ἔγραψα ... ἐγγραφέντων ... ἀντενεγράφησαν ... 2, διὰ προγραφῆς, 15.3, νόμους τε τοὺς μὲν ἀπήλειψαν τοὺς δὲ ἀντενέγραψαν; 16.1–4, λευκώματα αὖθις ἐξετέθη, θάνατον μὲν μηδενὶ ἔτι φέροντα ... εὐποροῦντας ἐς λευκώματα ἐσγραφῆναι.

[57] Cf. Hinard (1985) 17–32.

called 'M. Terentius Varro had done no wrong, but bore the same name as one of the outlawed except for his *agnomen*, and was scared something might happen to him like the fate of Cinna, so he put on public display a *notice*, clarifying this very fact (γράμμα). And for this he incurred amusement and derision.'[58]

In Appian's *'script' On Rome* (συνέγραψα ... συγγραφῆς, *Praef.* 1.6), Sulla likewise modulates to graphematics: a grateful People voted him an equestrian statue, 'with the *subscription: Cornelii Sullae ducis Felicis'* (ὑπέγραψαν): but, he wonders, is it clear 'whether the *inscription* was their satirical joke on the great man, or them buttering him up' (παρα-σκώπτοντες ἢ ἐκμειλίσσομενοι τὸν ἄνδρα ἐπιγράψαι)? Whether or not the oracular writing on the wall addressed to Sulla may have read the way Appian writes it up, for sure Sulla's reading of it had him send a crown and axe to Aphrodisias, with the *writing on* it that he cites (ἐπι-γράψας τάδε).[59] We are, like Sulla, emphatically, to *read* Sulla.

Appian studs his Coming of the *IIIuiri* with *writing*. They '*assigned* their vets. the pick of Italy' and '*co-authored* a manifesto of their plans – *read out* to the army by Octavian as consul – all but the death-sentences' (διέγράφον; συνεγράψαντο; ἀνέγνω, 4.1.3). 'In conclave, they *compiled* the death-sentences ..., *listing* their personal enemies, ... and one batch after another later *supplemented the list*' (συνέγραφον; καταλέγοντες; προσκατελέγοντο, 2.5). 'They *imposed* very heavy taxes on both People and matrons ... and by now folk got *proscribed* for the loveliness of a villa or *domus*' (ἐπέγραψαν; προέγραφη, ibid; also τῶν προγραφόντων). They 'delayed the bulk of the *proscriptions*. ... Every-one thought the flying squads were on their trail because it was known massacre was afoot, but none of the condemned had been *proscribed*.' So 'Pedius *proscribed* the seventeen [marks] as ... the only ones con-demned ... in ignorance of the triumvirs' slate. And that night Pedius expired, of... "exhaustion"'' (προγράψειν; προγεγράφθαι; προύγραφεν, 2.6; προγραφαί, 2.7).

'The *proscription/edict* itself ran thus: "the senate *outlawed* us ..., ... we had been *named in* Caesar's will ..., and the army was *outlawed* ... Our policy is to *proscribe* rather than arrest unawares ... A blessing on

---

[58] Dio 47.11.2f.
[59] *BC* 1.11.97: Herodotean hamming (à la Croesus) – from Appian? from his 'sources'? from Sulla?

this: let no one hide, evacuate or take a bribe from any of those *written infra* on this screed ... On pain of us putting them among the *proscribed*. ... And no recipient of bounty will be *registered* in our records/ accounts, so they cannot be traced." So ran the *proscription-edict* (suffering only from translation).' (ἡ προγραφή; ἀναγεγραμμένῳ; πολεμίους ἀναγράψασιν; ἐγγράφεντες; ἐγγράφεντες; πολεμίῳ ... ἀναγεγραμμένῳ; προγράψαι; τῶν ὑπογεγραμμένων ἐν τῷδε τῷ διαγράμματι; ἐν τοῖς προγεγραμμένοις; ἐγγεγράψεται; ἡ προγραφή, 2.7–11: see *Appendix*.)

Mentions of *proscribers, proscribed* and *proscriptions* crowd together to overpower their text.[60] 'In many books, Roman writers have *compiled* many an anecdote ... but I shall *write up* a sample under each (be)heading' (συνέγραψαν; ἀναγράψω, this editorial's last word 3.16). The sequence of anecdotes heaps up references to proscription – that is what they are *for*.[61] As well, the matrons' finances are also *'proscribed'* (προύγραφον ... γυναῖκας ..., προγράψατε καὶ ἡμᾶς ὡς ἐκείνους, 5.32). Lepidus' *edict* orders celebrations at his triumph – or else 'be among the *proscribed*' (προυτέθη διάγραμμα οὕτως ἔχον ..., ἐν τοῖς προγεγραμμένοις ἔσται, 5.31). *Painterly-and-writerly imaginations* capture Aeneas bearing his load of father (γράφουσιν, 6.41). And, primally and ultimately, there remains Appian's own *writing* (ἀναγράψω; ἀναγράψω, 4.23, 36).

Sullan *proscription* always bleeds into the bloodstream of *'putting on public record'* – 'noticing' the terms of political existence. For writing history always is writing to death, as any Greek historian must proclaim, caught in the toils of translation into Greek, English, or whatever sociolect. It should be engraved on our memories that history is constitutively *'programmatic/proscriptional'* (τὰς αἰτίας προΰγραψα πρῶτον ...).[62]

---

[60] ἐν τοῖς προγράφουσι; ἐν τοῖς προγραφομένοις; τῶν προγράφοντων; τῶν προγραφομένων; πολεμίους ... ἐψηφίσαντο; ἐν τοῖς προγεγραμμένοις; ταῖς προγραφαῖς, 3.12; προγραφέντος; ταῖς προγραφαῖς, 3.14; προγραφείς; προγεγραμμένων, 3.15.

[61] προσγεγράφθαι; προγραφέντες ... προγεγραμμένῳ; προγεγραμμένος; προγεγραμμένων ... προγεγραμμένων; προγραφαῖς; προγεγραμμένον; προεγράφη ... προυγράφη ... τοῦ προγεγραμμένου; ἐγγραφέντος αὐτοῦ τοῖς πίναξιν; προύγραφον; προγεγραμμένους ... προγράψαι; τοῖς προγεγραμμένοις; τῆς προγραφῆς; προγραφέντα ... προγραφείς; τῶν προγραψάντων; προγραφέντα; προεγράφη; προεγέγραπτο ... τῶν προγεγραμμένων ... τῆς προγραφῆς; προέγραψα ... τῶν προγραφέντων; προεγράφη; and a closing editorial, τῶν προγραφέντων, 4.18; 22; 24; 25; 26; 28; 29; 5.30; 35; 6.36; 43; 44; 46; 47; 49; 50; 51; 7.51.

[62] Thuc. 1.23.

To *'make the point'* – *'set it down'*, *'keep it in the public domain'* – in the course of this narrative of *proscription*, here is a file of ten anecdotes from Appian that unmistakably button life/death struggles in the toils of proscription to scenes of writing/reading, to (y)our scene:

(i) The principal casualty Cicero lost 'the hand with which he *composed* his invectives against "tyrant" Antony, *entitling* them *Philippics* in imitation of Demosthenes' (συγγράφων ... ἐπέγραφεν, 4.20).

(ii) On the other hand, 'someone else' (nameless) 'ran up as his brother was being arrested, not to know he had himself been *proscribed* together with him: he told the squad, "Kill me first"' (πρὸ τούτου = before him/instead of him). 'The centurion holding the accurate *print-out* said: "A reasonable demand from you – *inscribed* before him", and as he spoke he killed the pair of them – by the book'! (προγεγράφθαι ..., τὸ ἀκριβὲς ἀνάγραπτον ..., πρὸ τούτου γέγραψαι ..., κατὰ τὴν τάξιν, 4.22). Here the semantics of προ/γράφω are cracked open to make a joke between temporality, formula, and human sociality, while tyranny paradigmatically dictates 'order' through textual power.

(iii)–(v) First, 'Caesennius and his hunters. He ran for it and yelled he wasn't *proscribed*, but was being framed by them for his riches' sake; but they fetched him to the *blacklist* and told him to *read* his name. They topped him as he *read*.[63] Aemilius, unaware that he had been *proscribed*, saw someone else being hunted down and asked the centurion hunter who the *proscribed* was. The centurion recognized Aemilius and said "You and him" – and killed two birds. Cillo came out of the senate-house with Decius. When they found out their names had been *added to the list*, though no one was after them, they began to flee in disarray through the city-gate. It was this bolting that betrayed them to the centurions who intercepted them' (προγεγράφθαι ..., ἐπὶ τὸν πίνακα ..., ἀναγινώσκειν ..., ἀναγινώσκοντα ἔκτειναν; προγεγράπται ..., ὁ προγεγραμμένος; τοῖς πίναξιν ... προσγεγράφθαι, 4.27). This triptych forcefully dramatizes the

---

[63] As Hinard notes (1985) 241 n. 65), only in this story is the killing done in central Rome; otherwise, heads only were brought to the triumvirs.

terms of proscription textuality – read it, ask what it says, heed it: anyhow, it *writes* you *off*.

(vi) Messalla 'ran to join Brutus. The triumvirs were afraid of his mettle, so they *published an edict/proscription*, so: "Since his relatives have shown Messalla to have been away when C. Caesar perished, let Messalla be lifted from the *proscribed*"' (προύγραψαν οὕτως ..., ἐξηρήσθω τῶν προγραφέντων, 6.38). Written in, written out: erasibility is as arbitrarily reversible as inscription was. Neither suggests a threat has been *written off* (in any sense).

(vii) For the rest, the stories happily re-write the triumviral text: 'On Arrianus' tombstone there was *incised* according to his will: "The one who lies here his son hid, joined him on the run and saved his life: his son was *not proscribed*, he *was*"' (ἐν τῇ στήλῃ κεκόλαπτο ..., οὐ προγραφεὶς προγραφέντα, 6.41).

(viii) Vinius' 'freedman hid him right in the very middle of his home, in one of those iron trunks people have for the safe-keeping of valuables *or books* ...' (6.44).

(ix) 'Varro the philosopher-historian *writer*, a fine soldier and general besides, was therefore, it may be, an enemy of autocracy, and *proscribed*' (συγγραφεύς ... προυγράφη, 6.47).

(x) And in the end: 'when the despatch was sent by Caesar with news of Antony's débâcle, Cicero's son *read it out* to the People and publicly exhibited it on the rostra where before his father's head had been publicly exhibited' (ἀνέγνω, 6.51).

Now this scroll of tales is only where Appian's proscription saga *explicitly* situates writing/reading as the *locus* of triumviral terrorism and response to it. The social 'text' encompasses a far wider range of hermeneutic registers than this. But see already how the narrative unravels the document it promulgates – and substitutes parables of deconstructive dissemination and of inescapable elimination for that mortal list of names from 43 which, in refusing to reach a definitive form, modelled the unwritable illegibility of oppression. The episode engrossed Augustus, the Julio-Claudians, all the Emperors, Pollios, Appians, Dios, and the rest. The 'list-lessness' of its death-sentences haunted – haunts ancient Rome, endlessly.

Appendix: Translation of the proscription edict of 43 (Appian, *Civil wars* 4.2.8–11)

8. And the proscription ran like this: 'Marcus Lepidus, Marcus Antonius and Octavius Caesar, elected to harmonize and set to rights public affairs, declare as follows: "if villains had not begged in bad faith and been shown mercy, but when they got it, became their benefactors' enemies and then plotted against them, neither would they have done away with Gaius Caesar – those he took prisoners-of-war but rescued them with mercy, made them his friends, and took forward *en masse* to office, distinction and bounty – nor would we be compelled to deal so broadly *en masse* with those who have insulted us and proscribed us as public enemies. But as it is, seeing that those by whom we have been plotted against and at whose hands Gaius Caesar suffered have a viciousness that may not be gentled by humane treatment, we choose to get in before our foes rather than suffer. Now let no one consider our action unjust or savage or immoderate, seeing on both Caesar's and our part the sort of treatment we have suffered. Gaius, now, was both dictator and *pontifex maximus*, he both subjugated and annexed the tribes most to be feared by Romans, was both first of mankind to pioneer the unnavigated ocean beyond the pillars of Hercules and discoverer of a land unknown to Romans: in the middle of the declared holy ground of the senate-house, under the gaze of the gods, they slew him with twenty-three insulting blows, these people who had been taken prisoner in war by him, been preserved, and written onto the list, some of them, of heirs to his estate. While the rest, instead of punishment, sent out those polluted with this desecration to office and command – which *they* have both exploited to seize public moneys and gathered an army from them against us, also seeking another army from the barbarians who are always hostile to our rule, and they have both burned down or flattened or razed communities subject to the Romans, or else scared them and are leading them against our native land, against us.

9. We have wreaked vengeance on some of them already; the rest, with the assistance of god, you will presently see paying the penalty. While the most important affairs have been brought to completion by us and are under our control, viz. Spain and Gaul and the home front, one matter is still outstanding, to campaign against the assassins of Gaius across the sea. On the point of hazarding this war abroad on your behalf, we judge it a security risk both on our part and yours to leave other enemies behind us, for them to trespass on our absence and wait on opportunities materializing from the war's progress; the same goes, too, on the other hand, for delaying on *their* account in the midst of so great an emergency, rather than getting them out of the way *en masse*, considering that they started the war against us, when they voted us and the armies under us public enemies.

10. As for them, they were wiping out ever so many thousands of citizens along with us, regarding neither vengeance from the gods nor the hostility of mankind; whereas we shall go hard on no swathe of people; we shall not regard as personal enemies all who opposed or schemed against us; nor for wealth on its own, or opulence, or status, or in the numbers that another supremo before us killed, when he too was ordering the state in a civil war, the one you dubbed 'Felix' for his success – though three must of necessity have more enemies than one. But we shall punish solely the worst and most guilty of all – this for your sake just as much as ours, for it is necessary that while we are in dispute all of you must suffer terribly in the cross-fire, and it is necessary that there should be something by way of consolation for the army, insulted, provoked, and proscribed as a public enemy by our common/public foes. While having the power to arrest by main force any people we decide to, we choose to give notice by proscription rather than arrest them still unawares – this too for your sake, so that it may not be possible for the legionaries in their wrath to go over the top with the innocent, but having them counted off and circumscribed by name, they may leave the rest alone in accordance with orders.

11. A blessing on it: let none host any of those written below on this bill, nor convey them anywhere nor take hire for their pay. Whoever is shown to have either preserved or afforded aid or been in cahoots, we assign them among the proscribed, taking account of no pretext or pardon. Let those who kill them fetch the heads to us, free men at 25,000 Attic drachmas *per caput*, slaves at his personal freedom plus 10,000 Attic drachmas and his owner's citizen status. Informers will have the same going rates. Also, none of those who receive rewards will be written down in our accounts, so that they may have no publicity." '

So ran the proscription edict of the triumvirs – so far as translates into Greek from Latin.

2   XPDNC: writing Caesar
(*On the civil war*)[1]

Julius Caesar (the *memorable* Roman Emperor)[2]

Appian was the latest, and Julius Caesar is the earliest, writer considered in this book. His *On the civil war* (*BC*), as we shall see, comes
to us as a continuation of his *Gallic wars*, which celebrates his ten-year
conquest of vast territories in furthest Gaul for the Roman Empire. His
campaigns are still presented as if they are despatches from a governor
reporting back to the senatorial government. Caesar narrates his invasion of Italy with as little fuss as can be, as if his *Blitzkrieg* was all in the
line of duty. His writing fights for Rome in the most literal sense, for
writing Caesar shows how important the war of words is in campaigning through a world he could never resign as enemy territory.

We shall consider how his narrative is written round the letter he
sent to Rome for the new year of 49, his eleventh-hour effort to proffer
terms for holding back from the brink which meant to invent some
moral high ground for him to claim as opening shot in the propaganda
war. Writings of all sorts thread together the battle for hearts and
minds across the face of the Roman earth, mediating between Caesar's
missing and scorned letter in the narrative, and the literary *coup* of
Caesar's narration.

The circumstances, timing, and (so) the thinking, of Caesar's writing
(up) these *Commentarii* are, we shall find, hard to recover. They present us with the self-invention of the key prototype for the emperors
to come, facing some of the same challenges to blend claims to Republican traditionalism with the demonstration of the power to push
through a Roman revolution as would confront (post-)Augustan ideology. Was Julius the first emperor, or the road not taken? We shall
find (in chapter 5) that Julius' war against Pompey and/or against the
Roman Republic, could construe as the decisive episode in all Roman

---

[1] 'XPDNC' spells 'expediency', with Caesarian expediency.
[2] Sellar and Yeatman (1960) 9.

history: a century and a half-dozen emperors later, Lucan's epic could strive to re-open the fight for Rome against Caesar – and against writing Caesar; and, living through the frenetic complexities between the Rubicon and Actium, a particular generation of survivors who told and re-told their stories from Pompey, Cato, and Julius, through Brutus, Cassius, and Antony were, for ever, enshrined as the 'classic' phase in Roman culture (chapters 3–4). Julius himself could not know he would himself never die – enshrined by triumvirs as the Roman deity *Diuus Iulius*, and soon an imperial dynasty's founding father.

Caesar's writing pretends to be anything but a speech before the Senate, yet in miming as his provincial 'governor's report' to the house, it supposes we will recognize it as performatively nothing else. Through the insufferable third-person mock-remoteness of his power-driven prose, we should listen to the history Caesar would compel to follow along the tracks he has imposed, and reflect on how briefly that story retained its pertinence to the political agenda at Rome; but, yet, how centrally its hero's self-profile would persist through so much of Roman and Western ideology.

O THE BRIEF

> Like many who believe their own propaganda, [he] often used the Caesarean third person.[3]

Whereupon Henderson rose, in his place, to speak his motion (*surrexit sententiae suae loco dicendae*). And moved (*pro sententia sua hoc censuit*):

* that: Caesar's *Caesar* tells of a peace-keeping war[4] which didn't have to be, yet had to be, fought over the 'self-regard' the world owed him and his Caesar self – his *dignitas*. 'Not status for Caesar but something approaching self-respect' (his apologist might aver) 'and knowledge of his actual worth and the offices it entitled him to seek, meaning more to him than life itself.'[5] From the horse's mouth, what Caesar is worth, what a Caesar *is*.
* that: the monological, even monomaniacal, myth of Caesar's

---

[3] Montefiore (1992) 67.

[4] Caesar 'fights for peace', Collins (1972) 957. For the liveliest introduction to *BC*, see Richter (1977) 166–79. On the opening chapters, cf. Oppermann (1967). Wensler (1989) stresses how Lucan's version of Jan. 49 BCE plays up his sources' independence from Caesar's account. (Livy? So Pollio? Or Pollio? And/or . . . ?)

[5] Raditsa (1973) 450f.

writing puts his *Civil war* in denial. Fiercely dialogical protestation powers and motivates every turn of the rhetoric, not
despite, but through its repression. The dispute between Caesar
and his world occasioned a welter of writings; parasitic on them,
Caesar hides his parade of self where you must not miss it.

* that: Caesar's *Commentarii* run, and should be read, together:
  Gallic wars and *Civil war* claim a scandalous continuum.

* that: Caesar, 'whose every word denied the inevitability of such
  an outcome',[6] wrote all over the *imperium*. Caesar wrote *Caesar*,
  onto the world, until the world, and all the writing in it, was
  his. This writing won and lost a world war.

* that *BC* reinforces Caesar's thinking over Caesar's thinking. In
  the protestation of a Roman identity, the masking and marking
  of iconoclasm with conformity.

I CROSSING OUT THE RUBICON (*FAC ET EXCUSA*)[7]

The Man who is born to be a dictator is not compelled; he wills it. He
is not driven forward, but drives himself. There is nothing immodest
about this.[8]

'The letter from Caesar was successfully delivered to the consuls and
the utmost exertions of the tribunes just about got it read out to the
Senate; but nothing could get a motion arising from the letter put to
the Senate. Instead, the consuls put to them the national interest' (*BC*
1.1.1f.: *Litteris Caesaris* ...). *Not*, then, the letter of *Caesar*, the letters
written by Caesar, Caesar's writing; but the *res publica*. So begins the
text of Caesar, *BC*, at once opening the rift that would tear down
SPQR and write up *Caesares*.

Readers are never to have this letter from Caesar to the Senate read
out to them. One had to be there. Some editors cannot believe this is
not the chance injustice of scribal accident.[9] They cannot believe how
unlucky Caesar's *Bellum ciuile* has been, to be deprived of its opening

---

6 Ibid. 448.
7 'Act now, justify later.' For Caesar's 'ben calcolata reticenza' on the Rubicon, cf.
Pascucci (1973) 519f.
8 A. Hitler, *Der Hitler-Prozess*, in Bullock (1962) 117.
9 To start with *consules* is the Roman way; but *unnamed* consuls are an odd way to begin –
as adrift as the Republican calendar, which Caesar would soon reform: the timing of
the *BC* would then require rescheduling, commandeered by Julian temporality from
46/5 (chapters 3, 5).

paragraph, or so.[10] 'The contents of Caesar's letter were very important and however hastily Caesar may have written the *BC* it is almost
inconceivable that he did not spell out the offer he was making: that
either he should be allowed to retain his command, or that all holders
of commands should lay them down.'[11] The majority view, however,
has been to accept this abrupt opening as Caesar's, to the letter.

The abruptness of the denial of debate on the matter of the letter
from Caesar stands, in any event, as the symptomatic gesture that inaugurates *BC*, just as it initiates the civil war.[12] The consuls of Rome refuse
to comply with Caesar's written will. In so doing, they treat his letter as
the report of a magistrate to the government; chivvied by the tribunes,
they give the despatch an official hearing, despite pressing crisis; but in
so far as Caesar's writing required to be handled as a proposal from afar,
an *in absentia* representation to the Senate seeking to determine a vote, it
is disallowed. Instead, a procession of senior figures produces an array
of *sententiae*, from which the presiding consul selected the motion 'that
Caesar disband his army before a certain date, on pain of being seen to
act against the national interest' (1.2.6).

The veto from two tribunes on this successfully carried proposal
was a week later dealt with by passage of the 'emergency decree' (*illud
extremum atque ultimum senatus consultum*), according to which the
magistrates should protect the national interest from damage. The
inscription of this declaration of martial law (*perscribuntur*) issued
instantly in the *flight* of tribunes (i.e. as if '*the* tribunes') to Caesar at
Ravenna (*profugiunt*, 1.2.7, 5.3). The consul who blocked Caesar's
written will was Lentulus Crus. He is to die a short way from the end of
Caesar's text, 'arrested by a king', the Pharaoh of Egypt, 'and executed

---

[10] Esp. Carter (1991) 28, 'All surviving manuscripts ... lack the beginning of the work';
cf. 153f. for 'strong reasons for believing that at least several sentences have been lost
from the start of the book'. Gelzer (1969) 190 n. 5, 'Unfortunately the beginning of
Caesar's *bellum civile* as preserved in our manuscripts is defective, and the end of
Hirtius' *b.G.* 8 is also missing.' Brunt (1986) 18, 'The end of Hirtius' narrative and the
beginning of Caesar's are both lost.' Raditsa (1973) 439, 'The mutilated state of the
end of *bG* 8 and the beginning of *bc* 1 make it difficult to assert with full confidence
that Caesar omitted the contents of his letter to the Senate.' The MSS have the irritating intrusion *a Fabio C.* between the opening *Litteris* and *Caesaris* (= *a Curione*? Cf.
Richter (1977) 175).

[11] Carter (1991) 153.

[12] Barwick (1951) 17f. argues that Caesar withholds the contents of his letter because, or
lest, they might seem tantamount to menacing arrogance.

in confinement'.[13] The proposer of the motion against Caesar was Metellus Scipio, joined in his resistance by Cato, through discussions convened by Pompey in an after-dusk unofficial meeting of senators. Both of these survive Caesar's text, though not before Cato has been humiliated when he flees Sicily before a shot is fired, complaining of being 'abandoned and betrayed' by Pompey,[14] and Scipio satirized as first a 'self-proclaimed *imperator*' after some setbacks in Syria, then the would-be despoiler of Ephesian Diana, and finally hybristic contender for Caesar's priesthood, counting chickens before Pharsalus.[15] Caesar's text is to cease – abruptly – with Pompey's killer, Pothinus the Pharaoh's eunuch guardian, himself 'put to death by Caesar' (the last words of *BC*: 3.112.12; Pompey killed at 3.104.3). Yes, up to a point, the *Civil war* hangs together. Caesar picks off both the villains he stigmatized to begin with and the villains he picked out along the way.

All Caesar's writing in the *BC* constitutes a commentary on that first, slighted, text of his, suppressed from the historical (i.e. written) record by the enemies of Caesar in the Senate. This is indeed Caesar's own claim, regularly and insistently reiterated throughout the three books. His text bears witness to his keenness to propose a cessation of hostilities, until this becomes the theme of his pre-battle speech to his army before do-or-die Pharsalus (3.90). Much of the text's business is taken up with supplying terms for that missing, and/or suppressed, opening letter from Caesar, from the paraphrase he gives to intermediaries to take to Pompey at the outset, 'when he sent a letter to the Senate "that all should leave their armies", he couldn't even get that'.[16] The lists and précis lengthen and shift, asserting, or betraying, a range of self-estimations: '... asserting the right to freedom of *himself and the Roman People* from oppression by a minority wedge', for example; or '... the senators should prosecute the national interest and govern together with himself; but if they ducked it for fear, he wouldn't shirk the burden and would govern the *nation on his own account*'.[17] Caesar himself sails

[13] 3.104.3. This event is marked out by *necare*, a *solitarium* in *BC* (Opelt (1980) 112).

[14] 1.4.1–3; 1.30.5. Cf. LaPenna (1952) 194.

[15] 3.31.1, 33.1f., 83.1f. Cf. Eden (1962) 115f.

[16] 1.9.3: *ne id quidem impetrauisse* here amounts to a back reference to the opening sentence of *BC*. Cf. Kraner, Hofmann, Meusel and Oppermann (1959) 12f. and the versions collected in the *Appendix*.

[17] *se et populum Romanum*, 1.22.5; *per se rem publicam administraturum*, 32.7: 'Half way between a threat and a promise', comments Collins (1972) 957. That is, a threat – all the way (*docet*, wrote Caesar, 32.2: 'a lesson').

close to the wind at Massilia: 'You should follow the authority of all Italy rather than *defer to the will of a single person.*' And the game is all but up in Greece, when Caesar tries to give his final warning through Vibullius and his message shows Pompey his *alter ego* as would-be cosmocrat: 'if fortune gives just a bit to one of the two rivals, the one who seemed superior would not abide by the peace terms and the one who was confident that *he was going to be master of the universe* would not be content with even shares'.[18] As shall be seen, the telegraphing of terms comes to founder on talks about talks, the slippery, practical, business of framing the exchange of terms. But terms *are* formulated, throughout this process of deferral, terms that set Caesar's self *before* the Roman state.

If every action in the text is a shot in the word war, each ascription of a view, position, or identity also colours its representation dialectically. The writing of *Bellum ciuile* is strung, like all discourse, between (i) the selection of actional terms that determine reality and its mutation, and (ii) the supply of relational terms which establish a modal set toward the contest of wills:[19] thus (i) Caesar, of course, plainly polarizes (his own) 'set-back' against (their) 'disaster', 'elimination' against 'massacre'; (Pompeian) 'flight' against (Caesarian) 'withdrawal', 'boast' *vs.* 'pledge', etc.; but (ii) he also implants *attitude*, by dramatizing acts of judgement, reactions and responses: his account of his adversaries shows them to think, speak and write in self-seeking hatefulness. *They* brutalize themselves, they drag everyone they can down with them, they monger war from nothing; whereas *Caesar* wants no enemy, reinstates order and ideals, stays warm, human and social. All the solidary sentiments are his, the violence and tyranny theirs. This work of euphemism and denigration is passed off as description, while Caesar creates a profile for his Caesar from negative ventriloquism of his opponents. His Caesar thus depends dialogically on the projection of unattractive images of power and knowledge onto the othered. Not Caesar but Cornelius Lentulus, for a start, lets the biggest cat out of the bag: 'hyping himself to his cronies as a/the second Sulla, for *imperial mastery* to revisit'.[20]

---

[18] *unius hominis uoluntati obtemperare*, 35.1; *qui se omnia habiturum uideretur*, 3. 10. 7. For the terms stipulated by Caesar, cf. LaPenna (1952) 196–8, Barwick (1951) 47–70.

[19] See Hodge and Kress (1993) 162–4.

[20] *summa imperii*, 1.4.2. On the Sullan typology, cf. Collins (1972) 961f., cf. 3.18.2, *summa imperii*; 3.83.

In the course of the narrative, it becomes clear how writing has, if it has, a role to play in (the) *Bellum Ciuile*. On the one hand, letters are centrally important, and the letters that compose them carry the brunt of the campaign; for this war is, before all, a war of words, where the prize at stake in the *Kriegschuldfrage* ('Who started it?') is, more than diplomatic victory in psychological warfare, the very stairway to world supremacy.[21] The stated, proclaimed, bandied platforms formulated by the combatants would win, accredit or dispute, and would set the seal on, interpret and calibrate, the victory. Moreover, Caesar's own text is itself nothing other than the most lengthy version of the case he put forward before the Senate, before the descent into hostilities, before the text could start. The vindication of the 'truth' of Caesar's glaringly missing letter is the work set for the narration at the outset.

The writing of letters plays a shaping role in the fighting, as the war accumulates archival substance for the eventual writing: this *dictator* could dictate four letters to four different scribes at once – something of a strategic advantage, the smart weapon of smartness.[22] In this world, commanders report to base, just as proconsul Caesar had written his despatches from Gaul to the Senate through the 50s. They communicate and share knowledge – to provide for detailed calculations of movements and counter-moves, and (counter-)intelligence on both sides. But most typically they bear orders, or requests for orders, and are themselves borne by messengers as the most authentic versions of the will of the generalissimos. Letters are written and conveyed by messengers; the messengers carry *mandata*, whether in writing or for oral delivery is often unclear, and perhaps still more often an immaterial triviality; crucially, most of the messages are in the imperative, and, harbingers of an imperial future of *fiat* and decree, they make things happen – if only their delivery.

But, even so, in this world writing is on the other hand also, paradoxically, at a discount. This is a world of action and of reactions, where the *œuvre* of Caesar displays, not the literate orator and man of writing-culture, but his giant manoeuvres athwart the empire. A chief-of-staff's ciphers must deliver on this, or be dead letters.

Yet, since the *Iliad*, the business of war-correspondence has always inescapably *moralized* culture through the blockage of communication,

---

[21] Cf. Collins (1972) 945f.   [22] Plin. *Nat. Hist.* 7. 91. Cf. Rambaud (1966) 23.

through the blockade on colloquy. Thus, a certain L. Caesar began the invasion (so to say)[23] by arriving at Ariminum with business to discuss (1.8.2–11.3): 'he finished the conversation that was the reason why he had come, then indicated he was instructed by Pompey to speak to Caesar on *private* business. Pompey wanted to be clean in Caesar's eyes, in case he took for an insult what Pompey had done for the *nation*: he had always held *public* interest above *private* ties.' Further assurances of the same kind were added by praetor Roscius. Caesar's response is a paradigmatic display of acuity wrapped in statesmanlike courtesy, marked by his characteristic concessionary gesture,[24] despite his own better judgement: 'although these doings seemed without relevance for easing the wrongs done Caesar, nevertheless he took the opportunity of these suitable people to be intermediaries for delivering his will to Pompey. He asked the pair of them, since they had brought Pompey's message to him (*mandata*), not to shirk taking his demands back to Pompey, too (*postulata*), in case with an ounce of effort they might be able to get rid of a vast quarrel and so free all Italy from terror ... So that all this might come about more easily and on settled terms, and be sworn on oath, either Pompey should come closer himself or allow Caesar to come; it would turn out that all the quarrel would be settled by talking with each other.' No cloak-and-dagger shabbiness from *Caesar*, but all the graces, and, congruently, the offer to short-circuit hostility and hostilities with face-to-face companionability.

The ethos at the other end of this mission earns writing Caesar's ire: 'taking the instructions, Roscius with (L.) Caesar reached Capua and there found the consuls and Pompey; he announced Caesar's demands. They pondered the issue, replied and sent back through them a written message to Caesar (*scripta ... mandata*), summarized as follows: Caesar return to Gaul, quit Ariminum, dismiss troops; if he did this, Pompey go to Spain. Meantime, till pledge were received that Caesar would do what he promised, consuls and Pompey not to desist from levying.' Where Caesar self-deprecates his fraternal greetings as *postulata* but dignifies the terse insults that returned as *mandata*, the generosity of his fulsome self-declaration to the go-betweens damns the cold inhumanity of his adversaries' intransigence not least by the modality encoded in the contrast in syntax. As Caesar's *Commentarius*

---

[23] For close reading of 1.8.1, see Pascucci (1973) 517–19.
[24] See the important paper of Batstone (1990).

comments, 'An unequal exchange, these demands ...' Dutifully rebutting the proposal point-by-point, Caesar saw the strangled message screaming through the laconic formality: 'Not to find time for talking together and not to promise to come brought it across that there was serious giving up on peace.' With the famous pendent 'therefore' at this juncture (*itaque*, 1.11.4), the drive is on, and will not stop before Suez. So see how it all started here, when Pompey traded on the separation of young L. Caesar from his father, Caesar's legate, and their need to talk, but himself failed to meet even the basic etiquette of agreeing to meet with his old partner.

At the end of the road, Pompey will find himself obliged to 'send a request to be received in the name of guest-friendship and friendship with the host's father ... The people sent by Pompey did their diplomatic job, but then started chatting all too freely with the guards.' The result: 'those who were sent by Pompey were given a generous *up-front* reply and were told to tell him to come. But the same people began a plot and sent *on the quiet* – a pair of heavies to kill Pompey' (3.103.3–104.2). Messages bring finality.

Between these moments, letters and instructions divide the sides in antipathy, even as they both pull their separate business together. 'Domitius sent to Pompey in Apulia people who knew the area, for a large bonus, plus a letter to beg and pray for help ... When the town was mostly enveloped, those sent to Pompey returned. After reading the letter, Domitius started acting ... Pompey had written back that ... if there was any chance, Domitius should come to him with all his resources. Not that he could ...' (1.17–19). The letter gets through, but only to draw a blank, or worse, and decipher as betrayal.

Later, the grand pattern of hybris is marked by 'the letter and messengers that brought word to Rome', 'written out by Afranius and Petreius and friends in anything but the plain and dry style'. This started a dash of runners to Pompey in Greece, 'some bent on being first to bring such news, others worried they might seem to have waited on the out-turn of the war, or to have come at the end of the queue' (1.53).

The same communiqué, 'written out really expansively and windily by Afranius', set Varro in further Spain 'to dance to fortune's dance', into self-deflating mockery of resistance to Caesar. His downfall is sealed by a letter from the people of Gades to say that they were joining Caesar, which prompted him to 'send to Caesar that he was ready to hand his remaining legion over to anyone he told him to'. Script for a farce.[25]

The tragic equivalent: 'Caesar's messengers and letter announcing (genuine) victory in Spain', which inspired his lieutenant Curio to fatal over-confidence in Africa – disregarding the messages that reached Curio and his opponent at the same moment, to the effect that Juba's vast hordes were at hand (2.37.1f.).

Readers regain the narrative track, when 'Caesar's letter arrived, informing Calenus that the ports and shorelines were all occupied by the other side's fleet', just as he put out to sea with the reinforcements embarked, 'in accordance with Caesar's orders'. One private vessel under its own steam went ahead: every last human on board was executed, to the very last one (3.14). This was, truly, a red-letter day.

Polarized parallelism between the principals goes on through the contrasts between their correspondence: 'Pompey's admirals were torn off a strip (*castigabantur*) by a volley of letters for failing to stop Caesar's crossing'; 'troubled by developments, Caesar wrote pretty strictly to his men in Brundisium' (3.25.2f.). In his bureau as all else, Pompey is an outmanoeuvred but considerable opposite number – worth writing a war with, a decent way to write Caesar, the best of a bad job.[26]

Through all the deadlock and circling, the consul Caesar parleys unilaterally, for the duration. Two matching episodes tell of perfidy within the business of negotiation: first Caesar picks twice-pardoned Vibullius 'to send with instructions to Pompey, summarized as: both men to bring their obstinacy to an end, walk away from war and risk fortune no further ... Vibullius heard the account and thought it no less necessary for Pompey to be informed of Caesar's sudden approach (*aduentu Caesaris*), so that he could take counsel for that, before any dealings began on the instructions' (3.10.2–11.1). Then, 'informed by letter about the demands of Libo and Bibulus', Caesar calls them 'for talks'. Caesar had to excuse Bibulus, 'whose reason for shunning the talks was in case a matter of the greatest hope and greatest expediency

---

[25] 2.17.4–20.7. For the farcical treatment of Varro, cf. Haury (1966), LaPenna (1952) 194, Eden (1962) 116. See Rowe (1967) for the articulation between the dramas in nearer and further Spain. Avery (1993) urges that Caesarian reverses under Dolabella and C. Antonius were a lengthy episode lost from Book II.

[26] Respect for Pompey: Collins (1972) 954; irony: Perrotta (1948) 2of.; satire: LaPenna (1952) 193f. In *BC* III, Caesar writes the pair 'Caesar and Pompey' into all but parodic parallelism, e.g. 45.1f., 76.1f.

might be hog-tied by his wrath'. They said they wanted 'to learn Caesar's demands and send to C.-in-C. Pompey', but Caesar sussed them out by requiring personally supervised 'safe-conduct for representatives to Pompey'; Libo 'would not receive Caesar's representatives nor assure their safety, but referred the whole matter to Pompey'. So 'Caesar realized that Libo had started up the whole scheme in view of the danger he was in ... and was coming across with no hope or term for peace' (3.16.2–17.6). *Waffungstillstandsunterredung* (peace process) was only a pretext for playing for time.

Furthermore, when Scipio entered the frame, Caesar 'didn't forget his original strategy', but sent him a mutual friend, Clodius, 'handing him a letter and giving him instructions for Scipio, which summarizes as: Caesar had tried everything for peace, and reckoned that the zero progress was the fault of the people he had wanted to take responsibility for the business, because they were afraid to carry his instructions to Pompey at a bad moment ... Clodius delivered these instructions to Scipio', but 'he wasn't allowed to join any talks ... and went back to Caesar in failure' (3.57). The breakdown in communication has now itself broken down. And, this time, Caesar's message is a masquerade – really a string of bare insults.

But the mail will get through, eventually: though Pompey 'never got used to writing-in his acclamation as *imperator* as his letter-head' (3.71.3), the victory he won it for was quite wrongly diagnosed by his officers, who therefore turned it into defeat (in analysis)[27] and the occasion of their own fatal and final hybris: 'just as if they had won by their own courage and as if no change of fortune could occur, they celebrated that day's victory all through planet earth, by word of mouth and by letter' (72.4).

Now this climax to Caesar's chain of dramatic tales of reversal[28] makes big big waves: 'Pompey had sent out letters through every province and township about the battle at Dyrrhachium, and rumour had hustled far more extensively and windily than what had actually happened: Caesar repelled and on the run, most all his forces lost' (79.4). This hype, the telltale miscommunication that betokens a fake sociality, the Pompeians' spurious bid to speak to and for their country, and *not* the actual battle at Dyrrhachium, threatened to break the inexorable pattern of the narrative. Caesar was obliged to force it back

---

[27] Explained well by Eden (1962) 108.　　[28] Rowe (1967).

into shape, encouraging a fresh spate of loyalty to himself by sensational but (he has said) *controlled* aggression. As Henderson will have demonstrated, they *must* have brought it on themselves, when Caesar must take out a people's town: regrets, he had a few – but then again, almost too few to mention.

So Caesar writes his instructions, demands, letters. They invite readers to come to talk, if only about talks. His *Commentarii* do not pretend to be other than documentary drafts, a condensed saturation of documentation, intermediate between the utilitarian pragmatics of the performative world of reports to HQ and orders to units, and the elaborated synthesis of a historian's finished text.

The *Commentarii*, that is to say, pretend to be no other than rough drafts, a provisional string of raw documents, indeterminate between the signals telegraphed from generals to soldiers and back, and the clamorous prosecution of a raft of conditions for a new political order.

'In a real sense, as long as Caesar could write this narrative, the Republic still existed. For such writing would show it was still possible to know the public interest rather than simply to idealize it.'[29] Or, rather, as any less partisan view would have it, writing Caesar turns on disavowed will to power.

2 MIGHT IS WRIT –

> As when [Shakespeare] said in the person of Caesar, one speaking to him, 'Caesar, thou dost me wrong' – he replied: 'Caesar did never wrong but with just cause.'[30]

The most obvious place to look for Caesar's missing letter is *not* in the putative preliminary lacuna, where the reader was not privileged or entitled to hear its wording before the senatorial meeting despatched it to the rapidly filling wastebasket of Republican history's might-have-beens, but rather in every letter he goes on to write as commentary on his claimed attempt to stave off the need to fight, write and right the Civil War. Caesar has hidden the letter of his law where it is most easily overlooked, on display through the pages of his public record.[31]

---

[29] Raditsa (1973) 434.

[30] B. Jonson, *Discoveries*, in Wilson (1969) 245.

[31] The modelling of the transference, the repetition compulsion, within reading staged in Poe's *The purloined letter*, the 'figure in the text, something hidden in full view as one reads', is summarized effectively in Wright (1984) 66f., 113, 114–16, cf. Henderson (1986) on 'epistoliterarity'.

His account might easily read as, exactly, confirmation that his initial representation of the sending of this first-ditch letter as an attempt to pull everyone back from the brink to safety was itself the prototype for all his subsequent barrage of *déformations* of the historical record.[32] In any event – and this is the point, certainly the predicament readers are in – every re-formulation of Caesar's terms in the course of the three books is put across as a raise on the same stakes he began with. Readers begin with the question of his sincerity, the authorial sincerity embodied in the promissory terms of the pledges he vouches for. As the opening episode means to suggest or impose, this intersects with the question whether sincerity from Caesar *could* affect the reception it was possible to give him, once the Senate conspired to cross its Rubicon and quarantine contacts from him. This compounded question will never be left behind: it extends, unfolds and articulates to become the question of the *BC*.

So can be read the first displacement operated by this project of writing Caesar in that opening blockage of any motion based on Caesar's letter. According to Caesar, even those who blocked serious consideration of the missive, Lentulus and Scipio, told the house they and Pompey might or might not do a deal of some sort with Caesar, take it or leave it; and a series of senators nevertheless ventured proposals pacific or appeasing (1.1.2–2.4). The text indeed wades straight into efforts by the players to interpret Caesar's will and read Caesar – while the attendant events were being shaped to exclude effective moves to meet him half-way. By the time Caesar supplies readers with that first, foregrounded, summary of his letter's drift (1.9.3), he has shown how irretrievable a situation had (been) developed, and has obliged his reader to reflect on the momentum endemic to the escalation from entrenched antagonism to all-out war.

The letter of Caesar had been a text and an affidavit: could he be held to it, or did the spirit which prompted its sentiments belong strictly to that determinate instant of history? Could letters hold on to what they meant in a context of slide and slippage into crisis – or could no one dare credit them with meaning what they (would have) said?[33] A letter belongs to its moment, even if that moment never arrived.

---

[32] The classic prosecution of the guilt of Caesar *scriptor* compounding that of Caesar *imperator* is Rambaud (1966).

[33] Raditsa (1973) 439f. shows brilliantly, as Caesarian partisan, how the narrative mimes the impact of the events on interpretation of those events.

However, *this* absent letter presences the eternal moment of Caesar's text.

Neither the momentaneous *Caesar* the Romans of the time were 'reading', nor the *Caesar* that he was and is writing, were invented from scratch. Rather, this is the proconsul of Rome, victor over Gaul and Germany, proved in a series of wars and ordeals against the age-old barbarian threat to Roman Italy, the unprecedentedly acclaimed *imperator*. This is the hero of a thousand despatches, written up as the mastermind of his sevenfold *Gallic wars*, equally apt to write as to fight. This same exemplary citizen and would-be servant of Rome is now the victim of his own success. Writing just one more epistle back home, he is feared and cold-shouldered. As if he leads a Gallic tumult, or as if the Roman government were tribal chieftains intimidated by the approach of the Roman Caesar they had learned to know and (rightly) fear. Yes, the trace of Gaul will persist in *BC*.

In time, Caesar's lieutenant and amanuensis Hirtius would ape the *hupomnēmata* of Alexander's marshals, plug the gap in his leader's story, in his text and in his rhetoric. But when he did that, with *BC* VIII, the Caesar he would be writing for would have moved on many a mile. The project had become to complete the record of Caesar's progress to full 'rationalization' of the Republican system of a bouleutic Senate supervising its temporary and inducted magisterial representatives – and the eventual nemesis of assassination by former associates and adversaries in coalition. The loyal Caesarian Hirtius' mimetic project of marching behind Caesar in filling out the record of his campaigns,[34] provisionally working up the most suitable primary despatches he could solder together into a supplementary *Commentarius*, may have been completed under the aegis of the dictator, as he seems to claim. Or the project may have been finished after Caesar's example, by the compilation of the remaining episodes in the *corpus Caesarianum*, up to and including, or down to, Caesar's ultimate battle of Munda, at the world's edge (*BG* 8.*Praef.*). Something an administrator *could* delegate, perhaps. The effect, at any rate, is to complete the soldierly biography of the soldier Caesar, as if the completion of his world conquest

---

[34] Cf. Tatum (1989) 208 for the compulsive drive of the bioscript primer: At the end, 'the text of the *Cyropaedia* dissolves in mimetic replication of Cyrus, with his lieutenants and satraps doing what Xenophon's readers may now do in turn: imitate Cyrus'.

remained primarily a military matter, the progressive consolidation of exploits from *prouincia* to *prouincia*. But, it is patent to all, the geo-politics of Caesar's career invaginate any such portrait.

At any rate, the story Caesar made true by fighting, then writing, the Civil War down to his victory over, and vengeance for, Pompey made Caesar himself into an over-achieving *imperator* who could scarcely – and this on the most optimistic reckoning – take one more step without confirming the fears he has rejected so firmly from the outset.[35]

By the end of *BC* III, the fame of *Caesar* meant the world was his oyster, as he (correctly as ever) reckoned, 'all space shall be indif-ferently secure for Caesar' (3.106.3), even if he does contrive to cam-ouflage this new omnipotence adequately behind his cliffhanger of a finale: Caesar's back to the wall in Egypt. Romans must see that *he* is the new Saviour: Pompeius – never called *Magnus* in *BC* – has (it could seem) been cut down to size in the city that is the necropolis of Alexander, whose degenerate Ptolemaic wardens must be punished for the hybris they dare commit on the person of the great Roman Pompey, and then on the majesty of the serving consul of the *populus Romanus*, Caesar (the Alexandrians killed Pompey 'because the *fasces* paraded before Caesar ... This was treason against the [*videlicet* Egyptian] crown', 3.106.4). At this juncture, Caesar, come from the other end of the earth and its untamed barbarians of Britain, all the way to the corrupt hyperculture of Egypt's eunuchs, queens and boy-kings, stands forth as beacon to all those in peril on the political main: he takes charge of the Pharus (112) – though, ironically, he could not himself sail out of Alexandria against the prevailing winds (107.1), the political winds that had blown him clean across the map, blowing with him until the end-point where *he* had prevailed over his Roman adversaries.

On the one hand, the victory at Pharsalus turned Caesar into the (double) saviour of Ephesian Diana (105.1–3), blessed by annunciation across the Hellenistic East of the Macedonian diadochoi – from Olympia to Antioch to Ptolemais to Pergamum to Tralles – blessed, that is, with the charisma of a new super-Alexander (105.3–6). On the other, Caesar finds himself, for the first and last time in the text but, fatally, not for the last time in his life, as over-confident as any of

---

[35] Contrast Collins (1959) 117, '*BC* is a work *republican* through and through; ... it neither contains the spirit nor the foreshadowing of the "monarchial" or "imperial" idea' (discussed by Mutschler (1975) 198f.).

his Roman adversaries had proved, and by 'trusting in *fama*' gets out-numbered and bottled up 'with troops no way numerous enough to trust in' (106.3, 109.2). For all the world, if one knew no better, like some second-rate Pompey.

As Caesar plays the perfect Roman magistrate in Alexandria, he gets the chance to re-play, his way, the Lentulus scene where he and writing Caesar came in. In Egypt there is, naturally, civil war, fought between kin. First, brother and sister; then another sister joins in, but soon disputes break out *de principatu*, and the united front needed to face the alien Roman teeters on the edge of collapse – just as Caesar's text gives out. *These* disputants *were* all *reges* – whereas Julius would continue, less and less plausibly from this moment on, to repeat to his subjects *Caesarem se, non regem, esse.*[36] Caesar thought the quarrel 'involved *the national interest and his own*, as invested in his office'. He also had a personal stake of honour, in the shape of past connections with the disputants – just as in that opening chapter of *BC* Lentulus had, he said, had with Caesar (1.1.3). Caesar knew the solution: 'Our recom-mendation is that Ptolemy R. and Cleopatra his sister *dismiss the armies they have*, and negotiate their differences before himself at law rather than between themselves at arms'. This time the solution doesn't work because *this* state is indeed truly rotten, and needs saving from itself.[37]

Caesar in Egypt faces the classic impurity of molten civil war: a rabble of Gabinius' former troops now married to natives, spawning hybrids as they unlearned 'the name and norms of the Roman people' and turned to Alexandrian ways of licence. Add a heap of bandits and robbers from all over, rootless flux. Stir in lots of criminals with a price on their heads, chuck-out exiles. Every runaway Roman slave made a bee-line for the foreign legion at Alex. Long decadence had made civil war a way of life: in the anti-politics of chaos, these forces stuck together, settling the hash of courtiers, extorting bonuses from the palace, and even king-making.

These experienced mercenary muckers made of Caesar what civil war threatens to make of any commander, or disputant: a street-fighter, Caesar must descend to messy working from house to house, must turn the apparatus of orderly civic life into so many sordid for-

---

[36] Suet. *Diu. Iul.* 79.2: 'Caesar – not some dime-a-dozen king', cf. Dio 44.10.

[37] *ad populum Romanum et ad se*; 3.107.2, *exercitus quos haberent dimittere*; cf. *BG* 8.55, and *BC* 1.9.3–5, *omnes ab exercitibus discederent ... ipsi exercitus dimittant ...*, etc.

tifications and foxholes – theatre, palace, harbour, docks, lighthouse. Egypt ultimately makes of Caesar (a parody of) the Sulla he had always absolutely abjured to become.[38]

But this, the start of the *Bellum Alexandrinum*, was not a *Roman* civil war.[39] Here, Caesar could insist, was Caesar the servant of Rome still, carrying on where he left off in the wastes of the north, down in the post-civilized pit of the south, standard-bearer for the ethical centre of the Roman world, upholding the order of Republican institutions. Best if the writer Caesar desists here. Rather than take his readers and his notes up the Nile, to serve Clio by living it up and writing it up on Cleo's barge.

Besides, the wars to come, in Africa and Spain, were both easy and impossible to tell as un*Civil wars*, with too many eminent Roman deaths, among them the suicides of the greatest Republican names alive, the aristocrat in spades, Metellus Scipio, and the walking legend Cato the martyr; and worse to come, with the unglamorous chore of mopping up Pompey's litter. No doubt it could be done, by Caesar, rather than botched as it is by his loyal lieutenants. But whatever the causation, the question should be asked, just *what* flows from the fact that Caesar's text stops where it does, delegating the task of completing the campaign report to adjutant acolytes in the secretariat?[40]

Henderson's story had to be that the débâcle in Alexandria caps Caesar's denial that he has fought a civil war. He may have been dragged involuntarily into circumstances that look mighty like civil war, but anyone who should take the trouble and take up the challenge to write up these drafted *Commentarii* will find that Caesar has consistently and resolutely engaged (us) in, at most, an involuntary series of wars way short of civil.

There *is* civil war in the *BC*. But it appears just where Caesar doesn't.

---

[38] Anarchic confusion in arming slaves formulaically tars the opposition with making war on the *ciuitas*, e.g. 1.24.1, 3.22.2, 3.103.1, Rambaud (1966) 339, Collins (1972) 953.

[39] Cf. Ahl (1976) 307. E.g. Ogilvie (1982) 284f. accepts the incomplete state and status of *BC* III. Barwick (1951) 93–106 argues cogently (if only the uncanny or poetic be banished from our order of history) that *BC* is a finished, not an uncompleted, work. Carter (1993) 233 notes laconically, 'Caesar's narrative stops here, in mid-course.'

[40] The argument that Caesar's greatest reader and interpreter, Lucan, makes much of the point of termination of Caesar's *BC* in his own *bella plus quam ciuilia* is more than presentably set out in Masters (1992) 216–59, 'The endlessness of the *Civil war*' (chapter 5).

Inside the walls of Corfinium, under Caesar's blockade (1.20.3); in the mutual destruction of ships bent on battering the enemy in Massilian naumachy (2.6.4); and in Thessaly, where the Pompeian leader must be like Pompey, so 'one of the *ancien régime*', and his Caesarian rival a 'budding aristocrat's aristocrat' (3.35.2). The pattern where fraternization threatens to dissolve hostility into integration, but is foiled by desperate officers, *does* threaten to bring the horror too close to Caesar: in Spain, 'civil war', a sedition within the opponents' camp, has the troops 'look out and call for anyone in Caesar's camp they knew or who came from the same town ... , complaining of bearing arms against people who were close to them and related by blood'. 'Two camps were just looking like one', when the Pompeian generals returned, to turn it round with savage war-crimes and cursed oaths (1.74-6). In return, as was noticed, Curio off in Africa had to scotch Varus' efforts to seduce the former Pompeian soldiers he once messed with at Corfinium (2.28). And in Greece, 'between the two camps of Pompey and of Caesar, there was one river alone'. The soldiers kept talking to each other. Caesar sent Vatinius to the bank to yell out awkward questions about 'why *citizens* couldn't send representatives to *citizens* ..., especially when the object was to stop *citizens* fighting a decisive war *with citizens* ...' Talks got as far as fixing venue and time, hopes ran high, but *BC*'s villain, Labienus, pounced, as mysterious missiles hailed down, and told them off: 'Stop talking about a settlement; for there can be no peace for us without *fetching* Caesar's head *back* with us' (3.19: *capite relato*).

This near thing is twinned with Pompey's immediately preceding declaration, in response to proposals to discuss Caesar's instructions: 'he interrupted him in full flow and barred him from another word, saying, "What use do I have for life or citizen status if I seem to have them by Caesar's favour? That opinion of the matter will be ineradicable, when ... I'm thought to have been *brought back* to Italy"' (3.18.4f., *reductus*). So civil war is waged in *Pompey*'s camp; and Caesar is involved only as disputant trying (so Caesar writes) to end the dispute.

Otherwise, so Henderson observed, civil war in *BC* abides where it should – in down-town Alexandria. And the equable and equitable Caesar searches only for 'a farewell to arms on equal terms', as he is led West to 'learn the lie of the land / his opponents' position' and offer battle in Spain 'on equal ground', then as consul establishes 'evenness' in the civil administration (3.20.2), he pleads for an armistice while the balance between the two sides was still 'even', and still, at the death, offers battle 'on even ground' against Pompey in Greece: although Pompey 'kept drawing up his line at the roots of his hill, waiting to see if Caesar would subject himself to uneven ground', 'one fine day Pompey's line advanced a little further beyond its daily routine, so it seemed possible for the fight to be on ground that was not uneven'. Pompey had all along 'refused to let anyone get even with him in dignity'.[41] The rest, the text leaves to be gathered, is history.

3 LE PORTRAIT DE CÉSAR, C'EST CÉSAR[42]

... ut de suis homines laudibus libenter praedicant ...[43]

In (his) truth, Caesar stoutly avoided invading his country; and neither has he left it, at the death. He was no Gallic barbarian; he is no Oriental Sultan. Instead, his orders have consistently preserved Roman order, in the lines of his regimental formations,[44] the precision of his circumvallations, the organization of supply, engineering, logistics.[45] And performatively his writing gives the order to relate his orders to the national interest. This, Caesar's message runs, is how these three books of *writing*-talk come to exist.

The author Caesar does not tell all that Caesar the actor did or was. In particular, his Caesar is not sighted composing the two books *De analogia* on crossing the Alps between winter-quarters and the front

---

[41] *aequ-*: 1.26.4; 41.2f.; 10.7; 55.1; 85.1, 3; 4.4.

[42] See Marin (1988) 206–14, esp. 213, 'to paint the king's portrait is to make the portrait of all possible future kings'.

[43] '(These things were extra windily recounted by them) the way people do speak out freely in their own praise', 2.39.4: displaced away from (= onto) Caesar, as reflection on Curio's cavalry.

[44] *suos ordines seruare*, e.g. 1.44.3 and *passim* – military morality.

[45] Caesar writes of engineering feats, instead of Caesar fighting, from Corfinium (1.21.4f., 19.5) and Brundisium (25.5), to Spanish ditch *without* rampart (41.4: a ruse), multi-channel ford (61), or the staple *uallo fossaque* (81.6; cf. Rambaud (1966) 248–50, 'Travaux et flottes'). War at Massilia, when out of the shipyards, consists in fanatically devoted description of fiendish towers and ramps (2.8–13.1, 15f.). In Greece, the 'new-fangled war' is an inventive sapper's paradise (3.47.1, 50.1, cf. 39f., 43.2, 44.3, 46.1, 54, 58, 63.1). Beats civil war (like other ways in which mass-killing can be re-charged in telling of derring-do: for example, the race for the pass in Spain, 1.70, and the cross-country dash, 1.79).

(spring 54). Here *Caesar the* purist *man of letters* once told Cicero's Empire how to speak Latin, in no uncertain terms.[46] He could make words stick to the world, close up description and prescription so tight that *nomen* and *nominatum* must bond in unique propriety.[47] *Commentarii* in this stylistics could slough or veil their definitionally subjective particularity as a species of memoirs, for their narration blanks out marks of personality, limiting the narrative to an ascetic régime of reportage paradedly shorn of palpable *mentalité*.[48] What was done, not what was being thought of; tactics not strategy; a world of detail, observation, specification not overview, impression, valorization.[49]

The proconsul in this field is but *primus inter pares* among the characters, an agent with the same strong exteriority of an officer-administrator's accounts; the narrator with the omniscience of retrospect writes a Caesar strictly intent on his business, dividing and ruling tribes and chiefs in the time-honoured manner of the Roman commander.[50] *Any* officer might be compiling these reports from the frontier? Almost.[51] But the writing Caesar twins with the written *Caesar* in their shared manner,[52] of swift, forceful, precise, pointed application to the matter in hand, customized rhetoric indistinguishable from impas-

---

[46] Cf. Rawson (1985) 122, Hendrickson (1906), Oldfather and Bloom (1926–7); for political grammar, cf. Sinclair (1995) 93.

[47] E.g. Eden (1962) 86, 'the same words for the same situations ...'; ibid. 97, 'Caesar seems to have viewed the anarchic growth of language with disfavour, and in trying to bring order out of chaos to have applied almost a logician's insistence on having only one symbol for one concept or relationship.'

[48] The old style of scientistic study of Caesarian purism (e.g. Schlicher (1936) '... the low percentage of dominant verbs preceded by two or more subordinate clauses or phrases in Books i and ii is probably due to the greater brevity and simplicity of the sentences, which average 30.3 per 100 lines ...') has yielded to a more recent quest to tease out the self-disguised art of a plain stylist (Gotoff (1984) 1–18: 'Obviously the Commentaries are a form of self-advertisement; what form of self-advertisement is less obvious ... It may be that Caesar has succeeded all too well in disguising his art; that centuries of readers ... have failed to notice his diversity, his deceptiveness, and his power' (5f.)). 'Caesarian prose style', that is to say, still gathers formalist panegyric (cf. Williams (1985)) that is dead set against invasion by the politics of discourse.

[49] For narratological analysis, cf. Reijgwart (1993) on *BG*.

[50] Cf. Dyer (1990) 18 for the idea that Caesar's treatment of pacified Rome was on a continuum with the way he had earlier treated Gaul.

[51] See Bérard (1993) esp. 93, 'Il ne s'agit donc pas d'une autobiographie ... mais d'un autoportrait.'

[52] For the classic account of Caesar's style as mimetic of his generalship, see Fränkel (1967).

sive dash – 'il velo dell'impassibilità, dietro il quale lo scrittore si nasconde'.[53] One signifier per signified. And in the *BC*, the dyad will shoot the moon.

That tenacious construction, the conqueror of Gaul, must become the reserve of credit that the *BC* draws on. One complete set of *Commentarii*, one narrated *Bellum*, one Caesar. By analogical theory, *BG* and *BC* must bear the same referentiality, formal and actual, across the textual wound that is to be sutured by Hirtius. In this poetics, there will be no holding the boundary between Gaul and Italy, which Caesar and his texts must cross and re-cross as they progress their work.[54] The seven hundred and seventy-five occurrences of 'the letters of *C-æ-s-a-r*' (the letters of Caesar's name) that line up through *BG* and *BC* are one, in seamlessness.[55]

The narrative works hard to make the theory bite: features of *BG* litter the stages of *BC*. Guerrilla warfare in Spain has rubbed off on the legions 'because they have got used to fighting Lusitanians and other barbarians in a barbarian-style of battle: this is something that generally happens, that soldiers are greatly affected by the habit of the regions in which soldiers have matured' (1.44.2). Lusitanian and local troops found it 'easy to swim a river, because the habit of all of them is not to go on campaign without skins [for floats]' (48.7), while 'Caesar ordered his soldiers to make boats [coracles] of a kind that experience of Britain had taught him in earlier years' (54.1). To aid Caesar, a huge convoy of Gauls treks over the mountains – 'cavalry with long waggon-trains and heavy baggage, as the Gallic way has it ... All sorts of men, plus slaves

---

[53] 'The curtain of impassivity behind which the writer hides', Perrotta (1948) 27. Cf. Bérard (1993) 94, 'deux personnages, l'auteur-narrateur et le proconsul-protagoniste, qui se cachent mutuellement'. Adcock (1956) 76 manages to speak of written Caesar as 'the natural, almost automatic, expression of his conscious pre-eminence'. Raditsa – who took the notion that there must have been a *Machtsfrage* behind the Caesarian *Rechtsfrage* seriously: 'such statements have consequences. One sees them in the faces of one's students' ((1973) 440 n. 68) – admired Caesar because he 'distinguished thought from feeling but did not suffer their opposition. (Note:) Hans Oppermann [repeated, from 1933, in (1967) 497] has beautifully put this ...: "*Der wichtigste* (reason for the resistance to and murder of Caesar) *ist vielleicht die Einheit von Caesars Persönlichkeit ... ist Caesar die letzte Verkörperung der Lebensganzheit in der Antike*"' (442 and n. 74).

[54] Esp. Collins (1972) 932f., 942 puts notable effort into severing the limbs of the *Caesarian corpus*.

[55] The often-repeated count was made by Rambaud (1966) 196f.; *Caesar* is normatively salient in its sense-units, cf. Rambaud (1962) 67f.

and children; complete lack of order and discipline, with each person doing his thing and all of them travelling along without a worry in their heads – still practising the anarchy of earlier times and migrations' (51.1f.). Shades of the Helvetii: even at Phocaean Massilia, rough mountain tribesmen from the hinterland, called the Albici, put up a fine fight (34.4, 56.2, 58.4, 2.2.6, 6.3).

In Africa, Curio faced more othered 'natives': 'the Numidians bivouacked all over the place, no shape at all – that certain way with barbarians' (2.38.4), and the *déja vu* feeling is completed when Juba deploys the 'two thousand Spanish and Gallic horse' of his bodyguard, who did the traditional manoeuvre of fake retreat, before the sucker-punch (40f.). Greece had 'barbarians' of its own, of course, as at Salonae (3.9.1), but wherever Caesar, or indeed Pompey, go, still the familiar old braves who have stayed the whole distance in writing Caesar ride in from the pages of the *BG*: most memorably the two Allobrog troopers, 'men of unmatched courage, on whose top-quality services, best of warriors, Caesar had capitalized in all his *Gallic wars*' (3.59.1f.; cf. 63.5, 79.6, 84.5). With the assistance of these old totems, Caesar's old wars are reinscribed to make up his *Bellum [quam minime] ciuile* ('The war *non*-civil': see chapter 5).

4 MEIN BUMPF

Well, consider a quantificational translation of the description: say, $\exists x(\forall y((y$ was a Roman military leader & (y invaded Britain & y once decisively crossed the Rubicon)) $\leftrightarrow x = y)$ & ... x).[56]

In short, you can beat personality tests.[57]

Crude, violent, barbarous, the enemy has been cleanly divided from Rome; the mission of the *imperium*, a secure future behind pacified borders, has been celebrated for *Latinitas*; the moral centre has repelled extremism far away to the Atlantic margins, rectified by Roman order: such are the grand mythologizations of the 'realist' story of proconsular *res gestae* – the *Caesaris ... monimenta magni*.[58] Now the *Bellum Gallicum*'s greatest accomplishment, *Caesar*, must make himself count in a

[56] McCulloch (1989) 267: 'One inescapable point here is that we take a great deal on trust about how the world is and has been ...'

[57] Huff (1964) 110.

[58] '*Caesar* the Great's legacy', Catull. 11.10.

world bent on othering *him*, with ritual, with ridicule, and with righteousness. Caesar is The One, the same, in the field and on the page.
His meanings must prevail, as before.

The authorities at Rome determined to prevent Caesar from articu-
lating his case. They ruled out his criteria for making an intervention,
effectively banishing him from the *res publica*: 'they no longer lived in
the same worlds, even though the words they spoke, barely now more
than a convention, sounded the same'.[59] Like Coriolanus, Caesar must
invent a one-man collectivity where he may retort in defiance, 'I banish
you.' If this was to respond to elimination outside the state by setting
himself in its place,[60] he must transform the basis of his claim to serve
the Republic still, the proconsul's solidarity with his legions, into a
revisionary dispensation where Rome was retrieved from inimical
déformation and distorting *Tendenz* (sectarianism). Caesar's victories
will say what goes, what is what, and straighten out the rules for
wor(l)d-dealing in Rome.[61] It wasn't Caesar's fault. It wasn't Rome's.
Just a misguided cabal of losers.

So the arrogation of power for Caesarism must amount to a complete *bouleversement*, tearing up the codes of his defeated enemies,
reversing their verdicts, and yet, finally, dissolving the claim that any
revolution had occurred. No, Caesar was never enemy to Rome; his
vindication of the *res publica* brought no debt-cancellations – rather, he
brought restoration, repair and renewal to the city. Those lost ones had
done 'what had never happened before' and gone 'against all parallels
from Antiquity', 'introduced the political novelty of armed quashing of
tribunician veto', 'uttered new-fangled orders'. All over Italy, 'funds
were extracted from the townships, lifted from consecrated shrines –
throwing the divine and human rulebooks into confusion'.[62]

Contrast Caesar, who saved that 'holy of holies, the Roman treasury'

---

[59] Raditsa (1973) 449.

[60] Cf. Petrey (1990) 95f., 98f., Cavell (1987) 143–77. Raditsa (1973) 439 bites the bullet,
to show it isn't one: 'the Senate grew incapable of negotiations with Caesar, and took
unilateral steps toward war. It collapsed completely when it passed the *senatus ultimum
consultum*. In its threat, it forced Caesar, who did not take threats lightly, to act.'

[61] Caesar stresses he is the very model of the military *passim*, but esp. with his tactical
play with the Roman reveille (1.66.1; 3.37.5, 38.1). 'Military disgrace' at Dyrrhachium
hurt, 'never before in an army of Caesar' (3.64.4), but Caesar's 'Up and at 'em'
speech before Pharsalus was perfect: 'when he urged the army to battle in military
style' (3.90.1).

[62] 1.6.7f., 7.2, 85.8; 1.6.8, cf. 1.32.5, *omnia permisceri mallent* ...

(1.14.1), as he will restore his bullion and dedications to Hercules of Gades (2.21.3); later, a letter's opportune arrival from Pompey, urgent because of Caesar's lightning approach, 'saved Diana of Ephesus' ancient vaults' from Scipio – shortly before another timely letter, from Favonius, turned Scipio's course, and 'so Domitius' energy saved Cassius, Scipio's velocity saved Favonius' (3.33, 36.6f., 105.2). The one-and-only, true, Caesar.

That 'Caesar's arrival caused panic flight' of his opponent as he violated every code ('arrival', or 'epiphany': *aduentu Caesaris*, 105.1) is the refrain established from the very start, where Caesar's adversaries are swept away in flight by his very proximity.[63] So all fund-raising activities come not from Caesar, who only rewards his troops' efforts above and beyond the call of duty, but are, without exception, desecration: illegal expropriations meant to bribe the world's population to face Caesar.[64]

Caesar's sanctity (he *was*, since 63, *pontifex maximus*) is further entrusted to narrative in military dress through the medium of the military oath of loyalty, named *religio* (1.67.3): his opponents stopped fraternization between the two camps dead by exacting 'an oath not to desert or betray the army and generals, and not to plan their own individual salvation'; combined with their terroristic reprisals, the 'unprecedented sanction of the oath' prevented progress to peace (1.76.2–5).

On the other hand, when their old commander Varus talks over the former Pompeian troops by recalling their 'first memory of taking the oath', the failed Caesar-clone Curio bucks up his panicky squad by discrediting 'the oath dissolved by their surrender' in favour of the 'fresh oath' sworn to serve Caesar; in the teeth of disaster, he himself refused to come back without the army entrusted him by Caesar and went down fighting.[65] To stop his panicking army in Greece bolting from Caesar's approach, 'Labienus swore he would not desert Pompey and would take his chances with him, and the rest then followed suit'

---

[63] 1.13.1–3, 15.3, 3.12.1–3: see the powerful blueprint of Batstone (1991) esp. 128f.; Rambaud (1966) 254f. saw how the formula encompasses the entire narrative.

[64] See McDonnell (1990).

[65] 2.28.2, 32.9f.; 42.5. Seeing Caesar's Curio as 'ein jungeres Abbild seiner Selbst', Oppermann (1977) at 352, cf. Gärtner (1975) 122–5.

(3.13.3f.). But when crews surrendered on receipt of Otacilius' 'oath not to harm them, they were all led out and executed before his very eyes, in violation of the oath's sanction' (28.4): when his town came out for Caesar, Otacilius at once took to his heels (29.1). For the climax of Pharsalus, Labienus again dashingly 'took an oath that he would not return to camp unless victorious', and got the rest, including Pompey himself, to follow suit (87.5f.). Pompey precisely fled back to camp, in the 'rout' that ensued, whereas the Caesarian hero Crastinus showed how it should be done, with the simplicity of a promise – minus all the histrionics of oath-taking: 'I shall see today, my general, that you thank me alive or dead' (91.3). In the event, *Crastinus* ('Tomorrow's man'), 'was killed in combat, when a sword stabbed his face/mouth: and so it came true, all he'd said on his way to the fight ...' (99.2f.). Here the savage justice of slaughter through the mouth seals the 'truth' of his appeal to his ole buddies: 'Follow me, ... and give your general the service you pledged' (91.2). Self-reflexively, the character books his place in Caesar's heart, and record: an *exemplum* to be mentioned in despatches: *BC* is, not least, figured as Caesar's homage to his army, written *fides*.

Finally, 'the edict signed by Pompey, which told all males of serviceable age to enlist, whether Greeks or Roman citizens', failed, as Pompey was shooed onwards by Caesar's relentless approach and his 'flight continued past shut city-gates' as 'the word of Caesar's approach spread through city on city' (102.2, 4, 8). The only place on earth which would take Pompey in, perverse Egypt, duly did take him in, and treacherously executed him, too, at the hands of the Egyptian minion and of Pompey's former aide 'against the pirates', now turned pirate, not on the high seas but in a 'toy dinghy' – the state that Pompey's ship had shrunk to (104.3). The ultimate poetic irony, then, is when (it has already been observed) Caesar's 'approach' behind his *consular* fasces stirs this one township's population against Caesar, while he is kept from flight by the winds and, more than taken in by treacherous Alexandria's open door, he is holed up there at journey's end.

Now all this combination of sacrality and finance, words and bonds, that Henderson has rehearsed, goes to prove this was never a tale of civil war. Caesar did not engage in any such abomination, however it may have threatened to engulf and stain his majestic state procession bringing peace on earth. Those self-dramatizing oaths always figured in tragical narrative structures as prelude to nemesis, after fortune has oppressed Caesar, then capsized to punish his rivals for hybristic over-confidence on a Herodotean scale.[66]

Caesar made his righteousness plain to doubters among his readers when he assumed the *fasces* at Rome to inaugurate, bless, and com-mandeer *BC* Book III. As who did not know?, debt cancellation 'habitually follows *wars and civil fall-out*'; the unjustly condemned victims of Pompey's law Caesar 'put back into one piece again', by due process of magisterial legislation *ad populum*. When these unfortunates offered him their services 'at the start of the *belli ciuilis*' – one of the very few concessions Caesar ever makes to the stakes of his title and his predicament[67] – *he certainly did not accept*. Rather, he acted *as if* he had taken up their offer, though he had never fought dirty from the begin-ning of the troubles onwards. 'He had decided they should be restored by the verdict of the Roman People rather than rescued by favour of Caesar.'[68]

This from Caesar as legitimate and acknowledged *dictator* of Rome, and duly elected consul designate, to boot. Now for a negative proof, if proof could be needed. While he religiously held the elections and the Latin festival before duly abdicating the temporary crisis post of dicta-tor and setting off to campaign abroad, his own aide, Caelius Rufus, tried to stir up, as praetor, resentment against Caesar's new equity; failing to find cracks here, Caelius turned to legislative intervention but

---

[66] See Rowe (1967) 404 (but cf. the critique in Mutschler (1975) 222 and n. 1).

[67] 3.1.4. The *Bellum ciuile* is first registered as *bellum* at 1.25.3 (Pompey), 26.6 (Caesar; cf. 35.1, etc.). As throughout Latinity (Rosenberger (1992) esp. 158), euphemisms predominate, e.g. *conficiendi negotii, initio dissensionis* (1.29.1, 3.88.2; cf. Rambaud (1966) 66). At times Caesar talks as a military expert of 'war', *simpliciter*, for all the world as if circumstances don't alter cases – 'c'est la vie', 'these things happen', 'the old old story' (1.21.1, *quod saepe in bello paruis momentis magni casus intercederent*; 3.32.5, *quod in bello plerumque accidere consueuit*; 92.4f., *est quaedam animi incitatio atque alacritas naturaliter innata omnibus, quae studio pugnae incenditur ... neque frustra anti-quitus institutum est ...*). Very rarely, Caesar steels himself to slip in pontification that does belong in a *Bellum ciuile*: 'the usual, general, way of it' (*quod perterritus miles in ciuili dissensione timori magis quam religioni consulere consuerit*, 1.67.3), and *qui fere bella et ciuiles dissensiones sequi consueuit*, 3.1.3. In the latter outrage, one can't even tell whether to read in *ciuilia* with *bella*.

[68] 3.1.3–5. On Caesar's financial moderation, mimetically captured in the 'aptest of apt' syntax adapted in: *et ad timorem nouarum tabularum tollendum minuendumue ... et ad debitorum tuendam existimationem esse aptissimum existimauit* (3.1.2), cf. LaPenna (1952) 198–200.

was suppressed and suspended from office by consul and Senate; resorting to an unholy alliance with Pompey's discredited and banished former aide, Milo, he tried to stir up rebellion in Italy, while pretending to join Caesar. Their gladiators and *pastores*, debtors and armed slaves, and attempts to bribe Caesar's Gallic and Spanish cavalry, were scotched by local citizenry and a legion. Milo was killed by a rock flung from a town-wall; Caelius by Caesar's troopers. 'So it was that this overture to world-shaking events ... had a lightning and effortless finale' (3.20-2). Here, in microcosm, is the turmoil and contamination of civil war – what *could have* filled the pages of the *BC*. A caricature because a miniature, a storm in a might-have-been teacup; but, for all that, an exemplary lesson in the temperate abstention of the Pompey–Caesar dissension from the anticipated brew of social anarchy, opportunistic terrorism and cataclysmic mischief.

Above all, Caesar uses the Caelius–Milo sideshow to displace from himself the mindset of devilment. The minions ape the comradely conduct of war which the leaders manage to preserve between them through the narrative, as if by concerted arrangement. And Caesar begins his show-down campaign against Pompey as the moderate and balanced representative of legitimate Roman authority, impossible to confuse with any traitorous trouble-maker such as the *hostis* renegade Caelius (3.21.5). The 'secret messages' from Caelius to Milo (21.4), Caelius dissimulated virtually at once; Milo's 'letter', circulated to claim he acted under Pompey's 'orders' as the commission brought to him by an intermediary (22.1), cut no ice, so he dropped the idea on the instant. Contrast these botched perversions with Caesar's crusade of honest negotiation and sincere self-positioning ...

Well on the way to becoming *Caesar*, the consul installs the 'representational economy' of his self, plotting self-action in relation to his progressive escape from the bind of his framing as invader of his country, toward transcendence of the parameters within which civic identities should abide.[69] When writing Caesar prepares to leave him ice-cold in Alex, he has, for the first time, been disjoined from his armies. No longer the soldiers' soldier, he has not yet the autarky of the autonomous imperial ruler; but, now that there is no need to defeat Pompey, he must float upstream, and get ready to re-negotiate

---

[69] Cf. Battaglia (1995), 'Problematizing the Self: a thematic introduction', 2–4 for interesting (anthropological) rehearsal of this critique/jargon.

the terms of his interactive sociality with the rest of his world's *ciues Romani*. Readers know how far he is to travel toward arrogating the Pharaonic pre-eminence that commands official history in any autocracy. Caesar will dispense and *own* justice, his will to power coincident with the political will. For a short pancratic while, before the first Ides of March in Julian temporality initiated his ascension to divinity, Caesar could try out less deprecatory selves for size. It would be for Lucan to read/write back into the *Civil war* zone Julius' prefiguration of every monarch of the West (chapter 5).

Yet in the anathematic Caesarian third-person narration,[70] there already lurks the logic of a subservience of the world of writing Caesar to the writing *of* Caesar. The narrator's devotion to first-hand 'I'-witness depiction of the generalissimo in the ascendant threatens to model already the exclusive focussing of history on a Sun-King's self-orbiting.[71]

5 L'ÉTAT C'EST MOI

> Empires do not suffer emptiness of purpose at the time of their creation. It is when they have become established that aims are lost and replaced by vague ritual.[72]

Writing Caesar necessarily paints himself into a complex and contradictory corner between conflicting discourses. On the one hand, the armies he led were 'incomparably superior to any forces at the disposal of his adversaries'.[73] The celerity which gave him a bloodless occupation

---

[70] 'We thought him too cold or – shall we say? – "icily regular". We cursed his eternal third person' (Cooke (1925) 12, *cit.* Stray (1994) 204). This is all about power and the normative didaxis figured in this sadodispassionate 'set book': 'The first author read is Caesar – particularly adapted to disgust a twelve-year-old boy with Latin' (Curtius (1953) 51n. Cf. Owen (1935-6)). Lakoff (1990) 239-53, 'Winning hearts and minds: pragmatic homonymy and beyond', compares and contrasts Caesar's third person with that of Lieutenant Colonel Oliver North: North 'uses it to create emotional identification, "Caesar" detachment. But the positive impact of intimacy in a liteness style precisely parallels that of aloofness for a *gravitas* culture. The impact of each on its intended audience is similar. Both engender trust: *this is a good person* ... The plots are the same for both, and both shows are smash hits.'

[71] Cf. Marin (1988) 39-88, 'The King's narrative, or How to write history'.

[72] Herbert (1969) 47: '*Words of Muad'dib* by Princess Irulan.'

[73] Brunt (1986) 13, citing Cic. *Ad fam.* 8.14.3.

of Italy was not simply a genius' trademark;[74] it also labels the expediency of his cause: 'he would not yield the advantage that the rapidity of his offensive gave him . . . , never prepared to lose the momentum of his offensive'.[75] Military superiority must be veiled: this is *not* why Caesar would march on his country. Not that he ever did any such thing, nor does it in (that misnomer) the *De bello ciuili*.

No. Caesar has nothing to hide. Just not his style. As Henderson has noted and Caesar told, he nailed his colours to the mast, catalogues the Italian communities that spontaneously, enthusiastically, convincedly came over. Call it 'bandwaggon propaganda',[76] but these peoples of Italy were won over by the justice of his case, his forbearance, sensitivity, authenticity. The (discredited) government representatives disqualified themselves: they turned tail, ditched their men, abandoned their vaunts, saved their skins because they were found out, cowardly, inept, hypocritical. *None* of this was the result of the imminent approach of the largest fighting force on the planet (=*Caesar*), veterans of no-holds-barred massacre and all-out scourging of the Hun and the Gaul, not at all.[77]

Nothing to fear from their rapacity, not with this proconsul disciplinarian at the reins. (Actually, Caesar admits it once, 'urgently instructing Trebonius *per litteras* not to let the town be forcibly stormed, in case the soldiers . . . killed all the adults, which they were threatening to do, and were with difficulty held from bursting into the town'.)[78] Nothing to fear, for those who learned the dual lesson of the twin Thessalian towns of (i) Gomphi, where the approaching Caesar's response to being misunderstood and refused entry was exemplary terrorism *pour encourager les autres*, as 'he yielded the township to the troops for plunder' (3.80.6f.); and (ii) Metropolis, which was indeed

---

[74] For Caesar's mastery of the time-space-socio-political continuum, cf. Fugier (1968), and chapter 5.

[75] Brunt (1986) 21, 22.

[76] Collins (1959) 120f., (1972) 958f.

[77] See Collins (1972) 933f., for Caesar's atrocities and 'ethnic cleansing' in Gaul, esp. *BG* 4.11.5. Caesar would hold the world record for scalps in battle: 1,192,000 (Plin. *Nat. hist.* 7.92). Even beating the first Chinese emperor.

[78] 2.13.3f. This was Massilia, symbolic home of the free, as Caesar indicates, when 'he preserved them more for their name and fame in Ancient History than the way they'd treated him', 2.22.6 (cf. chapter 5); for Caesarian troops bent on plunder, cf. 1.21.2, 3.97.1.

encouraged by the chomping and gnashing of Gomphoi to admit Caesar, escape the same fate and provide the rest of Thessaly, and indeed the Roman and every *soi-disant* metropolis, with the moral (3.81). So: Caesar's men only behaved like those who crushed Gaul so they did not need to crush anyone (else). And, to read those who write *on* Caesar, it need never be known that this was a one-man superpower that tells the world it (he) was.

That is *not* what the row of flagwaving townsfolk lined their streets to say when they volunteered 'to do the things he ordered' – for all that this (abject, if momentary, submission)[79] is what it (and they?) meant: *sc.* (i) what the losers of Gomphi wanted to tell Caesar when they thought him beaten and shut their gates on him (3.80.3); (ii) the correlative of what the people of Antioch and its Roman citizens told the Pompeian fugitives, once beaten: 'If you approach, it will gravely endanger your necks' (3.102.6); (iii) *denique* (writes Caesar) what Alexandria did to fallen Pompey: 'just the way disaster regularly turns friends to enemies' (104.1).

It was *not* that Caesar's lightning trajectory promised all the world in his path that an open-arms welcome would help speed him on his way, the low-cost wait-and-see policy of prudence. Why, no one in *BC* supposes that this renegade Alexander controlled *only* his next host, while those in his wake hoped (erroneously) that Caesar could not be everywhere at once. The re-grouping of government troops in the West behind Caesar's lines awaits Hirtius' sequel, after the initial sortie to hunt Pompey down is brought to a satisfactory conclusion. Nor had Caesar, in pursuit of the soonest cessation of the troubles, left the new provincial front-line unforgivably bereft of legions – as he would accuse irresponsible Scipio of doing when he left the Parthians rampant in his rear, and *his* men muttered 'We'll go if we're led at the enemy, but we ain't gonna shoot no citizen, nor no consul, neither' (3.31.3f.).

For dutiful Caesar took care to leave regiments behind in Gaul, and had fresh outfits raised among the tribesmen. Not – not only – to block any assault from Spain (2.37, 39). Caesar's prompt siege also took Massilia out of the war, as the obvious port and springboard for any counter-invasion of Italy from the West. That this plan, the plan to

---

[79] 1.15.2, 20.5, 60.1, 3.12.4, 34.2. The terms belong in the minds if not the mouths of Caesar's soldiers, cf. 3.6.1, *imperaret quod uellet, quodcumque imperauisset, se aequo animo esse facturos.*

save Italy, continued seamlessly from the campaigns against the bar-barians, except that success in Gaul had brought Caesar enormous fresh reserves of recruits and levies to use *against* Rome, was a fact that must both be obscured and yet also, for other considerations, paraded.[80]

Caesar's command of his men rested on the mutual solidarity of loyal Roman vets. who had been through hell and high water together on an unconscionably prolonged tour of duty – 'nine long years',[81] 'something that had never ever happened in the army of Caesar' (3.64.4), 'Alesia and Avaricum ... conquerors of most mighty nations' (3.47.5), 'just like Gergovia' (3.73.6).[82] They had seen many a close-run scrap. He was one of the boys, engrossing them within his own name-and-fame (e.g. *frumentum ... reliqui si quid fuerat, Caesar superioribus diebus consumpserat*, 1.48.5, as if Caesar wolfed the lot), and never once tagging them *Caesariani*, but always *nostri*, in flagrant violation of his self-denying third-person autodiegetic narrative form.[83] His pro-consular dignity *did* at the outset repose on this guaranteed domain of mass approval: 'a victorious general who had served the state well', as the counsellors of Auximum (are supposed to) put it, 'with what great achievements' (1.13.1). One day's march was doubtless much the same as another, whether it took the standards into forbidden Italy or any-where else.[84] But this shower were not simply Caesar's might; this 'orrible lot (must somehow) model also his right. Not just because they were bonded by transgression, as full of mercy as anyone with a price on their head.

The same general who had (this must be so) mobilized and sum-moned his crack units from their original encampments to join him at the double, on the worst-case scenario, or the long-prepared plan,[85]

---

[80] E.g. the brace of Gallic chieftains who desert Caesar, 3.59; who later tip off Domitius, 80.7, cf. 84.4. Turncoat Labienus is wrong as ever, 'Do not think, Pompey, that this is the army that flattened Gaul and Germany ...', 87.1.

[81] As Caesar tells his troops, who roar approval, 1.7.7f. Cf. 1.39.2.

[82] An intertextual signal, cf. Gärtner (1975) 127.

[83] Cf. Perrotta (1948) 14f.

[84] Batinski (1992–3) shows how Lucan's catalogue of Caesarian troops (1.392–465) unmasks them as invading 'Gauls'.

[85] This suspicion is unsuccessfully neutralized by displacement onto Pompey: Caesar tells his troops the Spanish armies were 'fostered against him for full many a year ... The whole shooting-match was readied against Caesar' (1.85.5, 8).

of immediately overrunning all Italy, to wage his non-war of non-aggression, also made a virtue of his military ethos: straight talking and no taking needless risks or treating men as expendable cannon-fodder. This became and becomes the kernel of his pitch that *he* would avoid loss of life *on both sides*.[86]

Far from setting a fearful horde on the civilians back home, Caesar would fight the good fight, *no* fight. Not unless it was picked with him. Far from prosecuting energetic *Blitzkrieg*, Caesar was not even at war – let alone civil war. Instead, the diplomatic mission to secure fair treatment for himself and his band of triumphant heroes rested on a solid bedrock of orderly communications, a word that was his bond, orders that kept his myriads in order.

Written Caesar stands on his dignity, from unopposed pacifier of Gaul to consul cornered in the suburbs of Egypt. His writer sees to that any which way, somehow. Rhyming writer–reader relations with officer-men rapport, until none can either discern the last proconsular conqueror of the Republic or discriminate the first writer and mythographer of the Empire. Only (the titular) LETTER(S) OF CAESAR.

> Imagine that a general electroencephalocardiosomatopsychogram were possible.[87]

Appendix: Translated versions of Caesar's letter to the Senate

Here are translations of the five extant versions of 'Caesar's letter' brought to the Senate for 1 January 49:

0. Cic. *Ad fam.* 16.11.2, 'Caesar had sent threatening and bitter letter(s) to the Senate.'

1. Plut. *Pomp.* 59.2, 'For Antony also, strong-arming the Senate, read out a certain letter of Caesar before the People, containing some provocative incitements of the mob. For he proposed that both should leave office, dismiss their armed forces, leave it up to the People, and render accounts for their operations.'

---

[86] E.g. LaPenna (1952) 200 and Collins (1972) 96of. examine Caesar's abjuration of bloodshed (1.72, 74, 76, 3.90, 98 . . .), but without (Henderson thinks) getting *the* point: linkage.

[87] Derrida (1995) 144.

2. Suet. *Diu. Iul.* 29. 2, 'He begged the Senate's indulgence that the boon of the people be not taken from him, or else that the rest of the commanders should also quit their armies.'

3. Appian, *BC* 2.32, 'The screed comprised both a proud list of all that Caesar had achieved from the beginning, and a challenge, that he was willing to resign office simultaneously with Pompey, but while he still held office he would not only not resign office but would presently arrive with speed to avenge his country and himself.'

4. Dio 41.1.1, 3f., 'After this, Curio brought letter(s) from Caesar to the Senate ... In the letter was written all the fine public service that Caesar had ever performed, together with an account covering what he was being accused of. He promised both to disband his armies and to resign office, if Pompey too did the same as he. For, he said, while Pompey was under arms, it was quite unjust that Caesar should be forced to lay them down, so that he should not be delivered up to his enemies.'

5. Livy, *Periocha* CIX, 'The causes of the civil war and its opening sequence are recounted, and the disputes over sending a successor for C. Caesar, when he said he would not disband his armies, unless Pompey disbanded his.'

PART II

Horace

3   On getting rid of kings: Horace, *Satires* 1.7

Gossip is news in a red silk dress.[1]

From overview of two grand narratives, written at the start of the civil wars and long after their canonization, we now turn to close reading of two contrasting compositions by the Augustan classic Horace. One written before Octavian's defeat of Antony, the other timed to accompany the official return to consular elections and a renewed Republic – but under the aegis, or jackboot, of the life-president, Caesar Augustus. Horace does not narrate the wars, but impels his readers to scrutinize accounts offered by others. Every line he writes, however, thinks *with* the civil wars, not just *about* them. Reflects on how they become stories, speak otherwise to different people, and so incorporates the reception of his work into their agenda. The poems re-read hi(s)story for the first time – frame re-reading, have that for their subject and project. In minimizing the force of his own contribution, he draws attention to his own involvement, and puts reticent indirectness before us, to probe for its politics. Another writing, a Caesar otherwise (cf. chapter 2).

The two poems are in very different modes, and come from two of the different phases in Horace's life; they also colour the collections that include them. (We shall therefore look, 'through' *Satires* 1.7 and *Odes* 2.1, at the first book of *Sermones* and at the collection of *Carmina* I–III.) The successive publications of this poet map out between them positions that the emergent Augustan court could occupy, and pre-occupations they could share. Horace's poetry was always, whatever the topic in no matter what form, not least a profile of Horace – the creation of a (split) personality and projection of a (dual) subjectivity (chapter 4).

---

[1] News clip quoted by Spacks (1986) xi. 'Gossip gets its power by the illusion of mastery gained through taking imaginative possession of another's experience. People use this pseudo-mastery for their own purposes ... Unlike joking ... gossip involves unconcealed threat' (ibid. 22f., 51).

When Horace begins his writings (*Sermones* I was his first book) by turning back in the mid 30s to write around his brave and/or false start in fighting for Rome, where we found him listed among the proscribed of 43 (chapter I: no. xv), we are sure to demand whether he stays loyal to Brutus and Cassius and the rest of the freedom fighters of the Republic, still in favour of getting rid of kings – Caesars – as the only resort against tyranny; plays the convert, or turncoat, who warns how tawdry revolutionary zeal can swiftly become, what an avalanche of degenerating mimicry it unleashes, as assassination feeds on assassination, what juvenile *naïveté* the passing of time makes the violence of direct action (out to be); mutters or trumpets, still a small voice of Roman *libertas* worth defending to death, or now spokesman for the new Caesar no one would dare whisper should be eliminated like a Tarquin, that such whispers never die and will always have their uses, or have always been dangerous and deserve to be stigmatized as disreputable. Why, when we must know that Horace was there, does his Satire hive the anecdote off from himself? Why is this not Horace's story he is telling – when it obviously is? Why the arch innuendo, why so coy? Are his lips sealed? What is he telling us about himself and about triumviral Rome? What (Rome) is he fighting for? Why is he writing hexameters about fighting for Rome, but with the up-front brassiness of Lucilian satire, not gilded epic?

The satire has often been accounted a poor poem – repetitive, irrelevant, self-indulgent.[2] It is. And it is, rather, a cultured display of refinement as disguise, one that does not trade in the conversational idioms of Horace and his well-placed associates, but explores instead the 'loose talk' of plebeian gossip, and the fall-out that radiates from implication in it. The anecdote makes Horace, his intimates, and us take our view of the views of the populace, with no higher ground from which to measure off their abjection. The joke turns on the figure '*Brutus*', which noises a Republican politics of resistance to tyranny through what linguists term 'nonphonation'. A modern parable has it:

> There were press reports in 1986 that in a park in Zagreb, Yugoslavia, a young intellectual made a mimed protest speech before a crowd that

---

[2] E.g. Brown (1993) 165, 'shortest, slightest, and in my eyes least satisfactory . . . perhaps included as a make-weight'.

had gathered spontaneously, a speech without words (to avoid being accused of breaking the law). It seems, however, that the audience understood his message perfectly.[3]

As we shall find, Horace both tells a dummy tale about 'przemilczenie' ('not speaking about something', 'failing to mention something')[4] and at the same time performs a dumbshow of his own.[5] Whatever else we do, his audience must both have and lend ears to hear their (our) silent appellation as citizens. In the process, we have to address our views on satire, that implementation and so realization of freedom of speech in the polity, that divisive indulgence in degrading and destructive abuse – satire that sounds robustly independent and Republican, but satire that comes from sources close to the junta, and tells you it does, plays for approval from on high.

The poem messes with irritating parody of those who would drag Homer in to bolster arguments, dazzle jurors, eke out sententiousness. For content, there is just an infectious pun, or two – 'garbage', in Dryden's view, from nonce nonentities from nowhere interesting.[6] In form, this is basic scribble in hexameters, or piquant *Kleinigkeit* (triviality). As message, this is political aside, pegged to the eclipsed dateline of a *passé* international crisis. Worst of all, it could seem, the rhetoric delivers no proposition, but, infuriatingly, makes gestures in the direction of high ideological stakes that Romans could not ignore.

The joke – not-Horace's-joke, he says (or jokes) – entraps the reader into participation in the Roman, and thereafter 'Western', discourse on assassination/political martyrdom, demagoguery/Republicanism, tyranny/*coup d'état*. Going the rounds, *hi sermones, ... secreta haec murmura uolgi*,[7] deliver to the body politic the foundation myth of the Republic, without any legitimating authorization to control, direct and guarantee the narration. No one need spell out the transaction. It can't be pinned to anyone, only to everyone. Everyone else. Everyone who wants to be Roman, part of a continuing Rome. Anyone who stays out

---

[3] Manea (1992) 18. What did 'Yugoslavia' mean in 1992? 'In Zagreb'?

[4] Jaworski (1992) 108–15. Cf. ibid. 47, quoting W. Enninger: 'nonphonations ... are speech segments of high uncertainty'. On political silence, cf. Brummet (1980) 289–303, and essays in Tannen and Saville-Troike (1985).

[5] The normative force that governs 'How to Avoid Speaking' is explored by Derrida (1989) esp. 15 on 'Comment ne pas dire ... ?'

[6] Cf. Rudd (1982) 65.

[7] 'All this talk ... the mob mumbling up its sleeve', Juv. 10.88–9.

of the joke must be a lackey, living in an emirate. Who is saying that '*Brutus*' is dead: yesterday's news; an obsolete cliché: 'B' movie; consigned to a discredited past: ancient history? (Not-) Horace's joke rubs noses in solidarity: 'Why', prompts the adage with or without the comradely elusiveness it hints at celebrating, 'is it that the only people capable of running this country are either driving taxis or cutting hair?' (See the key v. 3.)

But this essay will fight its way back and forth over the grain of its text, so we shall need it before us without more ado:

> proscripti Regis Rupili pus atque uenenum
> hybrida quo pacto sit Persius ultus, opinor
> omnibus et lippis notum et tonsoribus esse.
> Persius hic permagna negotia diues habebat
> Clazomenis, etiam litis cum Rege molestas,   5
> durus homo atque odio qui posset uincere Regem,
> confidens, tumidus, adeo sermonis amari,
> Sisennas, Barros ut equis praecurreret albis.
> ad Regem redeo. postquam nihil inter utrumque
> conuenit – hoc etenim sunt omnes iure molesti   10
> quo fortes, quibus aduersum bellum incidit; inter
> Hectora Priamiden animosum atque inter Achillem
> ira fuit capitalis ut ultima diuideret mors,
> non aliam ob causam nisi quod uirtus in utroque
> summa fuit: duo si discordia uexet inertis,   15
> aut si disparibus bellum incidat, ut Diomedi
> cum Lycio Glauco, discedat pigrior ultro
> muneribus missis – Bruto praetore tenente
> ditem Asiam, Rupili et Persi par pugnat, uti non
> compositum melius cum Bitho Bacchius. in ius   20
> acres procurrunt, magnum spectaculum uterque.
> Persius exponit causam; ridetur ab omni
> conuentu; laudat Brutum laudatque cohortem:
> solem Asiae Brutum appellat, stellasque salubris
> appellat comites, excepto Rege; Canem illum,   25
> inuisum agricolis sidus, uenisse. ruebat
> flumen ut hibernum fertur quo rara securis.
> tum Praenestinus salso multoque fluenti
> expressa arbusto regerit conuicia, durus
> uindemiator et inuictus, cui saepe uiator   30

cessisset magna compellans uoce cuculum.
at Graecus, postquam est Italo perfusus aceto,
Persius exclamat 'per magnos, Brute, deos te
oro, qui reges consueris tollere, cur non
hunc Regem iugulas? operum hoc, mihi crede, tuorum est.'　　35

Proscribed Rupilius King [Rex] *and his infectious pus,*
the way Persius the half-breed gave him what he had coming, I guess
isn't news for everyone with bad eyes and barbers one and all.
This Persius was a rich man with real big business
at Clazomenae, plus a lawsuit with King that meant trouble –　　5
a tough guy, the sort that could beat [a] King for hatred,
assertive, puffed up, so acid a talker
he could zoom past Sisennas and Barruses on whitewall over-drive.
To get back to King. After zero agreement between the pair of them
is reached – you know all people are to the same degree trouble　　10
as they are courageous when head-on war befalls them; between
Hector son of Priam and between dashing Achilles
the hostility was so deadly that it took death finally to separate them,
for no other reason than that the heroism in the pair of them
was of the highest order: if a quarrel hassled two lay-abouts,　　15
or if war befell men in different leagues, as with Diomedes
versus Glaucus of Lycia, the more supine one would quit and go first
handing over gifts . . . – in the time of Brutus' command as governor
of rich Asia, the Rupilius and Persius match fight it out, so no
way was the bout Bacchius versus Bithus better billed. Into court　　20
they charge, on their mettle, an epic picture, the pair of them.
Persius sets out his case, is laughed at by the entire
gallery, lauds Brutus and lauds the staff,
dubs Brutus 'Sun of Asia' and 'Stellar Tonic'
he dubs the lieutenants, all bar King – who was 'the Dog,　　25
the star farmers detest, in its days'. He was spurting
like a river's onset in winter where the axe hardly ever comes.
Then, as he flooded sour and full-volume, the one from Praeneste
returns abuse pressed from the vineyard, the tough
grape-picker no one can beat, before whom many a time the traveller　　30
would back off calling at the top of his voice 'cuckoo'.
At this the Greek, after his shower in Italian vinegar,
Persius yells 'By the mighty gods, Brutus, I
beg you, you're used to getting rid of kings, why aren't you
slitting this King's throat? This job – trust me – calls for you.'　　35

I RIDDLE AND RIDDANCE

'Where's Ceausescu?/There's no more Ceausescu!'[8]

This little poem of Horace, briefest of the Satires, is a nasty piece of work which asks for good riddance: nasty, brutish and short. In it, a no-good nobody yells 'By the mighty gods, Brutus, I | beg you, you're used to getting rid of kings, why aren't you | slitting this King's throat? This job – trust me – calls for you.' Ruffian or martyr, a certain rough-'n'-tough brave called Rupilius *Rex* (='King'; no. (xxvii) among the blacklisted of chapter 1) is twitted for his name, by an opponent named *Persius* as if after the Kings of Persia, who throws around the sort of flattery usually lavished *on* a king of kings, to cap the altercation. (Not) much ado about nothing, or less?

The poem feints to disavow whatever it would be about. But in working to get rid of its power to mean or to matter, this satire reveals precisely what it means for the implementation of power that meaning be reviled, in a signal exemplum of the riddle as re-veiled meaning, the impulsion to veil the live evil of meaning. This, satiric revelling in this, does matter: to re-live this is to loathe it, every word of it. Not least for that hot potato, the ethics of criticism. Here Rome's repressed returns, and repeats in critical reaction and scholarship. Most commentary has obediently taken up the work of be-littling that the poem represents and in its work of representation incites. Anything to get rid of the damned thing. Its very opening words emblazon the poem 'proscribed infectious pus'. So let's 'Black it, then! Proscribe this poisonous putre-faction!' Reading of this (kind of) poem is bound fast to *resistance to* reading, to the impulsion to join in with the poem and get rid of its text. Reading reactivates the riddance which the anecdote has as its theme, repeats it at its own level. But what goes when '*Brutus*' goes?

This riddle incites violence – sucks on the jugular (*iugulas*, v. 35). But only verbally. Only as a suggestion. Neither prehistoric revolution

---

[8] The Bucharest shout of December 1989. Which echoes on, e.g. in Simpson (1991) excerpted in *The Observer Review* (27.7.91) 42, 'Saddam ... produced a picture of the executed Nicolae Ceausescu at a meeting of the Revolution Command Council to show his closest colleagues that what had happened in Romania could happen in Iraq as well.' A world war calls for this exemplary mytho-logic of replicative *dénouement*, which historians must promulgate despite themselves: narration does not mean to get rid of this climactic moment of *ultio*/'*Brutus*', far from it.

nor the now fast-fading day to forget at Philippi are on our minds or lips. Only as analogy and backdrop for a bad joke we can enjoy as a 'groan'. This is *not*, emphatically not, about a recent Ides of March. The joke is about *reges*, not *Caesar*. We recall (from chapter 2), that Julius of blessed memory – *diuus* since the triumphal triumviral settlement after Philippi – told us himself that 'he was Caesar, not king' (*Caesarem se, non regem, esse*).[9] And, no joking matter this, there is absolutely no connection between tyrannicide and the *name* '*Caesar*'. It is strictly off limits to dream that Horace, and of all people, Maecenas, Octavian's political spin-doctor, could ever think of slitting throats and Octavianus Caesar in the same thought. All this is irrelevant. In a word, the *mot juste* (and *don't* snigger), *proscribed*.

Snigger instead at the joke. The joke is non-violent interchange, the free bantering chatter of Romans about their daily lives (v. 3). Nor are we sniggering with the *hoi polloi*, we are condescending to lionize our new find, Q. Horatius Flaccus, a bright raw talent saved from himself (along with the state) by the clemency of the three members of the (duly appointed) crisis committee. We *Maecenates* are enjoying reading a poem: what could be less violent than that? Latin verse *is* fun. For instance, it lets you snigger *at* vulgarity without anyone thinking you are vulgar. Maybe it can give us street cred.

But the joke always does lend itself to its reception, that's what it's for: the joke is that it puts us all on the spot, including the jokester. That is what jokes are for. Which joke is it, *on* whom, *for* whom? The joke instigates a contest of values. Jokes are *also* ways to introduce brute violence *into* conversation, they memorialize, celebrate, naturalize and foster violence. Political jokes contest despotism when it tries to elide itself from criticism – including the application to itself of the language of tyranny. Even *mention* of tyranny is not enough of an exclusion zone. Innuendo is the creeping enemy – so hard to weed out. Or, to turn this round, tyranny can be *created* by aspersion. There is no despot until people throw the insults to match around. Jokes about the government contribute to a climate of oppression, justly or not. So jokes patrol (against) fascism, they are a barometer of public opinion, they foment stasis, in both senses – complaisance and dissension ... The question remains: what is *this* joke doing? (Who would you ask? Believe? Tell?)

---

[9] Suet. *Diu. Iul.* 79.2: 'I'm Caesar – not some dime-a-dozen king.'

At one level, the joke mobilizes an instance of the secret of power *as* the transmission of its secret, the secret that power is, the secret of representation. That is, the veiling and dissembling of meaning confers, and *is*, power over meaning. Representation *contains* violence, in both senses, transmuting but still intrinsically wielding violence.[10] The 'Brutus' anecdote shows up representation *as* itself violence. Something of this may be seen in the (dissimulated) violence of reactions it evokes and unleashes. Horace's riddle-me-ree works to get rid of its displayed veiling of violence, and that *is* its own violence. To write off Persius' purulent pun is itself a purge – a textual purge, but a purge for all that. If that's what you do, you are included with the *putsch* it performs, the *putsch* it impels us to repeat: 'Put it down! Put it down!' And if your politics are non-violent, you can side (violently) with the violence of liberalism: 'Down, in fact, with *putsches!*'

To do that is to take a representation that capitalizes on violence elsewhere – not here, not now, not us, nor ours – and allow it to disavow the violence *of* its representation, as if violence only existed to supply us with our dosage of representations, to replace us in the tranquillity of our peaceful lives. Which is to be complicit with the othering of violence in representation. Thus, the anecdote presses us to feel ourselves joining in – to 'other' Rupilius and Persius, Brutus and Horace, Asia and Philippi, together with the legendary downfall of kings, the murky drugstores and barbershops of down-town Rome, the whole shooting-match. For Horace to do that has to be self-laceration. But could any Roman get rid of all that and still be one? Is there nothing inalienable here?

Horace is re-telling (refuses to re-tell, disfigures) the Roman charter-myth of *ciuitas* as liberationist militancy. As such, his scrap of writing is at the heart of Rome. All the Romans had heard their fathers say, 'There was a Brutus once ...'[11] Whatever they might make of the civil wars, surely the one case of revolutionary uprising that would be hard to renounce was the '*Brutus*' narrative on which the *respublica libera* founded itself, the fable that sanctified violence in Roman politics? The anecdote cites, even if it does not recite, the traditional patriotic call to tyrannicidal direct action, the *exemplum* (moral imperative) trained into

---

[10] See Jed (1989). Discussion in this area centres on the work of Foucault (esp. (1981)) and of Gramsci (Crowley (1987); cf. Frow (1989)).

[11] *Julius Caesar* 1.2.157.

the *ciuis Romanus*' marrow. Does Horace dare distance and de-mystify this parable? Does he mean to purify politics 'here and now' of pollution by getting shot of the virulent old fable? Civic activism just a simplistic fiction, kept in misplaced currency by charlatans and knaves? Leave it where it belongs, in the dustbin of the past? Let it go – it always was a mockery, and has ruined generations of lives? The trouble is, '*Brutus*' had not gone out of style. He never did (see chapter 7). Funny, but true, that beards would return to royal chins just when Rome's emperor among satirists writes *quis priscum illud miratur acumen, | Brute, tuum? facile est barbato imponere regi.*[12]

The simplicity of the culture-narrative which equated the presence to society of a Brutus with the commandment to vindicate *libertas* from *regnum* had re-inscribed itself on J. Caesar's body. Such was the rule of thumb of, for instance, the people's couplet: *Brutus, quia reges eiecit, consul primus factus est: | hic, quia consules eiecit, rex postremo factus est.*[13] Still more eloquently (to add one further instance), the tyrannicide Brutus' dashed hopes of re-utilizing Accius' old play *Brutus* (for the *gens* it had first been written for) to top the bill of his *ludi Apollinares* in 'celebration' of the official 'birthday' of Julius on 13 *Quintilis* 44 *acted out* the political script of the foundation myth of the Republic. Whether or not Antony's brother (who actually held the games in this first ever *July* on the Julian calendar when Rome was too hot for that honourable man Brutus himself) literally cut *Brutus* and displaced it with Accius' *Tereus*, the horrible muting of the cry of 'Liberty' was violently projected round Pompey's theatre and amplified for all to read, in loud and clear silence:[14] '*Brutus*', name of the condition of resistance to despotic *force majeure*, the promise of redress, was revived for its public *in its cancellation.*

For the very name '*Brutus*' ('lumpen, dumb, mute, sub-human, macho') speaks even through the absence of its signified, as ever since

---

[12] 'Who marvels at the legendary subtlety of "Brutus"? It's a push-over to outwit a preshaving king', Juv. 4.102f.

[13] 'Brutus because he expelled kings, became first consul; | this one, because he expelled consuls, became finally king', Suet. *Iul.* 80.3. Cf. Dunkle (1967) 151f.

[14] Cf. Clavel-Lévêque (1984) 57, Evans (1992) 145–7. Clarke (1981) 140 n. 40 warns that the scrapping of *Brutus* may be 'simply a joke' remark from Cicero (so no *simple* joke). For 'Brutus' in the late 40s, cf. esp. Cic. *Epp. ad Brut.* 1.15.6, *consilia inire coepi Brutina plane (uestri enim haec sunt propria sanguinis) reipublicae liberandae*, Dio 44.12, Boes (1981) 164–76.

the beginning, and this is the signification of the veiling of language from power, the stolid power of those excluded from discourse which stems from their very exclusion. Showing a hack *Tereus* would only amplify the pain of muffled freedom.[15] Get rid of Brutus (from Rome, from the stage, from a story) and all that powers-that-be achieve is to re-activate the silent vocality of '*Brutus*' and all that that signifies, the legend, its compulsion toward self-realization in direct action, the liberation it bespeaks from the control of dominant hierarchies and their significations. Tyranny always surrounds itself with speaking silence, the eloquence evoked by the muted. And in return the mute mark out the tyrannical. This is the unofficial knowledge, these are the silent and deadly workings, of any Brutus anecdote.

Horace's jolly tale incisively juggles its own (Brutus') voice away, severs its Brutus from language: in the process, it courts re-activation of the founding principle of the assortment of meanings heaped together under the figure 'Brutus', *longe alius ingenii quam cuius simulationem induerat*.[16] And, to turn this round, in Horace's anecdote the Republican subtext weathers its repression, it dons the mask of a stupidity, the masking stupidity of a satirist's caricature. A story at once branded contraband: 'the outlaw (*proscripti*, v. 1) *versus* the half-breed' (*hybrida*, v. 2: 'the man of violence, of hybris, who transgresses against racist/ nationalist/whatever categories'). A dumb story handed us in preliminary précis, written off before we can even begin: this is, short and sour, 'revenge taken' (*quo pacto sit ... ultus*, v. 2). All over before we begin, so we can get rid of it all the more easily. 'Just tittle-tattle.'

If we do read on, it will be to get rid of annoying interest, despite ourselves, in what Horace means to irritate us with. And what he means by irritating us with it. In the eating, this pudding only clarifies this 'revenge' if we are prepared to force (do violence to) the text. We shall find that the punch-line won't help define the 'vengeance' *any*

---

[15] Even a snuff-*Tereus*' Philomela can get rid of a king. That is what she means, her message. Her silenced charade never stops beaming this message from victims to their oppressors, at all Caesars. Philomela makes tongues wag, then knives, cf. Richlin (1992) 162–5.

[16] 'Not half as dumb as the dummy he'd put on for show', Liv. 1.56.7, cf. Ovid's tale of *Regifugium* in *Fast.* 2.685–852, with *Brutus ... stulti sapiens imitator* ('wise mock-fool') v. 717, *Brutus adest. ... animo sua nomina fallit* ('Brutus' big moment: belies his name with brute courage'), v. 837 (cf. *edidit impauidos ore minante sonos; uirtus dissimulata; Brutus clamore*, vv. 840–9, with Feeney (1992) 11).

more closely. Readers duly fill in what Horace left blank for them. But this is ticklish: in *ultus* we are brought perilously close to confronting a (carnivalised) elaboration of a master-signifier of Rome of the 30s, core of the politics of Octavian Caesar. *Vltio* labelled *his* violence as a specific duty of pious counter-violence, a sanctioned filial vendetta against the self-proclaimed tyrannicides, re-written by triumviral *fiat* as *hostes* (public enemies).[17]

If we are to get rid of such leakage of meaning away from the skit scene of 'Persius versus Rupilius', we must fight off reading the satire as in any sense a cosmi-comic displacement of the struggle to control Rome, to control meaning in Latin. Tweedledum's pun avenges its match, Tweedledee's abuse. That is all there is to it – exactly what *ultus* was always already signalling, in advance (v. 2). 'Seen it. Case dismissed.'

2 SKUNKS AND SATIRE

It's a wonder that you still know how to breathe.[18]

Now we have got rid of 1.7 in just the way it does for itself, more silly silliness and sillier smelliness are to follow. In 1.8 *brut* Horace plays the jester 'Dickhead' (*Priapus*) and talks out of his backside for Maecenas, getting rid of some witches, the black magic and malevolent spells that afflicted Rome before Octavian;[19] then we (thankfully) climb up out of the gutter of Horace's youth into the light of day with 1.9's self-portrait.[20] Here Maecenas' poet-client will be back in person, as in 1.1–6, to confront one more *alter ego*, the would-be emulator 'pest'. On the *Via Sacra*, no longer the first damned spot that leapt to mind for getting rid of a king,[21] he defends civilization with the poetic justice of good riddance to more bad rubbish, as he wards off evil from (Octavian's) Rome. Here Horatius will begin to lift his head toward the vatic sublimities of (his) post-Actian maturity: Apollo closes the poem

---

[17] *RGDA* 2, DuQuesnay (1984) 205 n. 79.

[18] Dylan (1974) 'Idiot wind'.

[19] 'La raie de mon fondement à été publique, donc je suis la République' ('The crack in my arse has been made public, and therefore I am the Republic'), as one patient later put it (Redfern (1984) 116). See Henderson (1989) 60–3.

[20] Cf. Radermacher (1970) 277.

[21] Suet. *Iul.* 80. 4; another *alter ego* of Horace, another servile military tribune (cf. *Sat.* 1.6.46–8, Armstrong (1986) 271f., comparing Tillius in *Sat.* 1.6.24–5), gets his earful of *libertas* ('Freedom, free speech as invective') here in Epode 4.

to get rid of the pest, along with everything you can want him to represent. We can think, so throw, the pest, away, with all the spleen, gut
and groin of Horace's early writing (*Satires* and *Epodes*), the Horace of
the man-in-the-street's civic *inuidia*.[22] The scapegoat-reject will bear
off with him the virulence of the ulcerous world of chaos post-Ides-of-
March, enemy of peace and poesie. We *will* Horace to get rid of his
'shadow', and approve when the long arm of the law reaches out and
gets shot of the offender, of anyone who gives 'us' offence: behind the
placid exterior of flopsy Horatius 'Flaccus' is re-veiled the divine wrath
of triumviral justice, fighting invisibly to save Rome from the Romans.
Our part is to welcome, with or without recognition, the violently
suppressed repression[23] that Horace's poem works upon its readers. It
charms both this, the nuisance of the pest and us away.

We will, frankly, be glad to see the back of the pest, and that side of
Horace and our selves. And the pest stands for his era's back side,
when the 30s forced (even nice) Horace to take sides, and we are
forced, too, to back his side. If we have prized Satire's/our precious
freedom to speak out, still in 1.9 we feel with relief the glad sensation
that we need no longer exercise civic frankness. For to be civilized is,
exactly, to aspire to a *res publica* in which we are rid of the duty to be
unpleasant. Above nastiness, beyond dissension. Politeness polices the
polity – that is what '*Horace*' will stand for, in the citizens' arrest we
readers are softly con-scripted into making 'for' him, as his under-
studies. But if the claim is made that this ideal is now attained, then
...? To keep Caesars out of view, out of the reading of 1.9 / the reckoning, can prove just as violent an act of collusion in representation as
ever it was back in 1.7 / as it ever is.[24]

So readers of satire are co-opted into the persecution of the 'fall
guys', all the losers in the stakes of cultural capital. What is really being
(re)-produced in these poems is an orderliness, the seriousness of a
hegemonic mindset, as the blueprint for our work of interpretation.
You'll see, the *genius* of Horace was all along at the controls, soon to
shake free from the unpleasant bars of the musick of his youth. He
was using the image-repertoire of the *populus* all along, as a rhetoric
to heave civility up by its boot-straps. Wherever the early poetry could

---

[22] See Henderson (1987) for a reading of the *Epodes* through woman-hating Epode 8.
[23] Cf. Lecercle (1990) esp. 242f.
[24] See Henderson (1993).

appear to be immature, tasteless, offensive, this was really a lever for the decency and sweet decorum of civilized Moderation. Every bit of it, if we can pull that off: the first book of *Sermones*, pictured by 1.8 as 'a speech act in ten farts'. And then Epode 3's garlic model for its book of 'bad mouth in seventeen breaths'.[25] For the interpreter's challenge is to reclaim ubiquity for reason, to snatch control from the libertine disorder of brutish carnival.

In the classic script, the repressed must put in a rationed appearance, in order that it may be returned to its repression; the canonical text applies all the brute farce of an exorcism to banish from interpretation whatever mocks Reason. The irreducible residue is for us to marginalize, suppress one way or another, and scapegoat: 'Best of a Bad Job'.[26] What would we be saying/accepting about ourselves if we didn't help keep order in the best repair? And that includes hiding from view the unpleasantness of this work of 'purification' – what we might call the splashback pollution of expurgation.

One way to despatch 1.7, then, is to brand the thing the exception that proves the rule, a work of Horace that he wanted (meant) to get rid of. If (most) post-Victorians can no longer jettison it as an early, so hardly 'Horatian', composition, then, short of refusing to print its filth in our editions,[27] we can marginalize it as a meaningful dud: 'it was precisely for such nothings (*Nichtigkeiten*), or, to say it in Latin, *nugae*, as themes to be embroidered by him, that Horace was looking when he had decided to fill up his book of satires by the insertion of a few additional pieces'.[28] Thus Horace resorted to 1.7 as a last-minute expedient so that he could get rid of *the whole book*. This said, we can take up the 'trifle', as a relatively harmless nullity. Or else we can salvage the poem's 'literary/aesthetic' coding for Horatian/'Callimachean' poetics, and save the poem for Horatian tastefulness – save these ruddy

---

[25] Cf. Gowers (1993) 281–310, for the 'love–hate relationship' of (this) 'Garlic breath'.

[26] Cf. Wills (1989) 130f., White (1989), on the civilized internalizing and inhibition of the festal repertoire as our pollutant/purgation.

[27] The cut and trimmed 1.2 and 1.8 palmered off in old editions stage violence committed on slang, forcible repression of obscene language. The convention of 'obscenity' once had its civilizing way as the recognition, sanctification, of 'obscene language', masking – what it now marks – the singular importance of veiling the hard-core of gender-discrimination in the economy of traditional culture. Both poems become through cutting, if c**t-less and f**t-less, *none the less blatantly point-less. And that* no longer becomes the Bard, the Classic-to-be, our 'Horace'.

[28] Fraenkel (1957) 120f.

verses from dismissal as a 'trivial' 'failure',[29] 'an inept make-weight to fill up the book'.[30]

And yet. Even as we are led to ponder the significance of 'Rupilius *versus* Persius' – 'What they represent nags at our thoughts'[31] – we are still well caught in the work of repressing the text. The *joke*, i.e. the end of the poem's pun on Rupilius' *cognomen* of *Rex*, can't be what we're here for.[32] The humour must have some force beyond that. We can all test this out: 'with this poem one might start, at the very end as it were, by considering the effect produced on the reader as he (*sic*) completes the poem. The reader is left with a feeling of distaste'; once we have found the humour to be of the forced kind, we can allow the poem's 'jaundiced view' to jaundice our 'view of epic and its code of conduct'.[33] This de-mystificatory work of representation 'glittering in its epic pomp'[34] falls where it means to fall – which is to say, well short of real violence.

But, it could nag readers, isn't our fighting for Rome just saving a residue of the poem now? Forcing the thing to behave, to tell us something we can feel comfortable with, to feel we are nice, nice as Horace usually contrives to be? Seeing the characters as 'representing' at all, necessary if we are to see their story as vehicle to some underlying tenor (poetic, cultural, ideological, political, whatever), is by definition bound to be a way of getting rid of them in some measure, of discounting their excess, of trimming. For representation is clearly caught up in the drive to interpret, to recognize pattern, and the normalization at work in interpretation is targeted on satisfaction.

Strong will is needed to elicit satisfactory sense from the characters. Some readers try to affix values to 'Rupilius ~ Persius', as differentiated contraries and/or as a convergent pair. They look to educe a fruitful, or

---

[29] Rudd (1982) 66f., 'Having paid for a ringside seat we feel like demanding our money back.'

[30] Coffey (1976) 78: 'not' to be 'uncharitable', is his saving formula, the formula that would save him from his uncharity, if –

[31] Connor (1987) 106.

[32] It is anticipated at v. 6, *qui posset uincere regem/Regem* ('who had the beating of (a) king/King'), Van Rooy (1971) 74 n. 24, cf. vv. 29f., *re-gerit conuicia ... uindemiator ... inuictus*. For the currency of the pun in the late 40s , cf. Cic. *Ad Att.* 1.16.10, *Quousque, inquit, hunc [Marcium] regem/Regem feremus?*, Matthews (1973) 23.

[33] Connor (1987) 105f.

[34] Fraenkel (1957) 120.

frightful, dialectic by counterposing either one or the brace of them against '*Horace*', against 'Horatian' values.[35] But the poem, which may indeed recommend such dialectical evaluation by practising it, also puts paid to any notion that mastery of the representation is attainable. The poem's 'filling', vv. 10–18, ensures this, given over to the parodic, self-satirizing, turgidity of extended comparison of 'Rupilius *versus* Persius' before the law (*ius*, v. 20) with contrastive scenes of man-to-man combat from the *Iliad*, and their law (*iure*, v. 10). In the proportions 'Achilles : Hector' and 'Diomedes : Glaucus', there is imported into the anecdote an invitation to bring to its 'duel' the proceeds of your reading in literature – your cultural formation, no less. In the process, Horace's text opens onto that classic *locus conclamatus* of Homeric scholarship, the evaluation of Glaukos' exchange of arms with Diomedes.[36] This points straight to an abyss for interpretation: 'it is right to exercise some caution'.[37]

In the *Iliad*, 'Diomedes *versus* Glaukos' reads locally as a key move in the dialectical traverse from 'Sarpedon *versus* Tlepolemos' to 'Hektor *versus* Aias', wherein heroes negotiate recognition/killing in the face of mortality,[38] en route ultimately to 'Akhilleus *versus* Hektor', the critical moment of the narrative's exchange with its audience, interpretation's pay-off. More specifically, ancient no less than modern readers fasten on the *Iliad*'s own marking of 'Diomedes *versus* Glaukos' as a pregnant 'moment' of 'inequivalence ... in the exchange of arms'.[39] We can never be comfortably reconciled with the heroes' own reconciliation through reciprocal exchange of words, arms, recognition, for their narrator scandalously stigmatizes Glaukos. Horace in fact had no option but to join an acknowledged contest between interpretations – the contest of inter-pretation.

Besides, any mention of the Diomedes/Glaucus Affair would awake readerly suspicions of a leg-pull, for there were both (i) literary precedent for aping Homer's 'ridicule' for his own hero by picking out and picking on Glaucus as the epic's own figure of fun; and (ii) a (quasi-)proverbial currency for Glaucus' bad deal: χρύσεα χαλκείων ('gold for

---

[35] Kraggerud (1979) 95f., 98, Van Rooy (1971) 76 and n. 36.

[36] Along with the episode it climaxes, cf. Harries (1993), Maftei (1976) esp. 52–5.

[37] Van Rooy (1971) 75.

[38] Cf. Benardete (1968) esp. 29.

[39] Lynn-George (1988) 200.

bronze').[40] Thus the poem's bloated and self-indulgent aside on 'Diomedes *versus* Glaucus' injects a discordant note into the presentation of the 'Rupilius *versus* Persius' dispute.

Readers (readers at any rate with a nose for satire) must scent self-reflexivity, as the poem 1.7 offers us Horatian 'gold', the representation and its work of re-presentation, in lieu of the nasty civil war 'bronze' of its represented, as a stake in the deal by which it exchanges Homeric 'gold' for Lucilian 'bronze'. Thus, Persius' *flumen ... hibernum* ('a river's onset in winter'), v. 27, is interchanged through *salso multoque fluenti* ('as he flooded sour and full-volume'), v. 28, with Praenestine Rupilius' *expressa arbusto conuicia* ('returns abuse pressed from the vineyard'), as from a *uindemiator* ('a tough grape-picker'), with all his *Italo ... aceto* ('Italian vinegar', i.e. 'plonk'), vv. 29–32, and then switched back by *Graecus ... Persius* ('Persius the Greek'), vv. 32f., in his final 'exclamation'. Gold for bronze, for ...? We should wonder what this trade-off, of *sermonis amari* ('so acid a talker', i.e. 'bitter whine'), v. 7, in *sermo*, has to say to the presentation of early Horatian poetics: the abrasive sting of an adoxographic poetry *after* Callimachus.[41]

But we should (not) stop there – merely registering a literary profile for 1.7. Nor is it sufficient to sketch out a simple political intent for the poem. For in the ideological stakes of the work of representation, the 'gold' of *ditem Asiam* ('rich Asia'), v. 19, underwrites the valuation of *Persius ... diues* ('Persius ... a rich man'), v. 4. So does Horace satirically demand that his readers give him, in exchange for the 'glitch' of his throw-away lines, the 'gold' of their esteem for his performance? Does/n't the 'faint-hearted' poet 'quit', à la Glaucus (*discedat pigrior*, v. 17)? Duck a show-down with his critics, palming off on us an offer we can't refuse, the golden gift of a gilded suit of satirical armour (*ultro | muneribus missis*, 'go first | sending gifts of appeasement', vv. 17f.)? Is his initiative matched by *our* brazen complicity?

The requirement of in-put from the reader keeps the text live, open to reading and re-reading. It wears on its sleeve the slogan 'Gold for bronze', a disconcertingly plain warning that: 'Someone round here is being had!' Such nagging suspicions constitute satiric narrative as the implication of readers' values, sophistication, politics. They are,

---

[40] Lloyd-Jones and Parsons (1983) 120 on ?Callimachus? *fr.* 276.2, *heroa Lycium Lycio glossemate obiurgat*; Otto (1971) 82, s.v. *chrysius*.

[41] Cf. Scodel (1987).

precisely, what you cannot get rid of, what you can only wish good riddance.[42] In brief, no agreed valorization of Horace's combatants through comparison with Homer is forthcoming. A match (or is it a walk-over) between Horace's handful of debased satiric hexameters, and the *Iliad*?

Rupilius and Persius will not represent securely and we are *not* assured, through them, of control of the sense of their poem, of the joke they figure (in). If we press the final joke to get rid of the nastiness of their desperado-invective,[43] the violence of its demand for uplift all too easily will become palpable, even unmissable. For the text authorizes no estimate of the *impact* of the 'bad pun'. *None whatever.* The poem does not even warrant the understanding of Persius' 'exclamation' *as* a 'pun', of whatever quality, to whoever's ears – nor even as a 'joke'. If there is to be a 'laugh', whether of appreciation or of derision, on whatever interpretation or refusal to interpret, the text has been staged to get rid of it. Any smirks, groans, cackles, hoots, roars, brutific smiles must come, *if* they come, from the reader. The *text* just cuts out.

Most recent readers have got rid of the pun from their estimation of the poem's good offices precisely because they cannot, when put on the spot, abide by 'the fact [*sic*] that in the Roman world of the second half of the last century BC the pun on "*rex*" was in fact a very polished (and most popular) joke'.[44] Thus, what matters more than its 'quality' is the positionality of the pun: the pun that climaxes an anecdote is not *langue* but *parole*, it is not iterable but rather discursively set as a specific performance.[45] The pun, above all figures and instances of language, is not seized in the enumeration of its instances: its brute force resides in the grain of social drama. This is why puns can be like poetry.[46] And

---

[42] Cf. Marin (1978), Palmeri (1990) esp. 1–10, on 'open-ended dialogicality'.

[43] 'The bad pun devised by Persius as a last resort achieves more than he anticipated: the audience laughs at his enemy. No doubt, the audience was laughing at both foes, and the main result is that the pun reduces the tensions of the bitter dispute', Anderson (1982) 80. Doubtless 'No doubt' always gets rid of bother.

[44] Van Rooy (1971) 81. Insistence on '*the fact* of the matter' in fact always betrays strain.

[45] Goffman (1972) 65, 'The act of speaking must always be referred to the state of talk that is sustained through the particular turn at talking ... and ... this state of talk involves a circle of others ratified as co-participants'; cf. essays in Drew and Wootton (1988).

[46] Chiaro (1992) 34, quoting Sherzer: 'puns are seen as items which occur outside their expected habitat ... "precisely the Jakobsonian definition of poetry"'.

this is why it can only be a formalist misrecognition to declare: 'in itself the pun is not too bad'.[47] For it *has* no intrinsic self.[48]

3 RIDDLED WITH FICTIONAL BULLETS

> Am I so far gone, in my desperate need for meaning, that I'm pre-pared to distort everything – to rewrite the whole history of my times purely in order to place myself in a central role? Today, in my con-fusion, I can't judge. I'll have to leave it to others.[49]

As we remarked, anecdotes challenge their participants to ask first: 'Where is the joke?' One response, one blatantly pioneered by Horace, is to get rid of this question, lock, stock and barrel. For the poet has disowned 'his' anecdote, marginalized the 'joke' along with its deni-zens' whole world, disengaged from the whole shooting-match. 'It is not really Horace's garbage.'[50] That is to say, we cannot play blind to the fact that Horace has got rid of himself from Brutus' *conuentus* ('gallery', i.e. at the assizes, v. 23). In one effort to come to terms with this, we are told that: 'he cannot be accused of malicious invention: every reader knows he was there and that the anecdote has all the authority of an eyewitness account. In any case, we are assured that the tale is well known.'[51] But however reassuringly authoritative we find such assurances, there has to be both more and less to the re-presentation of the anecdote as the much-bruited common property of 'everyone with bad eyes, and barbers one and all' (*omnibus et lippis notum et tonsoribus*, v. 3), rather than as *Icherzählung* ('I was that soldier' narrative), than this.

---

[47] Rudd (1982) 65.

[48] Cf. Culler (1988) 4, 'The pun is the foundation of letters, in that the exploitation of formal resemblance to establish connections of meaning seems the basic activity of literature; but this foundation is a foundation of letters only, a foundation of marks whose significance depends on relations, whose own significative status is a function of practices of reading, forms of attention, and social convention'; Chiaro (1992) 39, 'Puns are two-faced. Their hidden meaning is brought out by the environment in which they occur.'

[49] Saleem, worried about getting the date of Gandhi's death wrong for ever, in Rushdie (1981) 166.

[50] Rudd (1982) 65.

[51] DuQuesnay (1984) 37f. In any case, whatever the force of '*in any case*' here or in any case, such assurances can, obviously, disconcert: cf. Brown (1993) 166 'he is obviously not going to devote a satire to a story which he really expects will be familiar'.

Horace is far from giving 'a direct and detailed picture of the republican side'. At the very least, 'he is playing a double game'.[52] We could decide to decide that Horace *writes the poem*, but that the people of Rome *tell the tale* through his voice. That is one valorization, of many. We may wish to be rid of the gaps that open up in this siting of the material as a relay, a (re-)citation. For example, have our Horace laugh *with* as well as *at* his characters and their repartee;[53] then decide for ourselves whether his derision of them is more savagely biting than their in-fighting is to each other, working out as we do so how to save the poet's seriousness for our own. If we can. For example, have the poet's good humour overcome the hatefulness of the era whose good riddance was Philippi – all that the nasty sting of Lucilian satire is best fit to evoke. So Horatian *sermo* gives up on spleen, bounces aggressive spite out of civilization.[54] Doesn't the story come right out with it and *say* it is both an eyesore looking for a poultice, polluted by the ailing point of view of the political body; and a contaminated bit of its ephemeral refuse, the unwanted facial hair that a cultured patriarchal citizen leaves with his (*sic*) barber as the sign of his purgation (v. 3)?

Decide, in the very best tradition, not to exceed what the text says.[55] And in so deciding, iron out the text so that it may, all the same, offer in caricature a serious assessment of Brutus, through the comic reflectors of his associates, the anecdote's exhibits. For 'at the centre of all this activity is Brutus'.[56]

Horace gets rid of important victims from this poem / his texts only so that he may the better home in *indirectly* on its/their target.[57] He conjures up the atmosphere of the civil war: 'the Republicans are depicted at each other's throats in litigation ... But he cannot be accused of malicious invention.'[58] Why not? Because ... he/we won't let ourselves accuse him of that. Because we won't read dissembled

---

52 DuQuesnay (1984) 36; Rudd (1982) 65.
53 Rudd (1982) 65.
54 Kraggerud (1979) 104f.
55 Ibid. 92f.: 'Wir sind deshalb nicht berechtig, Aussagen über den Ausgang des Rechtsstreites zu machen ... Wenn also der Dichter über den Ausgang schweigt, dann sollte auch der Interpret diese Frage nicht aufwerfen.'
56 DuQuesnay (1984) 36.
57 Kraggerud (1979) 95.
58 DuQuesnay (1984) 37, punning on Persius' *iugulas* ('slitting this King's throat'), v. 35, to cover the text seamlessly with its interpretation. Mimetic QED.

vituperation, verbal violence under cover of genial humour, as (violent) vituperation. Because we want to side with the representation. Whatever we may find ourselves making it say.

Yet we never can securely assign the voicing of the tale, as between (i) Horace's own waste product, and (ii) a favourite (much-loved/ -loathed bad?) joke from the people's repertoire, and this problematizes the whole tenor of the narration. There is, for instance, a 'clear' contrast between the *reporting* of Persius' first verbal salvo (vv. 22–7), and the *quoting* of his final exclamation (vv. 33–5).[59] The first sally, of Hellenistic-style, 'soteriological', flattery, is 'laughed at by the entire | gallery' (vv. 22f.): we may hear the laughter again, re-doubled, as the response to the 'yell' he ends with, this time in the very different terms of recourse to a quip in the rhetoric of Roman tyrannicide (vv. 33–5). Would the 'laughter' be just the same, for the diametrically different style of oratory? Or will any 'laughter', if laughter there is to be, from the *conuentus* and/or from its general, Brutus, be of a diametrically different kind, for Persius' equally derisory/risible/agreeable/cheery oratorical *tours de force*? Does Horace's repetitive style of reportage for Persius' first effort, *laudat ... laudatque,* | *sol(em) ... salubris* |, *Brutum ... Brutum ... salubris, appellat ... stellas ... appellat* (vv. 23–5), communicate long-winded prolixity, Persius droning on and on round the constellations, and so pre-figure a *volte face* in his pithy 'yell'? Does the vocally involving music of Horace's report create or evoke a style of (Asiatic) sonority, over against the Roman *tene rem, uerba sequentur*-style of Persius' later colloquial quip, if quip it be, his pseudo-atavistic thrust to Brutus, *ad hominem*? Is this the silver-tongued master of language – the Greekling to a *t*? ' "Indirect discourse" in narration never escapes some degree of implied "stylistic physiognomy" – the sound of the man's [*sic*] voice.'[60]

Shall we see Persius' first effort as setting in train a competition in the mobilization of power through nomination? When he calls Brutus and co. 'the solar system', he is binding '*Brutus*' to a burden of obligations: his deferential 'Salaam' accords supreme power its potential for

---

[59] By contrast, Rupilius' first effort is eclipsed by silence: its report even yields speech to the internal opponent, the 'traveller' who before 'backing off' before the 'grape-picker', is 'calling at the top of his voice' at him (vv. 30f.).

[60] Tannen (1989) 99. The poem is an echo-text à la *cu-culus* ('cuckoo'), cf. *conuentu ... cohortem; conuentu ... comites ... uenisse; inuis(um) agricolis sidus; inuis(um) ... uenisse,* vv. 23–6.

violence, but tuned to his own ends. Already, within his speech, Persius re-names his co-star Rupilius 'the Dog(-Star)', the place in the topology of the metaphorical firmament to which the outcast beast is driven by the force of analogy. So Persius already mobilizes the verbal pun against *Rex*, as he 'others' him from Brutus-the-'Sun'(-King). As he does so, he catasterizes, so mock-magnifies, his victim, however much those who identify with the 'farmers', those primeval bearers of culture, will join them in 'detesting' the coming of the Dog-Star (vv. 25–6). And Persius models already his later attempt to manipulate metonymy in place of metaphor, by complimentary naming of *Brutus* for the power and obligations of his pedigree. But do his two examples of the politics of rhetoric chime – or do they clash the one with the other?

Naturally, direct speech is withheld to the climax so that its mimetic force may the more effectively tie its reader into actualizing the scene, into 'living' it.[61] But how is the reader to flush away the (unresolvable) issue of how much, and how little, in the poem is ascribable to '*Horace*', behind and beyond his dummy narrators in the chemists' and barbers'? Rupilius and Persius, Brutus and the gathering, cannot, for example, have appreciated any verse-match of Persius' insult – 'the Dog' (*can(em) illum* |, v. 25) – to Rupilius' abuse, that 'cuckoo' call (*cuculum* |, v. 31). Only a telling of the story which features the 'comparisons' with the Homeric adversaries of Horace's poem could find an analogy for the 'traveller' in this image, who 'backs off', in the 'quitting' of 'the more supine one'.[62] Similarly, the Dog-Star is a favourite marker of early Horatian writing,[63] and only in a hexametric parody of the *epos* does Persius' canine abuse of Rupilius bespeak the Homeric imagery of comparison of serious heroes (Akhilleus and his understudy, Diomedes) with *Sirius*.

No. This narration blinks and blurs between its several narrators and its audiences. Different considerations may naturalize the 'pair' of combatants as either one-off eccentrics ('never seen the like') or all-too-familiar social stereotypes ('you know the sort'). But authorization

---

61 Tannen (1989) 25f.

62 *uiator | cessisset*, vv. 30f. ~ *discedat pigrior*, v. 17. The 'traveller' would be a shadow for Persius – were Persius just passing through Brutus' camp, bound for some trade-route, stumbling upon civil war and pitching into fighting (for Rome and) his own corner.

63 Oliensis (1991) esp. 120f.

for this is suspended indefinitely between (i) the characters; (ii) the citation 'for sore eyes' at the chemist's which has also been a close shave 'at the barber's' (v. 3); and (iii) the poet's voice. All three of them materialized in the writing. Even and especially the final 'yell', which we could well see as the *raison d'être* of the performance, demands that we hear in its foregrounded, ostentatiously *uerbatim*, quotation the proximate narrator *Horace*, rather than Persius' *ipsissima uerba*. For that is the rule in the anecdote – that in it apparent 'direct speech' is itself a species of 'fictive utterance', a form of 'constructed dialogue'.[64] Thus, for example, it is certainly not in my translation, but effectively, if not only, *in Horace's poem*, that the introduction of Persius as the man with '*real big* business' could be amplified through '*the top of* the voice' of the traveller who is 'calling out', to set up Persius' 'yell "By the *mighty* gods"' (*permagna . . . negotia*, v. 4, *magna . . . uoce*, v. 31, *per magnos . . . deos*, v. 33: marked out by the intertwined echo of *Brute . . . te*, in apotheosis by word-order; cf. *appellat . . . appellat*, vv. 24–5 ~ *compellans*, v. 31). *For Horace's reader*, the very wording of the 'yell' is itself part of the styling as well as the authorizing of the narration. For instance, '*permagnus*' does *not* have a *real big* distribution in Latin verse.

In short, we might judge that the anecdote arises entirely from Horace's desire to get what he has to say à propos '*Brutus*' said, and that all the rest is the *alibi* of 'reportage'. This whether or not it is at all *accurate*, in the senses (i) that it accurately reports a, or the, popular tale going the rounds – the tale whose entire *raison d'être* was to get what the people had to say à propos '*Brutus*' said –; and (ii) that that telling accurately reports what (some little bird said) Persius actually said at the time.

Thus the political force of this re-presentation of violent politics need not be purged from the poem. We can appreciate Horace's elimination of authorial explicitation by writing his authority back into the text in our reading. We can get rid of his withholding of the conclusion of his tale. And we can be subtle enough to leave (impel) our readers to draw the right conclusions as their own by writing in the name of

---

[64] Tannen (1989) esp. 110: 'The act of transforming others' words into one's own discourse is a creative and enlivening one . . . even if "reported" accurately. In many, perhaps most, cases, however, material represented as dialogue was never spoken by anyone else in a form resembling that constructed, if at all.'

Horace: 'Horace is subtle enough to leave the reader to draw his [*sic*] own conclusions.'[65]

Readers of the book of *Satires* should by all means appreciate the partisan force of the absenting of Horace from 1.7. Especially after 1.6, which just constructed the coherent autonomy of an *ego* for its Horace. The shift from 1.6 to 1.7 bespeaks volumes in mutual confirmation. The nurseling protégé of 1.6 appeared before the tribunal of his social father-figure Maecenas to declare his own function of modelling for the new dispensation. *quod eram narro* ('I told you what I was'), v. 60, was the self-reflexive point of the whole piece, where 'Mr Clean' Horace bathed his well-rounded self in the warmth of his representation: | *non patre praeclaro sed uita et pectore puro* | ('not by having a highly distinguished father but by decency of heart and character'), v. 64, *purus et insons* ('clean and above reproach'), v. 69, *obiciet nemo sordes mihi* ('No one will call me stingy'), v. 107, unlike *immundus Natta* ('that filthy Natta', so *Horace* calls him), v. 124. This is the *scriba* (penman, clerk) welcomed into Maecenas' *amicitia* (charmed circle) – talked in by his epic fellows', Virgil's and Varius', introduction, past the barrier of his unbirth, his lack of stemma made good under the new dispensation. He is the new blood of the new era which Horace here inaugurates through discussion around the structure of public service, focussed on the glorious arena of military command, to the disdain of *ambitio* (self-advancement).

Satires 1.6 narrated and relayed the making of '*Horace*', 'Horace' its narrator, as it welded narrator to narration beneath the approving eye of Maecenas. It is here that Horace fills in the positive 'I-deal' that is implied by his negative portrayal of the circus-parade of his satirical menagerie through the ten poems of the book. This catholic congregation is representatively and collectively catechized in 1.2.1–3, 'The federated flute-girls' union, pedlars of quack medicines, holy beggars, strippers, comics, and all that lot, ... Tigellius the singer', but appears *passim*. The cast of its narratives, in 1.5 along the length of Italy and then, in close-up, in the assortment of anecdotes 1.7–9, present the anti-world of Horace the singing mock-*flâneur*. He comes across the anarchistic swirl of the ' "street walkers" ', the beggars, the prostitutes, the old men and women ... , the rubbish collectors and street-sweepers, the itinerant vendors and open-air stall keepers ... and, last

[65] DuQuesnay (1984) 37.

but not least, the buskers and saltimbanques (itinerant clowns, singers, acrobats, and mimes)'.[66] In Book II, Horace will get rid of the risks of narrating altogether, under orders from his lawyer-censor Trebatius, who rules satiric self-exposure out of court in 2.1. Meantime, the writing rakes across the *ciuitas* as if in his name.

There could scarcely be a more pointed withdrawal of authorization *after 1.6* than Horace's ablegation of his next venture, 1.7. Here, the anti-types approach, not Maecenas' purse, but Brutus' tribunal: Rupilius joins Brutus' *cohors* or *conuentus* as 'outlaw' – *proscriptus*; the 'half-breed' Persius joins as 'Mr Moneybags'.[67] The unepic fellows Rupilius and Persius rudely 'introduce' each other only to incite *their* 'patron' against each other. 1.6 indeed always already showers 1.7 with cold disapprobation. In its dim view of Republican politics, *regnum* is the ancient history of Maecenas' forebears (vv. 1–4, 9–13); aeons before Horace's origins are conceivable, it was a Valerius who expelled Tarquin (v. 12); even (a) Horace has commanded a Roman army (v. 48), and *that* left its legacy of false valorization of past glories, for the Republic has been no more than the aristocracy's *ambitio*, the self-blind 'stupidity of elections – that mass weakness for labels and medals' (*populo qui ... stupet ...* vv. 15–17). So 1.6 has amounted to a forcible directive on where to read 1.7 from.[68] Horace performs still, as through the book, before the law of Maecenas – Maecenas, whose *scriptorium* pushes Horace's pen, expensive copyists turning out approved text. This is the invisible frame for reading 1.7, all the more securely in place for its invsblty.[69]

But even as we obediently follow the trail blazed by 1.6, to reclaim *risus* for *uerum*, 1.7's structure of address cuts our moorings. The suppression of a response to Persius' 'yell', whether (within the scenario) from Brutus and/or his *conuentus*, or (within the representation) from

---

[66] Maclean (1988) 56.

[67] 'A rich man with real big business', v. 4. Cf. the pest's wrong-headed approach to Maecenas' good-books, 'I'll bribe his servants', 1.9.57.

[68] See Armstrong (1986) for the political dialectic of 1.6. Links with 1.7 include recursive *Barrus*es, 6.30, 7.8, and the motif of recursion, *ad ... redeo*, 6.45, 7.9, cf. Van Rooy (1971) 68 n. 3.

[69] 1.6 has articulated the force behind 1.1.1's 'titular' ascription of the book to its controller, | *Qui fit, Maecenas ...* ('How is it, Maecenas ...'). Namely, the entitlement of Horace to speak, to speak in the name of his (satirically caricatured) *Iuppiter ... iratus* (1.1.20f., 'Jupiter ... in anger').

its narrator, or (failing him) from its narration, obliges the reader to do the dirty work. If we are supposed to know what (a) Maecenas can assume to be obvious, if we can presume on a *rapport* with him, in the meeting of minds that human(ist) nature timelessly posits, then to do the poem justice by reading its hints as assurances we must assure ourselves that 'we' belong within his fairy ring. We can tell a hint when we are given one, we can read in. But the bind of the poem is that it installs us as Maecenases, but *Maecenates* who are put through the mill of playing Brutus: we are made to put our *pauca* before Brutus' court and we await, forever, the *pauca* of Brutus' response (1.6.56, 61, 'a few words … briefly'), for the last word, all that counts, is this time his – just as in 1.6 the verdict on Horace was Maecenas'. Like the patron, but out in the *ciuitas*, '*Brutus*' is not someone (dead) we meet. He is, rather, the rhetorical figure we have been trying to get to grips with, an 'operator' or way of seeing, a viewpoint from where we can observe ourselves coming into view. As poets, citizens, readers.

But Horace's (un)civil poem demeans itself with the pun it is – 'the wit of crassitude'.[70] The joke shows that 'Rocky III' *Rupilius Rex*[71] is no more a 'King', and the hybrid-signifier *Persius* (half-Persian, half-Greek, half-Italian?) is no less a 'King of Kings', than any '*Brutus*'. All three are also 'tough guy' brutes (*durus … durus*, 'a tough guy … tough', vv. 6, 29). To confirm that he walks 'tall' as the parody of epic *uirtus* should, *Rex* comes from Praeneste:[72] where, as we saw in chapter 1, Sulla mowed down every last one of the locals, as his *coup* invented proscription. Before his suicide there, the younger Marius sent word to the praetor L. Iunius *Brutus* Damasippus to mow down the opposition – which he duly set about. And, though we know that 'it's the same distance from anywhere to hell',[73] Persius' business puts him to work at *Klazomenai* so that he may 'yell' with all the force of a kledonomantic tropology.[74]

As '*Brutus*' leaves the order of reality to join the specimen of low humour passed by Horace, he must become a verbal joke. This joke

[70] Ahl (1988) 32.
[71] *rupex*, 'ruffian/clown': *rupices a rūpibus*, Fest. 226L.
[72] *Praeneste* from *praestet* ('the big one'): *RE* 22.2, 1550, Bremmer and Horsfall (1987) 60.
[73] See Cic. *Tusc. disp.* 1.104, where 'Lord-of-Language' *Anaxagoras* of Clazomenae dies in the 'light' of *Lampsacus*.
[74] *exclamat*, v. 33; *Klazomenai* from κλάζω, as in Auson. *Epigr.* 93, *pace RE* 11, 554f.

would trivialize the tyrannicidal imperative: it goes right to the heart of that sanction of violence by figuring Brutus' act of violence as the act of verbalization, not his assertion of power on the Ides of March, but the political act of self-identification he performed when he verbalized – to himself and to others – the intent to get rid of the 'King'. That act was 'the verbalization of a political act' and it was accordingly 'itself ... a political act'.[75] It fused Brutus' subjectivity into the stereotype of '*a Brutus*', over against a, Caesar's, '*Tarquin*' and in that proportion Brutus made '*Caesar*' mean '*Rex*'. And *this* punning is a deadly serious play on wor(l)ds.

What Horace's spurious anecdote performs is the terrifying spectre of replicability in the violent power of evocation that inheres within the schema of tyrannicide. Persius is here to speak a hideous parody of and spin-off from Brutus' act of self-representation, the violence of his verbalization of tyrannicide, as (beyond the meiosis *tollere*, 'getting rid of', v. 34) *iugulas* ('(a) dagger for (his) throat'), v. 35. A paraded verbal violence which ascribes to the tyrannicide the violence that should destine a 'King' for the chop.[76] A bloodthirsty tyrannicidal avatar for M. Brutus would be his doubly-claimed ancestor Servilius Ahala, who skewered the 'would-be tyrant' Sp. Maelius in the Forum in 439, they said, for aiming at *regnum*.[77] Whereas Brutus the Liberator only *expelled* the Tarquins (put in 510). *Stricto sensu*, he was no 'tyrannicide' at all: 'if there is progress in history ... the abolition of the death penalty is the moment when a country really delivers itself of its kings. What has been said about this delivery, in history books or picture books, was only a lie.'[78]

Once the cry '*Rex*' is out of the bag, we must recognize, anyone can play '*Brutus*', play the demeaning game of euphemism. Here begins a nightmare of the mimetic contagiousness that plunges a tribe into an

[75] Pocock (1984) 25f., and Hampton (1990) 221, using the example of the stage Brutus.

[76] So in Cic. *Phil.* 3.8–10, where D. Brutus and Antony replay L. Brutus and Tarquinius Superbus, tyrannous Antony 'cut the throats and butchered' surrendered citizens (*iugulauit ... et ... trucidauerat*, 10).

[77] Cf. Plut. *Brut.* 1.2, Ogilvie (1965) on Liv. 4.12–16; cf. DuQuesnay (1984) 206 n. 89, *RE* 2A, 1771. He specially asked Atticus to trace the *Iunia familia* from stock to the present, Nep. *Att.* 18.3.

[78] Serres (1991) 135, cf. 167, 'Sextus Tarquinius is sacrificed at Gabii. ... He is expelled from the City ... Here is the condition of the new liberty, history says. Here is the sacrificial mechanism of the social pact, the anthropologist would say. Here is the requisite for the constitution of the world, the philosopher said.'

abyss of *anomie*. Horace's Persius shows us how tyrannicide perverts into a see-through verbal *alibi* for violence. He (mock-)proposes that his comrade Rupilius be slaughtered as if he were (a) Caesar, not the victim of Caesarism, and verbally replicates that killing for a name alone that is the *reductio ad absurdum* of mob violence, the *ultio* exacted *per errorem* (*cog*)*nominis* from the tribune Cinna by the rampaging Caesarian crowd on the Ides of March, as if from the conspirator Cinna.[79] Horace tells us, then, that Caesar was still less of a *rex* than was Rupilius. Rupilius at least owned (up to) the name '*Rex*'. Rupilius at least provided the minimal justification of a pun.

This *must* be why Horace has brought us to wallow in the mire of 'Rupilius versus Persius'. For this spectral scene of the body politic lynching (for the s(t)ake of) language. He makes a power-play for ideological high ground, as he exploits the tragic pathos of the proper name in just this sense: at the top of the spiral down through 'Brutus' to 'Rupilius' comes 'Caesar'. The proper name bulks large in any clash between monarchy and people-power, for the motivated (reified, fetishized) name of The King centres his 'symbolic world-order', makes the world his world, over against the democratic demystification of 'arbitrary' (conventional, mundane) nomination in the 'syntagmatic world-order' of *res publica*.[80] As chapter 5 (and the post-Roman history of the West) writes large, Caesar was and is (made a bid to be, insists on being) his name, the force of the name '*Caesar*'. The concretion of autocratic power resides in the naming that a Caesar enforces for himself. Caesar is, then, precisely to be killed for his name, for 'the great opinion | that Rome holds of his name'.[81] In the mimetic compulsion of violence, Brutus must kill for *his* name, and then, at once, 'Let him be Caesar ... ' So next on the hit-list, next for the chop, come Caesar–Rupilius and Persius–Brutus.

To take Horace seriously could mean we are committed to believing that in the case of (a) '*Caesar*' 'there is everything in a name'.[82] This is exactly what the Roman tradition offered its tyrannicides for precedent:

---

[79] Mistaken 'vengeance', so not vengeance at all. Cf. Suet. *Iul.* 85, Hampton (1990) 213, Morgan (1990).

[80] Serpieri (1985) 128–32.

[81] *Julius Caesar* 1.2.322f.

[82] Mahood (1970) 78, but adding '– for the ignorant and irrational'. Thus Plutarch's *Life of Caesar* culminates in Cassius' suicide 'with his self-same tyrannicide blade', and ends with Brutus' assisted decease.

everyone knew that '*Tarquinius*' had been expunged as clan from the body politic[83] and no less as name from the Latin language.[84] '*Antony*' is prime candidate to succeed the tyrannicides as '*Regent*' – or Pharaoh. In Brecht's play *Arturo Ui*, 'the gangster-Führer takes lessons in elocution from an old ham actor, who appropriately trains him on *Antony*'s speech to the crowd in *Julius Caesar*.'[85] See where this tends: if Brutus[1] gave Rome a good Republic for a bad king; and Brutus[2] took a good *un*king, the first Caesar[1], from a bad Republic: can Caesar[2] deliver a good Republic with(out) a good king? In the event, improbably enough, Octavian attained ' "the biological solution": the long-awaited and long-delayed death of the Leader'.[86] And left Rome with kings gone to the bad – under their new name of '*Augustus*'. But had Rome ceased to be Rome, and become a stranger to itself, Susa, say, Alexandria, or Parthian Ctesiphon (chapter 7)? Or overwritten and obliterated the Republic as an interlude, a blip in the history of regal Rome, the original, eternal and true Rome (chapter 8)? Fighting for Rome was either terminal or interminable.

But perhaps such politicization of Horace's jovial 'damp squib' is, for those with tasteful, floppily Horatian, ears, dispensable: 'Get rid of it!' Closer to the tone of the poem, one can find instead that one's urbanity is here taking an opportunity to show off its reach. Then, the poem is rigged as an occasion for urbanity. 'Indirectness (or, in formal pragmatics, implicature): conveying unstated meaning' is exactly the function of anecdotal exchange.[87] We 'Horaces' are here to play dirty, and play-talk *sermo* into a *Sermo*. Why else would we descend to the poverty, repetitiousness, self-indulgence, of the plebeian? We are here to talk rough enough to parade our comprehensive mastery of social

---

[83] So Cic. *De off.* 3.40, *cognationem Superbi nomenque Tarquiniorum et memoriam regni esse tollendam*, *De rep.* 2.53, *Collatinum innocentem offensione cognominis expulerunt et reliquos Tarquinios offensione nominis*, Ogilvie (1965) on Liv. 2.2. The myth requires that we keep mum about 'the fact that Brutus is also a Tarquin, son of the king's sister Tarquinia', cf. Kraus (1991) 320 n. 25.

[84] To prove the rule: how splendid that Cicero should contrive to unearth *quidam L. Tarquinius* 'arrested on his way to join Catiline's bid for Rome' (Sall. *Cat.* 48.3): McGushin (1980) drily comments *ad loc.*, 'Nothing else is known about this man.' Nothing, that is, bar his name: but that is the force of his existence, his part is to play the last of the Roman Tarquins, true to pedigree to the end.

[85] Heinemann (1985) 220.

[86] Manea (1992) 71, on Romanian hopes before 1989.

[87] Tannen (1989) 23.

discourse – but we are clear that it would be a ridiculously *faux pas* to suppose that this excursion could represent the subjectivity of any of 'us', anyone like us: along with getting rid of 'Getting rid of kings', we are here with Horace getting rid of *pu(n)s*, by ridiculing the idea that anyone (any one of *us*) could find this risible, or that it could be humorous to make a joke out of this material.[88] It could only be a joke to suppose that we, we who are constituted as a 'we' by our like-mindedness in this, could find this slanguage funny: 'a brute us'.

4 GOOD RIDDANCE

Senator, you are no Jack Kennedy.[89]

Even so, the story puts Brutus in the driving-seat. Even though Horace puts the civic lore of Tyrannicide in the mouth of the outsider *Graecus*, as just a twist from his orientalistically forked tongue in a rootlessly half-breed ethos, what he says does sign (off) the poem, self-reflexively, as a tribute to '*Brutus*': *operum hoc ... tuorum est* ('This job ... calls for you'), v. 35. 'This *opus* belongs to all Brutuses.' Reading dedicates us to the duty of finding the '*Brutus*' in us to act; the writing is a 'work' in so far as it works on and (potentially) through our 'works'.

Brutus presides, so he must decide (for example whether or no to decide). His verdict impends. The narrational structure of address makes readers presume what Rupilius and Persius represent for (their) Brutus, so what is at stake for him here, the urgency of his strategic dilemma. Put to the test, our political seriousness. Who can blink this, play blind to why this scenario is no joke for (a) Brutus, none of it is?

To take him first, the proscribed Rupilius[90] is a martyr for the Republican cause. Even if he is, even if he is in the eyes of Brutus (and co.), a hoodlum gangster who deserves all he has had coming, still the illegality of his triumviral damnation must make of him an invaluable walking indictment of the 'Caesarian' faction, with his place of honour on the roll-call of chapter 1 (no. (xxvii)). The Republic needed to maintain (t)his standing at all costs. In him, willy-nilly, is reposed

---

[88] For the constitution of a régime of *politesse* through evasion of explicitation, see Brown and Levinson (1987).

[89] Lloyd Bentsen. How long ago *was* that? Which election?

[90] Whether or no he is the *praetor designatus*, *RE* IA, 1231, no. 10.

and risked the force of tyrannicide, its currency as the creed of the Republic/*Italia*. Regifuge was the founding condition of the political system of rule by popular election at Rome of representatives drawn from an enfranchised Italy. No kings at Rome, (so) only citizens. It cannot matter what Rupilius is (*sc.* privately, or for real) for Brutus. As they say in casualty and the betting-shops, 'politics makes strange bedfellows.'

Do readers repress these considerations so as to get rid of the nagging thought of Horace the lickspit of a *junta*? Do we instead prefer obediently to second the despotic violence of Rupilius' blackballing, under cover of projecting violence away and onto him? And is this because we insist on recognizing the representation of violence *before* the violence of representation – before we recognize the complicity in violence (which is to say: the violence) of our own representation? How we *need* to be rid of the notions *both* that Persius' flattery of Brutus might shadow Horace's flattery of Maecenas/Octavian/power, *and* that Persius' and Rupilius' abuse might figure Horatian satire's vitriol, working unseen to poison the air for his Masters.

Now for Persius. Let us turn to consider, as if we cared, the logistics rather than the propaganda of the Philippi campaign. One tiff with this linchpin of the mercantile fraternity that controls the flow between the East–West halves of the Empire, and the Republic had as much chance of a successful crusade through Greece to march on Rome as ... the Kings of Persia. Less, indeed, for any general, any Good Soldier Schweik, knows that the trafficking tycoons of munitions and the magnate Mamurras of the supply network are the *real* masters of war. If he yel^1/$_p$s 'One out, all out!', then, requisitioning or no requisitioning, there would be no tide in the affairs of men and Brutus' Republicans would certainly lose their ventures. But, once more, to put it thus is, so far, to accept (impose, force through) a virulent, triumviral, representation: the poison of *our* in-folded acquiescence in the tyranny of the stereotype, in this case a prejudice against Business – Business in the hands of that Turkey, the alien entrepreneur.

For many readers, Persius' name has been enough to fix his number. And we must here own up that commentary, silently or otherwise, fails to object to, so ratifies, so relays, reinforces and forces through, the slurry of this story's slur on birth, as if the 'half-breed', as if the social code of breeding, is (still) an unproblematically descriptive category, for *us*.[91] The reporting of a slur is itself not simply exonerated from implication in the slur, as this nasty essay means to make abundantly clear. So do go ahead with imagining your Persius, join in, stamp on this king-pin *Pasha*: but see what you thereby say about yourself.

The Brutus you construe might conceivably agree with the poem's assessment of his predicament. Perhaps he was, in his own eyes as well as for real, doomed all along, a tragic misfit, with two jailbirds here hung round his neck to stand for all the albatrosses he accumulated: 'Pristine Reptilian + Personage from the Orient' (whether that was or wasn't just what Brutus had coming, all he deserved).[92] Either, then, your Brutus is one played false by history, (no doubt honourably) obeying his duty, living up to his name, but out of season, murdering the wrong man rather than assassinating the right tyrant, tarred forever with the recrimination of '*E-t t-u Br-u-t-e*', that sonically recursive complaint, with its suggestion of mimetic compulsion, an order to play Follow-my-Leader: 'Your turn next, Brutus'.[93]

Or else, we may decide, the so-called Republicans are a ratpack, birds of a feather, due for Caesar's *ultio*. Even a moderately sane Brutus must have seen in the 'Biff-and-Bash' (*compositum . . . cum Bitho Bacchius*, v. 20) of the gladiatorial *par* 'Rupilius *versus* Persius' the writing on the wall, for his gang as for its chief. This at any rate is the force of Horace's retrospect, the re-visionary view imposed on and through him by the violence of Philippi's victory for Octavian and Maecenas, and relayed to us through our (acquiescent, complicitous: violent) reading.

[91] 1.6 has indeed just re-valorized through its repudiation 'breeding' as the yardstick against which self-worth can be measured: must the *libertinus* Horace plead parity with the atavistically regal Etruscan Maecenas, or is that the ancient history of the *populus Romanus*? For the point, cf. esp. Greenblatt (1985) 29, quoting Kafka, 'we identify as the principle of order and authority in Renaissance texts things that we would, if we took them seriously, find subversive for ourselves . . . "There is subversion, no end of subversion, only not for us."'

[92] After the battle of Philippi (part 1) two POWs joked in the hearing of distracted Brutus' entourage: 'Casca – the one who struck the first blow in Caesar – protested: "Tu, *Brute*, will show how you hold commander Cassius' memory, by either punishing or protecting those who would mock and insult him."' Hardly noticing, Brutus lets them get led off for execution (Plut. *Brut.* 45, a reference I owe to John Moles). Another anecdote/albatross around the Liberator's neck.

[93] Caesar died silent, or his last words were the unRoman καὶ σύ, τέκνον (' "To hell with you, too, lad!" ' . . . In using this apotropaic expression, Caesar died with a curse on his lips', Russell (1980) 128). *Et tu, Brute* is first extant from 1595 (ibid. 124 and n. 7).

The important point here will be that, and how, Rupilius and Persius represent,[94] and what they represent turns out to be what they represent to Brutus, for Brutus, and so what Brutus represents to us, which Brutus we mean to be ours and what 'Brutus' means to us, and in turn what Horace's representation means to us, what represents us, what we mean. This is the force of this humorous writing.

And yet, still, the poem's structure of address occludes its vituperation of Brutus. This is a frame-up, it would de-throne '*Brutus*' from its mythic function. A 'king'-by-another-name, the power-bloc of Maecenas, the name '*Caesar*', hereby installs itself, declares itself already installed (as in chapter 2 we saw Julius write Caesar, until he made it true). '*Tarquin*' spells, is to be spelled henceforth, '*Caesar*'. Delete '*Brutus*' from the new era. But when Horace delegates authority for his narration to his chosen samples from the populace, getting their prescriptions filled and cocks combed, more and less happens than that he seals himself and all that he represents off from the nastiness he is about to perpetrate and than that he manufactures a solidary 'popularity' for the mud of *inuidia* (slings and arrows) that he means to slang in Brutus' direction.

For Horace won't get rid of Brutus' memory, of Brutuses, of the replicability of '*Brutus*', so easily as *ultio* got rid of Brutus. He can slap a writ from Rupilius and Persius on Brutus' court, stamp it out with their sickly abuse, their worse flattery and the killer *mal mot*, and he can stop Brutus' voice. But will this brutalization wash with the people, will it 'work' with your *ciuitas*? If we let (make) Horace's labelling in v. 3, 'everyone with bad eyes and barbers one and all', gift the anecdote to his *mechanicals*, (the representatives of) 'the people', then it acquires withal, along with *droit de cité*, the condition of the popular discourse it represents: the casual, formless, seamless, local, fractious heterogeneity and dispersion, the unruliness, of civic multiplicity. Here, there is no orthodoxy, no given hierarchy, no foregone conclusion. Proprieties and niceties of thought or language live elsewhere; respect for reputations, persons, the powers-that-be, cannot be read off from conversation in its natural habitat. You won't find any of that in the drugstore queue or at the barber's salon, only 5 o'clock shadow-boxing and evil eye. 'Trust me' (v. 35), just this once.

Make no mistake. To cut (even especially) Brutus down to size, mob

---

[94] As Fraenkel (1957) 120 proposed.

banter could caricature Brutus many times more nastily than Horace's niceness can bear to re-present and yet, even so, its caricature could serve as a tribute of respect. Indeed it could work precisely to worship his memory, exactly to preserve the operator '*Brutus*' as the collective sanction against the powerful, whoever that may be (pinned on), from time to time. Vulgar insults can and do cherish folk-heroes, trashing the lexicon with popular usage, the litmus of abuse.[95]

The people's '*Brutus*' need not speak his mind. There need be no valorized reading of 'Rupilius *versus* Persius'. No one may ever pronounce the last word on Brutus and his (civil) war; on the Ides of March (and their *ultio*); on the Republic and Republicanism; on Caesars and Caesarism. For what the *mobile uulgus* does, they say, is bide its time before getting its own back on the kings, those that citizens are disposed to damn and demonize with the title. We have seen that *ultio* is (like *talio*) an essentially self-regenerating structure within the power-relations of society, a discourse that cannot be settled. Thus what '*Brutus*' means is not what Brutus meant 'in himself' but what '*Brutus*' means 'in itself', what the cloaked dagger dumbly proclaims to the *ciuitas*.

Just why this anecdote, this 'yell', should (be supposed to) become the common property of the streetwise of Rome is not something you can read out from Horace's re-presentation. We can't screen out his version's, his comic inversion's, interference with the anecdote. Nor would any controlled reading be conceivable for 'the real thing', if any such thing be imagined – before inverted commas. For this is polyglossic discourse off the record, language at large, loose talk 'on the corner'. This is myth at work, not the citizen's acquisition of lore, but the lore 'actually acquiring him or her'. The following joke about power shows what is meant:

> FOUR-YEAR-OLD BOY: Dad, when is a bus not a bus?
> FATHER: I don't know, when is a bus not a bus?
> BOY: When it turns into a street.
> FATHER (*and other adults present*): Ha ha.
> BOY (*five minutes later, taking his father aside*): Dad, why is that
> funny?[96]

---

95 This is an aspect of the struggle for power over the dispersion of language through the populace, cf. Crowley (1989).
96 Leith and Myerson (1989) 36, 39.

Now the anecdote *form* of the tale is something we recognize as such and what it signals is the *nadir* of narrative-form. It is patterned in the basic 'priamel' structure of: '*foil*: (i) Persius[1] + (ii) Rupilius; *cap*: (iii) Persius[2]'.[97] But this story says nothing to stamp its meaning. Even if it did, stories that interpret their meaning within their own telling can only be seeking to expropriate, beguile, the audience with the force of representation. Every (re-)telling plays a new part in the drama of social intercourse, and street jive is always subject to the crowd's mêlée of interpretations. 'What, then, is so perilous in the fact that people speak, and that their discourse proliferates to infinity? Where is the danger in that ?'[98]

5 BAD RUBBISH

> When Rome, to end royalty, chases the kings out, it is not expelling royalty but defining it.[99]

As Horace moralizes, among the proceeds of his first book: 'humour ... cut(s) knotty issues'.[100] His shortest poem cuts the most ice. The silliest poem is 'real big business' (*permagna negotia*, v. 4), 'an epic picture' (*magnum spectaculum*, v. 21), 'calling at the top of *its* voice' (*magna ... uoce*, v. 31). The writing of proscription is (still) hard to come to terms with: for 'outlaw' (*Proscripti*, v. 1), try writing, then understanding, '*fatwa*'. Recall chapter 1, and write death, *quod scriptum est, scriptum est.* What has stopped us hearing any such thing is (the violence of) representation, all that makes us want to get into the socially shared universe of meaning that stands for a polite and decent world, the cultural domain coordinated by the contract between narrator and reader. Namely the power to evoke mimesis, the violence of concordance: 'reading Horace'.

The investment in self-preservation of the civilized (*sc.* the patronized) stops 'us' from leaving the table to join the powerless, self-condemned to an identification with what we all heard in the '*Brutus*' chant in Bucharest against the Roman(ian) 'King', Caesar-by-his-other-

---

[97] Cf. Nash (1985) 62f.; cf. 70f. on the taking *up* of the anecdote into larger and higher forms.

[98] Foucault (1981) 52 = (1984) 109.

[99] Serres (1991) 124.

[100] *ridiculum ... magnas ... secat res*, 1.10.15, cf. esp. Van Rooy (1971) 71, 77–81.

name-of-Ceausescu. The echolalia of a *glasnosty*, *un*British, shout: 'Liberty! Freedom! Tyranny is dead!'[101]

The catchword '*Brutus*' has its place in the contestation of representation that surges through the flux of civic discourse, the violence that powers society. The poetic *jeu* does not simply re-present the Ides of March. It is not just proleptic of Philippi. Horace is doing more than 'mediate' between these crises of the Republic, turning-points in (imposed) social self-conceptualization. True, his anecdote stages, together with its successors, the writing of his poetry as the purgative work of a political weave, away from deadly hostility between its writer and his mentor, and toward the cultured collaboration of their *amicitia*. But against its role of *epideixis*, 'the discourse of the flatterer', Satire trades off its generic abjection, shielding its work of representation behind a screen of disavowal, a comic show and undecidable relay of fictive authorization. After 1.6, as I saw it, '*Brutus*' is, even, a *put-off* for Maecenas.[102] If temporarily, ironic distortion grips together tyrannicide/butchery with suicide/*ultio* in one power-filled sweep of displacement and condensation.[103] Readers may feel, or play, 'Humble Joe' before the lability of popular politics, but the raw figure '*Brutus*' holds us, still.

Over at the apothecary, bleary patients expect *collyrium*, 'a topical remedy for disorders' (of the eyes),[104] and discuss – what? Cyanide capsules? While another stroppy queue makes barber's music as the stubble approaches the cut-throat blade: 'from 'ere to 'ere, like this!'.

'The King must die.' *Regifuge* is, soberingly, thin cover for *regicide*, both caught in the excentricity of mass will to any directive, risked to representation in every crisis, in all fighting for Rome. 'Then what does the exclusion of kings signify, if kings are kings precisely by being excluded? We are not so easily rid of them. Whether there are kings or not, there are always some.'[105]

---

[101] Cinna in *Julius Caesar* 3.1.78.

[102] As in 'Where are you going? – To see a man about a dog', Leith and Myerson (1989) 120.

[103] Cf. Marin (1988) 61, 'Thus the man of letters lures power with the lure of his instrument, discourse, meta-discourse, and its figures. Thus simultaneously, he obtains from power – and with his trap – the power of the power of the discourse that he holds.'

[104] *OED s.v.*; cf. *Sat.* 1.5.30.

[105] Serres (1991) 171.

4 Polishing off the politics: Horace's Ode to Pollio (*Odes* 2.1)

mortalium nulli uirtus perfecta contigit.[1]

Break on through.[2]

There was always another side to Horace. He wrote hexameters from *Satires*, through *Epistles* to *Ars poetica*, in a voice that busied itself with Roman life, then his own theory of life, and his theory of poetry, as he moved up from associate of Maecenas to reflective courtier, and laureate of Augustan verse (a composite Lucilius–Cicero–Aristotle self). He wrote lyrics from *Epodes*, through *Odes* to *Carmen saeculare*, in a voice that inspired itself with Roman gusto, then his own impressions of lives, and his vision of futurity, as he moved up from sidekick of Maecenas to perceptive courtier, and laureate of Roman song (a composite Archilochus–Alcaeus/Sappho (etc.)–Pindar self). The *œuvre* cumulatively synthesizes one subject: the subjectivity of Horace. However much individual poems shy away from, or get rid of, the personal, as in *Satires* 1.7, or outline Horace through the medium of his response to the subjects of his poems, as in *Odes* 2.1, they all colour the portrait. Lyric and hexameter Horaces always speak to each other – a *satire* always needs an *ode*, for dialectic, and *vice versa*.

Since the *process* of reading is vital to lyric poetry, to its definitive *mobility*, this chapter's close reading will present and muse on stanzas as they come to the reader. (The whole text is given in the Appendix, with running translation.) As we remarked (chapter 3), Horace will sing here about another survivor of the fighting for Rome: Pollio. Like Livy's account of the fighting for Rome (chapter 8), Pollio's *Histories* have perished – except in the form of traces in the narratives offered by such as Appian (chapter 1) and Lucan (chapter 5). But Horace's cameo catches up Pollio's project, as an investment of self in the life of his country by a famous soldier, statesman, poet and enthusiast for the

---

[1] 'No mortal is blessed with absolute virtue', Pollio ap. Sen. *Suas.* 6.24, *elogium* on Cicero (see chapter 8).

[2] The Doors (1967), 'Break on through (to the other side)'.

arts. He writes up a writer whose own writing writes up both their lives
– and everyone else's. Like Horace's, Pollio's writing fights for Rome,
from Julius to Octavian, from Brutus to Augustus: both have survived
the revolutions, the horror; both write (for) their lives. Now the tragic
historian must fight for comprehension of Rome, the lyric poet must
fight for the spirit of Rome. For their own sakes, and everybody's.

Like the Ode, and like Caesar's *On the civil war* (chapter 2), we do
best to plunge right in *ex abrupto*. Caesars make reader–writers (such as
Pollio, Livy, Lucan, Appian, Dio ... and Horace) work out, and work
up, their own finished versions. We must parade *our own* notions of
loyalty to / comprehension of Rome, the Republic, and '*Caesar*'. The
details, and what they mean, for players and readers, must come as
they are prompted. In *Satires* 1.7, elusive Horace did not write, but
wrote *about*, epic and power; here he does not write, but writes *about*,
history and power.

I IN MEDIAS RES ···

This poem flags Horace's innermost concerns: the central book in the
central work of his career will share with readers more of how he thinks
a civic poetic can bless his writing with significance produced in each
reading than any other he ever wrote. This proem must be read from
one end to another. It is *Horace*'s most explicit programme for reading
Horace. A poem which feels out what it is like to think as a quite other
poet, to operate as a poet who is presently writing poetry in prose – a
poet who is far more than a poet, and a poem which thinks about its response to writing and what that writing is about, in its own (re-)write.
This Ode teaches how Horace reads and writes, sees reading and writing, lives open to others' readings, of texts, politics, people and history,
and opens to his readers a sight of a life lived among others'. This is
lyric for Pollio: civic discourse. What '*Pollio*' stands for – the Pollio of,
and in, Horace – as figure for all Romans to think the fighting through.

> Motum ex Metello consule ciuicum
> bellique causas et uitia et modos
> ludumque ...   (vv. 1–3)

MOTION

> *Date-line, Metellus' consulate: commotion of the body politic,*
> *civil, too – war's causes; and crimes; and modes;*
> *the game, too ...*

Motum, the poet wrote: 'movement, emotion, tumult, trope'. *Motum*, the reader–reciter performs, 'gestural presencing' from the oratorical repertoire to fix the scene of utterance bodily to its participants. This is to be a Roman act of enunciation, 'public discourse between Romans': *motus . . . ciuicus.*

At Rome, a poet is supposed to have said, '*Metelli* become consuls by Fate.'[3] *Metello consule* spells no less than political life at the height of the Roman Republic. If it is to pin the start of the book to *a* Roman dateline, the flood of consular *Metelli* in Roman history means we need more to go on. As the second line adds its trio of further accusatives bound together by their common controlling genitive, the reference narrows to two possibilities.

(i) From the arrival in Africa of the consul Metellus (109) to shape up the army struggling with Jugurtha, there stemmed not just the victory memorialized in his triumphal cognomen *Numidicus*, but also the rise of both Metellus' client the *nouus* C. Marius and his aristocrat rival Cornelius Sulla. Readers could begin Sallust with his *Bellum Iugurthinum*, then read Sisenna's tale of the atrocities they went on to perpetrate in the 80s, or skip to his admirer and (?) continuator Sallust's *Historiae*, which began from the aftermath of Sulla's counter-revolution (chapter 8).

Motum . . . ciuicum | bellique euphemizes, on this account, unspeakable civil war (re-writes it, we could say), as well as accurately tracing it back to its antecedents in the 'turmoil' that upset the 'Metellan senatorial order' in so unpredictable a set of shifts, lurches and upsets.[4] The heyday of Q. Metellus Macedonicus (*cos.* 143) and his four consular sons Q. Balearicus (*cos.* 123), L. Diadematus (*cos.* 117), plain Marcus (*cos.* 115) and C. Caprarius (*cos.* 113), together with his brother L. Calvus (cos. 142) and *his* sons L. Delmaticus (*cos.* 119), Q. Numidicus (*cos.* 109), was over for ever – 'more than a dozen consulates,

---

[3] On Naevius' line, *fato Metelli Romae fiunt consules,* and the consul's reply, *dabunt malum Metelli Naeuio poetae* ('The Metelli will hurt Naevius the poet', Ps.-Ascon. on Cic. *In.Verr.* 1.29), cf. Goldberg (1989) 254f.: 'Verres possibly, and Cicero certainly, used this line against a Metellus. We do not know that Naevius did.'

[4] *Motus* for *bellum* brings a welter of added connotations and imagery-contexts: Lucan shows this in his epic's (re-)start with Caesar's 'bellicose emotions, war on its way' (*ingentes . . . animo motus bellumque futurum,* 1.184).

censorships and triumphs in a dozen or so years'.[5] Along came the 'shake-up in the *ciuitas*' which became the 'Social war', where Q. Metellus Pius must subjugate the Latin colony of Venusia and Sullan veterans be assigned its confiscated land, as a certain freedman Horatius somehow prospered in their midst.[6]

(ii) From the consulate of Q. Metellus *Celer* (60) stemmed the so-called First Triumvirate, which eventually and eventfully shaped the downfall of Roman order in the civil war between Julius Caesar and Pompeius Magnus. Another paradox of chaos, a pattern with a future. This time the spiral from *motus* to *bellum* all lay within the lifetime of the son of that Venusian freedman, Horace. If the story is scrolled on, past the ends of both Pompey and Caesar and through to the Second Triumvirate and the victory of Antony and Octavian, it reaches Philippi, which (we saw in chapters 1 (no. (xv)), 3) left Horace among the defeated and his Venusia expropriated by Caesarian veterans.[7]

The suicides of the consular commander Q. Metellus Scipio (*cos.* 52) and of Cato in their defeat by Julius Caesar in Africa were matched by those of Brutus and Cassius, the tyrannicides, in their defeat by Caesar's avenging successors, after an interval of wildly veering, kaleidoscopic, confusion. 'In the 12 years from 80 to 68 BC the [Metelli] held three consulships and a triumph, while four other consuls during that time – with two triumphs, and another one coming ... – were grandsons of Macedonicus and Calvus through the female line. In particular, three of the four sons of C. Metellus Caprarius (*cos.* 113) promised great things: Quintus [Creticus] and Lucius were consuls in 69 and 68, and Marcus, the youngest, as *praetor* in 69 was clearly destined for a third consulship at the earliest opportunity.'[8]

These moving stories account, between them, for the century that separated the Republican aristocracy's zenith, between the first and third Punic wars and their tail-piece, the Spanish victory of Scipio Aemilianus, a.k.a. Africanus Minor, which brought him the triumphal

---

[5] Vell. 2.11.3, cf. Plin. *Nat. hist.* 7.139–46, Wiseman (1974) 176–91, 'The last of the Metelli'; with stemma on 182f.

[6] Metellus: App. *BC* 1.53, cf. Fraenkel (1957) 2. Cf. Jal (1963) 10f. for Gracchan/Social war thresholds for the civil war(s).

[7] App. *BC* 4.3, cf. Fraenkel (1957) 13 and n. 6.

[8] Wiseman (1974) 177f.: Q. Pius was *cos.* 80.

cognomen *Numantinus*, from the rise of Octavian at the expense of his ally Antony, to metamorphose into Augustus through victory at Actium. A series of manoeuvres culminating in the restoration of consular elections from 23 worked to complete this narrative, with official restitution of the Republic – marked not least by the publication of Horace's three books of *Carmina*.

Sorting out how the past, and its past, was to be told, lay at the heart of the politics of the Augustan present. Disagreement about what had happened would perpetuate the conflicts strewn along the way, and unsettle the status of the *status quo*. Self-comprehension depended on establishing a narrative for the lives of former Antonians, Pompeians and Republicans, along with their ancestors, traditions, martyrs, regions, dependants, within some bearable version of the simple story of righteous triumph for the avenging son and heir of *Diuus Iulius*. If you could tell the tale of fighting for Rome, it must be over (chapters 5, 8).

Formulae of repetition, ironic symmetry, and tragic necessity were invoked, as they had been even in the shaping of the events by their actors. Pharsalus and Philippi could coalesce (chapter 5). Marian–Sullan *coups d'état*, proscriptions and massacres blurred into the (second) triumviral bloodbath (chapter 1). Historians could emphasize unity between various phases in the nightmare. Their activity could affirm that the dream was over, the turbulence spent. It was the time to talk down recent atrocity and revolution into brief ripples spreading no great distance across the great sweep of Roman time. Waves of inauguration followed by difficulties could be outlined, to link the deified founder Romulus–Quirinus, Brutus the Liberator, Camillus the second founder, with deified Julius and the saviour Caesar Augustus (chapter 8). Selective curtaining off, impressionistic sketching, metaphorized softening of detail could all help. And, as we shall see, the past could be washed in tragic solvent – just about everyone could be blind but true, patriotically misguided, heroically sacrificed to transcended causes.

Negotiating the present involved a constant and continuous monitoring of the past, amnesty's necessity to remember to forget, and not to forget to keep the memory trained on the outlook of the future. And yet of course, inhabiting every shift, hostility got smart, found cover, went underground. Fine-tuned courtiers watched (for) each other (to) go through the motions (chapter 7).

When Sallust died in around 35, leaving his *Historiae V* unfinished at

67 or so (from a start with the aftermath of Sulla, 78, and the damp squib of Lepidus' father), the newly retired Asinius Pollio (*cos.* 40, *triumphator* 39 or 38) could focus the seventeen books[9] of *his Historiae* on the Caesarian civil wars, from the Rubicon up to, or even past, Philippi,[10] with discussion of their aetiology stretching back to the originary moment of the First Triumvirate in 60; and still he could achieve *virtual* contact with his predecessor's work.[11] Metellus Celer, for example, had been the *praetor urbanus* of 63 active in suppressing the Catilinarians of Sallust's other monograph, the *Bellum Catilinae*, which lay just ahead of his *opus maius*. By the time that Pollio's writing reached Philippi, Actium was past and Horace composing his Augustan *Carmina*.

By the time of the completion of *Odes* I–III in 23, reference to the First Triumvirate as 'a perturbation *Metello consule*' took on the particular nuance of an epoch, now that Augustus had (if only) formally ended the suspension of the *res publica* in the martial law of the two Caesarian *juntas*. Long before *that* diacritical moment, the evocative power of the great senatorial name would eclipse its rival, *L. Afranio cos.*, the Pompeian commander in Spain who would be crushed by Caesar's *Blitzkrieg* (in 49/8),[12] since it was clear to see that the wars had to all intents finished the Metellan clan: true, one Augustan Metellus would become *praetor urbanus* and proconsul of Sardinia, and his adopted son Q. Metellus Creticus Silanus would achieve an imperial consulate in 7 CE. But the rest were consigned to oblivion – by the clan's independence, by its alliances with Pompey and Crassus, and by

---

[9] Suda *s.v.* Ἀσίννιος. Zecchini (1982) 1286 hazards a Caesarian rate of a book a year, from 60 to 44: but prefaces and preludes, epilogues and *envois* could spoil steadiness of that order.

[10] Cremutius Cordus in Tac. *Ann.* 4.34.4 claims Pollio presents a super *memoriam* of Cassius and Brutus; and (as we have seen) Pollio wrote Cicero's *obit* (n. 1 above). Cf. Haller (1967) 99–105, Zecchini (1982) 1284f., Bardon (1956) II 94.

[11] Fornara (1983) 68, 75f., sees Pollio as writing more of a Sisenna-like monograph on the 'subject of a single historical process' than a Sallust-like *continuator* (but cf. Zecchini (1982) 1281f.). More important to recognize that Pollio's was a story 'treated by [an] individual[] involved with, and suffering from, the very conditions they attempt to describe and analyse' (cf. Jal (1963) 268, Haller (1967) 214).

[12] Neither Livy nor the (discrepant) *Fasti* establish which in each pair of consuls was *cos. ord. maior* (Drummond (1978)); but (obviously) *Afranio cos.* would make for an *un*ambiguous dateline where *Metello consule* does the opposite. Pardoned by Julius after surrender at Ilerda in Spain, Afranius would escape from Pharsalus, but be caught and executed after Thapsus: no Augustan limelight, or twilight, for *him*.

its notable hostility to Caesar. 'Despite five consulates in twenty-three years, the Metelli soon found that their power was passing. Death took off their consuls one by one.'[13]

Which Roman could not trace a grand message of doom for the entire Republican aristocracy, from the heroic elimination of another Metellus – Metellus Scipio, father-in-law of Pompey, proposer of that vetoed motion of 1 January *Claudio Marcello Cornelio Lentulo coss.* (49) which terminated Caesar's command and so triggered the civil war,[14] commander of the centre at Pharsalus and generalissimo of the Republicans at Thapsus – back to the pathetic non-event of the decease of Metellus *Celer* before he could leave Rome for his province of Outer Gaul in Caesar's year of 59, his name left behind to mark the 'swift' moment in the annals of Rome when a Metellus must date the lightning ascendancy of Julius on all his successors' Caesarian calendar? Longer views back from the Caesars' triumph would see decline into internal dissension inevitably ensuing, once the anxiety of Carthage was stemmed. With the rise of the Metelli, associated with the Punic Wars through Macedonicus' grandfather L. Metellus (*cos.* 251, 247), and father Q. Metellus (*cos.* 206), came the Gracchan agitations and a century of disastrous entropy halted only by the Augustan 'restoration'.[15]

2 WATCH THIS SPACE

> ludumque F o r t u n æ grauisque
> principum amicitias et arma //

> nondum expiatis uncta cruoribus,   (vv. 3–5)

> *the game, too, of F O R T U N E; the weight, too,*
> *of leaders' alliances, and armaments*

> *not yet expiated blood for gun-grease, more blood*

---

[13] Syme (1939) 43, cf. ibid. n. 2.

[14] Lucan's presentation of civil war *nefas* stands a symbolic Metellus (Lucius, *tr. pl.* 49/8) between Caesar and the treasury of Rome – for a moment (3.114–40), as his tribune's veto fades on the breeze, taking with it his name and its Republican fame: the future spells *Caesar* not *Caecilius* (Metellus).

[15] The coward L. Metellus led the cowards who would have had Rome up and quit Italy after Cannae (Liv. 22.53, Sil. *Pun.* 10.420–48).

The lyric processes what it has to say through the rhythmic grid of the Alcaic stanza:

$$\times - \cup - - \,\|\, - \cup \cup - \cup \times$$
$$\times - \cup - - \,\|\, - \cup \cup - \cup \times$$
$$\times - \cup - - \qquad - \cup - \times$$
$$- \cup \cup - \cup \cup - \cup - \times \,\|\,^{16}$$

Metre (and alliteration) paired the first two lines. As the rhythm changes at the pivot *FORTUNAE*, the list lengthens: two more items in parallel with the second line as a whole (| *bellique ... , | ludumque ... grauisque; belli ... Fortunae ... principum*) and/or a second new tricolon in parallel with the first (*ludumque ... -que ... amicitias et arma*). These items amplify and colour the components of the first limb, or tricolon. They unpack the string of 'causes-and-crimes-and-modes' as we think them toward taking shape:[17]

(i) The *'causes'* of civil war can *in this context* well be typified by '(the) grave alliances between principals', for this very phrase would otherwise proclaim the aristocratic élite securely in command of the state, through their 'solemn political alliances'. The dynastic network motivating their solidarities framed long-term commitments across generations, with correspondingly high-tariff penalties for infraction. Perversion of this in the triumviral marriage-contracts between Pompey and Caesar's daughter Julia, then between Antony and Octavian's sister Octavia, made *these* 'alliances grave' indeed for the world, as they fought to eliminate all pretenders to the title of *'princeps'*.

(ii) The *'crimes'* of such civil war pair 'alliances' with 'arms' as horse goes with carriage, and/or as grossly excessive as their

---

[16] '||' indicates 'stanza end'. '×' indicates, in the first foot: 'usually a long syllable but sometimes short'; at line-end: 'a syllable long by position'. This scheme emphasizes the 'pivot' at the heart of the third verse of the Alcaic stanza, and stresses a 'rhyme' between the third line (the enneasyllable) and the fourth (the decasyllable); the counter-rhythm which gathers these two lines as one longer unit (still alive for Horace) stresses the tension introduced by the change of pattern at the pivot and builds the stanza to a closing t h u m p. It is in order to bring out more clearly the way the third verse begins with the same rhythmic pattern as the first two that I have throughout this chapter set out the Alcaic stanza with only the fourth verse indented, instead of in the conventional style. (Cf. Wilkinson (1963) 110–13.)

[17] For the articulation, cf. Nisbet and Hubbard (1978) 14 on v. 4, Nadeau (1980) 179.

continuation past the stanza-end, to the appalling extreme of 'blades greased with the gore of one massacre after another' ... The motive power behind this story, as we piece it together, is 'not yet' over, with a vengeance.

(iii) The '*modes*' of civil war flesh out as '(a/the) game of Chance': too complicated, too many incalculables. An unreadable lottery, where winning is good luck, losing bad; a sick procession of collisions and uncanny coincidences ...

Any lengthening list invites us to seek out organizing principle(s), segments and sub-groups, with inter-articulation between them – classificatory, serial, or narratival. We do our best. But the poet makes us clothe the bare bones of his list with our own ideas on Roman history, *before* we can have the least notion of how *he* would unpack the 'kit'. With the overspill into the *second* stanza, we run full-tilt into implicature in a 'not yet' assigned point of view: the linguistic 'shifter' *nondum* presses us to situate our relation to the utterance; we need to know 'where is here? – when is now? – who are "we"?' because someone is making *us* aver 'not yet'. But where is this story of bloodshed 'still not' done coming from, this day of atonement 'not yet' come?

3 WHATEVER YOU DO, DON'T LOOK DOWN

periculosae plenum opus aleae,   (v. 6)

a dangerous work full of throws of the dice

With this next verse, the utterance declares *its* 'work of plenitude' (-*osae, plenum*),[18] as the appositional verse- and sense-unit further stretches the suspense. This, the repeat-verse of the second stanza, parallels (*re-phrases*) what precedes. We are being told how we should have responded (and be responding) to the text's *effort*, as well as to its referent in civic history: the 'game of chance' is talked up by insistence on the 'gravity' which is *performed* in the over-running of the first stanza. The bulk of *p e r i c u l o s æ* fills out the lightweight *words opus*

---

[18] Cf. Sen. *Suas.* 6.24, again, on Pollio's 'full' elogium for Cicero, *testimonium ... quamuis inuitus plenum ei reddidit*, Tac. *Hist.* 1.2.2, (pun) *plenum exiliis mare*.

aleae, and it labels the paradox of civil war's deceptively trivial 'dice-box full of caprice' where every throw is lethal. Narrative historians normally 'have their work cut out, and hands full' of the 'task' of ordering material 'then . . . and then . . . and then . . .', infusing chronology into causation. But the list that *won't sort* is a sure way to capture the collapse of logic in civil war.

To take such a tack with the immediate past threatens to undo the apparent or achieved solidity of the present, shown up as the latest wasteland in a series of blundering lurches to no one's credit and everyone's loss. To write *Historiae* of the 50s–30s was (and still is) essentially to write of civic turmoil, with all the deformity, unseizability and nullity that this mobilizes. Whatever the treatment, the brute *non sequitur* of their succession would trade the relief it underscores in having survived the madness, against the cancellation of any satisfaction in having prevailed through the struggle. Is that it?

We need our bearings fast. And we can spot here an unforgettable beginning for a particular narrative of civil strife, even if that moment stands for *any* such conflict. It would be no surprise if Asinius Pollio's *Historiae* fastened on Caesar's crossing of the red-faced *Rubicon* in 49 as the decisive inauguration of *his* chosen theme, even if he did start with a preliminary 'archaeology' back from 59: when Julius had exclaimed 'Roll the die', the young and unnoticed lieutenant on the scene had taken note, shadowing his Leader's every movement, and the first-blush vignette passed from his account through the rest of our sources.[19]

Pollio's (Hi)story was exactly the *cursus* of his life. His adolescence saw the preliminaries (aged 16–27); his hot-house maturity the action (27–37, from [possible] *tribune* at 29 in 47, to *consul* in 40 and *triumphator* by October 39 or 38, then retirement at 38, before sitting out Actium at 45); his long old age the time for a consular historian's reflection (*obit* 4/5 CE). Thus history for Pollio was bound to the organic fallacy, orchestrated as a 'bio-script', the story of his own life as well as his city's, a citizen's civic record (see chapter 8). How then are readers to relate to this material?

---

[19] Cf. Plut. *Caes.* 32.7, cf. App. *BC* 3.35, Pelling (1988) on Plut. *Ant.* 6.1. Pollio translated the Rubic κύβος into Latin, so in *alea* we have very much *his word* for it. Writing Caesar never crossed the Rubicon (chapter 2).

4 FAITES VOS JEUX

tractas, et i n c e d i s per ignis
suppositos cineri doloso: //   (vv. 7–8)

to this you turn, STEP ON through fire on fire
submerged beneath ash so treacherous //

To begin in 49 with Julius' *iacta alea est(o)*, is to begin *again* – it could
only 'begin' because of what began in 60/59, with the compact between
three generalissimos. What Pollio put in the preface to his work must
have summarized this basic interpretative strategy. The historian must
convey to the reader advance notice of what to expect, particularly
defined in terms of the choice and conceptualization of its opening.
Now Horace apes something of the kind. His re-launch of *Odes* I–III
goes over the same ground that the historian covered in his preface,
before it was elaborated in his text proper. *This* is the 'kit' of materials
which Horace has put in the reader's hands, and set in 'motion'.

Just as you reach this second stanza's 'pivot', the material is positioned for your utterance, as all those accusatives are given their subject and their verb, with *tractas* (v. 7). As you turn onwards to the new
rhythms of the stanza end, the text makes you enact *its* movements.
INCEDIS hustles *per ignis* | on into the verse 'positioned below' it, |
sup-positos cineri d-..., as the stanza 'tucks the risk of fires back under
cover of a crust of ashes' to explain how the emblazoned danger lurks
in the work in progress: periculosae aleae ↔ per ignis | suppositos cineri doloso
//.

The poet set his readers moving through his evocative inventory as
their project of reading. Every device planted in the text is loaded with
dynamite, 'a trip through some bombed-to-hell city ablaze to left and
right, over a minefield that threatens to explode the ground beneath
your feet'. Trust nothing, for what looks dust can burn. Cremation is
no secure boundary between living and dead, the past awakes in your
singing of this lyric. This poem is *loaded*.[20]

---

[20] Cooler response to the delay in orientation from Fraenkel (1957) 235, 'Even before the
reader is able to penetrate the meaning of the detail he [*sic*] is impressed by the
largeness of the picture before him'; cf. Ross (1975) 142, 'This device allows Horace
to write of the *motum ex Metello consule ciuicum* at second hand, as it were', Porter
(1987) 110, 'The impact of these opening lines is the greater ...' Epode 2 is even *about*
the difference introduced by deferral of the positioning of readers, i.e. by the final

The poet foists the project on his reader – not ancient history, but the story of *his* lifetime: born *consule Manlio*,[21] so aged 5 at the first triumvirate, 16 in 49, 23 among the proscribed and at Philippi, when he entered history as *tribunus militum*, 34 for Actium, and 42 at time of publication of *Odes* I–III. For Horace's own memories begin with the beginning(s) chosen for this poem. He tells you how dangerous talking about his generation would be, not ancient history, but live *politics*.[22]

Rather than starting the perilous story at the beginning of Rome, with Aeneas staggering through the burning towers of captured Troy under the burden of his past and his son's future tugged along by his side, as Horace's daring friend, and originally Pollio's protégé, Virgil chose for the epic of Augustus he was composing while Horace wrote these words, *animae dimidium [su]ae*;[23] and rather than starting *Ab urbe condita*, from Remus and Romulus onwards, as Livy had begun in the monumentally definitive annals he was also producing as Horace's poem took shape (chapter 8), the lyric poet plunges us into ... his own lifespan. In so doing, he plays the singing historian. And opens the past into live purchase on his and your present, in the linked moment of his writing / our reading.

Egomorphic writing here proves that it is another way to relate suprapersonal concerns. The otherworldly poet musing contentedly in his musical entourage of nymphs and satyrs (1.1.29–34) unmasks himself as an 'I' with a history, a past that exceeds ivory-tower 'protection' from Maecenas (1.1.1f.). *Horace* does not begin with the *Odes* (except in editions such as the Oxford Classical Text), he belongs to a generation, just like everyone else in the crowd and in the parade at the triumph for Actium. Just like citizens glad to begin again in 23 to elect

stanza's re-positioning of their (re-)reading: how *could* a money-lender have sounded so like Horace – and *vice versa*? How could we get Horace *so* wrong? A nasty programmatic-propaedeutic trick from the nasty *Epodes*, biting on writer, character, and reader, all.

21 *Carm.* 3.21.1: Manlius Torquatus, no. (xxi) on the list given in chapter 1. His late spring poem from Horace, *Carm.* 4.7, aptly turns on the twists of time – return, recursion, reparation, restoration, liberation, delivery; and decline, loss, depredation, and death.

22 Cf. Poiss (1992) 136, 'Das Schreiben des politischen Historikers greift in die Wirklichkeit ein, ist Handeln, ist eine Form von Politik.'

23 '(His) *alter ego*', see Hor. *Carm.* 1.3, esp. 8, 25, with Porter (1987) esp. 53f., 58–65, 110f., 'both 1.3 and 2.1 are themselves but stages in Horace's own poetic voyage and ... these words of 2.1 [6–8] have their applicability to his enterprise as well as to Vergil's and Pollio's'.

(their) consuls, while reflecting how the days of the aristocratic government of the Republic would never return, and wondering how the new political settlement was meant to develop. How far it *could* be manipulated, and by whom – maybe to turn the clock back.

As this lyric flashes its miniatures past a Roman audience never exposed to such a performance before, it collects a chorus of voices which have their common origin in the experience of their writer. Just as Horace showed us first of all that the triptych of *Odes* I–III would imaginatively empathize with the whole civic range of personality-types as his own pleasure (1.1), so now he insists that when 'you the reader tackle this work', you are reading the history of your country – which reaches through the moment of your reading, and into your every next move. Lyric can inhabit the mindset of the grand prose narrator of history, so long as that is conceived lyrically – as a live personal affair. Indeed lyric *needs* history to model its own espousal of relevance to the public lives of its Roman reading culture. The genres are a surprise pairing, a package which wobbles undecidedly between host/parasite and host/guest – like a 'duck/rabbit' cartoon.

Lyric recognizes history only in so far as it can serve as another route to its own aims, of telling for everyone the tales where their experience can cohere. Autobiography learns where to situate the self precisely from the coordinates plotted by the grand narratives of history: 'Where were you when ...?', 'What did you do in the ...?' The historian is properly himself, from this point of view, when 'his' story represents the experiences of his community, when his representation represents the *ciuitas*, re-presents empathetically and authentically the stories lived by his fellows. Those killed by the story, all over again, as much (perhaps) as those who survived, prospered, and stand to profit from the story. The pledge of mass bloodshed in the pursuit of however misguided or perverted politics is there to guarantee the seriousness of this work of commemoration: the past can 'never yet' quite have received all it is due.

Does Horace's description of history stick in the throat, not just because lyric seems safe from recriminating retrospect and responsible seriousness, but because his account is partisan, loaded already in favour of a reading which would be equally unacceptable in a historian, or promising as controversial an account as would encourage or goad a reader to continue past the programmatic fanfare of a historian's prologue, to find out just what he meant by starting so pugnaciously, paradoxically and alarmingly? He has a challenging (lyric) vision of the historian's dare, to concentrate his readers on *their* dare: 'you' are here to read your way into *Horace*'s mindset, to explore the lyric imperative to risk relating to representation by another. This truly is a dangerous, chancy affair.

5A I WAS SO MUCH OLDER THEN, I'M YOUNGER THAN THAT NOW[24]

> paulum seuerae Musa tragoediae
> desit theatris, ...   (vv. 9–10)

> *just a little, let austere Tragedy's Muse*
> *empty her theatre stage ...*

Meet the Muse. The poetic for this poem is the formidable *doyenne* of austere Tragedy, that monumental *verse*-medium. She must 'for a wee while desert her theatre': for Horace to begin to write as *per* his announced programme, he must borrow the Hellenic mode of grand drama which dwelt on those agonizing horrors of Greek myth.

'Tragical history',[25] however exclusively Roman the subject, calls for pity and pathos, sobriety and severity – 'just a little', because Rome from 60 or 49 is not *so* very differentiated an ordeal; 'in between performances', because lyric, even when filled out to take on the burden of history, will *not* distend to take the hours required for a full Sophoclean tragedy. Expect an impression, a sketch, a cameo – to stand for the whole.

5B STRANGE THINGS ARE HAPPENING LIKE NEVER BEFORE[26]

> ... mox ubi publicas
> res ordin a r i s, g r a n d e munus
> Cecropio repetes cothurno, ∥   (vv. 10–12)

> *... in no time, once the public*
> *record's as you ordAIN, THE GRAND service*
> *you'll resume, towering tall in Attic costume*

---

[24] Dylan, 'My Back Pages', lyric (1964A).
[25] See Ullman (1942) esp. 50f., Nisbet and Hubbard (1978) 9. (A dimension, not a genre of history, cf. Woodman (1988) 116 n. 151.) Sceptical arguments from Sallmann (1987) 74 n. 20 (an important re-reading of the poem in its scholarship).
[26] Dylan, 'World Gone Wrong', lyric (1993).

The third stanza's pivot *ORDINARIS* gets a move on, hurries to interrupt the rhythm after the monosyllable | *res*. We turn *to* the Muse, after the politely indirect third-person request (*desit*). When tragedy has set the account of the Roman Republic straight, 'it won't take long', the show can go on as usual. The poet is playing at deprecating the politics, as he puffs mannered compliments, 'in Greek', to theatre's Grand Opera.[27] Yet the high tragic calling is not released from collective duties when the stanza cadence returns the masks to the mythic distance and mannered tread of their alien unreality (*Cecropio* ... *cothurno*). The tale spanning back from 'now', through the Rubicon, to the primal scene of 60/59, is 'just a jiffy' in tragedy's timescale – *sub specie aeternitatis*, from classical Athens back through the first king *Cecrops*, to gods, heroes and the rest of the cast. Just a step from the stage for those 'six-league boots' of tragedy.

Lyric here is getting into the mindset of tragedy, 'for a moment'. Lumbering grand politesse befits *Historiae* that are filled with civil strife. To get Aeneas through Troy burning about his ears *or* to propel the reader through the Roman revolution, no other register will do (*cothurno* || overlays *doloso* ||.). For all the apologetic deprecation of the task in hand, the question inheres: if the *Caesars* call for tragic weeds, no less, will you not find, *pari passu*, that tragedy only works through its applicability to whatever 'Cecrops' the audience finds in its commonwealth? *Attic* paradigms of bellicose *uitia*, quarrelling *principes*, insatiable blood-curses, have power precisely *because* of their transferability, their translatability.

Getting back to her *Cecropian* roots will mean Tragedy has successfully lent cosmic grandeur to the wars – and never left her theatre. At the very next 'showing' (*munus*) of drama, if only inside the auditorium of Pollio's recitation-hall, tragedy will be repeating what she helped her co-author, history, write: the names may be *Thyestes* and *Atreus*, but it will be the *Roman* theatre cooking, the Romans' own fratricidal hatred.[28]

---

[27] The oddly proportioned enneasyllable, v. 9, with its extremes of monosyllabic clipped start + grand pivot, *res ordinaris*, disjoined from the unusual double disyllables by phrase-boundary in *grande munus* |, acts out stilted tragedy's high-stepping *entrée*. Cf. Poiss (1992) 139 for *cothurni* ↔ *incedis*.

[28] Varius' *Thyestes* was produced for the Actian triumphal games in 29, winning its commissioned author a fortune from Octavian, for *its* polishing off the politics. Aper in Tac. *Dial.* 21.7 lumps Pollio's tragedy and oratory together as tough and dry (cf. Néraudau (1983) 1734f.). Cf. Accius' *Tereus*, as discussed in chapter 3.

Two stanzas drummed history; a third conscripts tragedy. These were preliminaries, still waiting for the balloon to go up. Is the poem ready to begin?

6 LA VIE E(S)T L'ŒUVRE DE C. ASINIUS POLLION

insigne maestis praesidium reis
et consulenti, Pollio, curiae,
cui ...   (vv. 13–15)

in court a beacon and shield for distraught victims,
for the Senate, too, the consultant, Pollio,
for whom ...

In austerely grand style, we *have* indeed now reached a true beginning to the poem. A customized re-working of the start to *Odes* I(–III): *Maecenas* was hailed as Horace's *praesidium*, breathing Etruscan excess in fancifully gross self-promotion, with personal vibes of pleasure, a frisson of aesthetic χάρις (grace; 1.1.1f.). By contrast, the orator consul Pollio is a bemedalled rock of Marrucine *fides*, a togate saviour in the tear-drenched courts of the *forum Romanum*; Pollio is 'a Senate on legs', repository of political wisdom (*consulenti*: this Senate refers questions to Pollio as a consul refers them to the Senate). Both grandees provide the same '*protection*', physical or whatever it takes.

So this triumvirate of celebrities is, then, as eccentric as any in the post-Metellan élite of Caesarian Rome: the good-as-slave-born pardoned poet, the *éminence grise* who had steered his prince all the way to the top without pledging himself to the slightest public career, the ferocious *nouus homo* with the stupid *nomen* whose son's name *Herius* broadcast his homonymous grandfather's tribal martyrdom as rebel Italian general against the armies of Rome.[29]

With the double-barrelled block of vocative honorifics in vv. 13–15, the reader must now begin all over again. For the positioning of the reader as the 'you' interpellated by the poet's 'I' is undone, and a more complex array of communication opens:

(i) The poem speaks *of* Pollio by turning *to* him: the pair preen before the reader, coopted to the joint business of eternalizing fame. The poet pens Pollio; Pollio graces the page.

[29] Liv. *Per.* 73.

(ii) The poem speaks *through* '*Pollio*', *both* as a specific dummy-perspective which the writer can help readers share, before checking out how that relates to themselves, *and* as a representative or paradigmatic channel for indirect suasion of the reader, who is not *entirely* other than Asinius Pollio, and will recognize much of what s/he sees through standing behind his eyes for a spell.

(iii) The poem treats Pollio as its *alter ego*, mobilizing him as one more set of its chords, another voice for lyric to mimic and explore, *both* like *and* unlike the writer – and his readers. Specifically, lyric will supply the lack in history; while history arms unprotected lyric – with solemnity.

(iv) Most critically of all, Pollio writes-and-lives in a 'here-now-us' present-with-a-past which does duty as surrogate for Horace to involve his readers in a consideration of the nexus of writing-and/as-reading. In '*Pollio*' Horace finds an operator through which to write of writing, without lapse from the performative mode. His reader commutes on the circuit between Horace as writer, Horace as Pollio's reader, and Pollio as writer-*cum*-reader of Rome.[30]

We have been reading all along Horace's re-presentation of Pollio's work-in-progress. Our reading of history has not been a programme to be realized later in Horace's poem, or poetry-book, but rather an outline, a précis summary of Pollio's *Historiae*, a lyric version of *Pollio*'s prologue programme. Horace has written a tribute, a history of Pollio's *Historiae*. The structural ploy of a beginning with 60/59, to phase in *the* beginning with 49, is specifically attributed to Pollio. *Pollio* was caught up in 'the aleatory fun of Fortune', himself 'an *amicus* allied with some *principes*' and as such 'bearing *arma* against others' '. *He* is the storyteller of 'danger, picking his way between the fires – tramping on through embers ready to burst back into flame': between all the lines he writes. The third stanza's second person was not Tragedy, but Pollio: 'Tragedy was to exit the theatre to assist' Pollio's politicking on the page. *He* would soon set down in *his* order the politics of Rome. Pollio governs Rome *in his writing* ...

---

[30] Citroni (1983) 154–6. Pollio was remembered as a literary enthusiast (Sen. *Contr.* 4, *Praef.* 2).

As the reading is re-motivated, over-writing Pollio into the place occupied by the reader, the temporality splashed across the first stanza-break in *nondum expiatis uncta cruoribus* now fissures. The 'now' is, now, 23. And this text has been writing about writing as *the process of writing*. What view or views is Horace representing for whom?

Did Pollio's preface write that 'atonement was still not over' as the bold stake of the *Historiae* as a whole *opus*? Or did this notion appear on a particular page, or fasten on to an episode in the course of the narrative? Did Pollio (only) claim, for instance, that the first triumvirate's legacy did not stop at Pharsalus? Or Julius' final victory, of Munda? Or on the Ides of March? Or did he remark that *both* triumvirates had it in common that they left long trains of 'unfinished business'? Was Octavian's inheritance from Julius blighted by 'blood calling for bloody revenge' – revenge for Caesar, *ultio* on Caesar's minions (chapter 3)? Has Horace discovered for himself, as *his* reading of Pollio, whether signalled by that text or not, that the overall message of history if not the constant refrain of the *Historiae* is that Pharsalus inexorably spawned Philippi; and, for all that anyone could do, Philippi bred Actium? Does Horace find this for himself because this is how he sees the story of his life and times, or was this what you would read too under Pollio's signature? But would 'you' find this analysis because he put it there, because Horace has pointed you at it, because that's the way you see it in any case, or because this *is* the world gone wrong – when citizens cease to treat each other as citizens?

These questions are (just) a start. Some of them could be settled if we could find a copy of Pollio's work – or agree on a reconstruction proposed by scholars working on later texts which re(-)cite, re-write or incorporate, his account (such as Appian or Dio: chapter 1). Others couldn't. But the point is, rather, the relationship which is constructed in the reading of this poem between the moments of Pollio's writing, Horace's reading/writing and Horace's reader's reading. That is what the Ode is doing, what its saying *does*.

Writing history must always be provisional. This condition is most visible where history presents its material as an account of what happened within the historian's *floruit*. Sooner or later, there will come the chapter where the historian takes his place on the page as an actor among the actors; and all along, we know that he saves his skin, he now lives and writes on. But could he know at the time that what he was caught up in would come to make a story he could write and others read? Did he only know in retrospect that it was a story? To see 'events' as *this* story, *so* conceived, you need to draw a line underneath them. Your writing must vindicate this discovery/imposition of a narrative 'beginning-middle-and-end'. This takes more than the few seconds it takes to read Horace's sketch, or the few minutes it would have taken to read Pollio's preface. What happens to your writing as history continues past your story's conclusion? Exclusive devotion to the past cannot insulate the historian's project from the continuing drive of 'events' (chapter 8).

Horace in 23 releases to an 'Augustan' public which probes the political import for their world of currently staged declarations of restoration the *thought* of Pollio at work on his *Historiae*. At the end of this book of *Odes*, and again in the *envoi* from *Odes* I–III, Horace will envision a future for his own work which will endure and extend through space and time to the global eternity of Rome (2.20, 3.30). Canonical status for Horace, and for Pollio, will depend, not just on whether Rome and Roman reading-culture lasts, but on how the Roman future pans out. Every contribution to the Augustan order bets *somewhat* on acceptance by the future of indelibly foundational status of the post-Actian ménage. Even the *Aeneid*'s chances would look sick if ever (say) the capital moved to Carthage, expunged *Iulii, Caesares, Augustus* from the panoply of power – and Horace's socially embedded gallery of contemporary *hombres* is perilously subject to built-in obsolescence. Even in 23, *some* of his addressees were only of interest *because* Horace had written about them . . .

Securing a future is very much on the agenda of both *Odes* and *Historiae*. To start from Horace, 'the date of Horace's ode cannot be determined with any certainty'.[31] That is to say, we are by no means agreed how to think of the writing of Horace's poems. We are sure that he made no further changes to the text multiply copied and distributed from the *scriptorium* of Maecenas in 23; we should envisage him working pieces up individually, in clusters, and in their eventual berths within the final triptych; inventions and decisions might, however, stem from considerations proceeding in the reverse order, and likely enough he would loop between macro- and micro-level composition.

---

[31] Nisbet and Hubbard (1978) 9: quotations below from 9–11. Cf. Zecchini (1982) 1282, Poiss (1992) 132f. Further arguments for 34/33 in Grimal (1990).

Negatively, we can be sure that the last decision was to *let it stand*, that is, neither to tinker nor drastically to cut or expand the Ode to Pollio / the proem to *Odes* II.

Nor do we know how to calibrate Horace's thinking in the Ode with Pollio's writing: his project may date from his post-triumph retirement in October 39 or 38; or from Sallust's death in 35. How far should we glean from the poem that Pollio's writing had got by when? We could suppose Pollio's preface to have been prefixed to a first gathering of the *Historiae*, presumably with a few books on the events of the 50s. Historians need not name their destination, which fresh events could shift, or the lottery of life foreclose on. An insider's proximity to Pollio, however, could mean that Horace could be privy to the work in progress well before it was released to any public. Thus even in 23 Horace could still be heralding an as yet unavailable, radically undetermined, forthcoming classic – not just for dramatic effect, but for real.

Focus on the proem of Pollio's work, or its early stretches, or its first main phase, *need* not be explained by the stage of Pollio's progress presumed, attested, or assumed, by Horace. It may represent Horace's best shot, or considered view, of the full sense of the whole project; Horace may see the analysis of 'beginning' as exactly Pollio's chief contribution to analysis of (the) civil war(s); or as the safest topic to highlight – and brand 'dangerous'. What *matters* is what we see Horace as committing Pollio's work to say.

If Pollio wrote of *principum amicitias et arma | nondum ... uncta* between 38 and 35, this would wrap the fight between Octavian and Pompey's son Sextus into a spin-off from the Caesarian triumvirate*s*. Between 34 and 31, it would brood on the final collision between the allies Octavian and Antony. Pollio himself may have written in anticipation of either show-down; his phrase might be ratified afresh by every crisis and cataclysm. Between 31 and 23, it might become still more of a sore thumb, sticking out in rejection of any sense or pretence of 'Augustan settlement'. In 23, the slogan would be telling the courtiers that this old campaigner knows that Actium is no more absolute a beginning than was the Rubicon; and the new restoration of a consular Republic can inaugurate no more than a further phase in the witch-hunt of the past, terrorizing on into 'an open-ended future of bloody atonement'. Whatever the track-record of Pollio's thinking (see chapter 8), and of Horace's thinking with '*Pollio*', the point that is exposed for our thinking with *both* of them is that writing has a live historicality of its own, always subject to re(e)valuation. Pollio names a trajectory: history's *momentum*.

7 POLLION POUVAIT DIRE: J'ÉTAIS LÀ[32]

> cui laurus æ t e r n o s honores
> Delmatico peperit triumpho.   (vv. 15–16)

for whom laurel's E V E R G R E E N *roll-call of honour*
budded crowns of glory, in Dalmatian triumph.

Pollio was already acclaimed a tragedian in the early 30s, in connection with his victorious celebration of Illyrian triumph, 'ivy creeping among his *lauros*'.[33] Tragedy therefore *did* indeed coalesce with the historian's ordering of *publicas | res* in the *œuvre* of Pollio. The politics of Pollio's tragedies and the poetics of Pollio's *Historiae* interfuse as the common matrix for a grim message of blood-curse doom, nemesis without end.

And Pollio's public and writing careers are continuous. Horace empathizes with Pollio's empathy with the tragically 'afflicted accused in court'; his role as 'the Senate's text-book and adviser' befits the consular historian. Prominent orator and senior senator, Pollio is praised for his completed card of Republican 'honours'. A boy 'when Metellus was consul', he stepped onto the world stage in 49 as a warrior, shone in the dignified domain of 'Tragedy', then 'governed the state' – as *consul ordinarius* (*publicas | res ordinaris*). *Patronus* and *iurisconsultus*, strong and wise, Pollio capped his omni-competence with the laurels of proconsular 'military conquest' (*praesidium, . . . triumpho*). As one of the Republic's 714th pair of consuls AUC, Pollio's name achieved eternal synonymy with our '40 BCE'. His name/fame would last as long as the Roman calendar (worked by Republican *consules*, cf. chapter 7). *Pollione consule* would be memorable and distinctive, a 'new name' on the list, to be succeeded, in time, by a stubborn dynastic sequence of descendant *Asinii*.[34]

What did Rome associate with him / his date? There is no (other)

---

[32] André (1949) 77 (whence the title for Section 6 above).

[33] If exclusively by Virgil (*Ecl.* 8.10–3, echoed loudly by Horace here) and Horace (*Sat.* 1.10.42f.).

[34] His grandson namesake would become *cos.* 23 and the first word of Tacitus, *Annals* IV: *C. Asinio . . .* (chapter 7).

evidence that Pollio ever pretended to any triumphal *cognomen*, but Horace flatters Pollio's victory *de Parthinis*[35] into a *Delmatic* achievement so as to bring us full-circle back to those *Metelli consules* we considered first – to L. Caecilius Metellus *Delmaticus, cos.* 119 (*triumphator* and, like both his great-grandfather, the L. Metellus blinded in saving the Palladium from a blazing Temple of Vesta, and his *triumphator* nephew Pius, Rome's *pontifex maximus*).[36]

The parallel lifts Pollio up to the heights, *Delmatico peperit triumpho.* ‖.[37] Surpassing the last stanza's *Cecropio repetes cothurno,* ‖. Next, the stanza shifts rhythms round the self-affirming pivot A E T E R N O S, before unwinding in its explication of the burgeoning of these *honores* as the outgrowth from victory in the Balkans. Unlike Metellus, the *nouus Pollio*'s soldiering truly deserved the sobriquet '*Delmaticus*'. With this, the encomium of Pollio's public achievements leaves the triumphal acclaim to resound, at stanza-end: *-o* . . . ‖.

Horace congratulates his model citizen on leading an exemplary Republican life in the eyes of all citizens, even through the darkest era of civil war on civil war. Never shirking 'danger', marching steadily on 'through the minefields', 'getting the nation's business back on the rails', 'defending friends and countrymen in need',[38] 'dispensing good counsel in the *curia*', Pollio wound up a match for any hero of the glory days back before the troubles. He helped see the traumas through, survived to write them into the record.

Forever, *Pollio*'s lifework and name/fame will signify the rightness

---

[35] Dio 48.41.7. Parthini cavalry fought, like Horace, for love of Brutus at Philippi (App. *BC* 4.88, 5.75).

[36] Delmaticus' victory was smeared as the self-glorifying contrivance of head-hunting natives (App. *Illyr.* 11, cf. Morgan (1971)). Horace would have the one and only Pollio '*Delmaticus*' join Metelli *Macedonicus, Numidicus, Delmaticus, Balearicus, Caprarius* and *Creticus*. Fierce debate ('The battle of Bosworth') is fought about the theatre of Pollio's operations in history – Illyria? Dalmatia? (Syme (1939) 222f. *versus* Bosworth (1972); Zecchini (1982) 1276f., Haller (1967) 72–6; important discussions by Nisbet and Hubbard (1978) 19f. on v. 16, DuQuesnay (1976) 27, 86 n. 30, and esp. Woodman (1983) 192–6 on Vell. 2.78.) This bears on Pollio's politics, but doesn't decide the force of *Delmatico* . . . *triumpho* in Horace.

[37] Book I's final Alcaic piece, the thumping Cleopatra Ode (1.37) had just acclaimed Actium as Octavian's victory over alien aggression, leading up to the absent presence of the mad-poisonous-unmanning-menacing scalp of the Egyptian empress led in triumph (*triumpho.* ‖). Book II starts again, further back in the Caesarian story.

[38] Pollio defended on 8 out of 9 occasions known to us (André (1949) 67–71, Haller (1967) 85–7).

of attempts to roll back civil *arma* by reconciling 'leading citizens in *amicitias*'. The circumstances of his activity as consul were critical for him, both as citizen and writer. Horace's implicit portrait has him begin making his move, joining Julius to march on the fatherland, against the *SPQR*; he ends up as 'the trusted counsellor of the *curia* and proud *triumphator*, quelling a trouble-spot as the legitimate commander of Roman legions'. But in between the Rubicon and the triumph, Horace does not spell out (his line on) Pollio's line on what led up to and resulted from events *Pollione consule*.

Enlarged by life, Pollio marched on Italy with Julius, fought Cato in Sicily, survived Curio's campaign in Africa, then 'was there' at Pharsalus, Thapsus and, as *praetor*, the last battle of Munda.[39] Governor in Further Spain on the Ides of March, Pollio had moved gradually and with as much wait-and-see non-committal equivocation as he could muster from the end of the earth back to the centre of world events. Playing a modest role in re-uniting the Caesarian forces of Lepidus and then Plancus with those under Antony and Vatinius,[40] he helped the legacy of the First Triumvirate to imprint events after the demise of all three partners. When Octavian came to join the alliance at Bologna, the Second Triumvirate drew up a five-year plan for Rome, bonded by vengeance for the tyrannicides' 'yet unexpiated' crime.

Promotion to the consulate for 40 was fixed for Pollio and Cn. Domitius Calvinus (*cos.* II;[41] on the black-list of proscribed, there appeared Pollio's father-in-law L. Quinctius).[42] In 42, Pollio may have held Cisalpine Gaul while Antony led the coalition's *arma* to victory at Philippi;[43] in the twisting and tumbling mess of fencing and facing down that lasted through the siege of Perusia, only Plancus' temporizing was said to have held Pollio and Ventidius from pitching straight through the centre of Octavian's legions to relieve Antony's brother:

---

[39] Suet. *Iul.* 30, Plut. *Caes.* 46.2; Plut. *Caes.* 52.8; Vell. 2.73.2, Dio 43.47; Cic. *Ad Att.* 12.38.2, Suet. *Iul.* 55.

[40] App. *BC* 3.81.97; cf. Vell. 2.63.3.

[41] The *Fasti* suggest that the senior consul was Calvinus, but *Domitio cos.* would be as ambiguous a dateline as *Asinio cos.* would be unambiguous.

[42] App. *BC* 4.12. In a storm, he abandoned ship without a life-raft 'when Pollio was consul' (ibid. 27).

[43] There is no evidence here, cf. DuQuesnay (1984) 27 and 86 n. 26, '... suggest Pollio had a sabbatical in 42'; all the same, 'Horace and Pollio ... had seen from opposite positions the *fuga* of Philippi' (Nadeau (1980) 182).

their beacons came within sight of the besieged. (That was Pollio's story, at any rate?)[44] Retiring to winter around Venice, Pollio (*he* said?) was prime mover in talking (the proscribed) Domitius Ahenobarbus into Antony's camp,[45] bringing in his navy's control of the Adriatic in time for Antony's arrival back in Italy. Instead of taking up his consulship in Rome,[46] Pollio locked horns with Maecenas, thrashing out terms for the Treaty of Brundisium in September 40, with L. Cocceius Nerva for broker.[47] The result was another pull-back from the very brink of full-scale civil war in Italy. The consequence was the formal demotion of Lepidus to make-weight status, the recognition that the *Caesarian* future was now conditioned as another bi-polar '*amicitia*' all too reminiscent of the First Triumvirate after Crassus' death, which had led to – signalled, so retrospect could see – the Caesar–Pompeius '*arma*'.[48]

The couple of months which could literally justify the dateline *Pollione consule*, before Pollio's departure for campaigning in Illyria, were blessed of memory for this saving grace of reconciliation between '*principes*'. Virgil's Fourth Eclogue strains itself forever, to sing worthily of *te consule . . . Pollio, . . . te duce . . .* (vv. 1–3, 11–13), marking the start of a final New Age when the scars of our wickedness will dissolve into a destiny sealed by 'divine, stable, destined, concord' (v. 47).

On his triumphal return from the Balkans, both Pollio and Virgil could enjoy watching the peace extend through the Treaty of Puteoli in summer 39 to bring Sex. Pompeius in as a genuine third partner for Antony and Octavian, instead of the Republican (and tyrannicide) leader of forces pledged to destroy the Caesarian concordat from their base of Sicily. Middle man Pollio had played no part in *these* negotiations. As he established Rome's first public library in his restored *Atrium Libertatis*,[49] the first roll in his catalogue would be Pollio's

---

[44] App. *BC* 5.31–5, Wylie (1993) 135; cf. Zecchini (1982) 1275, Haller (1967) 56–8.

[45] Cf. Vell. 2.76.2f.

[46] Pollio may *never* have gone to Rome to assume office: he was succeeded by a pair of suffect consuls before 'his' term was up (Dio 48.32.1).

[47] App. *BC* 5.64: chosen from Antony's side by Octavian's legionaries.

[48] Cato (also) maintained that the (First) Triumvirate, not the Rubicon, started the civil war (Plut. *Pomp.* 47). On Pollio's 'general thesis', as over-stressing 'the personal relationships of the great men [and making] them too far-sighted and clear-cut in their ambitions', cf. Pelling (1986) 164.

[49] Suet. *Aug.* 29.5, Plin. *Nat. hist.* 35.9.

own promotion, the pastoral of his protégé Virgil, pitying the sufferings of Italian minnows as the 'principes' fought over Rome, then settled their veterans, and placing fervent hopes in the momentum initiated by Pollio's peace.

Or, if Pollio's triumph graced October 38, not 39, he could reflect that Octavian had almost at once broken with Pompey and prosecuted the bellum Siculum. In 37, Octavian would manage to reinforce his alliance with Antony, by the Treaty of Tarentum, while Agrippa eliminated Sextus for him at Naulochus. Caesarian Pollio could incorporate this within his scheme,[50] and swallow the degradation of Lepidus to house arrest at Circeii as part of the flak from Octavian's suppression of the last of the Republican power-bases.

As he removed himself from the scene to write up his Historiae, somewhere between 38 and 34, history could seem to Pollio a successful march to total victory of the cause he had tried to prosecute, at times caught in hopeless dilemma and contradiction, since he first felt impelled to choose Julius over 'his enemies'. His writing could even contribute to 'straightening out the politics of the Republic' some more, by deploring the tragic ironies of the story of his lifetime at the forefront of events. If the movement of history could stop right there, and the rest of time abide by the story so far, it could seem that the nexus between 'amicitias and arma' had been broken, after all. So long as the 'principes' remembered they were Caesarians first and last. As Pollio did – and was making sure that 'Pollio' would mean.

If Pollio did, either of these things. At any rate, approaching the ripe old age of 45, he confined himself to his study, through the collapse of 'his' settlement into the Actium show-down. Either victor could emerge to complete the drive to unification in some world peace; but neither would owe the construction of his victory to Pollio, now just a be-medalled hang-over from history.[51] Was his historical account from 60 on, from 49 onwards, able to incorporate all eventualities? Did beginning a tragic parable of doom – 'Blood bays still for more blood' – become a tragic error? After Actium, would Pollio wish that he had not

---

[50] Back in Spain, 44, Pollio had been defeated – but (he might maintain) heroically – by Sextus (Woodman (1978) on Vell. 2.73.2, clarissimum bellum, versus Dio 45.10).

[51] praeda uictoris, he had called himself – to Octavian ('The winner's trophy', Vell. 2.86.3). Whatever the magnus ... saeclorum ... ordo born in Ecl. 4.5 had meant to him, he lived to witness authorization of state finance for Augustus' ludi saeculares in 17 (CIL VI. 1.877a).

declared open season on massacre, that he had not published the view; and Horace that he had not represented Pollio as saying any such thing, that he had dissociated himself from the view?

Or would either or both writers be glad again by 23 that the Augustan settlement *required* a measure (a modicum? a minimum?) of 'unnecessar[ ]y tactless[ness]'? 'It certainly would' *not* 'be hard to believe that he', whether Horace *or* Pollio, 'was still lamenting the civil war in 23 BC'.[52] Rather, *tragic* coloration could productively enfold all the traumas in the lives of every Augustan citizen and family with resuscitated pain and re-kindled asseveration of despair. Pollio had this to inject into thinking in and around the new court – besides his presumable refusal, *if* he wrote that far, to write Actium up as a triumph over Egypt.

Above all, '*Pollio*' signified, and his work articulated, a route through the contradictions between loyalty to the *princeps* and to self-consistency which afflicted the entire ruling class, bar Maecenas and Agrippa, Augustus' fast friends from the first. They *all* needed a line for why they hadn't died before coming round, and moving over to Octavian/ Augustus, whichever cause they had fought for.[53] Between taking the plunge with Julius and staying dry for Actium, Pollio's alternately hair-raising and perplexed negotiation of tortuous spates of splintering and realignment within the *Caesarian* constellation both before and after Philippi had been vindicated by his emergence as the spirit of concord and conciliation. Just how to construe Pollio's role from the settlement at Brundisium onwards is hotly disputed, but it is necessary neither to convict nor applaud him for 'going over' from Antony to Octavian: if not before, then at least in 23, it was possible for Pollio to remember himself as staying true and keeping faith throughout the troubles, and so for Horace to say so. *All* civic relations – at times those of the *princeps* included – had been out of kilter; only now was it possible for them all to vote together for concord, back finally *on the same side*.[54]

---

52 Nisbet and Hubbard (1978) 10. Cf. chapter 8 on Livy's *Preface*.

53 Two 'great orators' could be remembered *otherwise*, as *Asinium et Messallam, inter Antonium et Augustum bellorum praemiis refertos* ... (Tac. *Ann.* 11.7.2, 'stuffed with loot from the troubles').

54 In the debate over whether Syme romanticized Pollio's intransigence, Bosworth looked to show that Pollio 'went over' to Octavian – between Perusia and Illyria ((1972) 41–9), but the common problem of *all* the survivors was how best to represent to themselves and others their own trajectory – Octavian as much as Pollio or

In 23, Horace *should* welcome back a *Pompeius* to the fold, first out so last in, by recalling his own speedier trajectory, 'out' for Philippi and 'back in' immediately thereafter (2.7). For the 'fold' could be represented in 23 as allegiance not to Caesar or his heir, but to the (restored) Republic. The secret, '*Pollio*' meant, was that 'a breakdown in sociality' (*motum* . . . *ciuicum*) had made the most exemplary loyalty to the state take wildly contradictory forms. Could anyone have predicted that the *nouus* who crossed the Rubicon would *save* Italy from conflagration, in *his* fifteen minutes of fame?

But historians strike poses. They are rhetoricians by another name (chapter 2). Roman historians explained their works explicitly in prefaces, then developed the interpretive demand of their narratives by varying motley bursts of editorial and comment with stretches of low modality note-form and action sequences bare of frame or key. There is as little likelihood that readers of whatever chunks of Pollio's *Histories* were available in 23 would reach the same view of his import as each other, or as their readings of Horace's sketch, as there was of spectators of his tragedies agreeing what *they* 'meant', or of subjects reaching the same understanding of the Augustan settlement and nourishing the same hopes and expectations for its future.

This is what Horace's lyric is performing 'for' Pollio's history – focussing entirely on the historian's drive to stamp their own sense of what counts on the tale they tell, for all the layers of denial represented by the rhetoric of self-less facticity and Olympian panopticism. Enthusiasm is *bound* to get lyric 'into' however dry a narrative, as transcribed personal testimony – whatever person it is written in. So this is Horace's opportunity to smuggle in a historian's public frame for *his* fast-moving array of forty-second poetic stunts. Making each of us read, for all we are worth.

8 LIFE BETWEEN THE LINES

iam nunc minaci murmure cornuum
perstringis auris, iam litui strepunt,

Messalla, as much as L. Arruntius, C. Sentius Saturninus, Cn. Domitius Ahenobarbus, or L. Munatius Plancus and Q. Dellius, or Horace (Bosworth (1972) 449,
473; cf. Jal (1963) 350, Haller (1967) 96–9). For discussion of '*Polliotics*', cf. esp.
Woodman (1983) 232–4 on Vell. 2.86.3, Feeney (1992) 7f.

iam fulgor a r m o r u m fugaces
    terret equos equitumque uoltus,   20

audire magnos iam uideor duces
non indecoro puluere sordidos,
et cuncta t e r r a r u m subacta
    praeter atrocem animum Catonis.   (vv. 17–24)

Now, right now, a damning din from your sirens
scrapes across ear-drums, now bugles screech,
now the glare from A R M O U R is panicking
    terrified horses, the look on each horseman's face,

now I seem to hear great commanders,
dishevelled with dust that does them no dishonour,
with a whole P L A N E T 's subjugation
    – all bar the obsidian heart of Cato.

Horace's tribute to Pollio has given a relatively extended review of
the GOM's career which is not so far from the *elogium* a historian writes
for his principals[55] – except that annalists write necrologies, and an
obituary for Pollio would be premature in 23, at least in the literal sense.
In time, Horace's writing would keep them both alive, and Pollio's
pages themselves aspired to keep those crossed swords and buried
hatchets from rust for ever, 'never to be wiped clean and put away
greased for the last time'.

Horace has described, evaluated, related to, empathized with, stood
back from, and/or disowned Pollio's project, as *he* reads it. We readers
reached the proclamation of Pollio's crowning 'honour', the triumph
that attested five thousand and one dead Dalmatians. Whatever doubts
we may have about the prestige, particularly the lasting significance,
of any campaign in Dalmatia, we recognized that the triumph seals
Horace's encomium for Pollio. Next we are primed for action, 'now or
never': *iam nunc . . . , iam . . . , iam . . . , iam. 'Pollio'* brings our ears the
abrasion and dazzle of battle. His life charged from one massed terror
to another: the reader advances straight on from *triumpho*, so that 'fresh
leaves spring eternal on that bay-crown', every time the next lines are
read. It is only after we have 'toppled heroic generalissimos in not
inglorious dust' that it will become clear, at vv. 23–4, when *'Cato'* gets

---

[55] For Pollio's, and others', efforts on Cicero, again cf. chapter 8, and Pomeroy (1988)
180f.; his Pompey inspired Virgil's Priam, cf. Moles (1983).

the last word hard on the heels of some 'worldwide conquest', that the spine-chilling thrills must have been, not the stirring victories of the legions taking the good fight to the 'fair game' of Illyrian cannon-fodder, but Roman civil war, where we must say 'We've seen the enemy, they're us.'[56] Horace's writing traps us again – this time into taking sinful fratricide for the noble art of war.

After the run of vv. 1–16, we do not suppose that Horace's shifter *nunc* orients the text simply to *his* temporality (bidding us hearken to the war being won as he wrote – by Octavian in Illyria, or at Actium, say, or before Augustus' return to Rome in 24/23, in Gaul and Spain). Rather, we intuit that Pollio's perspective continues to be implicated. Horace therefore continues to *celebrate* the mimetic power (ἐναργεία) of the commander-orator turned tragic historian. For empathetic lyric, to think '*Pollio*' is the same as reading Pollio, or writing what Pollio will write, and/or is currently writing. Horace is cueing us to a triumph of historical narrative: what better credentials could a writer have than that he has fought through the set-pieces of his story, and lived both to celebrate his own victories, and to work up their re-presentation in his spectacular procession through Rome (chapter 2)?

But Horace takes no prisoners here: the more we warm to this choice sound-bite of pleasurable historiography, the worse the depressive shock of running into Cato's confirmation that this 'war' is sick.

We are subjected to a barrage of war from Pollio 'via' Horace; it could represent *any* battle between the Rubicon and the carnage in Illyria. Therefore any of Julius' battles from Pharsalus to Munda. Or the Caesarians' battle with the tyrannicides at Philippi. Or Pollio's own thwacking in Illyria. Or some (land-)battle thereafter. This is typical – or *choice* – material from Pollio's 'theatre', until the blast turns out (if it does) to culminate in Thapsus and the defiant suicide 'of Cato', in 46. So shall we suppose that the material must all along have been recounting the 'world conquest' of *Julius*, with never a hint of *Octavian*? Or does Horace, and did Pollio, decide that all the struggles to 'master the universe' were alike – wherever/whenever between 60 and 46/45/42/31 or 23 – in crushing every last loser?[57]

---

[56] Early 1970s button, *after* W. Burroughs.

[57] 'Except Cato.' Cato's war proves 'the exception', bound to lose the world but gain his soul, and live for ever more as *Uticensis*, cf. Lucan 2.247, *dux Bruto Cato solus erit*, with Ahl (1976) 235. Nisbet and Hubbard (1978) 22 on v. 19 put the case for Pharsalus as Horace's scene; Cato, left in charge at Dyrrhachium, was only at Pharsalus in *his* imagination – but that is what counts.

If the generalized evocation of battle transports Pollio to the panoply of scenes etched on *his* memory, those horses and riders must deliver the *eques* Horace back to *his* trauma of *Philippi* (Φιλ-ίπποι, 'the riding classes'), his only *militia* known to us.[58] War for Pollio ended with his triumph, he made sure (*not* Actium).

Readers triangulate their experience against these protagonists'. Even if *your* Pollio stages (Pharsalus to Munda through) Thapsus, you will have to banish, so entertain, thoughts of Horace, returned by reading or contemplating Pollio to the 'now' when 'here' meant the sights and sounds of 'his' battle, when he obeyed – 'listened to' – *his* 'great generals', before *they* nobly bit the dust at Philippi, inspired to follow, though never equal, the ultimate example of their forerunner 'Cato'.

Both stanzas make their own structuring frame perform, around their rhyming pivots *ARMORUM* and *TERRARUM*. In the first, the paired hendecasyllables blare out a rumble of brass, then re-double in quickened toots of rising alarm. The third line starts, as the rhythm ordains, in further parallel, with a third limb: | *iam fulgor* . . ., but then lingers on the pivot *ARMORUM* before performing a *visual* alarm that culminates in *uoltus* at stanza end.

This second half of the stanza 'films' the dazzle of battle. See *uoltus* as nominative singular, and battle is written into eloquently displayed chiasmus: *fulgor* ∼ *uoltus, armorum* ∼ *equitum, fugaces* ∼ *equos*, with at centre the displayed palindrome *ter-ret*: 'now the glare from *ARMOUR* and the look on each horseman's face are panicking terrified horses.' See *uoltus* as accusative plural, and battle collapses into undifferentiated panic, as the words chase on and away into rout, with horse and rider panicked as one – the mount bolting, while the human face betrays its fear: 'now the glare from *ARMOUR* is panicking terrified horses and the look on each horseman's face'.[59] Mounts shy at riders. Men run from dazzle like horses. Look at the faces that strike fear – they are the faces that are stricken with fear.

The next stanza takes up the stirring, then revolting, momentum. Mighty generals, heroes in 'the dust that does not dim their glory'. The

---

[58] Horace probably gained equestrian status with his appointment by Brutus as *tribunus militum* (Taylor (1925), Armstrong (1986), cf. Poiss (1992) 141), so *figuratively* he is visible among these cavaliers (Nadeau (1980) 181, stressing the Cato/Brutus association). Cf. Sallmann (1987) 75, on vv. 17–24 'Nein, hier spricht nicht Pollio.'

[59] *Voltus*: nominative singular, Shackleton Bailey (1982) 113; accusative plural, Nisbet and Hubbard (1978) 22 *ad loc.*

emphasis shifts from sheer sensation toward evaluative impression. 'Leaders' *contest* the label 'greatness' through their commands, bellowed exhortation and shouted orders, heeded once heard and never ever forgotten, not till the soldiers' dying day. Memorialized in the historian's testimony, ringing through Horace's stentorian evocation.[60]

Pollio/Horace envisage/heed, so this stanza reveals, no winning, no killing, only dying, only glory. In this vision of greatness, the epic-heroic stature of *magnos ... duces |* returns in the second line in immediate *meiosis*. This witnessed 'greatness' belies appearances, doesn't *sound* like greatness, isn't *proclaiming* greatness, but rather codes the (true) greatness that cannot be asserted: the martyr's non-victory in undefeat, the paradoxical re-writing of the story which insists that readers fill for themselves the gap which yawns between | *non* and *indecoro*.[61] The 'dirt' is the badge of valour.

The second half of the stanza re-doubles the force of 'paradox' within this play with/in the values of war. We lift our gaze from the '*duces*' with their armies locked on their familiar plain, to engross 'the universe' (| *et cuncta*). This struggle between the generalissimos is to eliminate rivals and become lord 'of all', blocked out as 'the whole planet' by the pivot *TERRARUM* (cf. the last great collective plural, *ARMORUM*; with *terret*). We move from specks downed in the dust-bath of individual death to 'the face of the earth subjugated', 'world-domination'. But just as the grand strategy is achieved, the crown is snatched away –

– and dented. Emboldened after the *meiosis*, the stanza's long last line enacts a revolt, or *volte face*, from | *praeter* to *Catonis. //*. The whole external world is subdued – but *not* 'the Stoic soul'. Whether 'the exception of Cato' proves, or smashes, the rule will depend on the politics of the reader, for, again, these descriptions-*cum*-evaluations come to us with indeterminate reference, and with undeterminable authorization as between Pollio and Horace, whose assessments of (the) civil war(s) may have found precious little common ground. Perhaps from first to last.

---

[60] Fraenkel (1957) 236 and n. 4 claims these for noises in (his) Horace's head, not the historian's declamation, let alone set speeches given his characters in the historian's text. Cf. Connor (1987) 171, also crediting Horace's imaginary; Nisbet and Hubbard (1978) 23 on v. 21.

[61] Poiss (1992) 143 asks the right (rhetorical?) question, 'Kann man um einem Bürgerkrieg *decus* gewinnen?'

Indeed, throughout the rest of Antiquity Romans would learn to *become* Romans precisely by *debating* the virtues of Cato, for instance as calibrated against Brutus. When they read Pollio, Horace, Virgil and when they wrote their own histories, poems, declamations.[62] Pollio had no love for Cato *in life*. At the age of 21 he had memorably prosecuted him (in 54) for malpractice as tribune. After Pharsalus, Julius sent him against Cato in Sicily. Pollio tries telling Cicero he had to join up with Julius to escape persecution by his *inimicus* (Cato?).[63] But Cato the martyr might still take a different role in the *Historiae*.

9 FIGHTING FOR ROME: LOSER TAKES ALL

> Iuno et deorum quisquis amicior
> Afris inulta cesserat impotens
> tellure u i c t o r u m nepotes
> rettulit inferias Iugurthae: (vv. 25–8)

> *Juno and all those other gods enamoured more*
> *of Africans once gave up, helpless in rage, unavenged left*
> *their land: the* C O N Q U E R O R S '/, *grandsons*
> *they now deliver, offerings for Jugurtha.*

From the wide horizons of the last stanza, we now soar high, moving heaven and earth to import further losers in the *ludus uictorum*. 'Juno and the alliance of pro-African divinities' were *not* exempt from the total subjugation *terrarum*, but once 'gave ground'. Still the legacy of '*arma*' (vv. 4, 19) is the debt of 'vengeance' (vv. 5, 26). *Iuno* is given her defining entourage – not the Capitoline protectress of Rome, but her twin, Tanit of Carthage; tragical epic's incarnation of implacable hostility; the anti-force pitted against Roman patriarchy's *Iuppiter Optimus Maximus*.[64] The text's paired hendecasyllables amplify the paradox of Cato's victory-in-defeat after Thapsus, as mastered 'powerlessness'

---

62 Juvenal could expect readers to recognize the desecration when he re-cycles Horace's beatificatory phrase *atrocem animum*, whether it was a Pollio-esque invention, a citation *after*, or from, Pollio, or a sympathetic chiming of encomiast with encomiand (2.12, castigating censorious Stoicizing from hypocritical preachers – like himself). *Atrox* is complimentary only by way of paradox, cf. Nisbet and Hubbard (1978) 24 *ad loc*.

63 Sen. *Contr.* 7.4.7, Cic. *Ad Att.* 4.16, Tac. *Dial.* 34.7, Gruen (1966), Haller (1967) 18–21; App. *BC* 2.40, Plut. *Cato Min.* 53.2–4; Cic. (Pollio) *Ad fam.* 10.31.2, cf. Bosworth (1972) 455 n. 90.

64 On *Juno* as resistance, cf. Feeney (1984), Spence (1988) 23–6, 134 n. 3.

ominously smuggles back 'unmasterable fury' in the last word: *impotens* |, 'helpless in (controlling their) rage'.[65] But once the text swings away from the rhythmic sequence apparently completed with | *tellure* . . . , the stanza *un*writes what we suppose that we have just read. Divinities *always* live to fight another day, a setback no more than a springboard for resurgence. The power of the gods defies mundane distributions of power 'on earth' as merely temporal junctures in a greater master-plot. Beware: the gods of Africa are '*no less* bound in allegiance to their own people *than they ever were*' (*amicior*); their 'retreat' was tactical – they bent, *but did not break* (*cesserat*); they 'took no revenge', but *therefore* eventual atonement lurks for some future: felt 'impotence' only fans 'uncontrollable' rage (*impotens*).

From the stanza's pivot, *im-potens* | is re-formed in *nepotes* |; | *tellure* is over-written as | *rettulit*. Finally, we encounter the figure of *Iugurthae*. //, come to implement the will of // *Iuno*. The African anti-world's re-figuration of the risen-again figure on the Roman side of triumphant defeat, *Catonis*. //.

Not Julius, but *Jugurtha*, won the battle of Thapsus, which *Cato* did not lose. So this was revenge on the 'grandsons' of those who took Jugurtha away from African soil, for execution to make a Roman triumph for Marius. *Metellus Scipio* lost Thapsus, *because* his grandfather *Metellus* Numidicus won his triumph and *cognomen* for driving Jugurtha out of his kingdom. Before that, his maternal great grandfather, and paternal great-great uncle, *Metellus* Macedonicus had opened the war in Numantia which was finished by Scipio Aemilianus, *Africanus minor* and thence Numantinus, with Marius and Jugurtha serving him side by side – fighting for Rome. *This* Scipio was the grandson of the Scipio who invaded African soil to defeat Hannibal and win just about the first triumphal *cognomen* in history: *Africanus*.

But in the awry world of cursed civil commotion, victories returned to haunt victors, and war became nonsensical, as difference collapsed into cyclicity. This is just what Horace has written into the poetic *coup* of *coups* in the treacherous pivot *VICTORUM*, 'THE CONQUERORS' = *VICTORUM*, 'THE CONQUERED'. Here 'the winners' become and are 'the losers'. No less, none more. (My translation will work this trick if it is read out, and you hear both/either 'THE CONQUERORS'', and/or 'THE CONQUERORS,'.)

---

[65] Cf. Woodman (1974) 124 on *Carm.* 3.30.12, Oliensis (1991).

Now it is not the case that with this twisting, twisted stanza, which takes its cue from the 'mindset' its precedessor inscribed in its perverse admiration for Cato's 'grim' Stoicism, Horace has moved away from Pollio.[66] Or moved Pollio away from Octavian, from Caesarian fratricide, or from Augustus' New Deal. For Pollio, a ring between Metellus Celer's '60/59 BCE' and Metellus Scipio's demise in 46 would awake the hold of the past on his lifetime. For Pollio, Thapsus spelled more than the demise of the Republicans under Numidicus' grandson Metellus Scipio and the suicide of Cato at Utica.[67]

The Pompeian King Juba of Numidia, proclaimed descendant of both Hannibal and *Iugurtha*,[68] fled on news of Thapsus, back to his capital Zama, scene of Scipio Africanus' defeat of Hannibal's Carthage, there to accomplish *his* suicide. Caesar's triumph in 46 saw this 'Jugurtha''s young son and namesake Juba paraded for his jubilee through Rome, but spared and brought up in Octavian's entourage, eventually fighting alongside him and earning restoration to the throne of Numidia. In 25, Juba had just been re-assigned to rule Mauretania, with Antony's daughter Cleopatra Selene for consort, a model imperial satellite and exemplary enthusiast for all things Roman.

The names *Utica* and *Iuba* would always traumatize *Pollio*, however, for what Pollio lived through in Africa, when serving under Curio in the Caesarian invasion of 49 while Julius dashed to Spain for Ilerda, before pursuing Pompey east for Pharsalus. Curio had taken Sicily, then landed at Utica to tackle the Pompeian alliance between the propraetor P. Attius Varus and King Juba's Numidians. After ostentatiously camping at Scipio *Africanus'* base for the Zama campaign, at *Castra Cornelia(na)*, where the sharp natives had poisoned the watersources, the sick army withdrew toward Utica and won a skirmish, but on false intelligence Curio then led the bulk of his forces to ambush an exposed enemy detachment. Saharan conditions and reckless overconfidence had him outmanoeuvred, encircled by cavalry, and driven

---

[66] *Pace* Syndikus (1972) I 349, 'Er denkt nicht mehr an Pollio.' On the contrary, we enjoy Pollio's company on past the poem's bitter-sweet end (cf. Nisbet and Hubbard (1978) 10).

[67] App. *BC* 2.98f.

[68] Cf. Ahl (1976) 89f. for the typology from Sallust's *Jugurtha* for Lucan's Curio. Jugurtha was where Sallustian history began; Juba was where Pollio followed suit. For the surrender of Jugurtha to Sulla as the first seed of Marius' hatred, cf. Plut. *Mar.* 10.5. For Jugurtha ~ Hannibal, cf. Hor. *Epod.* 9.23–6.

back toward higher ground, before going down bravely fighting to his very last soldier. Not one survivor returned to join the small squadron Curio had sent back to guard HQ Utica. Curio's head was fetched to Juba. The Roman admiral Flamma cut and ran without taking off a single soldier from shore.

Pollio knew about all this because *he* was the officer detailed by Curio to take charge of the camp. His *Historiae* (must have) told how he had taken a dinghy out to merchants moored along the seafront and begged them to put in and take the troops off; but when some did, by night, a rush sank some of the ship's boats, and of those who were taken on board, lots were robbed by the traders and thrown into the sea. The stranded remnant surrendered with the morrow to Varus, but Juba came up, lined them against a wall, and had them mown down, as the remainder of his victory. The two legions, plus cavalry, light infantry and batmen, who had invaded Africa were utterly destroyed. Such is Appian's faithful narrative.[69]

Civil commotion had made *Sallust* Caesar's *quaestor* in 49 with a legion in the North Adriatic, then brought him to the victory at Thapsus, to stay on as Caesar's chosen proconsular governor of Numidia when *praetor* (46). Prosecution for extortion on his return was discreetly leant on; retirement and the writing of history ensued. So successive stanzas slotting the 'heroes' of Sallust's two monographs, *Catonis.* //, then *Iugurthae.* //, in the same *sedes* to end their stanzas, speak volumes to Pollio the historian.

Pollio's own active career sped *him* from Caesar at the Rubicon in 49 to Sicily and Africa, then Pharsalus; back to Africa for Thapsus. On to Spain for Munda; next, governor of Further Spain, and manoeuvres from there to Italy; perhaps back to Macedonia for Philippi, perhaps not; then North Italy and Venetia, Brundisium, Illyria, and triumphal entry to Rome for his final bow. The ring of death in Thessaly – Pharsalia/Philippi: Brutus and Cassius' suicides – linked for him with his own double tour in Africa. First for annihilation, then for revenge – Curio's death and Thapsus: Cato's, Metellus Scipio's, Juba's suicides.

So in Pollio's narrative, *Africa* could justifiably stand for Roman history from Punic to civil wars, for the cycles and spirals of history

---

[69] *BC* 2.44–6: Caesar has the *quaestor* Marcius Rufus in the Pollio role, *BC* 2.33–44. Cf. Carter (1991) 228 *ad loc.*, 'Pollio may even have supplied the whole story'; Haller (1967) 27–30. Details about wipe-outs with no survivors invite *Quellenforschung*.

as the narrative of world conquest by, then of, Rome. *His* nightmare, history up-ended, and a sick vision of 'human sacrifice for Jugurtha'.[70]

10 PAINTING THE MAP RED

> quis non Latino sanguine pinguior
> campus sepulcris impia proelia   30
> testatur au d i t u mque Medis
>   Hesperiae sonitum ruinae?
>
> qui gurges aut quae flumina lugubris
> ignara belli? quod mare Dauniae
> non decol o r a u e r e caedes?   35
>   quae caret ora cruore nostro?   (vv. 29–36)

> *Where* doesn't *soil fed rich with Latin blood*
> *call each field of unholy battles' rows of graves*
> *to witness, and* IN EARSHOT *of a listening Parthian East*
> *the West – crashed about our ears in ruins?*
>
> *What churning channel, which rivers of lamentation*
> *know nothing from the war? Whatever sea by Italy*
> *has* not *gone discol* O U R *ed, bloodstains on the map?*
> *Which shore is missing out, on blood spilt from us?*

These stanzas pour out a tragic refrain of lamentation in a series of stricken challenges, a chant which continues the ritualistic damnation of all who listen. The *Latin* script splashes the downfall of its singer/s in a worldwide torrent of *Latin* blood.

The curse of Juno's stanza re-echoes on into the next (*quisquis amicior* | . . . | *tellure . . . Iugurthae* //) returns in *quis . . . sanguine pinguior* | . . . | *testatur . . . ruinae* //). 'Total conquest of the planet' turns now to killing-field graves exported from Italy to enrich every soil everywhere 'without exception' (*quis non . . .*). The self-laceration here catches us all up in its 'here and now'. Infects us with history. Every episode in Pollio's

---

[70] So Dahlmann (1965). As we shall see in chapter 5, through Dido's thirst for blood, Pollio's (former?) protégé and Horace's *alter ego*, Virgil, helps shape Lucan's project: 'That the Roman *civil* wars should be a blood-offering to the ghost of Jugurtha (or Hannibal) is an extension of the Virgilian aetiology of the Hannibalic war as satisfaction for the ghost of Dido (sacrifice calling forth further sacrifice in the manner of an Aeschylean tragedy)' (Hardie (1993) 29, extending Ahl (1976) 83f., 98f.).

Histories is a *topos* in the cultural poetics of 23 – his, Horace's, the reader's (*quis non . . . ?*).

Civil war taints the imperial atlas, as it stains the texts of Italy: Pollio's writing was an eyewitness' *affidavit* pledged at first hand. But so, too, is Horace's. And to complete the triumvirate, their intermediary Virgil has written *his* eternally present testimony to the unholy abominations of impious civil war. First the *impius . . . miles* turfing Meliboeus out of his grainfields in *Eclogue* 1 (v. 70). Then the whole project of the *Georgics*, written to acclaim the triumphal advent of Octavian after Actium, but steeped still in alarmed despondency in the wake of the Ides of March. The protreptic challenge to warm to the soil, and find 'happiness' in 'manure = grain',[71] distorts into the ordeal of facing living history, as the farmer's almanac weather-signs close the pilot book with a coda of evil omens remembered from the *impia . . . saecula* of 44 (1.470: 464–514).

Virgil and Pollio will have been reading each other, too, as Horace has been reading Virgil. Imitation of *nec fuit indignum superis bis sanguine nostro | Emathiam et latos Haemi pinguescere campos* ('Nor was it unacceptable to the gods above that twice with our blood | Thessalian arena and broad fields of bloody Haemus increase fertility', *Georg.* 1.491f.) is signalled for the Ode's catechism at its start, *pinguior | campus*, and the boundaries of the intertextuality are sealed between its *sanguine* and *nostro. //*. Virgil's next sentence looks forward to the nasty surprise awaiting the farmer whose spade will turn up giant skeletons, as his land proves, in the very last word, to be 'a graveyard': *. . . sepulcris. |* (v. 497). Virgil bids, in 29, to push this into the past with prayer in the name of the Man of the Future come to right the capsized times, *satis iam pridem sanguine nostro | . . .* ('Long since now with our blood . . . ', v. 501), but the repetition only enforces more rehearsal of the plight: *tot bella per orbem . . . , saeuit toto Mars impius orbe . . .* ('so many world wars . . . , the god of civil war's sadism unites the nations', vv. 505, 511), and his cursed world is in as great need of the re-birth he had offered Pollio in the vision of *Eclogue* 4.[72] Horace pulls his intertextual trigger (*testatur*)[73] to point up the work locked into his collocation of *| campus*

---

[71] *laetas segetes*, 1.1: *laeto*; *laetamen*, 'spread manure'; 'muck'.

[72] Cf. *impia . . . deuoti sanguinis aetas*, Hor. *Epod.* 16.9 (also putting 29 into words).

[73] For *testatur* as advertising intertextuality, cf. Catull. 64.357, Virg. *Ecl.* 5.21, Prop. 2.1.37, or the elaborate game in Ov. *Am.* 3.10.19–24.

sepulcris ‖ with *impia proelia* |, further echoes from Virgil's doom-laden set-piece. When, a dynasty of Caesares Augusti later, Lucan raved for the nadir of his impious *Bella per Emathios plus quam ciuilia campos* (1.1) on the death-toll of Pharsalia, he had been reading Pollio, and Horace, as well as Virgil (see chapter 5).[74]

In the Ode, burial-ritual sours warfare into the *impia proelia* of civic carnage. From the 'interment' of Metellus *Pius* Scipio in the prostration of *Thapsus*,[75] back to the victory of Sulla's best general in 82 at Faventia, against the Marians, and Scipio's adoptive father Q. Metellus *Pius* (*cos.* 80) ... – 'every' Caesarian battle in the whole wide universe (*quis non?*) staged again the Sullan slaughter fought literally on the plain of war, the *campus Martius* of Rome, wherever geography happens to set the scene.[76]

When this stanza turns on its pivot *AUDITUM*-, it tells us to amplify the shriek that fills its lines with scarring profanity into a hypersonic cry for the cosmos: 'the fall of the West', and a shock the world wide. (The word *ruinae.* ‖ sonically completes the offering to *Iugurthae.* ‖.) The ensuing stanza further whips up the poem's frenetic phonetics, on cue. A row of questions varies but repeats the outcries, matching the scenes on dry land arising from Cato and Jugurtha's African cemetery with a trio of watery graves, then the shoreline where the two realms collide, to fill in the rest of the map. Tears of rage choke out a broken 'swirl' of grief, 'rivers' spill basins of pain – no breath spare for a verb, or verbs,[77] before an ocean pours all over Italy: *qui ... aut* ‖ *quae ...* ; *qui gurges aut quae* ‖ *flumina lugubris* | *ignara belli? quod mare Dauniae* | *non decol-* ...

At this pivot, the Ode drawls expansively a mouthful of volumetric expatiation: *DECOL-OR-A-VER-E* (before the first strong break between the enneasyllable and decasyllable in the poem, between

---

[74] Tacitus inaugurates the *Annals* in the Augustan succession (chapter 7), when Pollio's son Asinius Gallus alarms Tiberius *tamquam ... plus quam ciuilia agitaret Pollionisque Asinii patris ferociam retineret* (*Ann.* 1.12.4, cf. Zecchini (1982) 1278 n. 57). A paraded citation from Pollio's *Historiae*, like or *via* Lucan's inauguration in hyperbole (chapter 5): *Bella per Emathios plus quam ciuilia campos ...* (*BC* 1.1, cf. Nisbet and Hubbard (1978) 11 on v. 1, Botteri (1989) 90).

[75] *Thapsum ... iacentem*, Virg. *Aen.* 3.689, as from θάπτω, 'bury' (cf. Isid. *Orig.* 16.6.35, *Thapsus ... iacens et planior, unde et nuncupata*).

[76] Cf. Lucan 2.223f., and chapter 5.

[77] Cf. Virg. *Aen.* 1.459f., (Aeneas) *lacrimans, 'quis iam locus, ...* | *quae regio in terris nostri non plena laboris?'* |, with Currie (1985).

caedes? | and | *quae* ...). The second line colours Marrucine Pollio's *Italia* with the affective term 'Daunian', for Horace's native Apulia and Virgil's Turnus.[78] The final (shore-)line gathers together all the oratorical momentum forced into two raw stanzas of fury, as your mouth must now heave five jangling gobs of raw blood: ... ‖ *quod mare Dauniae* | *non decolorauere caedes?* | *quae caret ora cruore nostro?* ‖.[79] The final word's long and open-mouthed vowels *-o-*. . . *-o?* ‖ catch up the howl of blood across two stanzas, from *sanguine* to *cruore*; catch up the echoing run of stanzas in *doloso.* ‖, *cothurno* ‖, *triumpho* ‖; catch up the doleful Virgilian intertext's *sanguine nostro* | ... *sanguine nostro* |; catch up the plaintive series of identifications bestowed on the reader – *Latino, Hesperiae, Dauniae*. Finally and ineluctably, the excoriation, lyric transport into emotionality, devolves on 'us'. Every reader-reciter in our West: ‖ *quis non* ... *nostro?* ‖.

I I THE GET-OUT CLAUSE: IT'S JUST A
SHOT AWAY ···

> sed ne relictis Musa procax iocis
> Ceae retractes munera neniae,
> mecum   (vv. 37–9)

> *But no foxy Muse never leave your teasing fun, re-*
> *turn the archaic dirge, service with a wail,*
> *join me* ... ,

Through tragic coloration in the poem's re-presentation of its battle(s), Pollio–Horace have now brought together experience on both – no: on *all* – sides of the civil wars, producing, instead of narrative *dénouement*, the chorus of citizen voices that share in the 'Amen' of *nostro.* ‖. The poem simulates 'Ending', as its drama exits in shared lamentation, marked off and completed by a final command to desist.

The poem's last stanza turns the page on Book I, into II, pointing up the 'excess' of pain invested in its flood of lament. This allows Horace to 'place' the preceding howl as a Simonidean ('Cean') dirge, a literary lyric equivalent for the Roman *nenia*, chanted wailing as a family

---

[78] Cf. *Carm.* 3.30.11; *Aen.* 12.723.
[79] Nisbet and Hubbard (1978) 29 on v. 36 point out the aural effects, and the jerk of the weak caesura, *quae caret ora* | cruore ....

escorted its corpse down through the *forum* on its way to cremation and the family tomb. But the rhetorical gesture of *turning away* signifies no less than a 're-engagement',[80] both within the ambit of the Pollio Ode and in its prefatory function, as programme for Book II. To ignore either function is to fail to read the rhetoric, and its context.

(i) Within the economy of 2.1, this last stanza *identifies* what has just been performed; and stops the chain of interrogations as they exhaust the surface of the planet. To add more could only be to repeat. So ends the lament.

The inspiration of Pollio, his life, works, and the evocative power of their mimesis matched by their subject, has carried poet-and/as-reader away. Horace's reaction has been a response, and tribute, to the affective power (and compelling analysis?) of the *Histories*. His coda affirms that *he has got the message*. Epinikia may halt their narrative transports to recall the praise-poem to its subject, occasion and opening, in ring-structure; just so, Horace returns here to the address to Pollio from which he soared to convey us to war.[81]

In turning to the Muse here, Horace also enacts what he promised Pollio for himself, namely a return to his poetry after the dutiful completion of the *Histories*. The subject has occupied Horace for this 'wee while' (*paulum*, v. 9), but he knows his Pollio. The poem is like both encomiand and encomiast, finding respite after traumatic ordeal, just as the political careers of both men have turned from fighting for Rome to the productivity of 'retirement'.

Thus he is not *simply* 'turning away from Pollio to himself',[82] nor are 'we' *simply* 'watching ... a point-by-point refusal to write like Pollio'.[83] Rather, the poem's 'refusal' signals the politics of Horace's '*Pollio*': profit from survival of the conflict, first by paying the dead their 'dues' – elogia, ritual offerings and funeral lament (*munera*) – then also by returning to the good life, once civic relations return to health.

Joining the ostensibly apolitical life after serious reflection on the troubles *could* signal Horace's dissociation from Pollio's dangerous anchoring of the present in the past; it *could* represent solidarity with him, giving notice that both writers will have done their duty by attesting the unfinished business of the civil wars; and it *could* co-opt

---

[80] Connor's apt term ((1987) 172).   [81] Fraenkel (1957) 239.
[82] Nisbet and Hubbard (1978) 29 on v. 37.   [83] West (1973) 31.

both writers for 'a politically expedient ... Epicureanism'.[84] It can glue all this to the ideological turning-point, signalled by Augustus' auto-biography, that 'the Cantabrian war made a very suitable point for Augustus to stop writing. It was his final campaign as a front-line commander and immediately preceded his *retirement* from the highest executive position in the state ... After this "retirement" his public accountability became less ...'[85] 'We can detect an "Augustan" message in this "republican" ode: that while it is not inglorious to have fought in all sincerity on the republican side, now the time has come to forget the civil wars and enjoy the pursuits of peacetime.'[86] But 2.1 insists rather that citizens of 23 *remember*, not simply forget, *the civil wars*, as necessary induction to the future.[87] Indeed the poem makes *this* the condition of entry to this book, and as such proposes param-eters for what is to count as '*Augustan*'.

'Not yet expiated ...; danger: fires; intransigent Cato; blood up to our global ears' – these motifs are seared into the poem's contract with the 'here, now, us'.

(ii) As programmatic quasi-*recusatio*, the Ode neither *simply* 'signals avoidance of *overtly* political themes in the rest of the book',[88] nor *simply* 'prepares for the movement by which in subsequent poems ... Horace will ... again *turn away* from such harsh confrontations ..., distancing [him] from serious themes such as those of 2.1, casting him once again as the poet of elegant trifles, and setting him apart from those who, like Pollio and Vergil, would dare the hazardous cross-ing.'[89] Rather, this preface declares, on behalf of the book that it begins, that its less gruelling contents (what could fail to be less gruel-ling than the civil wars?) come to you courtesy of memorious *retirement*. The lifetime covered by Pollio's life-work is Horace's, too, their every

---

[84] Leach (1993) 298 n. 60, 'Horace ... aims to extend the exhortation to Pollio in *Ode* 2.1 to *turn away* from the dangerous past.'

[85] Carter (1982) on Suet. *Aug.* 85.1. Augustus' grave illness in 23 (must have) prompted the retirement, the settlement, and the troubles in 23, cf. Poiss (1992) 133–5.

[86] Nadeau (1980) 181.

[87] Cf. Poiss (1992) 149, contrasting Labienus' *optima ciuilis belli defensio obliuio est* (*ap.* Sen. *Contr.* 10.3.5, 'The best justification of civil war – forget it').

[88] Santirocco (1986) 84.

[89] Porter (1987) 110f.

moment predicated on survival of *motum* ... *ciuicum* to tell the tale, whether in Pollio's tragedies in prospect, or in the Horatian lyrics ahead.

Now, in an intense burst of intervention, commentators argue fiercely the syntax of *ne* ... *retractes*. Does Horace mean/say that his 'Muse is not to go over again' (as he fears she will, and/or has) 'what Simonides handled in his dirges', i.e. what they have just been through in the last pair of stanzas, i.e. what Pollio handles in his *Histories*? Would the 'Muse be naughty if she forsook hanky-panky and took on the job of bringing lyric exsequies to Rome, to Latin'? Or is she 'a naughty Muse who should not therefore abandon fun and games to re-do Pollio in song'? Or what? ... Is this fumbling dither, or foreplay fun? At the heart of the uncertainty is telling mobility – signalled as such within the poet's *mot juste, retractare*. The world of Horace's '*Pollio*' is summed up in this one word.

(i) In a context of leering innuendo, you could not exclude the sense 'refuse, shrink back, be reluctant', so that here the poet wants the Muse to share the 'fun' with him, act up 'sexy', and 'not say no'. Or he could tell her 'not to say yes again' to demands. Whether the Muse thinks of giving up further serving the lyric of death, or considers giving herself to some serving of it, she is in touch with Horace – they can discuss it some more in private (*mecum*). Heads Horace wins, *tails she loses*.

(ii) But *retractare* spans the polarity 'repeat' and 'revise' in a range of contexts. In particular, when it comes to literary production, *retractatio* includes 'correction' and 'alteration', as well as 'producing a new draft', 're-doing' – as well as 'writing a précis', 'thinking out afresh'. Thus Horace's lyric 'reaffirms', even under the sign of negation (*ne*); but in the process, it 'revises', too.

   The *Ode* 'recites/re-cites/re-sites' Pollio's *Histories*, Pollio's career, Pollio's lifetime, into its own idiom, interpretation, response, reading of the figure '*Pollio*', and into its own author's own perspective. Thus Horace 'represents' but *eo ipso* 're-presents' Pollio – 'revises, alters, reclaims, recuperates, appropriates ...'.

   Between them, they have provided the Republic with decent burial and expert keening: Pollio has graced a Simonidean lyric dirge, Horace has heralded the definitive narrative of his generation; and readers have been required to invest their own reading with their third viewpoint. 'You' handle the poem and its Horatian re-cap/re-write of Pollio's pre-fatorial précis, his full narrative articulation of the tragedy, and/or his summary conclusion from an epilogue. We feel the re-reading in the writing and re-writing of history in the *Histories*, in the Ode, refracted again in Pollio's *Tragedy* and Horace's (*non-*)*Simonidean lyricism*, and ourselves re-write this in your (re-)reading.

(iii) *ne . . . retractes* stars, through the disarming camouflage of toying with a Muse, as the poem's figure for its own, and its (Pollio's) book's, poetics, politics, rhetoric, propaedeutic. The poet doubles back on himself to show how 'translation' of another engenders active reading as 're-writing', for, as we have seen, the task of rendering Pollio has evoked strenuous exploitation of features of lyric writing denied to the historian, and to the Roman tragedian, alike. Composition in Alcaic stanzas has produced an original Pollio which could *only* be a Horatian 're-vision' – in a poetic mode which Roman (and modern) readers must *learn by reading, and re-reading, these very Carmina.*[90] The poem names the process it initiates – for itself and for *Odes* II: '*retractatio*'.

The closing instruction to the love of poetry *does* look forward pre-scriptively; but close-(re-)reading shows that we must first look for 'measured measures' (*modos*) in which to 're-vise' our reading *of 2.1.*[91] The Muse must 'accompany Horace' in 're-tuning' their poem, for 'a lighter performance', with less of the 'Simonidean sing-song'.

Careful reading (= constant 're-reading') of the poem already finds that the lyric has not only been acquiring cumulative resonance as it progressed, but has been 're-presenting' its materials, with a different coloration, in a changed mood, set to new music. Since the shock of battle in the 'central' pair of stanzas' *repraesentatio* (*iam nunc . . . uoltus, audire . . . Catonis*, vv. 17–24), the song has been re-calling and re-issuing the terms and images of the opening salutation for Pollio (vv.

---

[90] Horace's Roman lyric translates Greek music and Roman thinking – and 'une "bonne" traduction doit toujours abuser', Derrida (1978), cf. Lewis (1985) 39f., 41.

[91] See esp. West (1973) 31f., Nadeau (1980) 178–82. Sallmann (1987) 78 highlights oppositions: esp. Fortune's game / Juno's wrath, the fires / the waters, *thea-trum/antrum*.

1–16), in a spate of internal *retractationes*, poetry *as* 'repetitions – with difference':

(i) *modos* we re-find at once on re-reading: in *modos* at v. 2, indicating the 'manners' of civil war.

(ii) The first provocation for *leuiore* was *grauis*, v. 3, qualifying the 'alliances of great leaders'.

(iii) The last and first words can now loop together, *plectro* // ~ // *motum*, for to strum on strings is, exactly, *plectrum mouere*.

(iv) The details relay reading round the circuit of the poem:
amicior (v. 25) re-presents *amicitias* (v. 4)
sanguine pinguior (v. 29) ~ *uncta cruoribus* (v. 5)
impia proelia (v. 30) ~ *nondum expiatis* (v. 5)
Medis | Hesperiae (vv. 31f.) ~ *motum ... ciuicum, amicitias et arma* (vv. 1, 4) – i.e. those who should fight *versus* those who did: the world gone wrong
ruinae (v. 32) ~ *motum, per ignis* (vv. 1, 7) – *ruina* may include the effect of a quake (*terrae motus*), as well as collapse in a fire, or sack
lugubris (v. 33) re-activates the music latent in *modos* (v. 2), preparing for *modos* (v. 40)
belli (v. 33) re-doubles *belli* (v. 2)
decolorauere (v. 35) restores colour to *uitia* (v. 2), as flaws in the *finish*; and saves for rust *arma ... uncta cruoribus* (vv. 4f.)
cruore (v. 36) echoes *cruoribus* (v. 5)
Horace's *Musa* (v. 37) over-rides Pollio's *Musa* (v. 9), and *procax* (v. 37) lightens *seuerae* (v. 9)
iocis (v. 37) brightens *ludum* (v. 3)
munera (v. 38) replays *munus* (v. 11), and *Ceae* + *Dionaeo* (vv. 38f.) *Cecropio* (v. 12)
re-tractes (v. 38) repeats *tractas* (v. 7), *repetes* (v. 12)
leuiore (v. 40) addresses both *grauis* (v. 3) and *grande ... cothurno* (vv. 11f.)
not up on the *Cecropio cothurno* (12), but down, under the *Dionaeo antro* (v. 39 ~ 12), and *sub antro* (v. 39), not *per ignis | suppositos* (vv. 7f.).

Every time the poem is (re-)read, the effort to conjure relief from gloom which through vv. 1–16 lifted foul civil war to acclamation of Pollio's Dalmatian triumph, leads in vv. 17–24 to the bright face of battle and glory, only for the mood to break on the grim thought of Cato's grim thoughts at v. 24. As defeat stares him in the face, his invincible gaze scorns our terror to right and to left (*Catonis* //, vv. 16 ~

uoltus //, v. 20). We struggle to enjoy the war-movie narrative and forget the narrated, all trumpets and cavalry-charges, honourable death and the glorious pall of dust; but, despite our best efforts, the burden of doom weighs down through the generations and delivers a blood-soaked page that only a gloating Jugurtha could enjoy. Every re-handled item, each echo, only makes the stain deeper – until the reading reaches the final exhortation to 'Try again, only *this* time *lighten up*.'

12 IT'S JUST A KISS AWAY (GIMME SHELTER)

mecum D i o n æ o sub antro
quaere modos leuiore plectro. //   (vv. 39–40)

*join me, where in*A M O R*ation grows down the grotto,*
hunt musical modes to lighten up our strum.

Already the stanza has been 'revising' its predecessor, which as we saw resumed the accumulated drive of the whole composition. This *retractatio* began with the displacement of *lugubris* | by its inversion *iocis* |. *Dauniae* | ... *caedes* | returned, with a difference, in the noises signalled and sounded in | *Ceae* ... *neniae*. Now the poem's final pivot *DIONAEO*, with its exotic run of sonorous vowels, cues the altered rhythm of the second half of the stanza to redoubled, revisionary, re-writing of the dirge's climax: ... *decolorauere caedes?* | *quae caret ora cruore nostro?* // is ironed out and its echolalia naturalized as the responsive environs of a devoted auditorium: ... *Dionaeo sub antro* | *quaere modos leuiore plectro.* //.

No sooner headed 'down', down from the heights, chilling out, and calming down, than the musical quest strikes gold: *modos* here is under the aegis, or blanket, of the pivot of 'Love' (*Dione* is '[mother of] love'). Under (her) cover(s) Muse and poet will play *Grecques* and Romans – his *ego* with her *Dione*; her *antrum* ready for his *modos*; between them the gentle hammering of gossamer lover with thrusting beloved, *leuiore* ↔ *plectro* (< πλῆσσω, 'pound'), in the slightly striking oxymoron of well-matched lovers' gently rhythmic bonking – *Flaccus* and his escort, the lovable *Mlle* Erato.[92]

But the musical strains of lust, love's music, chime, too, with the

---

[92] Cf. Minadeo (1982). For *modi* of musical erotics, cf. Hor. *Carm.* 3.9.10; of sex-'n'-rhetoric, cf. Ov. *Am.* 2.6.28 (with *tecum*).

love of sympathetic music, where *modos* signify the desideratum of 'moderation'. In musical culture (the modest musician says), civilization modulates passion into a well-tempered blend of a lovely tune with a measured beat. And in *quaere modos*, the text also motions the re-reader to re-examine the music, the text. We must look deeper, beneath the surface: *Dionaeo sub antro*. To build up the energy for his simulacrum of Pollio (*exaedificatio*), the kaleidoscopic 'modality' of Horatian lyric has pulled together chords from all manner of 'musical genres' – notably Thucydidean/Sallustian history, Sophoclean tragedy, Simonidean lyric – and his revisionary re-writing has used 'Callimachean' refinement to polish up his performance (*expolitio*). Exactly as befits Asinius Pollio. For in Latin, *pollio, -onis* signifies none other than a 'polisher'.

Just as *polishing* requires 'handling' and 're-handling', so Horace's mimetic re-presentation of the *Histories* has paraded before us *arma* in need of elbow grease (vv. 4f.), blinded us with *fulgor armorum* (v. 19), itched to bush up the glorious dead, *non indecoro puluere sordidos* (v. 22), and loathed the stained panorama, *decolorauere* (v. 35); with his (golden?) *plectrum* (v. 40),[93] Horace and the Muse will polish up their 'modulation' – next time, next draft, next performance, next '(re-)reading', of Pollio's poem, and of the rest ... – until it is *finished*.

So '*Pollio*' names the kinetic principle of 'revision', whether poetic-literary, cultural-ideological, civic-political. These *Carmina* create a shifting, symphonic *ensemble* beyond merely notational fixity and prosaically stable programming. And *Carmina* 2.1 imagines a Muse for their opera that we could call '*Polliohymnia*' – and entitles her poetic: *MOTUS*.[94]

13 UN COUP DE DÉS JAMAIS N'ABOLIRA LE HASARD[95] (*ODES* II)

The next poem at once puts the plan into practice, strumming out the jingle of lighter Sapphic stanzas in fresh *retractatio* of 2.1, after extra time. Specifically, the imposing noise of the penultimate pivot D E C O L - O R A U E R E, and the booming vowels of the final pivot D I O N A E O echo

---

[93] Cf. Hor. *Carm.* 2.13.26.
[94] *Motus* dances, then, toward meaning 'trope', the *différence* in poetic language.
[95] 'Writing will never obliterate the page', cf. Scott (1988) 145f.

on into the first line, and into the first stanza's cadence-sequence, of the
next piece, as | *non decolorauere caedes* | *quae caret ora cruore* returns, and
the last stanza's cadences, ... *iocis* |, ... *neniae* |, *antro* |, ... *plectro.* // re-
sound, to the different tune of 2.2's 'pick':

> Nullus argento | color est auaris
> abdito terris, inimice lamnae
> Crispe Sallusti, nisi temperato
> splendeat usu.   (2.2.1–4)

> *No silver is a silver* colour *when miser*
> *earth has it hidden away – down hard on metal for coin,*
> *aren't you, Wavy Sallust* Crispus? *– unless the tempering*
> *it gets makes it shine from all the use.*

In moving into the cave with the Muse, and finding this Sapphic tune,
Horace has not left Pollio behind, or history. For here is *Sallust's*
(great-nephew and adopted) son, and in its Alcaic companion poem,
2.3, will enter Q. Dellius, historian of, and deserter from, Antony and
Cleopatra, whose 'work ... supplemented Pollio very well'.[96] Horace's
tribute accordingly ends with allusion to the father of history Herodotus' story of the Sage unmoved by mere royal treasure.[97]

Stepping further into the collection will bring us alongside Horace
for his own retirement from the military fray and instructions for his
burial (2.6), then the twin welcome for Pompeius (2.7) – back at last
from an exile that stretched from Pollio's war and Pharsalus, through
Horace's war and Philippi, on through Sex. Pompeius' struggles and
Naulochus, before post-Actian amnesty brought him back to the fold
in time to join the restored Republic of 23, first out and last back,
so sign of re-integration. *mecum* in 2.1.39 sews the Pollio Ode to
this Sapphic–Alcaic diptych, core of Horace's entire *œuvre*: *mecum ...*
mecum, 2.6.1, 21 (last stanza) ~ *mecum*, 2.7.1, *tecum*, 9.[98]

As we approach the shift of rhythms with Asclepiads for Maecenas in
2.12, we (may have) visited in 2.10 *Maecenas' brother-in-law* L. Licinius

---

[96] Pelling (1988) 28, cf. *Ant.* 59, Strabo 11.13.3.

[97] 1.30 (Solon and Croesus). For *liens* between 2.1–2–3, cf. Syme (1986) 384f., 'All three
exhibit a conspicuous feature in common, namely changes of side in the wars, albeit
not quite with equal success and repute. Another link bound them, the writing of
history ... [Horace] must seclude Messalla Corvinus from this company.'

[98] Cf. Segal (1969); Moles (1987) argues cogently for paraenetic revisionism from Horace to, i.e. through, Pompeius.

Murena (adopted by a Terentius Varro) in the last Sapphic–Alcaic pair, twinned with Quinctius of 2.11, very likely *Pollio's brother-in-law* and son of the Quinctius proscribed by the second triumvirate[99] – the one drowned in Pollio's consulship.

Then the new start to the second half of the collection *Odes* I–III at 2.12 is paraded as itself *retractatio of the Pollio Ode*: its recipient, Maecenas, will have read over Horace's review of Pollio, and 'their' series of yin and yang lyrics leading toward the end of Horace (2.6) before re-starting with his first friend Pompeius' new start (2.7),[100] through the re-start of the second half of Book II with Quinctius following Licinius' parable of (polished) 'golden mediocrity/middleness' (2.10.5), and should have appreciated his own offering – which presumes to portray him as, exactly, *no Pollio*. Under the sign of negation, // *nolis ...*, Horace's first stanza in 2.12 offers a regressive catalogue, from the starting-point of Numantia, through Hannibal to the war with Carthage for Sicily, and so re-traces the three Punic Wars; the references thus work back from the starting-point of Pollio's starting-point Sallust, with the *Metello consule* that spelled Metellus Numidicus' Jugurtha, and *his* start at (Metellus Macedonicus') Numantia, the pride of Scipio Numantinus, grandson and facsimile of Hannibal's Scipio Africanus Maior.

The detail of the poem precisely re-reads the Pollio Ode. Only, in the case of Maecenas, Horace *turns away* still farther from wars fought in their lifetime, to reach further 'back' to the terror and danger of myth. The sea is still stained with blood, but Punic (2.12.3) not Latin (2.1.29), and declared *from the outset* to be wrong for soft lyric musical modes of moderation (2.12.3f.). The reader is positioned as addressee through all *this* catalogue of war, but this time the material is deplored throughout as savagery. When he passes on from this opening volley of rejection, he supplies his named addressee, the material for *his* project, and reinforcement of his own refusal of *all* empathy or share in it. The reader has been seeing through eyes which are now positioned as Maecenas', a felt absence from Book II so far.

Another forthcoming narrative of the wars of (a) *Caesar* is promised

---

[99] Nisbet and Hubbard (1978) 168.

[100] Octavian had taken care to choose already a certain Cn. Pompeius as a suffect consul for 31, the year of the show-down with Antony (cf. Syme (1986) 30, with 'The Descendants of Pompeius', 255–69, and *Tables* XIV, XVII; Augustus even managed to die *Sex. Pompeio consule*).

the public, this time from his first friend Maecenas,[101] but the subject is now denied to Horatian *verse* as the stuff for Pollio-style 'pedestrian histories', stigmatized as 'prosaic' material (vv. 10–12). Better that *Maecenas* will make a stab at this task (9–12). In the pivotal centre stanza (vv. 13–6) Horace gets the approval of his *Musa* to write sweetly, instead, of singing, dancing love (v. 13f.). To complete the poem, Horace re-writes the first three stanzas of harsh nastiness into a catalogue of the fun and games of *his* fancy. He repeats that Maecenas 'would refuse' (*num uelis*) to swap all this for the physiognomy of a Pollio's *corpus* (*pingues ... plenas*, 2.12.22, 24 ~ *plenum, pinguior,* 2.1.6, 29).[102]

The charade has *made a mock-Pollio of Maecenas,* and so immobilized the demand he represents. It heralds a revise for the rest of the book's poetry, a mock-grim procession of poems of fluctuating bulk, but mostly an assortment of Alcaics (2.13–15, 17, 19–20) that transport the poet to brushes with death (13, 16.29–32, 17) and visions of Hell's torments (13.21–40, 14.5–12, 17–20, 18.34–40), before lifting him through Dionysiac ecstasy (2.19) to wing his way skywards from the grave (2.20) – and then come back re-born as the inspired *uates* of Book III's exalted procession of massive oracular Alcaics, the Roman Odes (3.1–6). The progression will portray the resumption of Horace's joking intimacy with Maecenas,[103] whose influence will re-surface again with 3.8, and last to the end (3.29),[104] before Horace's epilogue signs off the whole collection (3.30).[105]

Turning away from Pollio with Maecenas, however, has polarized them as 'book-ends' dialectically framing the intricately interlinked 'mosaic' of alternating Sapphic–Alcaic 'tiles' which form a central 'gathering' within the collection between 2.2–11, strung into concentric rings around 2.6–7 and studded with verbal, conceptual, and thematic interlinking as intricate as Pollio's Virgilian *Eclogues*.[106] The

---

[101] So affirms the closeness of *Caesaris | Maecenas,* v. 10.

[102] Maecenas wrote, not patriotic histories, but exotic – neoteric – verse (Bardon (1956) II 13–19, André (1967) 104–14, 149–53). On 2.12 (~ 2.1), cf. Carlson (1977–8), Santirocco (1980) 223–36, Nadeau (1980) 202–4, Citroni (1983) 178–85, Sallmann (1987) 85f.

[103] Cf. McDermott (1992).

[104] 'The Maecenas *Odes* are ... dynamically disposed to chart the poet's gradual *movement* toward greater independence' (Santirocco (1984) 243).

[105] Cf. Woodman (1974).

[106] For the problem of *writing down* the mobile structuration re-vised in each reading of a series of the *Carmina,* cf. Sukenick (1975), '... the law of mosaics, or how to deal

Pollio Ode was not least the initiator of this, launching this first project of Book II and re-launching the tripartite collection, I–III, for its centrepiece.

For the first book began by showing the lyric poet able to envision empathetically the chosen lives of all manner of men, as his own peculiarly satisfying goal in life.[107] The second now promises to lift his overview back across the historian's span measured in the *Fasti Consulares*. Horace's new beginning is itself the trace of a past, just as his own life inserted him into a story already long under way before he came along. Just so, his new book picks up the patterns that took shape already in Book I, not least the alternation of Alcaic with Sapphic metres begun with 1.37–8 and to be continued between 2.1 and 2.11.

It is the specific function of 2.1 to institute a unique cycle of ten Odes framed between 'Pollio' and the re-launching of the collection with 'Maecenas' in the Asclepiads of 2.12. This batch of Odes sits precisely at the centre of the collection, with 38 poems in I, then 2.1; 2.2–11 (with 2.6–7 as the centrefold); 2.12; and 38 poems in 2.13–20+ III. Another centrepoint is emphatically marked in the 'golden meet-you-halfway' of 2.10, at the half-way point through the score of poems in this central book of the collection. And in the other direction, there are strong continuities between, particularly, the last cluster of poems in I (35–8) and the cycle that 'begins' (rather: recommences) in 2.1.[108]

Philosophy of life, love, friendship run by the reader of *these* idylls 'from the cave of Venus'. True, *Venus was* Caesar's goddess,[109] but this does not gather 2.1, or 2.2–11, for the proprietary benefit of Augustus.[110] *Venus* speaks no less of Horace's *Venusia*, twice despoiled by Pollio's civil strife. And, as we shall see, Venus belongs, too, with that staunch Caesarian–Republican *Pollio*.

---

with parts in the absence of wholes', and Miller (1991) 366, 'Each rereading is also a restructuring of the collection ... because the relays between the [poems] are so numerous, so subtle, and so overdetermined, that they can never all be present to his or her mind at any one time.' For the cycle of 2.1; 2–11; 12, cf. esp. Ludwig (1957), Eisenberger (1980), Dettmer (1983) 203–32, Santirocco (1986) 83–95, Porter (1987) 31f., 112–28.

[107] For the Horatian hallmark of responsiveness, see Nussbaum (1981).
[108] Cf. Porter (1987) esp. 111.
[109] E.g. *Dionaei ... Caesaris astrum*, Virg. *Ecl.* 9.47.
[110] *Pace* Nadeau (1980) 181, 'It is worth noting that the pursuits of peacetime are to be under the patronage of *Venus*, who is a Caesarean goddess ..., and symbolises by her position in the poem the ending of civil war by Augustus.'

As we read into 2.2's cameo for Sallust *Jr*, reading of the polishing of silver to shine bright in use, we shall find Horace minting maxims before depreciating the 'counterfeiting of language in popular abusage' (vv. 19f.), in favour of 'the bestowing of crown and laurel to the hero unmoved by great piles' (vv. 21–4). Horace gives notice that he is picturing Sallustius *Crispus* ('Crinkly') as *inimice lamnae* ('no friend to sheet-metal for coining; ... also in colloquial use for "cash"', v. 2), to stamp him with his role in the new coinage of Augustus; he will therefore coin for Crispus' song of moderation (*modos*) visions of 'blend[ing]/alloy[ing] ... in the minting process', *temperato*, v. 3),[111] opposed to the money-mad hoarder of silver in the ground and those with eyes glued on heaped treasure.[112] But he is also *polishing* up his gathering of verse, to shine for Pollio.

My Horace moves us along with the Muse down to the *Asini monumenta* next to the *Forum Iulium* in the complex around Pollio's *restoration* of the *Atrium* Libertatis.[113] Here you would find the memorial of Pollio: a public library full of polite letters (plus bust-portraits of dead authors),[114] and a polished art-display. The collection of marble statuary was a striking enough feature for Pliny specifically to list its highlights.[115] Was Pollio's collection arranged in a garden-site, for example a *nymphaeum* set in a grotto?[116] Once we envisage a programmed *ensemble* of marble set *sub antro*, in full view will appear a work by Praxiteles' son Kephisodotos: *Venus in Pollionis Asini monumentis*.[117] There was *no* state monopoly on Venus. No Roman, not Pollio, not Horace, not Caesar Augustus, could own *Aeneadum genetrix*

---

[111] *Temperato* is re-mixed for 2.3 as *mentem ... temperatam* (vv. 2f.), while *color* returns in *colore*, 2.4.3, *colore*, 2.5.12.

[112] See Wallace-Hadrill (1986) 87.

[113] Suet. *Aug.* 29.5.

[114] Plin. *Nat. hist.* 35.9f., Isid. 6.5.2, cf. Rawson (1985) 114; Isager (1991) 164f.

[115] Plin. *Nat. hist.* 36.33f., cf. Isager (1991) 163–7, 'The collections of Asinius Pollio'; Pollitt (1983) 75, 'The outstanding individual collector of the 1st century BC was Gaius Asinius Pollio...., friend of Caesar, Antony, and later of Augustus, scholar, poet, literary critic, politician, promoter of cultural activities in Rome, and conspicuous philHellene.'

[116] So Grimal (1943) 157 n. 8, cf. Zanker (1988) 69f. In Horace, *antra* double as the old Greek site for love/entrapment, and as places for inspiration, immortal poetry, and encomia (Leach (1988) 490–7; cf. Joly (1983) on Prop. 3.2.14, *operosa ... antra*, 3.3.27, *affixis uiridis spelunca lapillis*, etc.).

[117] Plin. *Nat. hist.* 36.24, cf. Isager (1991) 156. The only poetry we have from Pollio are the three words: *Veneris antistita Cupra*.

– or the cultural flow between philosophy and sex, friendship and politics, lubricated by living-as-loving: *Venus*. Even especially when Rome was acclaiming the restitution of the *respublica libera* and negotiating how a collective '*Augustan*' civilization might remember never to forget the civic strife preserved in Pollio's histories, tragedies, library, life – and now *on the move* in his *carmen*, the pivotal *Pollio Ode*. Monumental poetry in M O T I O N.

A final word – but the poetry moves onwards, always 'beginning' (again). 'Beginning' has been deconstructively explored in and as *Odes* 2.1 by recourse to the figure of 'history', in the sense of lived experience and bio-script over generations; in the sense of historian's narrative; and – by reference to Pollio's *Histories* – in the sense of the plurality of competing patterns of chance recurrence, tragic cyclicity, ironic reversal, fated inversion and arbitrary paradox, which are negotiated between history's texts and their interpretations. In the process, representation of battle has doubled for 'beginning' *and* 'end', and their lapse in war after war. The decisive knock-out battle at the outbreak of war joins the series of its predecessors – the same battle again (itself a synecdoche for the overall narrative of war), simulating in its termination (as event) the conclusion (as message) that the legacy of battle is *another battle*, the upshot of war is *more war*. Ultimate defeat is denied by its memorialization, total victory is undone by running the text on. As Horace/Pollio showed us with such mimetic power, trumpets blare, and *Cato* adds his body to the pile of citizens. But with his 'exception', the poem breaks the closure of 'ending', deconstructed as just one more 'résumé', the revenge of *Jugurtha*, the return of Hannibal ... and another 'beginning', the fall of Iuba, destiny of Metelli and Cornelii Scipiones, and the martyrdom of Cato ensuring the Ides of March, the Philippi of Cassius and Brutus, and the widening arc of blood poisoning the victors ready for Actium ... *nondum*. The civil wars were not done in 23–[118]

> Don't accept that what is happening
> is just a case of others' suffering
> or you'll find that you are joining in
> the turning away –[119]

---

[118] –but that is to begin (again, in) chapter 5.
[119] D. Gilmour, 'On the Turning Away', on Pink Floyd (1987).

Appendix: Text and translation of Horace, *Odes* 2.1

```
x – ∪ – – ‖ – ∪ ∪ – ∪ x
x – ∪ – – ‖ – ∪ ∪ – ∪ x
x – ∪ – –        – ∪ – x
    – ∪ ∪ – ∪ ∪ – ∪ – x ‖
```

Motum ex Metello consule ciuicum
bellique causas et uitia et modos
ludumque F o r t u n æ grauisque
    principum amicitias et arma

nondum expiatis uncta cruoribus,   5
periculosae plenum opus aleae,
tractas, et i n c e d i s per ignis
    suppositos cineri doloso:

paulum seuerae Musa tragoediae
desit theatris, mox ubi publicas   10
res ordin a r i s, g r a n d e munus
    Cecropio repetes cothurno,

insigne maestis praesidium reis
et consulenti, Pollio, curiae,
cui laurus æ t e r n o s honores   15
    Delmatico peperit triumpho.

iam nunc minaci murmure cornuum
perstringis auris, iam litui strepunt,
iam fulgor a r m o r u m fugaces
    terret equos equitumque uoltus,   20

audire magnos iam uideor duces
non indecoro puluere sordidos,
et cuncta t e r r a r u m subacta
    praeter atrocem animum Catonis.

Iuno et deorum quisquis amicior   25
Afris inulta cesserat impotens
tellure u i c t o r u m nepotes
    rettulit inferias Iugurthae.

quis non Latino sanguine pinguior
campus sepulcris impia proelia   30
testatur au d i t u mque Medis
    Hesperiae sonitum ruinae?

qui gurges aut quae flumina lugubris
ignara belli? quod mare Dauniae
non decol o r a u e r e caedes?   35
    quae caret ora cruore nostro?

sed ne relictis Musa procax iocis
Ceae retractes munera neniae,
mecum D i o n æ o sub antro
    quaere modos leuiore plectro.   40

MOTION

Date-line, Metellus' consulate: commotion of the body politic,
civil, too – war's causes; and crimes; and modes;
the game, too, of FORTUNE; the weight, too,
    of leaders' alliances, and armaments,

not yet expiated blood for gun-grease, more blood,   5
a dangerous work full of throws of the dice,
to this you turn, and STEP ON through fire on fire
    submerged beneath ash so treacherous:

just a little, let austere Tragedy's Muse
empty her theatre stage; in no time, once the public   10
record's as you ordAIN, THE GRAND service
    you'll resume, towering tall in Attic costume,

in court a beacon and shield for distraught victims,
for the Senate, too, the consultant, Pollio,
for whom laurel's EVERGREEN roll-call of honour   15
    budded crowns of glory, in Dalmatian triumph.

Now, right now, a damning din from your sirens
scrapes across ear-drums, now bugles screech,
now the glare from ARMOUR is panicking
    terrified horses, the look on each horseman's face,   20

now I seem to hear great commanders,
dishevelled with dust that does no dishonour,
along with a whole PLANET's subjugation
– all bar the obsidian heart of Cato.

Juno and all those other gods enamoured more   25
of Africans once gave up, helpless in rage, unavenged left
their land: the CONQUERORS'/, grandsons
    they now deliver, offerings for Jugurtha.

Where doesn't *soil fed rich with Latin blood*
call each field of unholy battles' rows of graves   30
for witness, and IN EARSHOT *of a listening Parthian East*
    the West – crashed about our ears in ruins?

What churning channel, which rivers of lamentation
know nothing from the war? Whatever sea by Italy
has not *gone discolo* U R*ed, bloodstains on the map?*   35
    Which shore is missing out, on blood spilt from us?

But no foxy Muse never leave your teasing fun, re-
turn the archaic dirge, service with a wail,
*join me, where in*A M O R*ation grows down the grotto,*
    hunt musical modes to lighten up our strum.   40

PART III

Epic

5   Lucan: the word at war

there is a word – which bears a sword – can pierce an armed man
it hurls its barbed syllables – and is mute again
but where it fell – the saved will tell – one patriotic day
some epauletted brother – gave his breath away[1]

Epic, the epic. As bearer of cultural messages the classical epic had a patriarchal prestige which no modern medium can suggest. It was the foundation of its cultures' education, of their culture. It was charged with the telling, reinforcing and empowering of the city's foundation or defence; and the *other* city's defeat or *un*making. Epic had in the *Iliad*, Ennius' *Annales*, and the *Aeneid* narrated the myth in which 'the epic hero's sturdy, battle-scarred body, like the city's ramparts, guards the tribe. His is the body statufied, the human life reprieved from its brevity and magnified into architecture.'[2]

Epics built The City, and their narrators manned the nascent walls, showed at the expense of the othered foe the eternal fame which attaches to all efforts to defend the tribe. They built monumental walls of words, fortified stockades built out of, not bricks, but 'character – heroes' (*moribus antiquis res stat Romana uirisque*, Enn. *Ann*. fr. 156 Skutsch). The institutions governing approved reading-practices inculcated an ethic that privileged narration as the social responsibility of commemoration – the reinforcement, perpetuation, establishment of the truth of writing. All in all, the educational mission was, another, then another, brick in the wall. The epic was the mark, norm and sanction of author/ity, literature, civilization. It was the decisive textual realization of cultural order.[3] Or was in theory. Should (must once) have been.[4]

---

[1] Dickinson (1975) 9. Written c. 1858.
[2] Conrad (1984) 3f.
[3] Cf. Hardie (1993), Quint (1993); Feeney (1991) 5–56, 'The Critics', Buffière (1956) on moralized ancient readings.
[4] E.g. Prop. 2.8 makes the *Iliad* fun by reading against the pedagogic grain. Dominik (1993) and Goldberg (1995) 83–110 show that Ennius' *Annales* must have pulsated

Lucan was post-Virgilian, and (so) propter-Virgilian (cf. chapter 6). But he is also post-Ovidian. Ovid in the *Metamorphoses* had flaunted his collapse of epic decorum into an *ego*-trip for the artiste-narrator; had treated world history as a 'perpetual' flow of poems pouring bodies into the path of his 'self-perpetuating' mind; had pronounced his own fame as the bequest of his metamorphic writing – the last word, *uiuam* ('I shall live'),[5] in one wor(l)d collapses the goal of his narrative 'the Age of Augustus' (*tempora*, 'times') into 'the brain of Ovid' (*tempora*, 'temples (of the head)').[6] Lucan shifts epic narration away from slighting insouciance – and into defiling disfigurement.

This epic's '*petulantia* espressiva [e] *tumores* soffocanti'[7] deface his city's walls, unmake its foundation and its history, implode its traditions and ideologies along with the documents which bear them. Lucan stains the language of public propriety, twists Latin into self-revulsion, writes the continuing aetiology of its own accursed Fall. His hilarious poem traces a subversion of the system of values, linguistic, literary, ideological and cultural, which 'should' be fixed in place, asserted and paraded by the epic tradition.

Specifically, this *Bellum Ciuile* trashes the *paideia* that is monumentalized and *statufied* in the massive, totalizing, articulation through the *Aeneid*'s twelve irrevocable books of all (you might put it) that can be implied in that slenderest of link syllables, the -*que*- in *arma uirumque cano* (1.1, 'Virgil's song: Arms-Man', or: 'Arms/Man – what poetry is for').[8] In the narration that sets up Caesar's 'greatness' for its 'Arms ~ Man', there is menaced the 'greatness' of much *more than* 'literature'. Lucan's poem is set against its own form. It will tarnish that commemoration of 'manliness' – ἀνδρεία or *uirtus* – which it must enact. It will foul the ideology which seeks to construct and regulate the social self within military codes; this chauvinism starts from 'maleness', and goes on to assert as the indisputably real cosmology the commitment of the bodies of citizen 'men' in substantiation of the fictions of the state, through violence and injury to self and other. The

---

vibrant with discordant energies – politics in poetry, not brute memorialization (cf. chapter 8). Virgil –

[5] For Lucan's version at 9.986, *uiuet*, read on – survive.

[6] 1.4, *ad mea ... tempora*, cf. the pointed recantation in *Trist.* 2.560, *in tua ... tempora, Caesar.*

[7] Conte (1968) 253.

[8] Cf. Martindale (1993) 48–53, 'Lucan-reading-Virgil'. Green (1991) reads powerfully Lucan's intertextual bout with the *Iliad*.

subsumption of the civic order within this imperative to die, and (so) kill, for your country enshrines, at a bedrock level way below the polarization of the inside and the outside of the City into *ciuis/miles* (citizen/soldier), the deconstruction of its own founding sanction: namely, the taboos which order the community in terms of regulation of how another person is and is not to be touched. This principle on which civilization is built uncreates the rhetoric of war, as its perversion.[9] Grandiose epic had been there to dip this mess in the charisma of 'greatness': simply 'the best' (of the Achaeans, of the Trojans, of the Romans ...), *sc.* 'in battle'. Fighting written up into ἀριστεία.[10]

The disenchanted *seizure* of 'greatness' by '*Caesar*' in Lucan's text exposes this: when the city knows itself to comprise the world, the binary polarity of self and other, inside and outside, is a failed rhetoric, a rhetoric enforced by the powerful in their own pursuit of 'greatness'. It wrecks the call on citizen-soldiers to consent to bring their city into existence through the materiality of their bodies. The charisma of the wound, the scar, and the war-memorial cannot survive their exposure in civil war: 'what counts as a state, what counts as an external enemy and what counts as a war are questions which all go together'.[11] In the madcap hysteria of Lucan's deformed epic *topoi* and their principle and principal, the counter-creative Caesar, make out an infectiously retroactive plague on the whole tradition, something of the 'Lucanesque', always already a (dominated) element in epic narrative, here released to curse the atavistic 'greatness' of epic. Fighting – but fighting 'for' *what*?

Essays on epic cannot work through their texts. In Lucan's case, this is in the spirit of his own disregard for the order of the narrated. His Latin will need to be worked hard. Remember, too, that 'you' in *this* domineering chapter is aimed at me *more than* you.

I THE WAR OF WORDS

> Because the sword never struck its original target, ... it remains for ever poised and threatening.[12]

---

9 Scarry (1985) esp. 121f.
10 Cf. Hardie (1993) 3.
11 Teichmann (1986) 52f. and *passim*. On civil war's moral contradictions embodied in the *hostis* who is a *ciuis*, cf. Roller (1996).
12 Ahl (1993) 130.

Read Lucan. You must read Lucan. His extraordinary poem breaks rules, inflicts pain and suffering. Don't bother to reclaim this classic in the name of a 'literature': this tyrannical text – wild, accusing, ranting – screams a curse on its readers and upon itself: it *challenges*. If you can grit your teeth and decide to see things Lucan's way, it will be all too easy to recognize your co-implication with the mindset that he denounces. It takes one to know one.[13] The curse of his subject – the curse of taking up the curse as his subject – has always already been at work denouncing its author, *bellumque trahebat | auctorem ciuile suum* (4.738f., '(The) civil war / the *Bellum Ciuile* was dragging off its author'). *BC* tells you it is a/the 'Roman poem' (1.66). It drove the writer to destruction, willy-nilly.[14] And found for *Latinitas*, the Latin language, denunciation of '*Romespeak*', the pollution of (Re)public(an) discourse by *Caesares*. The politics of 'post-Augustan' (ab)usage.

'Lucan's epic imperialism' is recouping canonical status in your *fin-de-siècle* times.[15] The sense that there is no one out there; spinning in a void and staring at the past which precludes a future; hyperbole which insists on its inadequacy to meaning; violent tearing at the protocols of traditional discourse; estranged irony that knows its decadence – all this reverberates within post-modern skulls. There is explored in *BC* a vision of Western cosmopolis in which you are the more implicated as you appreciate the centripetal vortex of 'One World' politics. Lucan's Caesar, seen as the representative *ego* at its ultimate extreme of success-as-futility, forces the question of your future. The ideology forged to bridge from the order of the City of Rome to that of the imperial World State is exposed as a schizo drivenness, as the cult of aggression and 'Oneness' leads to a logical end in suicidal implosion. And Lucan offers no remedy, no alternative promise.[16] You are lost, too, in this

---

[13] Cf. Martindale (1993) 69, 'Is that what Henderson-reading-Lucan could be asking us to ask ourselves?'

[14] Masters (1994) 171: 'The poem became, simply by virtue of the changed circumstances of the writer ... a shrill protest against tyranny ... The poem became, by coincidence or design, a litmus test for the character of the Neronian Principate.' 'Principate' –

[15] Levin (1953) 49; for the impact of 'The War' – 'World War II' – on German scholarship in the 50s, cf. Rutz (1970) 6, Syndikus (1958). Ahl (1976) was a post-'Nam bolt. The 90s brought civil war itself back into fashion in the global village.

[16] Against schemes of 'oppositional ideology' (e.g. Pfligersdorffer (1959)), set the plasticity of Lucanian *libertas*: so Narducci (1979) 14.

'failure' of vatic powers.[17] *BC* foretells, all too well, your History. With the epic prerogative to tell fate, Lucan offers death as the cultural wish of humanity: *fatum* throughout this text will beat 'Fate' to 'Death' (= '*Deathstiny*'). Civilization is just an orgiastic procession of self-mutilation, built on the self-falsifying logic of war: were you to write the history of the world from a United Nations perspective, you would find what Lucan saw when he wrote out *Roma quid esset* (7.132, 'what Rome was'). In the fearful terror of human minds and the ghastly torture of human tissue, Lucan directs the movie after all the Star Wars have been lost and won: One, caved-in, World.

For the poem surges out way past its represented civil war, the events of 49–8, to offer, not 'the civil war', but 'civil wars', i.e. 'the (Roman) civil wars' and 'Civil War' (chapter 8). Like the voicing (*canimus*, 'our song', 1.1), the subject – given in the poem's first word *Bella* – is conspicuously *plural*. These 'wars' will be 'civil war the phenomenon', 'The Horror, the horror . . .', that serial killer.[18] War is laid bare in its scandal and all the lies you have made for yourselves fail. Conspicuously, with a fanfare. (All) war is 'civil' – it always already has been ?civil?, the figuring and disfiguring of civilization as an absurd process of unmaking. The cult of war has at its base a perverse barbarism, not that of the savage but that of the conquering hero. Who marks his success in the memorialization of the opened and defaced bodies he appropriates for his mission.[19] And desires more – *more than* that. In reading Lucan's poem, you of the First and Second Worlds cannot but confront your 'post-War' heritage, feel your collusion, still, in the charisma of pre-atomic conflict. You are all impressed by dynamism, by manly epic action before smart weaponry. *More* crucially *than* this, Lucan cannot escape epic, and you cannot escape complicity in the charisma of 'heroism' on the part of the media you have for comprehending historical reality. When victim is victor, when the differences constructed and confirmed by war have shrunk toward zero,

---

[17] Cf. O'Higgins (1988) for the *uates* whose powers succeed by failing; Ormand (1994) for the characters' 'deviant focalization' within *BC*'s warped narration: 'Lucan has at last succeeded, after a fashion: we believe in the unbelievability of narration, granting our credence to Caesar's utter failure to convince'; Bartsch (1997) chapter 3 for the narrator as his lead role.

[18] So Conte (1968) 240, 'che cosa sia la guerra civile'; Martindale (1981) 138f., ' "civil war" as much . . . as "the Civil War" '.

[19] Scarry (1985).

when there is only one side ... – you have no way to tell the story. This is not what narrative can narrate. Such is the imperious '*Caesar-Epos*' of Lucan – a bully-boy of a monster-poem that drills you in the imperative mood.

Now, as was traditional and 'right', writing the epic killed the poet (arrested adolescent, declaiming apt poetry on death row at $25\frac{1}{2}$).[20] The weight of standing-in for culture, of assuming the voice of a collective wisdom, of a totalizing concretization of its vital mythologies made epic projects as good as *unfinishable* (cf. chapters 6, 8). The obligatory authority and stature of maturity pressed the poet toward the risk of interruption by mortality. In Lucan's case, the self-assertion of this schema at once in and despite its transgression remains the mark of his poem's sincerity, beyond all trivial intentionality at the level of the author's awareness. This boy-wonder genius orbits round his adolescent emperor Nero, flattered by the *libertas* of his (*their*) unbounded outspokenness (chapter 7).[21] His Neronian poem courts Caesarian death for its own deathstiny.[22] As if to corroborate its analysis, the writer proceeds towards a goal of premature termination, eventually imposed by outside force. If you accept that Lucan cannot have *meant* to continue the linear trajectory of his writing only to the point where his text is stopped in its tracks in its tenth book, then it is irresistible that you recognize that Caesarism, true to the poem's indictment,[23] *meant* to impose this limit as *telos* to its own story. The imperialist, indeed 'post-imperialist', story of worldwide (re-)appropriation took back for its own the double-edged tribute of *BC*'s triumphant self-mockery. Emperors must always subordinate as minor characters in their story the clustering generals, ministers and poets: they insist, when possible, on each of them cutting their bodies and themselves out of the plot. Just as Nero cut all possible rivals, his entire family, out of history, and so presently terminated the dynasty in his own suicide on behalf of them all (chapter 8). Battle could then recommence. *Bella plus quam ciuilia*: in 69 CE, the 'Year of the four emperors'.

[20] On 'Lucan's last words', cf. Introduction, with Hunink (1992A).
[21] Masters (1994) 171.
[22] Masters (1992) 216–59 pushes for a *planned* 'endlessness' for *BC*, programmed to expire alongside Caesar's *BC*; cf. Haffter (1957). Was it Nero or Lucan or deathstiny that 'planned' Lucan's own end? Is *that* the *plot*?
[23] Martindale (1984) esp. 75.

As Julius Caesar pursues mastery across the world, from Rubicon to Brundisium to Spain to Brundisium, via Pharsalia to Egypt,[24] see that the 'Emathian' battlefields of the poem's project (*per Emathios ... campos* |, 1.1, 'through ?Emathian? plains') were only *concretely* to be identified with the 'plains of Thessaly' where Pompey the Great was defeated in book VII. Conceptually, the battle functions as the threshold for the transformation of the Roman world into a new absolutist empire on the model of Alexander the Great: Caesar, the new and transcendentally final, 'Great', processes through the East to Egypt and the mausoleum metropolis of the ('truly') 'Emathian' boy king, the Alexandria of the 'Macedonian' Alexander (e.g. 10.58). Lucan's text stops where Caesar's had stopped: the new master of the world is under threat, contained and pent-up in the palace next the beacon of Pharos by attacking Egyptian minions and renegade rabbles.[25] Caesar will survive the texts (chapter 2); but at just this point in the writing – symbolically and (why not?) actually pen-in-hand – Lucan is in 65 CE terminally arrested by Caesarian guards for conspiracy against the life of 'his' Caesar, the divine Caesar Nero,[26] who serves as (suitably crazy?) inspiration and Musagete for this (berserk) 'song, or spell, of Rome'.[27]

As Lucan took the liberty of making his poem wall Julius in with its lines, he halted him to consider the choice 'whether to fear or pray for death' (10.542f., *dubius ... timeret | optaretne mori*). Lucan faced the same options that his written Caesar imposed on the world of his poem. At the end, his pen wrote that he – Lucan–Caesar – 'looked back', over the text,[28] to see his finest creation, the accursed Caesarian

---

[24] O'Donnell (1978) 236: Lucan has already toured the globe within books I–x.

[25] Cf. Masters (1992) *passim*, esp. 17, 'Lucan's *Bellum Ciuile* is a deliberate counterpoise to Caesar's *Commentary* of the same name.'

[26] The blunt *Neroni* of 1.33 yields to *Caesar* at v. 41 (and v. 59), inserted tellingly between Julius' career from Pharsalia to Munda (v. 40, *ultima funesta concurrant proelia Munda*: 'ultimate Munda, foul end of the *mundus*'), and Octavian's Perusia to Actium/Naulochus.

[27] 1.63–6, *sed mihi iam numen, ... | tu satis ad uires Romana in carmina dandas* |, 'But I have divine power already ... You can give all the strength Roman poetry needs.' Cf. Häussler (1978) 45f., Feeney (1991) 300f., Hershkowitz (1995) 212. Cf. Ahl (1984) 198f., 'To talk extravagantly of the emperor's divinity is ... to control by flattery and, simultaneously, to mock ... his divine pretensions. Flattery is a kind of aggression.' The obvious question: how can anyone know this?

[28] At 10.543, *respexit* is (concretely) 'looked back', but also 'thought of' (cf. 6.185). 'Through the text' (v. 543, *in agmine denso*): a ten-book 'choker' of poetry refusing fine-spun Callimachean texture.

soldier-hero Scaeva, undead and at Caesar's back. Ready to repeat his cameo, which had turned against Pompey 'the Great''s trampling underfoot of Julius' breached beleaguering walls, resistance in the form of a renewed one-man siege,[29] back at the start of what stands for ever as the second half of Lucan's work, book VI. You should regard the extravagant episode too.

Lucan had there used his entire armoury of hyperbolic and perverse *colores* to upset the epic *topoi* of a hero-warrior's *aristeia*. He convinced his characters, his readers and his narrator that Scaeva had attained immortal fame at the usual price of death.[30] Indeed every time that Scaeva had spoken, he had 'death' left on his ill-omened lips: *dum morimur, mortis honestae* |, *mortis amor* (vv. 165, 235, 246). After he 'collapsed' (*ruis*, v. 250), he was shouldered by his mates, who 'compete to pluck the missiles from his stuck limbs and adorn the gods ... with his weapons' (an inverted *tropaeum*, vv. 251f.). As if a thing of the past, he receives a quasi-formal *elogium* (vv. 257–62): a scream, from the μακαρισμός opening: 'Scaeva ... *blessed* with the fame of a famous name', to the sententious climax: '*Unblessed*: with all that courage you set up a master' – all in the space of six hexameters (*Scaeva ... felix hoc nomine famae* | *si* ... ↔ | *infelix quanta dominum uirtute parasti* |). And so you left Scaeva, 'Caesar's Left Hand', personification of Lucan's anti-epic staining, all-unknowing 'how great a crime courage is in (the) *Bellum ciuile*' (vv. 147f., *in armis* | *quam magnum uirtus crimen ciuilibus esset*).[31] *More than* incarnation of the Roman exemplificatory rhetoric of hyperbole, Scaeva is unanswerable argument 'of whether heroism caught by odds and terrain offers *more than* death' (*numero deprensa locoque* | *an plus quam mortem uirtus daret*, vv. 168f.). Here is Lucan's abusive inversion of the purple-patch *schemata* and clichés of the 'One-for-all' epic/historiographical scene of heroic self-sacrifice – 'for the good of the cause' –[32] one *more* image of the *plusquam* of (the) *Civil War*, Lucan's objective for the *Bella ... plus quam ciuilia* advertised in his first verse ('Wars ... *more than* civil').

'*Scaeva*' – 'Sinister, ill-omened' – is your bad luck. What you have

---

[29] Paraphrase Lucan's last verses here, 10.543–6.
[30] E.g. Saylor (1978) 244, 251 n. 16 speaks of 'Scaeva's death'.
[31] Conte (1974) 35 = (1988) 67f. discovers the poetry of this hyperbaton, *uirtus* ringed by *magnum crimen* ringed by *in armis* | ... *ciuilibus* framed by *nesciret .. esset* |.
[32] See Marti (1966), Conte (1970) 133 = (1988) 26f., Lausberg (1985) 1590 and n. 96, Ahl (1976) 117f.

coming for reading *BC*. It is unlikely that mere readers can learn aright
from the fatal mistake of the cannon-fodder character *Aulus* ... *infelix*
('Unlucky Joe' – fancy running into 'Mr Bad Luck', Scaeva playing
possum, v. 236). The writer has drawn his 'hero' (in 6.203–50) from
'disdain of self-defence with his left (shield-)hand'[33] through exhausted
'choice of an enemy *in quem cadat*' ('someone he can ... fall on') to an
arrow homing into his left eyeball.[34] Only slaughter and shed blood
kept Scaeva going strong (vv. 240, 250). It all fulfilled the centurion's
initial promise, 'I would head for the shades *more* blessed *than* a saint,
if in Caesar's face ... I shall fall, to applause from Pompey' (*peterem
felicior umbras | Caesaris in uoltu* ... | *Pompeio laudante cadam*: vv. 158–
60. But this is also: 'I would attack the dead, chase shadows, fight Hell
...'). All Lucan's rhetoric could not overcome one hateful Hon.
Mention by Caesar: 'when Scaeva's shield was brought, 120 holes were
found in it'; Caesar rewarded him as Scaeva had deserved 'by his services to him Self and to the State', with money, praise and promotion
(*BC* 3.53, *quem Caesar ut erat de se meritus et de re publica* ...). As
Scaeva the bodyguard human shield is conjured up by Caesar's backward glance in Alexandria at the end of Lucan's *BC*, enter the Caesarian guard – to arrest the pen and the (left?)[35] hand that held it.
Walking off the page and into Lucan's life, '*Scaeva*', that 'missing link'
between Caesar and his standing epicthet *saeuus*.[36]

Scaeva names 'obsession'.[37] For *Scaevam perpetuae meritum iam
nomina famae* (10.544) directs you back to the start: *Scaeva* ... *felix hoc*

---

[33] S-c-a-e-v-a's options, *laeua* ... *u-a-c-a-s-s-e* | *aut culpa u-i-x-i-s-s-e sua* spell a deviant
choice to either side of *u-i-c-i-s-s-e*: either 'to lack his Scaeva', 'to have been lacking
with his Scaeva', 'to have given his Scaeva exemption from military service'; or 'to
have survived through the fault of Scaeva', 'to have stayed being Scaeva by being
Scaeva' ...

[34] *in Scaeuam* ... | *in caput* .... *oculi laeuom* ... *in orbem* / (6.215f.) stakes out the set of
equivalences: 'Scaeva', Caesar(ian army), anti-*uirtus*, set up to be 'head' of a Scaevan,
'sinister', cursed, Caesarian 'world'. So the arrow is *omni certior uoto*, 'surer than any
could wish', homing in on the particular truth of *BC*, *deuotio* for *deuotio*, a 'curse' for
the hero, not his own 'vow'.

[35] Yes, I write left-handed. 'You don't say.' (But I type–

[36] Cf. Newmyer (1983) 238 n. 17: esp. 5.303, 308, 310, *Caesar versus* 315, *saeue*, 364, *saeua
uoce*, 369f., *Caesar* ... *saeui* | ... *ducis*; Scaeva as bear, 6.220, is, inevitably, *saeuior*.

[37] 10.546, | *obsedit*, 'besieged'. Same pun in Saylor (1978) 250. *mortis honestae* |, 10.539,
triggers 6.234f., *sit Scaeua relicti* | *Caesaris exemplum potius quam mortis honestae*, 'Let
Scaeva be an *exemplum* filed in the manuals under "Betray (your) Caesar", not – or
"*more than*" – "How to die well".'

nomine famae (6. 257).[38] *Scaeva* meant *infelix* all along; or rather, to get closer to the war within the word, *Scaeua* says *both* 'left-handed, so ill-nomened, inauspicious, unlucky, gauche, stupid, perverse, instinctively choosing what is wrong' etc., *and*, precisely, 'auspicious', as well as, on another level, 'just like the archetypal *uir* Mucius *Scaeu*ola, who fought for *uirtus* and the fame of his name, his pseudo-etymology of a nickname, by "hostile acts directed against himself rather than against his enemy"' (Livy 2.12.14). So Scaeva was 'just like the return, revenge and excess of (the hypocorism) *Scaeu-ola*. He is the archetypal warrior of the *BC*, for the con-fusion of torture with war is not the exception that proves the rule, but the name of the game: fighting for Rome, with the kid(ology) gloves off. In Lucan, the sadomasochism of the cult of 'manliness' is laid bare to make an ideal, an (abusive) *exemplum*, on and beyond the model of Mucius: 'I am a Roman citizen, he said, they call me Gaius Mucius. As enemy to enemy I determined to kill, and I now have as much nerve for death as I had for slaughter: Rome is all about bravery – active *and* passive.'[39] So truncate the body, burn off the bodily tissue which makes it possible to win *uirtus*, the right hand, kill your own feelings, be a sacrifice, be a *Roman*. Fight for Rome.[40]

Lucan's poetic ruthlessly denies his characters proper names throughout,[41] but *Caesar* already withheld Scaeva's (tyrannicidal)

---

[38] 'Scaeva who had earned the fame of a famous name back in book vi' ∼ 'Scaeva, blessed by the fame of a(n in)famous name'. So Marti (1966) 256.

[39] Livy spells this out in the simplest – 'read my lips' – Latin: *Romanus sum, inquit, ciuis; C. Mucium uocant. hostis hostem occidere uolui nec ad mortem minus animi est quam fuit ad caedem: et facere et pati fortia Romanum est* (2.12.9). Scaeva is already in Caesar treated as a 'lucky charm' – '*scaeuulae* are small phallic ornaments supposed to have magical properties', Ogilvie (1965) 266 on Livy 2.13.1.

[40] See Quint (1993) 140–7, 'Broken bodies' on Lucan's mutilation of (the representation of) war in the mutilation of its Light Brigades; cf. Most (1992) 397–400: not heroic victors striking home, but poor victims sliced to pieces; Johnson (1987) 57; Bartsch (1997) chapter 1.

[41] Lucan can treat names as noises, e.g. 2.544–6, Camíllis | ... Metéllis |, ringing Cae*sar* magnisque, ad Cinnas Mariosque (with Ormand (1994) 44); he can create sardonic fusion, e.g. his *Cordus*, the quaestor come to 'cremate' Pompey's corpse (8.715–20; cf. v. 744, *cremantis*) can but suggest Cremutius Cordus, forced to death by Tiberius Caesar, his Pompeian *bella ciuilia* officially burned (Brennan (1969), chapters 7–8). But *more than* crucial to the project of *Bellum Ciuile* is the melt-down fusion of contemporaries, relatives, generations, countries achieved through restricted nomination: Marii, Antonii, Bruti, Lentuli, Pompeii filii, Phocis/Phocaea ...

nomen,[42] pointing up the centurion's magical *cognomen*, even for the formal medal-ceremony, Scaeva's phrase-long second of immortality. Promotion to the position of *primipilus* made of Scaeva and his shield the badge of courage and *nomen/omen* of Caesar's army, and the defence of his *castellum*, his 'shielding' of this 'shield' of Caesar('s army), in which 'every-man-jack had been hit, while elsewhere 2,000 *Pompeiani* fell, but 20 or fewer of ours went missing', was gathered by his leader into the most pregnant of his rare but strategically disposed narrative nodes of epic significance, so that you may learn *more* clearly *than* ever why Caesarian *uirtus* is deathstined to win the war (*BC* 3.53).[43]

In Caesar, then, Scaeva commits himself and his 'name' to Caesar, as Scaeuola committed his body to Rome; in Lucan's language, the sign '*Scaeua*' commits suicide, although its bearer survives, to be spotted, one-eyed, in Alexandria. For the word is caught up in the 'civil war' of Lucan's text, where opposed senses tear themselves up and rip the signifiers away from signification. Thus with *Scaeuam perpetuae meritum iam nomina famae*: the 'fame' of the famous 'name' he bears is its 'infamy' (*fama*); he has only the 'name' of 'fame', not the reality, 'fame' is only a 'word' (*nomen*), Scaeva's 'fame' is only a 'story' – just that old narrative (*fama*). And this is all that he 'deserves', just what *he* has coming to him. His final bow recaps the *aristeia* which began from Scaeva's 'deserts': 'the man's name was Scaeva; he had served in the ranks (*mereo*)' (6.144, *Scaeua uiro nomen: castrorum in plebe merebat*). When Scaeva lives up to his name, the process by which the discourse of the warrior generates and circulates value in its own image is on view: *merebat/meritum/meritus* are terms caught up in a 'commerce-of-war' image-repertoire, the vocabulary of 'losses and gains', the 'buying' of glory with the 'price' of death, all that: *caput mundi, bellorum maxima merces,* | *Roma capi facilis* ('head of the universe, the greatest prize of wars, Rome – effortlessly headed into captivity', 2.655f.: *caput /capio* a focal resource of signification in the poem).

In Scaeva, the 'Ro*man*', the soldier-patriot, is given the poisonous

---

[42] Marti (1966) 262: *Scaeva* in Caesar, Lucan and Appian; *M. Cassius Scaeva* in Valerius Maximus, *Cassius Scaeva* in Plutarch and Suetonius, *Scaevola* in Florus.

[43] More such 'B-movie' omenclature in Caes. *BC* 3.91.3, of the 'hero' 'Crastinus' (chapter 2): *faciam, inquit, h o d i e, imperator, ut aut uiuo mihi aut mortuo gratias agas;* Lucan picks this up for extended sarcasm in 7.470–5.

BC treatment: 'forever cursed' (*perpetuae ... famae,* 10.544, is (in) the gift of immortalizing epic's *carmen perpetuum*). He stands for *more,* though, *than* this. Lucan sours the subject of (epic) narrative, the relations between 'Arms' and 'The Man', with Scaeva's *pharmakon* (potent chemistry) of a name: | *Armis, Scaeva, tuis* ('With your – yours, Scaeva – arms', 6.257). In the process, he subjects to abuse its discourse of conquest, 'fame' as victorious impression of Roman arms upon the world as terrain, as the 'Emathian' *locus* of Scaeva's exploit is decanted into | *ad campos, Epidamne, tuos* ('by your – yours, Epidamnus – plains', 10.545: recall the *Emathios ... campos* of 1.1 and read their displacement throughout epic space). For this 'song of Rome' divides and conquers the signs it traverses, splitting the town called *Dyr-rachium* (6.14) into a bilingual *nomen/omen*: Ἐπί/*ad* + δάμνε/*damne*, where Latin forces the Greek verb of conquest, ἐπιδάμναμαι, into its own 'loss, damage, condemnation, damnation'.[44] With Scaeva, Caesar, imperial space, and Lucan–Caesar's world.

2 THE WAR IN WORDS

There had never been a death more foretold.[45]

> ... one does not burn something unfinished, and in a few months, even weeks, you will have got this little piece of work behind you ... so even though you may be in haste to die, you must still hold out that little bit longer... to finish? to have finished? verily he had finished nothing.[46]

From the same equation of Scaeva's time with his deserts, his 'military service' with his 'fame' (*merebat/meritum*), unpack the narrational law which should regulate the concrete 'success' of conquest. Progress through Lucan defames the 'success' of 'succession' – history's story of the winners – into 'successiveness', failure to escape 'successors'. Epic, too, and historical epic doubly so, trade in fame and fortune – the construal of fame and success contour the grandness of their poetics. *Felix,* Latin for 'productive, fertile, prolific', is accordingly one of

---

[44] Cf. Mela 2.56, *Romani nomen mutauere quia uelut in damnum ituris omen id uisum est.* Keller (1891) 232f. rightly objects that δυσ-ῥήγνυμι is just as ill-omened, and posits a dis-recognized Illyrian name.

[45] Marquez (1983) 50.

[46] Broch (1983) 208.

Lucan's central concepts and, *exemplum sui*, it is itself *more than* productive, fertile and prolific. It stands, or rather falls, as an operator that
neutralizes epic closure, its mobility unravelling the narrative's drive
to affix values and discriminate end results.[47] 'Anyone who is *felix* is
earmarked for disaster since the *felices* are under the vacillating tutelage
of a capricious power, *Fortuna*.'[48]

Consider some felicitous strands in the dense knot of senses which
crush together through *BC*. When every bullet aimed at Scaeva found a
billet, *nulla fuit non certa manus, non lancea felix* ('No missile launched
at Scaeva missed', 6.190), the words of war unerringly fitted the attack
onto the attacked in a perfect match of civil war logic: the sure (right)
hand of each assailant attacked 'Left-Hand', *Scaeva*, and hit the mark;
no spear launched by these hands was 'unlucky', because it hit its target and its target was 'Unlucky Scaeva'. As *C/ae/s/ar*(ian), '*Scaeva*'
participates prominently in a major set of schemata built round the
nexus 'Luck/Fortune/Success' (*felicitas, fortuna, c/a/s/us*, etc.). One
particular manifestation is the anxiety – self-fulfilling prophecy – that
'*Caesar*' re-cycles '*Sulla*', whose success was marked by the fake-name
'*Felix*' he won 'For Luck'. When Sulla's anathema Marius is (savagely)
labelled *felix* (2.74), see that both were caught on the same spiral, but
Sulla made a 'name' for himself out of his success; when Alexander is
called *felix praedo* (10.22), the success marked out by his 'name', 'The
Great', received the kiss of failure in the form of *his* successor, Pompeius '*Magnus*', 'The Great'. And now there shall be '*Caesar*', *more
than* special among 'names'. Caesar will be caught on the spiral of civil
war only concretely, for the *name* '*Caesar*' will succeed, where *Felix* and
Μέγας/*Magnus* failed, in transcending the failure of succession: by
re-cycling itself.[49] The five *Caesares Augusti* that Lucan knew (just
Augustus and Nero answering to originary connection with *Iulius*). Six
less than Statius (none Julian). And Tacitus, and Appian –

Sulla, then, figures as (a) Caesar *avant la lettre* (cf. chapter 1). He
represents *bellum ciuile* to Caesar's *Bella ... plus quam ciuilia*. Lucan
articulates this idea of anticipation in a fearsome howl of epic energy in

[47] Cf. Hardie (1993) 1–18, Quint (1993) 147–5, 'The never-ending story'.
[48] Dick (1967) 237. Cf. Ahl (1974) 314f. on 7. 727, *felix se nescit amari* of Pompey. Sulla/
    Pompeius/Caesar ...: see Ahl (1974A) 574f., (1976) 287 and n. 24.
[49] Sulla's failure helps elect him to Elysium's *felicibus umbris* (6.784; cf. 301–3, *felix
    Roma, si ... Sulla*), cf. Ahl (1976) 139; heirless Alexander died young as Nero and
    Lucan: 10.43–5.

Book II. Hammer this excerpted scream of paranoid whinge / visceral pain, from survivors of civil war – characters really looking forward to (being in) Lucan's epic:

> 'hisne salus rerum, felix his Sulla uocari,
> his meruit tumulum medio sibi tollere Campo?
> haec rursus patienda manent, hoc ordine belli
> ibitur, hic stabit ciuilibus exitus armis.
> quamquam agitant grauiora metus, multumque coitur   225
> humani generis maiore in proelia damno.
> exulibus Mariis bellorum maxima merces
> Roma recepta fuit, nec plus uictoria Sullae
> praestitit inuisas penitus quam tollere partes:
> hos alio, Fortuna, uocas, olimque potentes   230
> concurrunt. neuter ciuilia bella moueret,
> contentus quo Sulla fuit.' sic maesta senectus
> praeteritique memor flebat metuensque futuri.   (2.221–33)

> *'This way did Sulla deserve the name "Salvation", this way "Felix",*
> *this way a mound to raise for himself in mid* Campus?
> *This suffering awaits all over again, this sequence of war*
> *will be how it goes, this outcome for civil conflict will hold.*
> *Yet still worse stirs terror – gathering together is much*   225
> *of the human race, for battles, with its much greater loss.*
> *To the Marius exiles, wars' greatest pay-off*
> *was Rome reclaimed, and no more did victory bring Sulla*
> *than to get rid of the hated* bloc:
> *these men, Fortune, you beckon elsewhere – powerful long since*   230
> *they are collision bound. Neither of the two would initiate civil war,*
> *if they were satisfied with what did for Sulla.' So despondent elder(s)*
> *were wailing, remembering the past, afraid of the future.*

Freaked survivors – vets – knew already their nightmares were ready (loaded) for a re-run, they skip the proscriptions (chapter 1) and fixate on the massacres – at Praeneste, 'a people extinct in an instant's single death' (v. 195: cf. chapters 1, 3) and on the *Campus Martius*: 'All this, then, entitled Sulla to be called "Salvation"? This ... to be called *"Felix"*? | This ... to raise a mound for himself smack on the *Campus*?' (vv. 221f.). Here *felix* ... *uocari* means 'to receive μακαρισμός', to be acclaimed, to be acclaimed, as '*Felix*', as 'The Acclaimed' – exactly as Appian's triumviral proscription-edict will/had put it (chapter 1). In Lucan's *Sulla* hear *salus*, and reflect that the 'salvation' Sulla brought was his own 'tomb' (*tumulus*) – he died (in 78) soon after his 'successful' fight for Rome (82/81).

The 'mound' he raised re-presented 'all the heap ... of Sullan bodies' whose memory the poem has just waded through: Tiber 'received' an *accumulatio* of epithets pinned to corpses: *congesta* ... | *omnia* ... *Sullana cadauera*; the river of bloodshed 'poured through the whole plain' (*campum* ... *effusa per omnem* |) to join Tiber, whose banks could not contain its 'river' (*amnem* |) and so perforce it returned 'the corpses to the plain' (*cadauera campo* |, vv. 209–18). So you move from *campus* ('plain'), itself a warping of the (cosmic) 'epic battlefield', those *Emathios* ... *campos* | of 1.1, straight to the *Campus Martius* in Rome and Sulla's memorial, from Sullan corpses to corpse of Sulla. 'Lord of Luck' piled men in heaps and this is what his memorial memorialized. 'Heaps', unordered amassing, pile up Lucan's writing-desk, clogging and crushing his world.[50]

This implosive scene in the 'middle' of the campus, the 'battlefield', the *Campus Martius*, is the setting for a terrorstruck effort to comprehend the logic of civil war: 'these things are waiting to be our sufferings again, the war'll go | this way, this'll be the end of all Civil Wars' (vv. 223f.). 'Here', then, 'will be where all civil wars will stay', and where they will all 'stop' (*stabit*). In Rome. *All* 'battlefields' in *BC*, however 'Emathian' at the concrete level, will take place on, on a displacement of, the *Campus Martius*. This is the arena, wherever the war for Rome merely happens to be fought, because this is the centre, and the point, of Roman/world civil war. So, 'the weapons of civil war will not leave Rome, but will stop right here' means 'no one leaves, get it?' 'Here, Rome, will be the end of civil war, civil war after civil war after civil war after ... ' – for this is the only 'end' (*exitus*) of civil war: *not* to end. That is 'the logic of civil war' (*hoc ordine belli*).

In vv. 221f., the *his* ... *his* ... *his* were all the same *his*, namely 'what Sulla did to deserve his 'name(s)'. The *haec* ... *hoc* ... *hic* of vv. 223f. now say that *BC* will all be the same *his*, however concretely different each case may fall out to be (at the merely concrete level). 'These things' are here again, 'waiting to be suffered, this (counter-)logic of war is the way it will go' (*ibitur*) and if this is the way it will 'end' (*exitus*), it will 'go away' (*exitus*) because it will 'die' (*exitus*) and the

---

[50] See Masters (1992) 145 and n. 119. For 'cosmic dissolution' imagery in vv. 214f. see Lapidge (1979) 363.

'suffering in store' will be 'death' (*exitus*). War *can't* die – it *is* Death.
The death caused by Sulla, the death of Sulla. The 'success' (*exitus*) of
Sulla *Felix*, his final 'solution' (*exitus*). In the word, *more than* Lucanian
'deathstiny'. The permanent 'Sullution' will be: 'No Solution', permanently.

'*Sulla*' spells 'civil war'. And he spells *more*. For Sulla's enemy,
the Marius 'exiles' (*exulibus*, 'exiles': say 'ex-Sulla-s'; Lucan means
Marius' adoptive son, their followers, *and* no doubt old Marius' un-
quiet shade), 'pay-off in war was above all re-taking Rome, getting back
(to) Rome' (vv. 227f.). Their return to Rome was their 'departure,
their death' (*exitus*) and then their removal by Sulla: 'nor did victory
give Sulla *more* | *than* to wipe out the hated opposition' (vv. 228f.).
'Worse stirs terror' as 'terror stirs worse' as 'worse stirs t–', and besides
'Formations group for battles, with much greater loss of human-
ity', 'Much of humankind groups | for battles, with still greater
dam...nation' (*multum ... coitur | humani generis maiore in proelia
damno |*, vv. 225f.: remember *Epidamnus* and cf. 9.986, *damnabimur*).
'Damage', indeed, '*to* epic battles', because they are civil. In speaking
these lines, the characters are 'fearing' i.e. 'promising' that *BC* will
deliver 'damage *greater than* ... the greatest gain' that the last cycle of
civil war could manage (*maiore ... damno | :: maxima merces |*). When
'much', a great part, 'of the human race unites for battle(s) that cause
much greater loss of humanity', epic 'meets' in battle its own dead loss,
as 'greatness' turns turtle, and founders.

Hos alio, Fortuna, uocas ... ('These men, Fortune, you summon
elsewhere ...', v. 230). 'Marius and Sulla are called away, they must
leave' – to find their 'fortunes' together, make their pile, attain success,
become ?*felix*?. You realize *only at the end of the elders' speech* what you
were reading here, with 'These two wouldn't get civil war going | if they
were satisfied with what satisfied Sulla' (vv. 231f.). Not about Caesar
and Pompey. Instead *hos alio* ... displaced and *re*-placed Marius and
Sulla. The speech that began with the words | *Non alios* ... (vv. 68), as
the old man/men looked for similarity – for 'parallels for *great* fear'
(*magno ... exempla timori*) – now ends in difference: | *Hos alio* ...
These *hos* are, it transpires (already), a re-cycling of Marius and Sulla.
They are the 'sameness' within 'difference', the spiral of civil war, the
identity within *hos* of those *his his his*, *haec hoc hic*. *They* are 'called'
elsewhere, *their* fighting for Rome will, 'concretely', be 'Emathian', will
not be fought on the Campus Martius, will be global, anything but

fought in Rome. And that is precisely what the elder(s) fear(s) here.[51] Yet in Roman civil war, *all* wars are fought in Rome – where else? – there *was* nowhere 'else', 'there was nowhere to go'.[52] Your 'temporary' mis-reading of *hos* entraps you in the (mis)reading of the old man/men, the effort to see through antithesis between Sulla/Marius and Caesar/Pompey to analysis of that collapse of the antithetical, the 'mound' of civil war.

'Ever since time began, the powerful clash' (vv. 231f.; *olim ~ hos alio*). And, specifically – once you read this as of Caesar/Pompey – 'these two have long been powerful and are long since set on a collision-course'. The old man/men hint/s that the shared *dominatio* of the triumvirate has bound Caesar and Pompey together, so they are bound to *fight together* – that densification in *concurrunt* (v. 231). The whole speech has 'failed' to find an adequate *exemplum* in Marius/Sulla and collapses in repeating just what his/their predecessors, the young recruits fresh to civil war, concluded by saying in *their* speech (vv. 60–3), as they cursed both factions, leaders, and so themselves.

Listen to Lucan, before he pushes the button and declares *BC*. Listen to them (all). The difference between the Marius/Sulla and Caesar/Pompey civil wars will be ... *inexpressible* difference – *beyond* words = Lucan's *plus quam*. By the 'logic' of civil war, the law of its repetition, and its difference, Sulla *Felix* transcends Marius in his relations with 'Fortune'; Pompeius *Magnus* transcends him; and *Caesar* transcends all, transcendentally. This is how *BC* determines to mock its efforts to express, bound and limit the *plus quam* of its multiplying wars. *BC* narrates its failure to articulate this *as its own (anti-)narrative*. The series of scenes to open Book II, like the concatenation of portent and prophecy that wound up Book I, offers a choir of voices which amplify the detonation of *BC* in all its difference. They distract narration away from its narrated events, and smash the denotation of its language. It serves, like the rest of the epic, to beggar (its own) description.

'*Beyond*' Sulla, lie Scaeva and the success of the Caesars. *BC* cuts off before the poem can drive Cato into mad suicide, vindicate inalienable autonomy for human agency as victory for *Libertas*, defeat Caesar in his

---

[51] See Conte (1968) 243 on the perfection of v. 233, its metrics, composition and projection of meaning through past–present–future (cf. Lounsbury (1976) esp. 237f. for a similar view of book VII as a unit).

[52] Ahl (1976) 22 > Martindale (1993) 72.

decisive, but merely military, hour of triumph – the universe enslaved, with his exception (chapter 4).[53] Cuts off, too, from the mere exit of Caesar on the Ides of March. From Caesarian victory thereafter at Philippi, where the dynastic series constituted itself, its perpetuation, in the repetition of Pharsalus. From history, past, present, in the making. In his memorial poem for Lucan, Statius interprets what cut short the epic itself as martyrdom to Caesarism in mimesis of its characters (chapter 6).[54] The Pisonian plot in which Lucan was fatally involved (chapter 7) itself pre-figured the uprisings which prevailed over Nero, made him last of the Julii, copy of the premature decease of 'his' poet. To repeat, the cycle enforces itself afresh, the obliteration of Nero itself caused, exactly, *Bella … plus quam ciuilia*, in 69 CE. The text's undecidably voluntary / decisively involuntary *aposiopesis* reverberates with poetic (in)justice, aping and mimicking the successful *Latinitas*, the powerful facility and felicity, of Julius' *Commentarii*, those monuments to narration-as-success (chapter 2). The very choice of Pharsalus proclaims how centripetal the world built round the signifier '*Caesar*' had, lastingly, become.

Even providing its own 'blurb', *BC* reaches out to engross every reading of its words, taking *more than* liberties with the impersonal norm of epic narration: 'Lucan's *Bella … plus quam ciuilia* offers readers a charge of passion; excites emotions and surreal investment in the development of the plot; transports engaged readers into the present of the text, as partisans rooting for the losers' (7. 210–13, … *cum bella legentur, | spesque metusque simul peritura que uota mouebunt, | attonitique omnes uelut uenientia fata, | non transmissa, legent et adhuc tibi, Magne, fauebunt*). A proud boast of mimetic power, out to dominate us, all the 'us'-es (cf. Horace on Pollio's *Histories*, chapter 4). But, even so, the reader – and *reading* – is mocked.[55] And (as you shall see) '*Lucan*', whether text, classical author, narrator, actor in history, *ciuis*,

---

[53] Hershkowitz (1995) 234–50, 'Cato *furens*', shows how 'even the wise man is mad' is infected and infectious with the Lucan–Caesar virulence that colonizes *BC*'s cosmos.

[54] *Silu.* 2.7.107f., cf. Malamud (1995), esp. 170, 'Are we celebrating or mourning Lucan? Is he alive or dead? Do these distinctions matter or do they not?'

[55] Henderson's Lucan warms to Pompey, as ever, and forever, *gratus popularitate Magnus* (Stat. *Silu.* 2.7.69), and to Cato – *once they are ciphers (nomina)*. Masters (1994) 158–63, 'The representation of political bias', produces an ironizing reading of this preemptive reading of reading. Bartsch (1997) chapters 4–5 reclaims the 'political ironist': Lucan–Cato 'engages in ideology in cold blood'.

courtier or conspirator, will march into eternity hand in hand with absolutist Caesarism: 'posterity will read the pair of us' (9.985, *uenturi me teque legent*).

BC has always already anticipated the story it was prevented from telling. Interminably, unarrestably. Just as much of the poem is taken up with recall, the repetition with difference of a cyclic link with earlier civil war, so the poem proliferates prophecies and manifold other forms of anticipation.[56] Its constitutive principle, indeed, is that what (little) is to be narrated, the build-up to, account of and sequel to Pharsalus, is one representative slice through a spiral.[57] This serves to obviate the need to extend the text to reach some further historical moment. Philippi, Cato's suicide, Caesar's assassination,[58] the succession and successiveness of emperors – all this is forecast before Lucan is intercepted. Indeed, BC throughout jettisons narration through time to descant instead on all Antiquity, back ultimately to Priam's Troy, Atreid Mycenae, Oedipus' Thebes, the Argonauts' Quest[59] and whencever, as well as the future in imperial perpetuity unto cosmic conflagration.

Why? The poem abuses narration precisely so as to interrupt its telling of the tale. A chief objective of the recalcitrant bard is to impress upon you the unequal struggle which his text fights to the death, his death, against the mercurial felicity of his Caesar's lightning. This narrator loathes the progress of his story of Caesarian triumph, loves *mora*, delay, obstruction, diversion: whether physical and external, or internalized as doubt, hesitation and other forms of paralysis.[60] Where the *Iliad* must keep its mega-hero πόδας ὠκύς (run-them-down)

---

[56] Dick (1963) 49: prophecy is 'used for the ulterior motive of showing its futility'. Cf. Narducci (1985) 1545f.

[57] Ahl (1985) 280f., cf. chapter 4. *Series*, whether of *Fatorum, Caesareae ... domus*, or of *laborum* (1.70, 4.823, 9.295) ..., is the principle of epic narration as of Stoic concatenation (5.179, Lapidge (1979) 368 on *rerum series*).

[58] Ahl (1976) 314f.; 318 and n. 23, Dick (1963) 47f.; Ahl (1976) 319 and n. 27, Dick (1963) 48f.

[59] Lausberg (1985); Häussler (1978) 75, Hübner (1976) 112f.; Ahl (1976) 120; Shoaf (1978), Ahl (1976) 225f.

[60] Grimal (1980), Narducci (1979) 98; Masters (1992) index, *s.v.* 'delay'; psychic *mora*: Miura (1981) esp. 210, 214, 217. Thus, at 10.542, *dubius*, of Caesar held up besieged in the text, stuck fast by the text's 'running out' on him, would be the *telos* of this theme, if –

Achilleus penned up in the confines of his tent if the poem is to persist until it has become an epic, a totalizing representation of ἀνδρεία and vision of (fighting) humanity, before he proleptically sacks his city, Lucan's preternatural Caesar cannot be held in check by his writer, the 'city' is now co-extensive with the 'world', and the epic must despite its own best efforts tell of *uirtus* it knows to be the *crimen*, the *scelus*, of Caesar's wor(l)d.

Mora begins as the external spatio-temporal resistance of 'Everything' to Caesar's *cursus* (onset); it charges Caesar up to a paroxysm of *furor* worthy of epic; then correlatively and consequently it is internalized within 'Everything' as stalling, self-doubt, fear, and terror. *Mora* issues in its paradoxical other, *fuga* (flight), as the world runs to stand still, and Lucan hates, spurns, defers, and resists his projected narrative. But Caesar will be here for ever, as Lucan–Caesar dins into his readers: ... *nec meus Eudoxi uincetur fastibus annus* (10.187, 'I own Roman time. The calendar is mine, yes, just one more Caesarian *ueni, uidi, uici*: in the naming of Time, that measure of fame, the Julian year will defeat its Greekling rival and put down the cal...lousness of *Eudoxus*, 'Mr Famous' *fastus/fasti*'). Post-Augustan readers know that Caesar wins (every) time: Lucan wants 'his bad, bad epic' (*Phars-alia tanti | causa mali*) to oust the uncanny word *Allia* from the Roman calendar's blackspot highlights, but in vain (7.407f.). As the first bookroll gives out, Lucan's celestial expert Nigidius Figulus' '*domino*-theory' of an incomprehensible possibility of pluralized temporalities to keep Caesar at bay, *ad infinitum*, will flag, and the game is up: 'Mad war is on its way, military might forcibly obliterating all right, Romespeak converting unspeakable *scelus* into *uirtus*':

> ... multosque exibit in annos,
> hic furor. et superos quid prodest poscere finem?
> cum domino pax ista uenit. duc, Roma, malorum   670
> continuam seriem clademque in tempora multa
> extrahe, ciuili tantum iam libera bello.   (1.668–72)

> *'It's going to outlast many many years – and* more *– ,*
> *this collective seizure. And praying to heaven for an end is not an option.*
> *The peace-treaty will be struck between slave and owner. 'Line up*
> *   disasters, Rome (to stay Rome),*   670
> *in a continuing chain. The triumph of evil for aeon after aeon –*
> *drag it out. As of now, Rome is only free while there is civil war.'*

Which is to say: Lucan fights for Rome in striving heroically to stop the clock. No one loses their freedom in his company – it's not over while the fat book sings. So:

> This epic outburst will take me years to write, take you ages to read, mountains of paper. No divine machinery in this poem; and no death wish: I promise never to stop. When you break up the session, it's back to post-Augustan life. This song of Rome is programmed (here) – a filibuster line-up of tragic episodes; a triumph of language to spin it out from one recitation-date to another. Escape now, from bio-degrading mundanity outside the text: stay with the ablative absolute, and surround yourself with the *Bellum ciuile*.   (1.668–72).

BC sets out to pre-destine incompleteness as its objective. The triumphant *uirtus* of Lucan's (anti-)epic[61] failure is to make writing itself the drama of political resistance in the name of history. Lucan exactly fights for Rome in that he 'refuses to narrate': 'not one word from *BC* on undescribable civil war' (7.556), *quidquid in hac acie gessisti, Roma, tacebo.*[62] Just one terminal speculation, among many: ' . . . or is it so that Fortune can carry through the work of the sword of vengeance, the penalt*ies* for psychose*s*, autocrac*ies* returning again to avenging Brutus*es* – Apollo's silence?' (5.206–8, . . . *regnaque ad ultores iterum redeuntia Brutos, | ut peragat Fortuna, taces?*). And with that, eloquent silences.[63]

Yet Lucan *himself* melts down into his '*Caesar*'. Either/both 'may seem to be starring in a great world-wide film about himself'.[64] Caesar transgresses all conventional codes, social boundaries, linguistic categories; re-deploys around his name all meanings; fixes a new centre from which all discourse is oriented and enforces his signs absolutely. When Lucan–Caesar feels the atavistic tug toward the still unmastered source of the Nile in what proved their last book together – like Nero,[65] as well as like manic Czars such as Alexander, Sesostris and

---

61 So Marti (1975) 76, 'almost an anti-epic'; cf. Narducci (1979) 15.

62 Bramble (1982) 540; cf. Masters (1992) 148, Ormand (1994) 53f., Malamud (1995) 183.

63 O'Higgins (1988), esp. 214: at Delphi, 'The Pythia's name, Phemonoe, may be translated as "speaker of thoughts". Speaking her thoughts is precisely what she is not permitted to do.' Lucan's use of the 'poetic plural' adumbrates the multiplier-effect in myth and in-

64 Harland (1987) 172.

65 Cf. 1.20 and e.g. Plin. *Nat. hist.* 6.181.

Cambyses[66] – he is irresistibly cast as that tyrant-self driven ever on-wards to appropriate his world, *beyond* its limits, *further than* its origins: 'What could be more conducive to expansion and achievement and aggression than a kind of desire that nothing can ever truly satisfy?'[67] Is this not the West? *Finis quis quaeritur armis? | quid satis est, si Roma parum est?* ('Define arms-limitation? What is enough if the planet is not?', 5.273f.) Lucan was just as driven, another Caesar in writing: 'Epic (*arma*) *never* ends. *BC* is a Roman song – and (so) wants *more than* it can be.'

Lucan's epic curses itself, for its Caesarism. And yours. Read Lucan. And 'be damned'. With poet and Caesar: *damnabimur* (9.986).[68]

3 THE WARP OF WORDS

so hold me mom
in your long arms
in your automatic arms
in your arms
in your petrochemical arms
your military arms
in your electronic arms[69]

Lucan's difficult language is strange, foregrounded in reading above the tale it tells: 'making of its own rhetorical figures a comment on its subject-matter'.[70] You need to (de)familiarize your self with it. The struggle to forge a new (anti-)poetic, and escape belatedness, begins in the rhetoric of hyperbole and *Extremformel* announced in the first verse as *Bella ... plus quam ciuilia* – 'wie ein Motto des lucanischen Steiger-ungswillen'.[71] Probably a tragic invention of Pollio's *Historiae* (chapter 4), the phrase dares you to name this excess, this *plus quam* – the code

---

[66] Cf. Ahl (1976) 222f., 10.189–331: 191f. 'Let me count on seeing the springs of Nile and I will leave the poem', and esp. 269f. See Irwin (1980) 79f. for discussion of '*Nilosis*', that quest for origin-ality, where –

[67] Harland (1987) 41.

[68] Cf. Johnson (1987) 118–21, 'Caesar is, in fact, Lucan's Muse', Masters (1992) 212, Malamud (1995) 182, 'Writing about Caesar makes him somehow complicit with and analogous to Caesar.' Between them, these colleagues pois(e)on the universepic. The outburst in IX will recur below.

[69] L. Anderson (1982), 'O Superman'.

[70] Bartsch (1994) 182; cf. Hershkowitz (1995) 200 on this 'metapoetic'.

[71] Hübner (1972) 582; Martindale (1976) 48f.; Hübner (1976) 113; 'a kind of motto of L.'s will to go one further', Seitz (1965) 221 n. 2.

of (social) 'kinship' with Caesar–Pompey as *socer–gener* (affinal relatives); the paradox of *Roman* civil war fought out in *alien* Thessaly; the
sheer scale of *world* civil war; or whatever.[72] But the force of Lucan's
hyperbole is *itself* the point.

You hear that ranting/hurt *voice* in such excesses as:

> maius ab hac acie quam quod sua saecula ferrent
> uolnus habent populi, plus est quam uita salusque
> quod perit: in totum mundi prosternimur aeuum,   640
> uincitur his gladiis omnis quae seruiet aetas.   (7.638–41)

> *The peoples of the earth are dealt a* greater *wound by this battle*
> than *their own ages could possibly bear;* more than *life dies*
> *and salvation is lost: we're flattened for our universe's*
>   *whole eternity;*   640
> *conquered by these swords are all future, forever subject, generations.*

Lucan twists epic mimesis into an insistent performance of all that
resists objectification, of all that shrugs off the power of language
to normalize, by naming, the inexpressibility of pain.[73] Rhetorical
(dis)figuration aims to resist being brought into the fold of 'literature'
by interpretation: there is always that residue, that excess, language –
electrifying language.[74]

The narrator attacks his (traditionally omniscient) epic authority,
subjecting you to its 'master-trope', a barrage of apostrophe;[75] persis-
tently figuring as the Neronian Lucan who rages at his heritage of
Caesarian subjection;[76] but also inventing a(n anonymously limited-
consciousness) voice which lives the drama of the narrative, in ignorance of its eventualities – despite the betrayal of *BC*'s 'counterfactual'
wishes and pleas that history could have been, might have been, otherwise.[77] The irritant – aggravating – narrator forces you toward intervention, the risk that you may find your self in agreement.[78]

This poem doesn't wish to comprehend, but disowns its patrimony

---

[72] Father-/son-in-law: Jal (1963) 19, 27f., Häussler (1978) 69f., Ahl (1976) 313f.; Graeco-
Roman: Hübner (1972) 593; scale: Hübner (1984).
[73] Seitz (1965) 219. Cf. Scarry (1985) 5f.
[74] Hübner (1972) 578. Hübner's volley of early 70s 'cold war' papers single-handedly
revolutionized grasp of Lucan's rhetoric.
[75] Martindale (1993) 67; Marti (1975) 82f., Ahl (1976) 117f.
[76] Pfligersdorffer (1959) 347f., Dick (1963) 46f., Marti (1975) 84f., Masters (1994) 161.
[77] Marti (1975) 86f., Masters (1992) 5f., 78f.
[78] See Frieden (1985) 161 for this argument.

of power/knowledge.[79] *BC* curses *poetry*: 'Just look at Caesar betrampling the ruins of Homer's Troy, doesn't it make you see that poets have their greatness, their works are sacred/cursed: you're the one that rips Everything | from deathstiny, you hand eternity to the peoples of the earth despite their decease. | "Caesar, don't let it get to you, no need to be jealous of sacred/cursed fame |"'' (9.980-2, *o sacer et magnus uatum labor: omnia fato | eripis et populis donas mortalibus aeuum. | inuidia sacrae, Caesar, ne tangere famae |*). In the fracture of the signifier *C/ae/s/a/r* into its split-and-doubled twin *s/a/c/r/ae*, a scandalous incest within the sign disseminates the assertion of power along the linguistic chain: 'The Sacred' bears along with it the deconstructive freight of Lucan's *carmen*, 'The Desecration' of *Pharsalia*' s own *inuidia* ('malevolence').

As Lucan's voices weld epic, hero, poet and readers together into: *Pharsalia nostra | uiuet* ('our *Pharsalia* will live', 9.985), *Latinitas* conquers the 'Emathian' sign, Greek *Pharsalia*, in abusive appropriation for *Romespeak* as *pars alia nostra*.[80] *La bataille de la phrase*[81] grips the internal divisiveness of *Bellum Ciuile* within *pars alia*, together with its implosiveness into a Caesarian 'Everything' within *nostra*. In this textuality, Lucan–Caesar's outburst at the origin, the Trojan origins of Rome, Latin and the Caesars, the origins of classical literature in Homeric–Virgilian classical epic, the origins of classical order in culture as The Walled City, all that makes the memory held in the narration transcend the narrated, that empty name – ruined oblivion of the past –, site of Lucan's ascension as epic immortal – in this textuality is figured that revulsion from the narrative which in *BC constitutes* the narration.[82]

So the rhetorical figures of Lucan's text are salient, gesturing toward the *more than* sayable. Absurdist paradox[83] puts a mock- or para-logic to work for the poem's design: *urbe relicta | in bellum fugitur* ('The city is abandoned, | and off to war – in flight', 1.503f.), for example, abuses

---

[79] Cf. 1.127, *scire nefas*. In general *nescio* is a key term in *BC*; Häussler (1978) 60f., Marti (1975) 76f., 85.

[80] I liberated this from Masters (1992) dedication. You're an accessory now.

[81] French metaplasm: Simon (1969) 'La bataille de *Ph-a-r-s-a-l-e*', discussed by Heath (1972) 161.

[82] Cf. Opelt (1957) 437, Johnson (1987) 118–21, Green (1991), Bartsch (1997) chapter 5. At Troy, Caesar unfounds Rome and the *Aeneid* (Hardie (1993) 107, Green (1991) 251–3) and becomes Alexander ready for the Pharaohs (Zwierlein (1986)); and he shows 'what kind of a' (wilful) 'reader' he is (Ormand (1994) 51).

[83] Conte (1968) 230, Martindale (1976) 45f. 'Epic of ideas', '*concettismo*', 'cerebral intellectualism', 'mannerism', even 'expressionism' are attempts to name the unnamable *more*-ism.

the pious *fuga* of the Odyssean *Aeneid* into the pattern of Pompey's retreat from Rome, Italy and the West rather than face Caesar in civil war. The pattern of *mora* – as the most that the universe can throw up by way of resistance to Caesar's 're-founding' of Rome – takes the surreal form of 'flight'. Normal subject–object relations are often disrupted, as in *modo luce fugata | descendentem animam* ('a soul on its way down | having just put the light of day/life to flight', 6.713f.).[84]

The obsessive practice of 'negative enumeration' ('Negations-antithesen'),[85] where the text mentions epic material only to repudiate its adequacy to represent civil war in the *Bella ... plus quam ciuilia*, highlights Lucan's deformation of the tradition,[86] and wrests the narration away to imaginary worlds *beyond* words. At the same time, the poem turns on the power to name which is proper to mimetic representation, to uncreate the world.[87] A Spanish instance, of Lucan's geophysical poetics, saturating the world with war:[88]

> placidis praelabitur undis
> Hesperios inter Sicoris non ultimus amnes,
> saxeus ingenti quem pons amplectitur arcu   15
> hibernas passurus aquas. at proxima rupes
> signa tenet Magni, nec Caesar colle minore
> castra leuat: medius dirimit tentoria gurges.
> explicat hinc tellus campos effusa patentis
> uix oculo prendente modum, camposque coerces,   20
> Cinga rapax, uetitus fluctus et litora cursu
> Oceani pepulisse tuo. nam gurgite mixto
> qui praestat terris aufert tibi nomen Hiberus.   (4.13–23)

Pompeians versus *Caesar: armies encamped on hills across the valley of the bridged R. Sicoris, which opens out onto the extensive plain bounded by R. Cinga, minor tributary of the Ebro.*

– or, rather *more than* this:

> *Gliding past, the calm waters*
> *of more than the last river of the West: Sicoris*

---

[84] Hübner (1975) 209: *BC* as 'die Erfüllung des Lebens im Tod'; cf. Saylor (1990) on Lucan–Caesar's light in death (= life).

[85] E. J. Kenney *cit.* Martindale (1980) 374; Conte (1968) 245.

[86] Nowak *cit.* Bramble (1982) 544 n. 2, *q.v.* 543f., Martindale (1976) 49; for deviant similes, cf. Miura (1981) 229f.

[87] Hübner (1975) 201f.

[88] See Masters (1992) 52f.; 43–90 on *BC* IV.

– a bridge of stone hugs him with each mighty arch;
he'll endure the rains in Spain. Well, the adjoining crag
received the standards of Pompey the Great ∼ Caesar alighted his camp
on a greater – not lower – hill. In between, maelstrom split tent from tent.
From here a flood of terrain unfolds wide-open plains for battle,
– the eye hardly grasps their limit, and the plains for battle you hold down
    in thrall,   20
you robber Cinga, forbidden to beat waves and shores
of Ocean with your onset. You see, the maelstrom merges
so . . .

        the one who grants it to the land,
              steals yours from you,
            the name in both cases,
       the one being Hiberus
                    (Iberian river,
                            Iberian Spain).

In this morsel, see Pompey the victim – in fact not Pompey but only the sign *'Magnus'* is present at Lucan's Ilerda. He names what is at stake, 'greatness' – his force 'held prisoner' by Lucan's syntax: | *signa tenet* ∼ | *castra leuat.* 'Magnus' is a subject skewed into dependence on a mock-object in one-sided *BC*, facing the energy of *Caesar/castra*, subjectivity as active agency,[89] lifting lightly the weight of an army. In the litotes *nec . . . minore, BC*'s *plusquam* projects Caesarian greatness, onto the map he is re-drawing: in Sicoris and its litotes *non ultimus*, Lucan portrayed domesticated Pompeian sluggishness; the destructive Caesar river Cinga did *more than* 'separate the Roman rivals'; in 'flooding out the land beyond the horizon, before confining the visual field', Cinga evoked elemental *BC*.

Book IV is introduced with *Caesar . . . maxima . . . fati ducibus momenta* (4.1–3, 'Caesar . . . the greatest shifts in the balance of death-stiny for the leaders'). Ilerda will make *'Caesar'* (mean) great. In the repetitions *gurges/gurgite, campos/camposque* read the terrain of civil war, its 'Emathian' *campos*, the multiplier-effect of chaos in cataclysm. Read *plus quam*, as elements (are) saturate(d), they divide/destroy, extend and compact, their domain. But, *more than* this, the double-act of *Sicoris* and *Cinga* have the map pulled from under their feet, as the marauder is robbed in turn by the greater power of the Hiberus. The 'Pompeian' *gurges* loses the agency of its *cursus* when its, and its

---

[89] For 'Caesar : subject : : Pompey : object', cf. Rosner-Siegel (1983) 171f.

'Caesarian' superior's, *gurges* mingle in the 'unity' of *BC*, where one side will confiscate the identity of its opposition, stamp its own 'name' on the Roman world, supplant every Latin 'word' 's meaning (*nomen*, 'word') with the connotation 'Caesar's – Everything is Caesar's.' The point of the suffocated rhetoric of the last verse here, where the subject–object relations of normal 'description' are disrupted as the 'tributary' does not lose its name, but yet the main river steals it away, holds up language itself as what is at stake in *BC*.[90]

The paragraph of topographical nonsense amplifies with its scenography the introductory programme of vv. 1–10, which opposed *Caesar ... saeuus ... non multa caede* (vv. 1–2, 'Caesarism – more gore coming') through the link *ducibus* (v. 3, 'leaders') to the army of the consuls Afranius and Petreius (vv. 4–10). Here, in the imagery of *castra*, *BC* pictured and painted over the Republic. Sketching Rome as *concordia* and/as *custodia*, the give-and-take binary oneness, the exchange, sharing and dis-course of power that is the sign of Republican collegiality (*iure pari ... in aequas ... uices, alterno ... signo*), discipline (*imperium*, *paret*), duty (*peruigil*), communality (*commune*), those walls (*tutela ... ualli*), Lucan also perverted the Republic of *BC*, with 'Latin battle-lines' drawn up *alongside* the natives, *within* one *imperium*, *uallum* | *castra* | *moenia* | *urbs* | *orbis*. His voice rose to the last limb of a tricolon crescendo: ... | *Gallorum Celtae miscentes nomen Hiberis* | (v. 10), echoing on into Book IV's guerrilla war. Here, 'refugees from an ancient tribe | of Gauls' mash Caesar's *Gallic Wars* into the shattered post-conquest world of *BC*: the 'name' *Celt-* 'merges' its self, its identity as a 'word', into the 'name' *Hiberi-* to 'unite' in the mutilated *plusquam* of the *nomen Celt- ... -Iberi*. An ethnemic drama within the sign set to rhyme with the erasure of the name at the second climax: *mixto* | ... *nomen Hiberus* |.

The *nomen Hiberi* was already pseudetymologized in *hibernas ... aquas* ('wintry ... waters', v. 16) to forecast half a book of Spanish cataclysm. Winter's inundation in *BC* (vv. 50f.) will 'merge the boundaries which mark out the world' (*rerum discrimina miscet*, v. 104), so 'the hills' and 'all the rivers' are lost in 'one huge swamp' (vv. 98f., *tumuli collesque*, cf. *colle tumet ... tumulo*, vv. 11–12). Lucan drowns Caesarian *f-u-l-m-i-n-a* and *f-u-lg-u-ra* in *f-l-u-ct-u-s* and *f-l-u-m-i-n-a* (vv. 77f. ~ 81, 89, 98, 117), before his Caesar's 'Everything' (vv. 143f.),

---

[90] Hübner (1975) 201f. for this and other 'points' about *nomen*.

omnia fatis | Caesaris, re-distributes the boundaries – 'stealing away' (*abstulit* ~ v. 22, *aufert*) the *campos* and trapping the Republicans into water-denied surrender on these very 'hills' (*collibus*, v. 263, etc). In full view of Sicoris and Hiberus (v. 335).

Half a book awash with *non multa caede* (v. 2). Lucan's abuse of Caesar's *clementia* ensues. Mixed up Republicans and Caesarians merge like bloody rivers in liquid fraternization/surrender,[91] before a shipload of slaughter, 'enough for Caesar to call it a loss' (v. 514, *damnum*), exemplary Caesarian killing, begins in earnest with the spectacular mass-suicide on Vulteius' Raft of State (vv. 402–581).[92] Here *Bella ... plus quam ciuilia* pull out all the stops, as 'the slayers slay the slain slayers in an equation of death' (vv. 558f., *pariter sternuntque caduntque, | uolnere letali*). Trapped Caesarians take all the parts here, showing off their *uirtus* as '*Kampfwut*' (combat frenzy), *BC*'s speciality of *amor mortis* (lust to die).[93] In *Vulteius*' 'face' (*uoltus*), *you* must face *uolnus* (wound) as pure 'will to power' (*uoluntas*. His endless last words: *se uelle mori*, v. 544). The defiant mass-suicide is more than *success* for Caesar – Vulteius says it all, ending his call to become a *magnum ... exemplum* with the *mot*: 'Success is dying' (v. 520, *felix esse mori*). Total victory means seizing the role of victim from the victim. That Caesarian, Lucan, is solid with Vulteius – also 'committing epic suicide ... by writing about the civil war'.[94]

All Caesar's victories over Roman discourse, *ius ... datum sceleri* ('legality given to wickedness', 1.2), warp *uirtus* into *crimen* and *nefas*. These are 'Justice War''s assizes (*iudice bello*, 1.227).[95] Success would mean a general subversion of cultural values, of greatness and goodness.[96] Even to accept that civil war is 'war' is, already, to side with

---

[91] Saylor (1986) on winebloodwater, and Masters (1992) 72f., 110f., 170f. on mixing: vv. 22, *mixto |*, cf. 190, *mixtique ... concordia mundi*, 198, *permixto Baccho*, 283, *miscendae copia mortis*, 320, *immixtum uenenum ...*

[92] On Vulteius, see Ahl (1976) 119f., Saylor (1990), Hershkowitz (1995) 215f.

[93] See Rutz (1960), whence the main impetus for ?post-war? Lucan studies. Cf. Pfligersdorffer (1959) 350f.

[94] Masters (1996) 13 and n. 6. '*Caesar*' 'transforms this centurion from a man whose *greatest* mark of distinction was that he had saved a fellow citizen's life into one who would willingly slaughter his fellow citizens for Caesar' (George (1988) 338 on Laelius at 1.357f.: *more than* this, 'Give the word and I'll stab brother's and parent's throat, plus pregnant wife's womb', vv. 376–8. An élite corps, this).

[95] Due (1962) 116f.

[96] Jal (1963) 537f., Marti (1966) 251f.

'*Caesar*' (chapter 2).[97] Lucan's deviant rhetoric unsmooths Caesar's path, subverting subject–object relations, standard tropes, and the norms of military narrative. Take the superannuated *imago* of *Patria* at the Rubicon, for example:[98] to usher in *BC*, she appears hugely to Caesar, 'pouring down white hairs with harmed tresses, by his side with arms unarmed, bared in crisis' (1.188f.). The dishevelled *matrona* called 'Father's (land)' is still recognizable as, say, the return of olden-times' mama Veturia come to meet another rebel Coriolanus: *quoniam armis uiri defendere urbem non possent, mulieres precibus lacrimisque defenderent* ... (Livy 2.40.2, 'since epic manliness couldn't defend Rome with rockets, women's rhetoric of pathos should step into the breach'). Lucan's *Patria* annunciates *BC* as *ultra*-civil war: *Quo tenditis ultra? | quo fertis mea signa, uiri? si iure uenitis, | si ciues, huc usque licet* (vv. 190–2, 'Where is your *over*-reaching to end?', she punctuates with unVirgilian[99] sobs, 'Where are you men bearing my standards? If you come within the law | and as citizens, *BC* 1.192 is as far as you can go.' Here *mea* disrupts the 'Roman signs' of the cliché '*signa ferre*' ('to march'), so that para-logically the owner of arms is also the target of those arms. *BC* – truly, 'Your mother's arms'.

But read on, fight for Rome with Lucan and Caesar. You must combat re-description, the art of military narrative, which supplements paraleipsis[100] – 'When All about are Losing their Heads (in the metaphorical sense: nothing so nasty as decapitation ever creeps into a citation' – with the power-play of metaphor, creating those colourful 'lumbering' giants or 'scuttling' ants, non-sentient 'harvests' and colourless 'neutralizations', and with the rhetorical ruse of metonymy, dispersing the personness of lacerated, mutilated, unmade bodies. Their pain is to be at once the object and the repressed of war, along a chain of substitutions whose objective is to displace agents with weapons, that bizarre 'exchange of idioms between weapons and bodies' which must threaten the very relations between The Arms and The Man that the cult of manliness seeks to enforce. 'Although a

---

[97] *BC* begins 'in the tenth year of war' (1.283, 299f.): i.e. Caesar's objective all along was (his 'Troy') *Rome*. Cf. Green (1991) 233.

[98] Narducci (1980) and (1985) 1558f., Feeney (1991) 292–4, Masters (1992) 1–10, *q.v.*

[99] Narducci (1985) 1560f.: comparing Virg. *Aen.* 8.112–14.

[100] Scarry (1985) 63f., 'The main purpose and outcome of war is injuring. Though this fact is too self-evident and massive ever to be directly contested, it can be indirectly contested by many means and disappear from view along many separate paths.'

weapon is an extension of the human body (as is acknowledged in their collective designation as "arms"), it is instead the human body that becomes in this vocabulary an extension of the weapon.'[101]

BC shoves its tropes into self-defeat: the mass of personified weapons, those *signa*, *aquilae* and *pila* of his Proem (1.6f.), takes shape in all the *gladii* and *enses* equipped with properties and epithets, governing verbs, and dominating their lines *more than* you can blink.[102] Absurd relations between agency and object-world scar the memorialization, as in Vulteius' crimson patch, where 'the sword is punctured by the chest' (*percussum est pectore ferrum*, 4.561), or at farcical Pharsalus, where 'only the sword hates enough for this tale of one city: it guides right arms into Roman guts' (*odiis solus ciuilibus ensis | sufficit, et dextras Romana in uiscera ducit*, 7.490f.). Violent compression (verbal coercion) typifies *BC*'s atrocities done to epic language: *uolnera* ('wounds') in place of *arma* ('what wounds'); *manus* as all a *uir* is; *sacer* compacts its two faces, 'the gods / cursed': *tractentur uolnera nulla | sacra manu* (3.314, 'No one should fight the gods / may no hand touch the gods' wounds / don't wield the cursed weapons of Caesar's civil war / let none of our Massilian men pollute their arms in Roman civil war').[103] Poetic invention strains inside-out to build a word world for Caesar – in case his army won't fight: 'these arms will find hands, I'll reject you and then Fortune will supply enough men to go round the weapons' (5.326f., *inuenient haec arma manus, uobisque repulsis | tot reddet Fortuna uiros, quot tela uacabunt |*).[104]

Lucan's proem already promises *more than* the traditional form of battle narrative, the syntactic combat of polyptoton, a war-dance in rhyme: *infestisque obuia signis | signa, pares aquilas et pila minantia pilis |* (1.6f., 'offensive/deterrent words, the banners of war ..., warhead parity ..., first-strike missile-to-missile capability', 1.6–7).[105] This was

---

[101] Keegan (1976) 315; Scarry (1985) 70; 66f.; 67 *bis*.

[102] See Hübner (1972) 581 and n. 2. Cf. Scarry (1985) 15f. for the 'language of agency' drawing off pain as (if) 'in' the weapon.

[103] Cf. Green (1994) 223f. on the ritual compulsion in this apopemptic wish.

[104] Note *arma : manus : : uiros : tela*, in this scrambling of *arma uirumque*, Masters (1996) 16. In general, see Hübner (1972), (1974), using the umbrella rubric 'hypallage'. Bartsch (1997) chapter 1 canvasses 'inversion of subject–object relations'.

[105] For such polyptoton in Lucan e.g. 3.544, 694, 4.624, 783, 7.573, Bramble (1982) 552. On 1.6f., cf. Jal (1963) 322, Conte (1970) 136 = (1988) 30, Enn. *Ann.* 582 Skutsch, *pila retunduntur uenientibus obuia pilis*.

already, within its sentence, a climax in amplification, and is to be
further hyped in the poem's first developed simile, the pushbutton of
cosmic dissolution:[106] *omnia mixtis | sidera sideribus concurrent* ... (74f.:
'All the stars, star upon star: *ad infinitum* collision / total fusion'). Here
Lucan – dismaying Bentley and Housman, neither of whom lived
wave/particle indeterminacy – writes in the end of classical meaning, as
he crushes incompatibles to head his litany of apocalyptic promises. In
this crash of syntax with concept, as in the opening sentence's climb
from *plus quam* to *pares*, do not miss the poetics of totalizing, civil, war.

4 THE WORLD OF WAR

> Occasionally, the whole class struggle may be summed up in the
> struggle for one word against another word. Certain words struggle
> against themselves as enemies. Other words are the site of an ambi-
> guity: the stake in a decisive but undecided battle.[107]

That word in Lucan's post-Augustan world is the name '*Caesar*'. *BC*
works toward tearing off the value of 'Greatness' from '*Caesar*'.[108] This
is Julius, and the 'Greatness' he made his name mean. It is his fame
and it became the mark of the greatest form of fame for the rest of
Roman time, the future of Latin. Caesar becomes a 'transcendental'
name, spells κράτος, the name which all Western names should love to
be: a name which means power, the power to name 'Power' for itself,
the appropriation of significance, the denotation which enforces its
own power to assign meaning. '*Caesar*' will be the signifier that projects
into the totality of the discourse of the Empire the assurance that
all discourse orbits around and radiates from Caesar. The master-sign
will dispense legitimacy, propriety, identity, the right to exist, to own
a name, the Word-of-the-Father to Roman culture, that is to human
culture.

Fighting for Rome left this *imprimatur*. From the late 40s, when
Antony could freely say, and Cicero could (no) less freely repeat, of
Octavian *o puer qui omnia nomini debes* ('O boy, you owe all – like,
everything – to a name, that name', *Phil.* 13.24), through the early 30s,
when Caesar's testamentary son could begin to enforce his imperial

[106] 1.72–80: Lapidge (1979) 360f., Miura (1981) 208f.
[107] Althusser (1971) 21, 'Philosophy as a revolutionary weapon'.
[108] Feeney (1986A), Ahl (1976) 218.

claims with the 'name' *Imperator Caesar*, '*Caesar*' passed from traditional *cognomen* to the scandal of a dictatorial title that took a grip on
the Roman world which was never relinquished. At the material level,
reckon in millions the estates of settlers and their posterity dependent
on the continuing propriety of a grant in the name of (a) Caesar. Note
the proliferation of communities labelled *Caesarea*. In reading-culture,
Augustan texts permanently model the dynastic transmission between
'*Caesar*' and (the next) '*Caesar*'.

Nero lionized his paternal descent from the Domitii Ahenobarbi
(chapter 7). When Lucan's choice of *BC* for theme brought him to
choreograph his indomitable / often pardoned Domitius' last words as
the only notable casualty of Pharsalus recorded in the histories, he
chose to have him 'welcome death', as he told gloating Julius, 'while
Caesar was still obstructed from power' (*dubium*, v. 611) '– before the
republic was beyond hope' (7.615, '. . . *cum moriar, sperare licet*'). What
would stop Nero enjoying this pretty (sick) chivalry? In fact, Lucan has
just played the '*Brutus*' joker: his fancy has Brutus in pleb disguise
getting near to Caesar, to 'get rid of more kings' (*Caesaris intentus
iugulo*, vv. 586–96: chapter 3). An emperor could nod at the admission,
'this was the last to bear the name of this key clan through the ages'
(v. 589). He could share the glee at 'Tarquin's Brutus, the only shade
in Elysium glad to be in *BC*' (6.791f.). And Lucan's 'complaint that
the Brutus*es* and their Republic have only interrupted Roman slavery'
is doubtless a rousing conceit (7.437–41: *de Brutis, Fortuna, queror* . . .).
But Lucan's surreal mandate to Brutus, to wait for Philippi and keep
his knife sharp, for when 'Caesar has reached the summit and burst the
bounds of humanity – and earned the deathstiny of so glorious a death'
(vv. 593–5), could only make a *Caesar Augustus*' shoulder-blades itch:
uiuat et, ut Bruti procumbat uictima, regnet (v. 596, 'Let Caesar live, let
Caesar be king – then he can topple, sacrificed by Brutus'). *Regnum*
could force Nero to choose – no Caesar could afford to play Domitius
without jeopardizing his neck along with its 'greatness'.[109]

'Greatness' is what Lucan has Caesar fight for (*more than* his life).
Every mention in the narrative of value, significance or power, every
estimation by the narrator of size and scale, every performance by

---

[109] On the question of Domitius (Lucan's version of 'Crastinus'), cf. Lounsbury (1975),
Masters (1994) 163–8, Hardie (1993) 55f. On Lucan–Nero's Brutus, cf. George
(1991).

the narration of epic 'magnitude' relates to this objective. Fulminating Caesar pursues through the text (what happen to be the poem's last words) *calcantem moenia Magnum* | ('Pompey stamping down the walls', 10.546). *BC* sings the razing of Rome, as Caesar gobbles up Republican, Sullan, Pompeian, 'greatness'. Lucan unmakes the *Aeneid*'s 'walls of sublime Rome' (1.7, *altae moenia Romae*). In fact friction with these Virgilian walls is a principal target of Lucan's poem.[110] An example is Caesar's first approach to the city of Rome, where Lucan writes a 7-verse 'delayed proem' that teems with speculations, in so far as it can be understood at all – a commentator's fantasia:

> iamque et praecipitis superauerat Anxuris arces
> et qua Pomptinas uia diuidit uda paludes   85
> qua sublime nemus Scythicae qua regna Dianae
> quaque iter est Latiis ad summam fascibus Albam,
> excelsa de rupe procul iam conspicit Urbem
> Arctoi toto non uisam tempore belli
> miratusque suae sic fatur moenia Romae: (3.84–90)   90

> *By now Caesar had both surmounted the headlong bastions of Anxur*
>   *and where the swimming lane parts the Pomptine swamp,*   85
>   *where sublime grove*
>   *of Scythian Diana,*
>   *where empire*
> *and where is the way for Latin* fasces *up to highest Alba:*
> *now from a cliff of eminence far off he sights the City*
> *– in the time of his wars never seen, in all his campaign north –*
> *and he made this astounded speech to the walls, his very own Walls*
> *of Rome:*   90

Caesar('s army) climbs up these lines to a vantage-point, then on to Rome. Caesar plays a Hannibal that *takes* Rome.[111] Caesar presses further his conquest (*supero*) of physical geography, scaling an Italian citadel; taking Jupiter Anxurus' Olympus in black revenge for Gigantomachy. This 'sheer' ascent fits Caesar to his world, 'headlong in flight before him'.[112] Caesar charges up from Brundisium to Rome,

---

[110] E.g. 3.296–9, ... *omnia Caesar* | ... *praestitit orbem* | ... *trepidantis moenia Romae* |, cf. Ahl (1976) 202 on 1.345, *quae moenia fessis* |.

[111] V. 84 epanaleaps back to the start of Lucan's narrative, 'Now Caesarspeed had surmounted the Alps' (1.183); for *C-a-e-s-a-r* / *c-u-r-s-u-s*, cf. Miura (1981) 217f.

[112] *Praeceps* as epicthet for Caesar, Newmyer (1983) 238 n. 17, Quint (1993) 149, esp. 2.656, *Caesar in omnia praeceps*.

climbs over his cultural heritage, every Latin name standing for Rome, for all that he displaces, for 'Everything': *C-ae-s-a-r* / *a-r-c-e-s*. Lucan's additive string of unpoetic 'and's (*qua* ... | *qua* ... *qua* ... | *quaque*, vv. 85–7) has *qua* ... *uia diuidit* match *quaque iter est*, around the verbless v. 86 as centrepiece: a divided line embodying the *BC* in miniature. This *nemus* is 'sublime' because it is epical, (*the*) *Nemus* of Diana, *more* of a haunt *than* other sacred groves for *numen*, *religio*, *pietas*, as the age-old venue of the Latin League, evoking Latium, Italia, *imperium*, Roma. This is Diana's *regna* because *regnum* is why the 'grove' belongs in *BC*: the *rex Nemorensis*, the runaway-slave-*cum*-priest who slew the slayer and will become the slain, presides here, and fits Caesar's journey toward *dominatio*. The verse invokes the Graeco-Roman world of myth/ritual to curse this little '*Reisegedicht*' (traveldogguerel) with its mash of barbaric human sacrifice, spectacular serial cycle of slaughter, kings and/as slaves, plus the tug of the familiar, close to home and steeped in folk tradition and history.[113]

Lucan departs here from the Virgilian *color* of his précis of the Catalogue of Italians roused up to fight against the founding 'Caesar', Aeneas.[114] In *uia diuidit uda paludes*,[115] the topography crushes more *BC* into his words. The division of civil war muddies/muddles the triumphal road leading to Rome, now the *uia* of Caesar's lightning-course to *regnum* (from 1.150 to 10.538) out of clear referentiality, for *uia* ... *uda* forces parallel lines together in one phrase: (i) the great Via Appia; (ii) the Decennovium canal across the swamp between the Temple/Grove of Feronia, 3 miles from Anxur, and Forum Appi, alongside the Via Appia. The road was often too wet to be a road – 'often eroded or even cut through by torrents coming down from the Apennines; and people preferred to go by water'; the canal was itself a *uia*, but one made out of the waters of the marshes and their rivers, which it 'divided'.[116]

Caesar reaches *summam* ... *Albam* – Alba Longa and Mons Albanus.

---

[113] Ov. *Fast.* 3.271f., *regna tenent fortes manibus pedibusque fugaces,* | *et perit exemplo postmodo quisque suo*, Strabo 5.3.12; cf. *Met.* 14.331, *Scythicae stagnum nemorale Dianae*. Green (1994) esp. 214–16, shows how much power this ritualization of Caesar's march on Rome sheds over *BC* in re-presenting the *coup d'état*.

[114] *quis Iuppiter Anxurus aruis* | ... | *qua Saturae iacet atra palus* ... | *quaerit iter*, *Aen.* 7.799–802; Aricia and Diana at 762–80.

[115] Cf. Ov. *Fast.* 6.401f., *paludes udae* with Ahl (1985) 316f.

[116] Chevallier (1976) 211 n. 19; cf. Strabo 5.3.6, Hor. *Sat.* 1.5.

Matrix of Rome and destroyed by Rome, last of the Latin cities Rome
founded. The heartland of Roma, *Latinitas*, entrée to the *Aeneid* (*urbem*
| ... *Latio* ... *Latinum* | *Albani* ... *altae moenia Romae* | (*Aen.* 1.5–7).
And Caesar runs head-on into the procession way from Rome of the
magistrates and Senate of the Roman Republic, as they travel the Via
Triumphalis to spend the night of the *feriae Latinae* at Alba in the
holiest and hoariest of state sacrifices, to Jupiter Latiaris on the Alban
Mount.[117] Julius' Olympian speech from his epic vantage-point will
take further his sacrilegious translation *into* Jupiter Tonans of Rome.[118]
Finally, the walls of Rome become in prospect 'Caesar''s – not Virgil's
altae but Lucan's *suae*. BC tears up the world of Rome, all Latin culture, 'Everything'.

This *aduentus* to Rome will see Caesar brush aside the *res publica*,
in the guise of its tribune *Metellus*, who would defend the 'Saturnian
temple' (treasury/Golden Age), but has his most aristocratic of names
(chapter 4) sonically ejected from Lucan's text / Rome's imperial
future (3.114f., ... *Metellus* | ... *reuelli* |, and as written Caesar lapses
into writing Caesar's insufferable third person of himself (chapter 2),
139f., '... *Metelli* |, ... *tolli* |'). Ever since Caesar's usurpation, 'the
majesty of the Romans in the time of the empire was wholly in that
house: *omnia Caesar erat*'.[119]

'*Caesar*' = 'Everything'. 'He wants to *be* power, he *is* power.'[120] Re-
jigs the force of 'every Latin word': *tunc omne Latinum* | *fabula nomen
erit* ... , under the Caesars, the 'names' of 'all that once comprised the
Roman state in its widest definition, will be just a string of empty
nouns' (7.391). 'The whole Latin league' (*omne nomen Latinum*, Livy

---

[117] Cf. 5.400–2 (this held up Caesar's *cursus* for ... 3 verses, v. 403) and Caes. *BC* 3.2.
See too 7.395f.

[118] *procul iam conspicit* hands Caesar divinely powerful lenses, cf. Virg. *Aen.* 12.134, *At
Iuno ex summo* (*qui nunc Albanus habetur* | ... *monti*) | *prospiciens tumulo* ... *sic est
adfata*: .... Cf. Caesar's prayers at the Rubicon, *o magnae qui moenia prospicis urbis* |
Tarpeia de rupe Tonans ... *et residens celsa Latiaris Iuppiter Alba* | ... *summique o
numinis instar* | *Roma* ('O you who look out to the walls of great Rome from the Tar-
peian crag, Thunderer ... and Jupiter of Latium reclining on sublime Alba ... and
you, too, image of the highest godhead, Rome', 1.195–200). On Latiaris and Tonans
in the Julio-Claudian armature, cf. Feeney (1991) 292f.

[119] Dryden (1970) 261, citing 3.108. Caesar is the epic 'superlative one' who subsumes
'the many' into his 'totality', cf. Ov. *Trist.* 4.4.15, *res est publica Caesar*, Hardie (1993)
7f., (1993A).

[120] Johnson (1987) 74; cf. Ahl (1976) 198, 'energy incarnate'.

1.38.4) will be just a fringe of 'ghost-towns'. The big prize of Virgil's Italian Juno is unmade, de-memorialized as ideological construct (*ne uetus indigenas nomen mutare Latinos* | ... *iubeas, Aen.* 12.823f.). 'The Republic is but folklore.' 'The map of Latium is blanked out.'[121] *BC* stakes its claim to be the moment when fighting for Rome transformed Everything. Watch the Senate become a curio in a gilt flash: | *Curio Caesarei cecidit pars magna senatus* | (5.40). 'Caesar's Curio' – *Scribonius* Curio, killed in the massacre in Africa (chapter 4), whose 'name recalls the *sacerdos curio sacris faciundis*, the priestly *curio* in charge of sacrifices'[122] – 'has fallen'. And, with him, 80%, 4 letters of 5, of what he converted from the 'Greatness of the (pre-)Pompeian *curi-a* into the decadence of the Caesarian Senate |'.

The Senate meets and means for the last time, in 5.1f., halfway through your text, already decentred to 'Emathian' Epirus, to usher in the decease of Roman time. Rome's last consuls formally convoke the venerable order of 'fathers', the last meeting of its last year of existence, as the moment comes to 'give new names to the calendar' (v. 5) and Lentulus 'puts the last motion' (*consulite in medium, patres,* v. 46). These fathers must (i) decide *nos esse senatum* (v. 22, 'we are the Senate'); (ii) order ᵐ/ᴍ*agnum* ... | *esse ducem* (vv. 46f., 'their appointee-leader to be great', 'Pompey the Great to be their leader').[123] For the last time, 'Greatness' is in the gift of the Senate? No, already there are already *curia* ... *illa* and its *patres* back in Rome (vv. 32f.); the Senate minus its curules has already sat in the *curia* (3.107f.); and when the dictator 'makes the calendar blessed with himself for consul' (5.384), the end of 'every Latin word' will have been projected onto/into imperial time. Indeed that projection is to *be* imperial time, the invention of a new order of signification and power-structure: 'All words, all the words you and I lie with to our owners through so *great* an age now, this time first invented' (vv. 385f., *omnes uoces per quas iam tempore tanto* | *mentimur dominis haec primum repperit aetas* |). Like the year of Pharsalus, every year from 48 onwards will be

---

[121] Lucan goes on to revise Virgil's mantic catalogue: | *hi tibi Nomentum* ... | *hi* ... | *haec tum nomina erunt, nunc sunt sine nomine terrae* | (*Aen.* 6.773–6); cf. Ov. *Fast.* 4.905f., *Nomento,* vv. 937–42, | *tum mihi* ... *ait* | ... *nil nisi nomen habet* |, Feeney (1986) 7f.; note also *Collatinas* ... *arces,* Virg. *Aen.* 7.774. Cf. Ahl (1985) 308f., (1976) 215f.

[122] Ahl (1976) 113.

[123] So Feeney (1986A) 240.

named *Caesare consule* (5.387–92), unless (a) Caesar farms out the date, that *nomen inane*.

So Lucan's poem freezes the death of Republican meaning: *usque ad Thessaliam Romana et publica signa* (7.164, 'Before Lucan, (en)signs spelled *populus Romanus*'). In the 'Emathian fields' of Pharsalus (v. 152, *Thessala rura*), 'Roman standards bowed their bearer's head, much *more* heavy *than* ever before, only just torn up from the ground and soaking him with tears, depressing his life' (vv. 161f., *uixque reuolsa solo maiori pondere pressum | signiferi mersere caput rorantia fletu*). 'The signs that spelled *SPQR* until *BC* 7.164 grounded the signifier fast in the *greatness* of their dead weight – signs out to drown their signifier in an engulfing flood of its own ocean of Wonderland tears.' The fatted bull of Lucan's massive epic 'shattered the altar, took flight, dashed for Emathian fields headlong' (7.165f., *discussa fugit ab ara | taurus et Emathios praeceps se iecit in agros |*). It played the Pompey (*fugit*) and staged the Caesar (*praeceps*), then 'vanished, beyond imaginative reach' (v. 167, 'and no victim was found for the death rites'). In a sense, the poem disappeared at 7.167, as it does at Pharsalia, and at those other deaths of the text through to 10.546. The measureless, Borgesian, moment when the Republic died, when the possibility of memorializing its epitaph was denied by the very circumstance of its death.[124]

Where the epic holds to the register of *bella, pila, triumphos,* and the rest (1.1–12), the world as Arms-and-Man, you must amplify the imperialism within these signs, these Western standards, until they interpellate you in your civic subjectivity. *BC* subjects you to this interrogation: *Quis furor, o ciues, quae tanta licentia ferri? |* (1.8, 'Citizens, all who participate in and are comprehended by Latin culture and Roman civilization, feel this madness, the anarchy, the killing, the *greatness*.'). Lucan uses the voice of Virgil's doomed *uates*, ardent Laocoön of Troy. Oedipally doomed to take his family-future pair of sons down with him, civically doomed to unmake his polity into Julian Rome, his every patriotic effort only made his undoing more certain: *o miseri, quae tanta insania, ciues? | (Aen.* 2.42, 'My home town, figure of epical pathos and

---

[124] Borges (1970) 118f., 'The Secret Miracle': Jaromir Hladik finds 'the physical universe came to a halt' as *inter alia* he 'repeated (without moving his lips) Virgil's mysterious fourth *Eclogue*' and managed to finish the play he was stuck on, in that instant when the squad fired. Now –

pity; your sublime dementia past human intelligibility'). This is no Homer/Virgil appeal to the Muse, but horror of the inconceivable[125] and programmatic collapse of reader into character into text. No one stays out of this story, you all fight each other, your brothers, your selves at Pharsalia, as Pompey forces you to recognize: *Quis furor, o caeci, scelerum? ciuilia bella* ... | (7.95, 'You can't see, can you?, crazy for madness, wickedness on wickedness? *Lucan* | ...').

BC fulfils the curse of Dido; terms of Juno; menace of Jugurtha; appeases Hannibal; Gauls, Cimbri and Marius; badmouths its own topics from Thessaly today to Crastinus ...[126] It is made from 'allusività antifrastica'.[127] In this poetic, Pompey, the resisting, delaying, yielding, deferring object of the narrative quest for satisfaction, plays a Virgilian Aeneas in reverse, driven like him, but Eastwards.[128] Never to be re-fashioned into the subject, the agent whose decisions weld the epic action around him. But to end a decapitated Priam at the end of the Roman World.[129] '*Magnus*' operates as if it were a 'noun' and a 'name' (*nomen*) throughout the text. But it names a 'fame', a 'greatness', throughout, and cues the question of *BC*'s epic greatness.[130] If Pompeius and Caesar fought a war, then it was a struggle for this name *Magnus*: *si meruit tam claro nomine Magnus* | *Caesaris esse nefas, tanti, Ptolemaee, ruinam* | *nominis haud metuis* ... (8.549–51, 'If it was the lucidity of his name Magnus that made him worth Caesar's dreadfulness, aren't you, Ptolemy, afraid of the fall-out from so great a name's crash ?').

---

[125] Hershkowitz (1995) 201f. explores also Ascanius' belated attempt to intervene in civic self-destruction: *quis furor iste nouus? quo nunc, quo tenditis?* ... | *heu miserae ciues?* (*Aen.* 5.670f.).

[126] Virg. *Aen.* 4.624f., cf. Ahl (1976) 187f., *Aen.* 7.317, *hac gener atque socer coeant mercede suorum:* | *sanguine Troiano et Rutulo*, cf. Narducci (1985) 1543; Sall. *BJ* 35.10, cf. Ahl ibid. 89f.; 4.788f., cf. Ahl ibid. 216f.; Ahl ibid. 105f.; Seitz (1965) 216f.; 7.395f.

[127] See Narducci (1979, 1985), Bramble (1982) 543, Ahl (1976) 64f., 115f. Lausberg (1985) esp. 1616f. rightly declares that counter-imitation of the base-texts Homer–Virgil needs no *verbal* citation. So –

[128] E.g. 2.730f.: Virg. *Aen.* 2.707f., 3.4ff. esp. 7 : Virg. *Aen.* 3.522f. In the Adriatic storm (5.560–677), you see 'Caesar's power ... is just as great as the power of a storm; in fact, it *is* the power of a storm' (Hershkowitz (1995) 230 – blowing East.

[129] Narducci (1973), (1985) 1545f.

[130] Feeney (1986A). E.g. Brennan (1969) 104 on 8.717, | *infaustus Magni fuerat comes* ~ Virg. *Aen.* 6.166, | *Hectoris hic magni fuerat comes*; cf. 7.379, *ᵐ/ᴍagnus, nisi uincitis, exul*.

'One's name was often a military object of great value.'[131] Pompeius fought Caesar to make his 'name' mean, what *'Caesar'* is to mean – namely the sky, κράτος, the lot: *Romanum n-o-m-e-n et o-m-n-e | imperium Magno tumuli est modus* (8.798f., 'What makes Rome Rome, the wholly Roman Empire, every word of Latin, is the limit of Pompey's grave, is the way to bury Pompey'). Caesar hunts down *Magnus*, to make of it a dead 'name' (9.2, *tantam ... umbram*). But Pompey was defeated and predeceased, a 'shade' and the 'insubstantiality' of a mere shadowy 'name', from the start: *stat magni nominis umbra* (1.135, 'He stands, but the shadow of a great name, of the name *Magnus*'). *BC* targets the *Aeneid*'s last word, *umbras*: with Pompey exits *a* Rome, the one which spells *Libertas*: *Roma, tuumque | nomen, Libertas, et inanem ... umbram* (2.302f., 'Rome and your name, Freedom, a shadow without a body'). *'Greatness'* belongs to the 'shades', for they are *maiores*, the dead Republican *mos*: against their praises, Cato downgrades *Magnus*, as *multum maioribus impar* (9.190, 'greatly inferior to the past'); in their place, Lucan would have liked – but for history – to put the *magna ... fama* and *tantum ... nomen* of Cato (9.593–7).

But there is no competing with Caesarsuccess seizure. Lucan arranges around Caesar a world already empty of significant opposition: from Virgil's contagious phrases *paribus ... telis* and *paribus ... in armis*, the full-blown delirium of *BC*, where both sides face themselves and – snap – they *are* each other, those *pares ... aquilas* (1.7, 'twin eagles'), those *tot similes fratrum gladios patrumque* (7.453, 'rows of identical blades – brothers', fathers'').[132] Incorrigibly, literally 'one-sided':[133] 'you win, you lose' screwed into 'Caesar chops, you crash'. If ever it appears that there are rivals, *pares*, 'a pair of matched contenders', struggling 'not to be equal' (1.125f., *nec priorem ... | ... parem*), nevertheless it was always 'no contest' (1.129, *nec coiere pares*). For all that the narrative may toy with relapse into the sense of a 'fair' fight (e.g. 5.3, *seruauit Fortuna pares*) as if bespeaking a gladiatorial duel (e.g. 6.3, *parque suum uidere dei*, cf. 4.708f.), the terms have always

---

131 Turney-High (1949) 204.
132 Virg. *Georg.* 1.489; *Aen.* 6.826; Jal (1963) 416.
133 See Bramble (1982) 551f., Due (1962) 112, Ahl (1976) 145. Dickinson (1975) 15 – written *c.* 1858, first published in 1945, sums it down: 'We lose – because we win'. She –

imploded, since 'under normal circumstances ...' gladiatorial *paria* 'were equipped with different weapons; they were often of different nationalities'.[134]

The charge into bi-polar formulae[135] which seeks to preserve against the very logic of civil 'war' the necessary oppositionality for an intelligible ant/agonism, con/flict and its narration is crushed into one decisive process of deathstiny. The 'defeat' of Vulteius and the 'victory' of Pharsalus are all the same, there is just Caesar, *C-ae-s-a-r* and his metaplasms, *c-a-d-o*, *c-a-d-auer* / *c-ae-d-o*; *BC* turning over and over the figure at the level of the epic 'Man' of the 'walled city' 's uncreation – the *ruina* ('crash') of the 'corpse' – as itself the principal 'Arms' of the 'Imperial Mission'. In sullen death, 'the dead deal out death' (2.205f., *peraguntque cadauera partem* | *caedis*), 'the hordes of the dead ... are so great a heap that after the slaughter they can hardly fall' (2.201–4).[136] You have already seen the paroxysms of Scaeva's seizure, when 'he took a stand on the crashing' (*ruenti*) 'siege-wall and first rolled out corpses' (*cadauera*) 'from the loaded towers, crushed' (*obruit*) 'the advancing enemy with bodies; all the crashed debris' (*ruinae*) 'armed the Man' (6.169–72); and 'the corpses' – far from falling/crashing – 'move wall and ground together as the heap grows' (vv. 180f.).[137] *C-ae-s-a-r/c-ae-d-o* mash Rome into monology.

> both read the same bible and pray to the same god,
> and each invokes his aid against the other.[138]

---

[134] Ahl (1976) 88, cf. 84f.; cf. Barton (1993) 36–9, 'The arena of civil discord', Plass (1995), *passim*.

[135] Scarry (1985) 340 n. 65, with a Lincoln anecdote to the point: L. 'writhed at a phrase in Meade's general orders about "driving the invader from our soil". "Will our generals," he exclaimed in private, "never get that idea out of their heads? The whole country is our soil."' Try: The whole planet is your –

[136] 2.203, *caede peracta*: cf. vv. 210f., *cadauera ... cecidere*; 134f., *cecidere cadauera ... cateruas*; 150f., *ceruix caesa ... cederet ... ceciderunt*; 169–72, *caesi ... cadauera ... ceruice recisum*; 178–81, *in corpore caeso ... cecidere manus*; 192, *caedes*; 197, *concidit*; cf. Hübner (1975) 210 n. 66, Narducci (1985) 1551 n. 16.

[137] Cf. vv. 151–63, *Caesaris ... cadauera ... Caesaris ... cadam ... ruinae ... Caesaris*; 199–206, *obruat ... stat ... in quem cadat eligit hostem*; cf. 4.787, *stetit omne cadauer* |; 6.755–7, *cadauer ... terraque repulsum est* | *erectumque semel*; 6.822f., *cadauer* | *ut cadat*. More in Hübner (1972) 596. And yet more in Hübner (1975) 210.

[138] Lincoln's 'Second inaugural address', in Pratt (1952) 375.

5 THE WALL OF WORDS

a world war can be won
you want me to believe.[139]

One-World War, then: *certatum totis concussi uiribus orbis* ('struggle:
all the world's forces in fits', 1.5). *Ubi non ciuilia bella?* ('Lucan's
universal poem', 10.410). *Toto simul utimur orbe* ('Hands around the
Earth', 7.362). *Omnia Caesar* |, ... *orbem* | ('Everything–Caesar–
World', 3.296f.). The structured process of war – duality leading
through binarism to self-cancellation and the unitary, made real by the
aggregate of corpses whose memorialization validates the structure[140] –
caves in before the concussion of civil war. Those hills and rivers
swamped, road and marsh merged, the river and the plain and the
wall and the ground undifferentiated in the piles of bodies, referentiality spilled in the heap. Rivers or blood ∼ rivers of blood: which?
Undulating hills and valleys, or are they heaps of corpses and the
subsidence of putrescence (7.789f.)? The grounding differences of
Roman thinking turn turtle: Greek ∼ Roman, obliterated, for example
at Massilia – where the war may have seemed *un*civil – in unsightly
mutilation;[141] inside ∼ outside; self ∼ other; magistrates ∼ generals;
citizens ∼ soldiers; *Urbs* ∼ *Orbis*; *castra* ∼ *campi*.[142] Imperial space
annuls distance: Pompeian *fuga* finds those walls of Rome deconstructed, both besieger and besieged caught in a co-operative duet but
also storming/defending a wall which has only one side.[143] Lucan's
lines are down, Rubicon fails to mark off Italy from the provinces, lus-
tral *amburbium* cannot strengthen the *pomerium* (sacred perimeter of
Rome) between city and Italy as Rome flees from the protection of the
walls.[144]

Caesar's *BC* narrates the impersonal efficiencies and wooden complexities of siegework improvisation in deflection of the brutalities
of civil war (chapter 2), but Lucan strips, fells and hacks truncated
bodies, makes of this imagery both the dehumanized Caesar/Scaeva-
wall and the defaced victim/trophy Pompeius. 'Since military history is

---

[139] Dylan (l963), 'Masters of war'.   [140] Scarry (1985) esp. 115f.
[141] 3.758f., cf. Rowland (1969) 208.   [142] Cf. Brisson (1969) 12, Scarry (1985) 88.
[143] Saylor (1978), Newmyer (1983) 237f.
[144] On the *amburbium* at 1.593f., see Rambaud (1985) esp. 289f.

primarily concerned with the claiming of space by force',[145] read *BC* as a black hole swallowing the coordinates of sense, *ubi solus apertis | obsedit muris calcantem moenia Magnum* (10.545f., the *finis*). Here Caesar/Scaeva 'opens the walls', i.e. 'the siegeworks', and 'besieges Pompey who is stamping down the walls', i.e. 'the siegeworks'; the *muris* and the *moenia* combine opposed reference to the same constructions and opposing reference to the opposing constructions and counter-constructions, the walls within walls of the Caesarian and Pompeian engineers. The conceptual labyrinth of a one-man siege; a one-man siege taking over from the breached siege by Caesar's army; a siege prosecuted against Pompey after Pompey's defences were already breached; a siege prosecuted after the besieging walls of Caesar had been breached by Pompey; a siege prosecuted when the besieged already stands contemptuously upon (not just his own defences but also) the besieging works. The syntactical (counter-)construction of *apertis | obsedit muris*, where within the absoluteness of the ablative there insists the instrumental sense, 'besieged *with* open walls', oxymoronically figuring in Scaeva 'walls which don't work the way walls do, protections that are unprotected, closures that aren't closed . . .' All to show Caesar encircling and slaughtering a numerically superior with an inferior army, from Hannibal's Cannae to Schwarzkopf's Desert Storm.

No limit. Everywhere, then, is Rome: Brundisium or Massilia; Ilerda or the *castra Cornelia*; Dyrrhachium or Alexandria. For the centre, the narrative focus of the epic of civil war, is a *political* construct, the construction of a political contestation: for Pharsalia, *hic Roma perit* ('Here dies Rome', 7.634); for Pompey, Lesbos, *hic mihi Roma fuit* ('Here was my R-o-m-a', 8.133, the island harbouring Cornelia, so his *a-m-o-r*); for Caesar, Troy, *Romanaque Pergama surgent* ('Rome's re-birth, Asiatic', 9.999).[146] Rome is 'movable', whether as in Roman legend in the form of the Italian threat of the Samnite Telesinus to shift the 'capital'; or as the quibbles locating the city with Camillus in Veii not on the Gaul-occupied Capitol; or in Greek lore, as with the shift of free Phocaea to become Massilia, and resist Caesar, not flee the Persians; or in the form of Delphic assistance to 'whole city shifts, like Tyre's'.[147]

[145] Davis (1985) 56.

[146] Ahl (1976) 76f.; Rowland (1969) 205f.; Saylor (1982) 173; Saylor (1978) 253f.; Ahl ibid. 209f.; Jal (1963) 156, Ahl ibid. 177f., comparing *Aen.* 4.347f.

[147] 2.136–8, cf. Vell. 2.27.1; 5.27–9, *illic Roma fuit*, Livy 5.19f.; 3.340, *post . . . translatas . . . Phocidos arces*; 5.107f., *totas mutantibus urbes, | ut Tyriis*.

On one side, *BC* destroys any fixed 'Emathian' centrality which might attach to Delphic 'omphallibility', the principle that the word is whole, the language tied to the navel of a culture, with the inevitable price that its operators validate its mantic riddling by misreading (5.73f.). Book V indeed makes of this destruction of the order of truth the centre of the poem, as Appius ends by the Euripus maelstrom at launchpad Aulis (vv. 234-6). The Pythia is forced by him to select his little deathstiny from her memorious totality, that 'pile': 'Every age assembled: one, congested, heap' (vv. 175-8, *uenit aetas omnis in unam | congeriem*).

On the other side, that same central Book V decries the traditional antithesis which had constituted the focal immobility of the *Urbs* out of the dissemination of power from *curia* to *Orbis*. The waves of *SPQR signa* that had built, and shifted ever outwards, the absent presence of *Roma*. Those ephemeral lines of the *castra*. Now mixed up with the curia in that last Republican senate in Epirus – 'Who would call "*castra*" this army of axes bared by right, all these *fasces*?' (5.12f.). Lucan even displaces silenced Delphi as primal, originary, source of Truth – to his privatized 'Emathian voice', Thessaly's night-witch Erichtho (6.425).[148] *BC* would like to supplant Apollo further with Alexander's Sahara oracle of Jupiter Ammon, astronomically sited omphallibility, 'where the ring of the Solstice on high, the tropic of Cancer, smashes home through the World of Signs, bisects the Zodiac' (9.531f.). Here Cato 'should' be vindicated as the central *oraculum*, his *pectus* (heart and soul) the infallible truth of *uirtus*, his life a narrative journey toward this transcendence of 'Rome' through Latin philosophy. Once he stops being Lucan–Cato.[149]

But Caesar's dizzying spin around the globe (1.683-94) binds the world with his *nomen* from Spain to Egypt, catching up the centrality of *Roma* into the wake of his own transcendence: *BC* is monitored by the ultimate displacement of omphallibility to Caesar – to Nero as Lucan's *numen*, in refusal of Delphic Apollo (1.63-6). *Bella per Emathios ...* (1.1) – in Virgil's phrase, *tot bella per orbem* (*Georgics* 1.505). War had

---

[148] *More than* a witch, 'she lives in nightmares only ...–, an image of malignant power, a permanent enemy of the bases of social existence', Gordon (1987), O'Higgins (1988), Masters (1992) 91-149, 179-215.

[149] Cf. Viarre (1982) esp. 105f. on Cato's barred journey to Virtue; Ahl (1976) 261f., George (1991).

once provided the coordinates of Rome, military narrative had made
names in Latin, and empire had ridden on the back of the legions,
'through' the conquest of the Greek World toward the figuring of these
'conquests through the Greek' medium of epic poetry. *BC* makes of its
names a world of words where *bella* fail to signify 'conquests', where
the onward drive of the narrative – that *per* – takes you through its
series of *campos* |, but occupies only the *Campus Martius* interminably
mapped across the world: once you have read Caesar through I–IV as
the Hannibal curse homing in on Rome, you are ready to launch
out East for Caesarian *Blitzkrieg* in the wake of Great 'Emathian'
Alexander. From Emathian Macedon, Epirus, Thessaly, shift from
Pharsalus to Pharos, on to Emathian Alexandria.

As we saw in chapter 4, Lucan read Pollio and Horace – and found
BC spelled out in four cantatory lines of Virgilian multiple-vision:

> ergo inter sese paribus concurrere telis
> Romanas acies iterum uidere Philippi;   490
> nec fuit indignum superis bis sanguine nostro
> Emathiam et latos Haemi pinguescere campos.   (*Georg.* 1.489–92)

> *So Philippi saw again Roman armies*
> *clash together matching missiles.*   490
> *With God on our side, Emathian battlefields stretching out*
> *beneath Mt Haemus rich, twice, in our blood compost.*

Lucan's response is *more than* audible:

> quae seges infecta surget non decolor herba?
> quo non Romanos uiolabis uomere manes?
> ante nouae uenient acies, scelerique secundo
> praestabis nondum siccos hoc sanguine campos.   (7.851–4)

> *No grain will rise unblighted in the blade, free from rust.*
> *No plough-share will miss desecrating Roman dead.*
> *First, fresh formations will rendez-vous; for crime #2*
>   *against humanity*
> *Thessaly will lend, still drying from Pharsalus, Emathian plains.*

Lucan 'anticipates' Virgil's 'secondary' pietism, deploring Philippi
in advance, as the *Georgics* deplored Pharsalia in retrospect. Lucan's
Pharsalus book ends with *his* blighted prayer, aborted in the utterance:
'Why do you gods condemn the whole planet, so acquitting it? | The
disaster in the West, the sea of Pachynus' grief, Mutina, Leucas – they

have absolved *Ph...ilippi. //'* (vv. 870–2). He sees Munda in 45, the *Bellum Siculum* against Sex. Pompeius in 38–6, Antony's fighting in 43, Actium in 31, *totum ... orbem*, as the one battle: Pharsalia/Philippi.[150] In *BC*, *'Phil-ippi'* must raise the spectre of lines of Emathian 'Alexanders' watching ghoulishly their repetition and revenge in the Caesars. *Philippi* records its foundation as city in the prototypical world of Emathian conquest by the second Philip of Macedon, by *'Philip'*, name of dukes and princes, a(n aristocratic and Greek) name for κρά-τος whose proliferation grew it to 'greatness'. Consider Q. Marcius Philippus' dealings with Perseus, son of Antigonid Philip V and last King of Macedon; L. Marcius Philippus stepfather of Octavian Caesar; the first-century Seleucid Philips I and II; the Herodian Philip; and, inevitably, the third-century CE 'Philip the Arab': *Imp. Caesar M. Iulius Philippus Augustus*. From Attic to Roman failure, φιλιππισμός to Cicero's Antonian *Philippics*, that *per* ... No, the blood of Actium grew the *Georgics*; but history circled on.

Lucan privileges the name *Emathios ... campos* | (1.1 to 10.545). But Caesar's arena coagulates in words of blood, as in the Virgilian mountain of gore – *latosque Haemi sub rupe Philippos* | (*BC* 1.680) – and clots into 'Emathian' Thessaly, as *Haemonia*.[151] The 'Emathian' remains the core of Lucan's textual reactor, the signifier which grounds the Caesar quest for mastery. In the modelling of *BC* over against Roman *bella* overrunning the Greek world and the world of Greek; over against the Macedonian Alexander's monarchic 'greatness'; over against the imposition of Alexandria upon the 'anti-World' of Phar...aonic Egypt. In the subsumption of Epirus, Macedonia, Thessaly into one 'Greece' as hysterical site of all-Roman 'war'. Pharsalus as 'Emathian' principle of the collapse in totalizing world war of escape via displacement, evasion through distance, narrative *per* difference. And within the word, the epic*t*het 'Emathian' catches up the 'pulverization' of *BC*: the ruination of ruination; the *puluis* of battle and of duststorm; the *harena* of shore, coast, desert and amphitheatre; the *cinis* of the uncreated City; ashes for cremation-confetti; ritual dust for unburial; the unfathomability of *Ammon*; the breakdown of One, Stoic, World of inspired

---

[150] Cf. Ahl (1976) 280f., 324f.
[151] Haemus/αἷμα, e.g. Apollod. 1.6.3, cf. Mayer (1986) 49; *Haemoni-*: 6.394, 442, 480, 486, 694, 765; *Haemonid-*, vv. 436, 589, *Haemus*, v. 575; cf. ibid. 49f. For Lucan's *sangre y arena*, cf. Ahl (1976) 99.

matter in collision and collusion between the elements.[152] (The) Earth is decomposed and mushed into the Lucanian broth: Tiber plain, Ilerda, *via Appia* and all.[153]

Lucan's amplification of the military to the cosmic order disorients citizen-readers, making Caesar's victims more 'Antaeuses', uprooted from Rome, Sweet Rome, losing themselves, their heritage, as they lose their territoriality, get out of 'touch' with their land, eternally alienated from their language, discourse and culture.[154] Round Pompey imaged as tottering oak-tree *truncus*[155] crowd the array of tropes for the mutilated victim world, struck by the Caesar bolt of lightning, 'paradigm of the immune, inanimate, inhuman', the indifferent, the irresponsible, the 'unpunishable', the 'unreconstructable' – ' "stupidity" ... as a descriptive term for the "nonsentience" or "the lack of sentient awareness", or most precisely, the "inability to sense the sentience of other persons" that is incontestably present in the act of hurting another person'.[156] The congested crush of *BC*, the collapse in word and world,[157] robs 'war' of its necessary externality, its necessary separateness, and compresses it into a monstrous global mutation of its Other, namely the pain of torture:

> Its sheer aversiveness, negation; the double sense of agency; the sufferer, dominated by a sense of internal agency, feels not the knife, nail or pin but one's own body, one's own body hurting one, annihilated, by inside and outside alike; an almost obscene conflation of private

---

[152] Emathian sand: Strabo 8.3.14. Why Homer called Pylos ἠμαθόεντα, cf. Schol. Hom. *Il.* 9.382. Cf. Mayer (1986) 49 (coyly), 'No Hellenistic poet ... would let the word gather dust'; 9.969, *etiam periere ruinae* |; *puluis*: framing 'Scaeva', 6.162, 247; duststorm: 9.485–7, *harenae ... pulueris*; desert: 9.394–5, *harenas ... puluere*; amphitheatre: 4.708, *fatalis harenae*; 9.990, *di cinerum*; ashes: 2.334, 336; 'dust' for Pompey's *pompa*: 8.730, 733, 774, *cineres ... harenas*; Ammon/ἄμμος: 9.523, 525, 527, *puluere* |, *Hammon* |, *harenas*; zoom from particle to cosmos and back, the *continuum* in Lucan and Seneca: Ahl (1976) 283f. Cf. Bartsch (1997) chapter 1 on *BC* as 'boundary *crossing*'.

[153] Add Monoecus' tidal shore, 1.408–11; cf. Isthmos and cataclysm, 1.101, Newmyer (1983) 249.

[154] Saylor (1982); on 'losing touch', cf. Narducci (1985) 1552.

[155] 1.136–43. Cf. Caesar as Erysichthon at Massilia, Phillips (1968), and Ammon's *nemus*, 9.522f. On Pompey's *Eichengleichnis*, cf. Rosner-Siegel (1983), Miura (1981) 211f., Newmyer (1983) 228f., Ahl (1976) 156f. and n. 18, Narducci (1985) 1553f.

[156] Scarry (1985) 294. On Caesar's *Blitzgleichnis*, 1.151–7, cf. Rosner-Siegel (1983), Miura (1981) 213f., Newmyer (1983) 229f., 249f., Ahl (1976) 198f.

[157] Buzzwords in Lucan include *calco, coeo, concurro, densus, non uaco*.

and public; its ability to destroy language, the power of verbal objectification; its obliteration of the contents of consciousness; its totality.
Pain begins by being 'not oneself' and ends by having eliminated all
that is 'not itself'; terrifying for its narrowness, it nevertheless
exhausts and displaces all else until it seems to become the single
broad and omnipresent fact of existence; one of its most frightening
aspects is its resistance to objectification; real to the sufferer, it is
unreal to others; this is magnified in torture because instead of the
person's pain being subjectively real but unobjectified and invisible to
others, it is now hugely objectified, everywhere visible, as incontestably present in the external as in the internal world, and yet it is
simultaneously categorically denied; torture aspires to the totality of
pain.[158]

And *you* are Lucan–Caesar. Auto-crat, the self as master. The individual subject who would position what is good in relation to himself as
the selfsame, to him as centre and horizon: *toto iam liber in orbe solus
Caesar erit* (2.280, 'Caesar, sole free agent in the whole world: the
future tense'). You must read of Caesar monomania, from Monoecus
in decisive invasion to Scaeva, solo agent forever at Caesar's back, to
the end.[159]

> your gaze scans the streets as if they were written pages:
> the city says everything you must think,
> makes you repeat her discourse,
> and while you believe you are visiting Tarnara
> you are only recording the names with which she defines herself
> and all her parts.[160]

> *each line is a fresh corpse*
> ...
> *each word is another bruise.*[161]

---

[158] Condensed from Scarry (1985) 61, 52–6, 55.
[159] 1.407, *solus sua litora ... Monoeci*, from Virg. *Aen.* 6.830, *socer ... arce Monoeci |
descendens*; Scaeva *solus*: 10.545 ∼ 6.205, 249. Cf. Ahl (1976) 200, 'Caesar a-l-o-n-e is
fighting for h-i-m s-e-l-f.'
[160] Calvino (1979) 15, 'Cities and Signs 1'.
[161] Manhire (1985) 'On originality', 24f.

6   Statius' *Thebaid*: form (p)re-made

numquamne priorum
haerebunt documenta nouis?[1]

BERLIN WIRD MAUERFREI
Die Mauer ist in euern Köpfen.[2]

We know it, he didn't. Lucan was really a Flavian writer who died before his time. Around five years his junior, Statius was closer to his age than Domitian was to elder brother Titus, Nero's classmate. The other side of the civil wars of 69 CE, Rome's second dynasty began with the twin assets of Vespasian's already mature or maturing sons, walking security for the success of succession.[3] Yet when the epic that Statius began on the apotheosis of Vespasian in 79 CE was completed, twelve years later (a book a year, he claims, 12.811), it was just five years before the assassination, in an enigmatic palace knifing, of Domitian and the decease of the greatest poet of his court, Statius (in 96 CE). The dynasty folded in on itself, two generations of Flavii compressed into one of Rome; another Nero – *posthumously* mocked as 'Nero minus the hair'[4] – expired without issue, and only the women of the family left to mourn their passing. We know it, Statius could but guess.[5]

We find Statius turning for his dazzling mythological epic to the canonized unreality of an age-old saga of fratricidal civil war. The sons of Oedipus were cursed by their father to fight *between themselves* for Thebes. The horrors of partisan conflict, where all valour is atrocity, family are the foe, and winning is losing, stir portrayal in a massive over-kill of effect, as doomed to self-incriminating absurdity as it is to

---

[1] 'When will we ever learn?', 11.656f.
[2] 1988 graffito and scholion on the Berlin Wall, Waldenburg (1990) 67: 'Berlin's now wall free – The wall is in our heads.' Swinburne *cit. OED s.v. Thebes*: 'Thebes, by the way, was Dryden's irreverent name for Cambridge.'
[3] No Julio-Claudian emperor had had his own son or sons succeed.
[4] *Pace* Braund (1996) on Juv. 4.38.
[5] See Dominik (1994) 130–80, for all-out 'Political relevance to contemporary Rome'.

rending plangency. *Thebaid* outplays Virgil's (unfinalized) *Aeneid* I–XII by shifting sights still further from Roman civil wars, CE *or* BCE, from whichever Caesar (Augustus), by moving to the generation before Homer's Troy. But rounds off twelve post-Virgilian books of glittering Latin with a devastating accumulation of frames that bring the project right back home, with Ovidian-style *Prologue* and *Epilogue*. The last great 'mythological' epic, Ovid's (always under revision) *Metamorphoses* had, in taking the topic of universal change since time began, found itself including its own belittled version of the *Aeneid*, and found its ending in the apotheosis of Julius Caesar, with reflections on his own, and Augustus', anticipated ascensions appended. As we noticed from the other side of the divide (chapter 5), Myth (whether Greek or Roman) transforms History into brain-fodder, setting the mind to think its own predicaments; just as history invites mythologization.

Statius' *Prologue* and *Epilogue* bring him close to *his* Caesar – Domitian, dedicatee and 'first reader': *Prologue* walks brashly in Lucan's footsteps; *Epilogue* tells the poem to dog Virgil's tracks. In his other career, Statius the Flavian Horace uses one of his lyrics to monitor his progress in epic, and so critique *Thebaid*, as in another he had read Lucan's epic in celebration (before his widow) of his undying poetic power – beyond the purchase of 'rabid tyrant' Nero (*Siluae* 4.7; 2.7.100, 119) – and so through empathy outlined (*mutatis mutandis*) a reception for his own *maius opus*. Here, then, Statius and Lucan are another Horace- and -Pollio dyad (chapter 4) – although this time the lyric poet also writes in the same genre as his respected elder 'brother'; in another sense, Statius is himself a condensation of Horace and Virgil, and further fuzzes the demarcation lines between epic and lyric;[6] and his writing acts out in its own divided belatedness the configuration of his royal clan, as they slide toward instant extinction. Statius could write with the presumption that he and his emperor might be read – as Virgil read Augustus? Lucan Julius? – not least as lyric Statius proposes to read *BC*, and, by co-implication, *Thebaid*.

Like its twin (chapter 5), this essay does not attempt to run through the poem (or run the poem through) – although a plot-summary will be provided, to show how inherently and infectiously contentious any Theban narrative must be. Our focus will be the division of the narration between the dazzling gloss of Statius' most *finished* of epic poems, and its anxious struggle to repress the grotesque surfeit of

---

[6] Cf. Brown (1994) 188–220 on the interpenetration of *Thebais* and *Siluae*.

damned violence bursting through all the textual relations involved in recounting a *Thebaid*.

We write this time in a precarious first person plural (not just for the double-U). And we shall use the symbol '/' – for 'Antithesis'[7] – to suggest a constant alternation/fissure in the voicing of *Thebaid*. Theban feud impacts the Latin between the polarized/convergent views of all the 'Eteocles' and 'Polynices' characters/interpreters/dummy-readers in the text, but also between warring textual forces, such as *uirtus*, the proper régime of martial epic, and *planctus*, its subsidence in / sublime / collapse of warfare into the killing fields of the fighting for Thebes.

/ No one wanted to. / But everybody once knew this tale, and what it was *for*. However conformist Statius may be in returning the epic to its ancient ways and means, modestly restoring Virgilian classicism after the follies of exiled Ovid and Lucan's performance as 'human bomb', / we will find this schizo/phrenic poetic of Oedipodonian frenzy diagrammed in our heads. Lasered there, indelible, through macabre oceans of narrative:

> alter(n)- / gemin-
>   patr-, gen- / fratr-, german-
>   tenebr-, / noct-
>   dir- / ir-, fur-
>   unc-, ungu- / scrut-, rim-, quaer-
>   ocul-, uid-, lumin-, luc- / plect-, nect-
>   matr-, par- / soror-
> ei mihi, heu, gem-, plang-, quer-, lament-, fle-, dol- / ( )

> Alternate, the Other's, amoebaean / double, twin, dual
>   father / brother
>   dark / blindness
>   curse / anger, mania
>   claw / rummage
>   violate sight-light / hug
>   mother / sister
> pain / [silence]

---

[7] Cf. Barthes (1975: i.e. *S/Z*) 27: 'The Antithesis is the battle between two plenitudes set ritually face to face like two fully armed warriors; the Antithesis is the figure of the given opposition, eternal, eternally recurrent: the figure of the inexpiable. Every passage through the wall of the Antithesis thus constitutes a transgression ... The narration is always contested.' (Cf. Leith and Myerson (1989) 160.)

/ Docile Neapolitan courtier Statius gears up Homeric-Virgilian machinery, into 'a cascade of absurdity'.[8] Expect miles of post-Homeric machinery: Olympian inserts, twin catalogues and teichoscopy, necromancy and underworld scenography, funeral games and *aristeiai*, prayer-sequences and prophecy, tragical included narrative and aetiological hymn, developed formal similes, battle-*Sturm und Drang*, mountain vastnesses tipping out torrential volumes of surging verse by the dozen, the whole works. Statius could fiddle while *Thebaid* burns.

In a word. Renovation / Enervation.

Thebaid is not just to be read between these alternative positions, / they do more than alternate through a reading. Mutually constitutive, binary/eristic, as any sons of Oedipus, they are out to alter the (/ our) 'I's.[9]

I GATEWAYS TO THEBES / INTO THE STATIAN

> And the walls came down
> All the way to hell
> Never saw where they were standing
> Never saw where they fell.[10]

/

We must want to get to the end as much as Aeneas did.[11]

We will / might / find the 'counter-reformatory' view, of Virgilian classicism resurgent, outlined by the poem in *Prologue* and multi-tiered *Epilogue*. We also find support in Statius' own self-portraiture in his collections of occasional lyrics, the *Siluae*.

Prologue Statius (1.1–45) offers a *recusatio*, his re-make of the poet's traditional 'apology' for his substitution of the work he can manage for the aspiration he can glimpse but not rise to realize.[12] We recognize the

---

[8] Vessey (1986) 3006. See Le Clair (1989) for our re-awakening to colossal composition; cf. Ahl (1989) 31.

[9] Dominik (1994) 135 n. 28, 'Henderson projects the so-called Harvard school/ European school views of Latin poetry ... upon Statius' epic through alternating voices of critical interpretation.' We may wonder if there might / not / be more to it.

[10] Lucky Wilbury on The travelling Wilburys (1988) 'Tweeter and the monkey man'.

[11] Gransden (1984) 3.

[12] See Schetter (1962) 204–17, Vessey (1973) 60–7, (1986) 2971–4.

decorum of an imperial subject's loyalty to Rome and its royals, when the poet proffers *arma ... | Aonia* (vv. 33f., 'the epic of poesy's Thebes') in place of what he marks as the goal deferred to the hope of his maturity, the real subject for epic, *Itala ... | signa* (vv. 17f., 'Roman standards: a patriot's Latinity'). *Thebaid* tells us it is but an earnest of what may one day be written of Rome's promised future, the dash of Domitian Caesar's campaigning toward a great imperial victory and its inscription in triumphant verse.

Thebaid's plan is to trim its aspirations, then, in a responsible fit of callow producer to product. *Pierius ... calor* (v. 3, 'Inspirational heat from Pieria, near-enough to Thebes') will orchestrate this score for a *chelys* (v. 33, 'The Greek word for tortoise, Greek noises to denote the lyre of art-writing and connote an aesthete's devotion to Graeco-Roman poetry'). As yet this poet's verses will not pretend to sing Rome with its Latinity. As yet he but brings the traditionally worthy but cul-turally non-pertinent saga of Thebes for a new lease of life within clas-sical art. *horrore canendus*, ends *Prologue*, promising to 'sing a horror-show' (v. 45) / and at once the poet's hand plunges his stylus into the guilty eyes of cursed Oedipus, to write | *iam merita ... dextra* (v. 46, 'with expert ... hand') of the post-Senecan horror of the King of Thebes' self-blinding (*scrutatus lumina*: see *Appendix*). / To exaggerate, / the narration will be this acid attack. / The poet knows that *Thebaid* is, for now, *satis* (v. 33, 'Enough'). The artist's 'Not yet'.[13]

Epilogue Statius will re-double the 'apology'. He breaks off his final scene, of post-bellum carnage, with *uidui ducunt ad corpora luctus* (12.796, 'The women home on the men, as ever: widowed wives cleave unto the dead bodies of their males; in processional grief, voice after voice oblating laments'). This poet moderates his transports by fixing the widows' pain as beyond his powers to narrate. He calls on epic's traditional *recusatio*-formula: the poet would need more than 'a hun-dred hearts' to do justice to this theme, more than a fresh shot of 'the Apolline' within his chemistry (vv. 797–808).

As it is, he speaks plainly and conclusively for himself, *mea iam longo*

---

[13] For evasive deferral, or 'sublation', with a *nondum* ('not yet'), cf. Virg. *Georg.* 3 *Proem*, Prop. 2.10, Calp. Sic. 1.1. So too *Theb.* 12.1, | *nondum cuncta*: 'Dear reader, we're nearly there, now. | A final book to cap all previous eleven.' Book XII will re-echo round our skulls, as we read past the narrative's final aposiopes –

meruit ratis aequore portum (v. 809, 'My craft has now run the long course of its ocean-text and earned its haven'). At this moment of apparently final release, reminiscent of the ending of Apollonius of Rhodes' *Argonautica*, where the Argonauts disembark back at Pagasae, Statius makes a further turn, toward his own heroine, '*Thebais*'. He tells his poem she is *multum uigilata* (v. 811, 'night after night of lucubration: the finished article'), i.e. she 'took lots of slog, growing up along with his wife' – this 'song from his lady of the night'![14] Initial reception at court and in Italy promises her a future, once the usual envy of the writer gives way to 'deserved recognition' (vv. 812–19): *meriti post me referentur honores* (v. 819, 'After I am gone all we have earned will be paid: honour after honour after honour' – the poem's last line). With the one modest proviso, however: *nec tu diuinam Aeneida tempta, | sed longe sequere et uestigia semper adora* (vv. 816f., 'Don't take on the immortal heroine *Aeneis*. No, follow at the appropriate distance behind; for ever and ever worship the ground she walks on – dog her steps'). Statius knows all along, and inscribes, his 'post-Virgilian, propter-Virgilian' status.

These are privileged, authorized, self-positionings of *Thebaid*. An 'ode' such as *Siluae* 4.7 can lend its voice in support. This poem dramatizes Statius' writing-career within his social ambience, picturing the friendship, that 'Horatian' nexus of companionship and literary advice, of Vibius Maximus as the essential spine of his productivity. He is foil for Statius' writing, as the poet tells us. Vibius helped *nostra | Thebais multa cruciata lima* (vv. 25f., 'Our *Thebaid*, all that plastic surgery | the torture of criticism') take on 'the daring challenge of Virgilian-style glory', and is now needed for further poetic midwifery as Statius is 'stuck getting past his second epic's first bend into *Achilleid* book II' (vv. 23f. Stuck there, on his abortive second epic – he already knew? – for ever). The charm – ingenuousness, camaraderie, urbanity – of this fetching piece adds the last touches to the self-portrait of a scholar in his verse-workshop, turning out neatly-crafted and self-critical works in tune with the canons of tradition and the best taste of the day. Would this poetaster not be satisfied if we found his

---

[14] Cf. Cinna fr. 11.1f., *haec .. multum inuigilata ... | carmina*, with Lyne (1978) 120f., on *Ciris* v. 46; *Silu.* 3.5.34f., *mea Thebais*; Juv. 7.82f., *carmen amicae | Thebaidos*.

epic progeny competent, declamatory entertainment for the Rome of the Younger Pliny – a sell-out fit to stir Juvenal's wrath?[15]

2 READING THEBES / STATUS OF STATIUS

The *Thebaid* cannot be said to be *about* anything.[16]

/

What is the *Thebaid* about? In a word: power.[17]

/ But the poem *knows* this 'humility' of its 'apologies', it knows that their rhetoric is deflection and meiosis, the characteristic décor of urbane discourse under the Empire.[18] From two points of view, at least, we can find that the poem's self-framing within its editorials even points directly to its undisguisably explosive potential to mean, within the Flavian cosmos.

When Neapolitan Statius promises his princeling > lord and master the delectation of literary pirouetting in mythical Thebes from a *Pierio ... oestro* (1.32, 'As Greek a gadfly as the Muses can buzz into poetic frenzy'), he does more and less than direct attention away from Roman reality: he as good as pins the label to his tale, 'Read this text in and through its address to Domitian: look here and see "what His Divine Majesty deigns to give his time to"' (12.814).[19] 'Think of the Flavians when we read this.' This is not to say what we are to find, only to frame us into finding *something*, a point in reading as searching to find 'it'. Since the Augustans, Roman readers of poetry had become used to the notion that a reading 'as if from, within, over against, the position of' a Caesar could produce a legion of tonal divagations, a proliferating

---

[15] Juv. 7.82–7. On the cultural matrix for Statius' repertoire and taste, cf. Hardie (1983) 1–102.

[16] R. M. Ogilvie quoted by Ahl (1986) 2808.

[17] Dominik (1994) xii: 'about power'-politics, in fact, *dominatio*.

[18] On the politics of imperial representation, see Ahl (1984), (1984A), Bartsch (1994). For Statius' adversions to Ovid's editorial figuration, esp. v. 819 ~ *Met.* 15.871–9, cf. Vessey (1986) 2974–6. | *occidet*, v. 819 re-words *Met.* 15.879, *uiuam* |, blended with Luc. 9.986, *uiuet* (chapter 5). Cf. Ahl (1986) 2835 n. 36, Vessey (1973) 61.

[19] Here *noscere ... discit* bid for imperial attention and schoolroom canonicity *after* Hor. *Carm.* 2.20.19f., *noscent ... discet*, superimposed on *Epp.* 1.20. On Statius' poetics of *oestrogen*: Malamud (1995) 172f.

release of meanings (e.g. Horace, *Epistles* 2.1, a meditation on its own, and any, such performance; or Ov. *Tristia* II.). Statius' readers would need no explicit mandate to explore ways in which his poem was declaring to them at one and the same moment both that *Thebaid* was not 'about' their world and that it was not *not* about their world, too.[20]

In the second place, the story of 'Thebes' did not arrive on Statius' desk without its own set of meanings. A writer could insist, till he was black and blue in the face, that his treatment of this material was cleansed of any sociopolitical dimension, that he had only and precisely picked this legend because it allowed him to cut his teeth as a novice epic-versifier without taking a 'position' on anything, that ... – Only to find that epic form denies any such facile abdication from vatic authority. 'Thebes' remains a live, civic, paradigm, in no matter whose hands, under whatever waiver, in a declamation-hall, in a school text-book, in this book and in our life – but, especially, within any imperial order. We shall next explore both these points just a little.

3 ROMAN THEBES / EPOCH OF EPIC

The *Thebaid* is not a Roman epic, / it has no national or patriotic motive.[21]

Thebaid's *Prologue* moves in the shadow of Lucan's. *More than* trumps *cognatas ... acies* (*BC* 1.4, 'battle-lines of kin against kin') with *fraternas ... acies* (*Theb.* 1.1, 'battle-lines of brother against brother'). But loses the edge of Lucan's *BC*, its ambition to represent the ultimate epic amplification, *Bella ... plus quam ciuilia* (chapter 5), as it disjoins its readers from its subject. In Lucan, as we saw, the key textual moment was the appellation of readers into their positions as citizens of Rome (*BC* 1.8). Statius himself as good as poses the problem for Flavian epic as: 'What has Rome to say after Lucan's end-game?' We could find to

---

[20] Cf. Lee (1990) 83, quoting Schechner, '"All effective performances share this 'not – not not' quality ... inbetweenness. ... [Narratives] act inbetween identities" themselves, and also textualize this in the performances of their characters and examinations of subjectivity.'

[21] Vessey (1982) 572.

our chagrin that he has only the wet answer that his text displaces civic with kin war – and the promise of his pre-text that he will (try to) turn up the horror-controls.

Flavian subjects, however, could scarcely resist reading into their 'Thebes' that post-Lucanian tragedy of the Caesars of 69 CE, 'The Year of the Four Emperors', when civil war in waves of invasion found what could conceivably be told as supervenient settlement by a new 'Theseus' of suicidal internecine fighting à la *Thebaid*, when Vespasian finally arrived to conclude the carnage left after Nero's fall by the struggles between Galba, Otho, Vitellius – a Theseus that history would not re-cast as 'Oedipus' with the cursed brother-sons while Statius toiled, or spouted, on – not until they were all fresh in their urns. This is *not* what Statius says. He pretends *not* to write for us at all of father Vespasian's (Pisistratean) legacy of the Roman world-state, the City of Man, to his two sons for their rule.

But in his articulation of *Oedipodae confusa domus* (1.17, 'that chaos, the Oedipal ménage'), which the prologue presents as its designated *limes . . . carminis* (1.16, 'the line/limit/path/domain of the poem'), Statius' readers cannot avoid contemplating up close the collapse of a royal house, the end of such dynasties as the Julio-Claudian? And . . . – of whatever lineage will ever succeed it? The mass-destruction that absolutist monarchy must eventually spell for its cultural order, according to the age-old mytho-logic of epic Thebes. This was one secret of power at Rome that could never be concealed. Had some kind of Labdacidal 'tragedy' not befallen their Rome? Was it not all happening all over again, gathering strength to bring down Caesar–Statius, together?[22]

In *Siluae* 2.7, lyric Statius does not *not* write his own programme for (posthumous) appreciation of his own epic. In the guise of a strangely retrojected forecast of the short life in prospect for Lucan, alternately 'thundering' and 'lamenting' him as the master-poet of twin Caesar-lightning/Pompey-funeral pomp, the epigonous avenger Statius also protests, before the widow, that Lucan–Cato ascends to the ether from which the crazed tyrant Nero has been dejected (*detonabis, deflebis, seu*

---

[22] Cf. Ahl (1986) 2814 and *passim*; Malamud (1995) 190, 'Power relations in Thebes and power relations in Rome are not *un*related, history and politics cannot be neatly *ex*cluded from epic, and will not be *ab*sent from the *Thebaid*.' We can refer and relate to this.

rapidum poli per axem ... *terras despicis*, vv. 66, 71, 107–10). Statius plays the empathetic voice of a woman's grief for her dead baby, the plangent voice of *Thebaid*. But he also detonates the political power of epic poetry to overcome mundane corruption through the cosmos – the fight goes on, for Thebes, for Rome, for the City.[23]

Mythological epic – i.e., for Romans, the fiction 'Greece' – was never securely fenced off for formalist fiddling. At the very least, no one could ever be sure that myth was not the vehicle of civic thought. / Yes. Even in that imperial declamation-hall, in that school text-book. / Nor can we. Otherwise, *Thebaid* is dead. And so is our reading of Latin.

Thebes was a classic terrain for epic, as 'Homeric' as Troy. The Cyclic *Thebaid* has now all but vanished, though the opening verse survives – to set us to think hard and long: 'Argos sing, goddess, a-thirst from where chiefs | –'.[24] Ever after, the Theban story must consider its Argos, Argos embroiled in the Theban nightmare: innocent Argos?[25] Athenian tragedy, to which we must return, attests in full the aptitude of the cities of Oedipus and Tantalus for the release of the repressed. Among Hellenistic classics, Antimachus' *Thebaid* offered what we may guess to have been a massively recherché text of prevarication, starting from a grand 'Speak on, Muse-daughters of mighty Zeus, son of Cronus' and obstructing his Seven warrior-heroes from reaching Thebes with 24 books of preliminaries.[26] We know the bare existence of a string of other Hellenistic efforts – by Antagoras, a certain Demosthenes, and by Menelaus of Aegae[27] – before Rome's first dynastic inauguration called forth its *Thebaids*, in the early 20s: again

---

[23] We turn here to Malamud (1995), more eloquent than we can say: *quid maius eloquar?* Cf. Masters (1996) 5–10, esp. on *Silu.* 2.7.79f., *ipsa te Latinis | Aeneis uenerabitur canentem* ('*Aeneid* herself will reverence your song to Latinate readers'): 'No reader has dared to take this claim at face value', with critique of Van Dam (1984) 470. Cf. Dominik (1994) 169f., '... Statius' admiration of Lucan is based ... on his courage in writing an epic that more boldly establishes a connexion between tyranny and the Caesars than mythological epic.'

[24] Davies (1989) 23–9, 'The *Thebais*'. Brown (1994) reviews ancient *Thebaids*, *passim*.

[25] On the embroiling of Argos with Theban metaphorics, see Zeitlin (1990) 145–7, 'The Middle Term: Argos'. Statius makes great play with the 'Tantalid' connection of Argos, itself the tragically cursed scene of fraternal hatred between Atreus and Thyestes. His Polynices becomes an Argive for his Theban enemies Eteocles, then Creon, and for Jocasta.

[26] Tattered fragments in Lloyd-Jones and Parsons (1983) frr. 52–79.

[27] See Ziegler (1966[2]) 20–2.

we have nothing left to go on – so many textual *Thebaid*s as utterly destroyed as the house of Laius, more thoroughly than Alexander could raze physical Thebes. But it is worth taking a moment to wonder what Propertius' sparring-partner Ponticus can have been signalling by penning his epic of *Cadmeae ... Thebae | armaque fraternae tristia militiae* (1.7.1f., 'Cadmus' Thebes, where war turned sour on brothers-in-arms'). Was this but the re-cycling of re-cycled Greek melodramatics, a welcome reinvestment in the aestheticized sublimity of 'Classical Culture'? Or does Propertius find himself finding in Ponticus an explosive return to insistent relevance of those dinosaur alien cityscapes of early mythology, a theme for post-Actian Italy?[28]

4 *LE ROMAN DE THÈBES* / THE BASICS

L'anti-cité / la cité de la violence pure et de la stasis.[29]

'Thebes', then, was known throughout classical Antiquity as a central theme for epic narration, for representation of *cacotopia* in the wake of Homer. To an extent, it is but a trick of time that makes Statius' the first extant narrative. On the other hand, there are powerful reasons why this tale suited best the Attic and then the post-Attic (Accian, Senecan, Racinian ...) dramatic medium / why Theban narratives have died so many deaths and mainly survive to haunt theatre-scripts. In any case it is within the criticism of fifth-century Greek tragedy that the horror-show of Thebes has been most sympathetically registered. We next briskly summarize the 'story' and turn briefly to the Thebes of drama. / Later we shall return to the difference that narration, epic narration, of *Thebais* may make to its sense.

Here, then, we are given a paraphrase of the tale that Statius re-makes into his poem:[30] Oedipus carried within his nature, was, the curse of the family (of King Laius). Parricide, incest, horror. After his own self-recognition and self-blinding he damned his two sons to rule Thebes in his place. Their self-confuting agreement, to alternate power on an annual basis, broke down at the first try. Dispossessed by brother

---

[28] See Stahl (1985) 48–71, esp. 63–5 and 182, 'Will the same lasting praise be granted to the *Aeneid*? Or will it suffer the fate of Ponticus' or Lynceus' or Homer's *Thebaid*?' (For the enigmatic 'Lynceus'' *Thebaid*, cf. Prop. 2.34.37–40.)

[29] Vidal-Naquet (1986) 186.

[30] Apollod. 3.5.7–7.1 is the fullest ancient summary.

Eteocles, Polynices finds a band of guest-friends, new affinal relatives and warrior-comrades in Adrastus' kingdom of Argos, the 'Seven
Against Thebes', who will restore him to his throne. Considerable
delay and obstruction held up the assault half-way, around Nemea,
before catastrophic battle broke out, in which the armies of the Seven
and their opponents virtually wiped each other out. The climax was the
brothers' hand-to-hand duel, which closed in reciprocal fratricide. The
new king, Creon, denied burial to the invaders, but the women of
Thebes and of Argos called in the dashing King Theseus of Athens to
face him down. Thebes' royal house was as good as terminated in this
tussle. With lamentation from the bereaved ends the tale.

5 THE TRAGEDY OF THEBES / THE BEST

> C'est la *Thébaïde* / c'est-à-dire le sujet le plus tragique de l'Anti-
> quité.[31]

If we are to feel Statius' impetus, we will need to grant it something
of the form of attention which we habitually lavish upon fifth-century
Athenian tragedy, the presumption, that is to say, that in its struggles
to tell us its world, and in its own insistence that this is necessarily
and importantly an incomplete, suspect, and partial, representation,
'*Thebes*' resounds with political intelligence. In a magisterial essay,
Zeitlin (1990)[32] explores what '*Thebes*' meant for the δῆμος (people)
of Athens. She finds the boundaries of personal identity / alterity
annulled, the relational structure of the family imploded, and the city
system entropically closed, folded up from articulation and locked into
self-absorption:

> Thebes is the place ... that makes problematic every inclusion and
> exclusion, every conjunction and disjunction, every relation between
> near and far, high and low, inside and outside, stranger and kin ...
> When he ... alternates between a condition of self-referential auto-
> nomy and involvement in too dense a network of relations, Oidipous
> personifies in himself the characteristics that Thebes manifests in all
> its dramatic variants, through all its other myths, and through the
> extant work of all the tragic poets of Athens ... Thebes, the other,
> provides Athens, the self, with a place where it can play with and

---

[31] Racine (1982) 54, 'Préface' to '*La Thébaïde*'.   [32] Earlier version, Zeitlin (1986).

discharge both terror of and attraction to the irreconcilable, the inexpiable, and the unredeemable, where it can experiment with the dangerous heights of self-assertion that transgression of fixed boundaries
inevitably entails, where the city's political claims to primacy may be
exposed and held up to question.[33]

In Thebes, where father is brother, mother is wife, mother-in-law is
sister-in-law, nothing can add up and make sense. Internecine hatred
completes the undoing of the clan and its state. Barthes saw the confusion thus:

> Hatred does not divide the two brothers ... It brings them closer
> together; they need each other in order to live and in order to die,
> their hatred is the expression of a complementarity and derives its
> force from this very unity: they hate each other for being unable to tell
> each other apart ... What the brothers seek in order to vent their
> hatred is not battle, the abstract, strategic annihilation of the enemy: it
> is the individual clinch, the physical conflict and embrace; and this is
> how they die, in the lists. Whether it is womb, throne, or arena, they
> can never escape the same space that confines them, a unique proto-
> col has ordained their birth, their life, and their death. And the effort
> they make to tear themselves away from each other is merely the final
> triumph of their identity.[34]

We begin to see how powerful a scenario tragic '*Thebes*' can be,
through the eyes of the Athenian citizen we imagine ourselves to play:
the very dimensions within which we can find any relations thinkable,
the possibility for any story-pattern to be imagined – temporality,
space, generational linearity – spin at Thebes into re-cycled repetition,
glomerate in fusion. This is Statius' point of departure, the guilt of

---

[33] Zeitlin (1990) 134, 145. Cf. Euben (1990) esp. 99f., 133, Vidal-Naquet (1986).

[34] Barthes (1977) 61, 62f. Cf. Zeitlin (1982) 25f., 'Two sons must "fight not so much
to settle the differences between them ... but instead to establish through violence
a definitive difference – victor–vanquished – by means of which they can be distinguished each from each" [Fineman ... on Girard]. But Eteokles and Polyneikes, by
their mode of death, which I have termed reciprocal and reflexive, fail to establish that
difference between victor and vanquished, for each is victor over the other but each is
also vanquished by the other. This is exactly the meaning of their conflict, unlike other
conflicts between brothers ..., namely, that issue from an incestuous union cannot
establish any difference between its offspring, but can only produce sons who embody
the principle of difference, unreconcilable except through their inevitable identical
end.' In short: *alterna furentes* (7. 640) ~ *alterna gementes* (12.387).

Thebes – locked into circles of revenge in which everything can only happen again:[35]

> fraternas acies alternaque regna profanis
> decertata odiis sontesque euoluere Thebas
> Pierius menti calor incidit.   (1.1–3)

> *Battle-lines of brothers | the kingdom of alternation,*
>   *cursed hatred's final solution. | The guilty: Thebes.*
>   *On heat with Poesy – Greece! – My Mind. Falling.*

If the order here seems to be chronologically up-ended, so that the poem's first item must name its *telos*, the duel of Eteocles and Polynices, then the point will soon be clarified, when the voice of Thebes names as | *fraternas* ... *acies* those *Spartoi*, the 'Sown Men' of Cadmus with whose sowing and internecine strife the city came into being – total disaster from/as the start (vv. 184f.). An anonymous citizen reads Thebes for us as the abomination that lay at the end of founder Cadmus' 'search' (*quaerere*), the 'battle-lines of brothers' his dynastic legacy, the omen of dissemination (*augurium seros dimisit ad usque nepotes*, 1.184, 'He handed on the omen to reach right through to all his late-comer grandsons.'). It could still be the apogee of this senselessness that we come – perhaps with, perhaps in despite of, Theseus – to ponder on Statius' Killing Fields.

6 WAR AT THEBES / THE BASES

> War is, first of all, at war with the rationality of its own participants ...
> Hatred assimilates each side to the other, the *Wechselwirkung* becomes
> an oscillation as well as a mutuality, each side becoming the other as
> the sides work each other up to a resemblance in extremism. There is
> even an altruism of hatred, in which the other becomes more impor-
> tant than the self. One is willing to give one's life in order to take the
> foe's. This is the selflessness that gives war its weird and inverted
> nobility. It is, in Clausewitz's view, a necessary mark of fighting men.
> But it is hardly rational ... When we are most exalted by hostility and
> have the greatest sense of wielding war to serve our purposes, war is
> wielding us, carrying us away from ourselves in the nobility of self-

---

[35] See Irwin (1975) esp. 120 for 'revenge' as self-perpetuating loop of alternation.

sacrifice inspired by hate. Shoulder shoving, on the largest scale, has become an end in itself.[36]

/

And only one small boy,
who was not paying the least attention,
will ask
between two victorious wars:
And did it hurt in those days too?[37]

At Thebes we get to look at warfare afresh. A *Thebaid* is not cleanly the other of civic/patriotic/national/imperialist fighting. It does not simply stage a hyped-up mythic re-make of *BC*. Rather, it makes itself a messy collage from a cursed centrepiece of suicidal *Bruderkrieg* against the background of a (hysterically primitivesque) blood-brotherhood-in-arms. '*Thebes*' has that unsettling status of not *not* confounding war, revolution, civil war, and stasis. (Especially once Statian sabotage has deflated its shape, by un-featuring the walls, the gates, and Seven paired champions standing ready in the old story to structure a scene of attack/defence.)[38] We can scarcely agree with mad Capaneus that Thebes–Argos conflict does not count as civil war (6.737, *ciuili sanguine*, the only *ciuilis* in *Thebaid*). 'Cette lutte fratricide est l'image mythique de la guerre civile.'[39]

War is fought to decide a dispute, to impose a 'sense'. Thus the fighters fight to impose their reading on anyone left alive to dispute '*Thebes*'. We can set out some of the rival perspectives:

(i) For Adrastan Argos, this is a Just War. An obligation to a guest-friend, with God on our Side. And international Law. This blurs into: the Restoration of its own bonny crown prince to his full inheritance, (cloaked) military annexation. Not to mention: adventure for 'Heroes'. And: Alliance in operation.

/

---

[36] Wills (1983) 160f.

[37] M. Holub, 'A history lesson', in Heaney and Hughes (1982) 191.

[38] 8.353–7 is a trace of the old *Septem* schema; otherwise, Menoeceus' jumping, Capaneus' blasting and Theseus' storming from the (very same) ramparts survive to tell of the siege's symmetries (10.756–82, 875, 882, 12.706). Cf. Thalmann (1978) 38–42, 'The City's walls: inside and outside'.

[39] Petre (1971) 24 explores the half-truth of this her formulation.

(ii) Whereas, for Eteocles, this is a *coup d'état*, it must be stopped. So: patriotic Defence of the Realm. This is an elder son reclaiming his own rights; and he maintains Internal Security and restores Stability. An outlawed Enemy of the State leads an invasion, backed by the might of a Super-Power arsenal and economy, the Intervention is but papered-over self-interest.

(iii) For Tydeus, next, the attack is merited Revenge. The cause is that foundation of International Law, diplomatic Immunity. Theban Aggression assaults the Argive Nation when it assaults the person of its (second) crown prince-and-envoy.

(iv) Polynices? Polynices is out to direct his own script: of Restoration. He vindicates a Solemn Treaty, reclaims his Right to Rule, grants Thebes *Anschluss* with Argos, uses Minimum Force to punish the Usurper.

(v) For Creon, this is the story of his son's Sacrifice to save the walls; for him the Enemy is one alien undifference, set below Human Rights.

(vi) Loser Jocasta must re-play 'Veturia' failing to avert her 'Coriolanus' (chapter 5 on *Patria*: the mother whose son turns on his origins, his country, his people).

(vii) For Theseus, this is one more request to remake Man for clement Civilization. There is, to be sure, some (Regrettable) Loss of Life – from Hostile Extremists, naturally, condemned by World Opinion –

(viii) For the Cities, for their women, this is war – why discriminate further? This is that old refrain, 'And it's 1–2–3–What are we fightin' for?' '*Thebes*' is what takes the men away. It is why mothers bear sons: Victory, in that body-bag.

In war humanity orders and imposes a distribution of meanings around a dominant 'reading'. A final solution, a re-reading that 're-makes' / it says / a (stab at) truth. (As if there could ever be a dominant hierarchy that did not depend on the continuing resistance of the views and values it constitutively seeks to oppress. The defeated memorialize their stories even as they become cannon-fodder, notches on the belts of their conquerors. To each our role.)

We have perhaps thought we know why a wild west's Magnificent Seven, a world war's Dirty Dozen, must fight it out before us; why the champions of a *Thebaid*'s army of Argives must live their face-to-face

code of 'heroism' for us. This Western discourse of warfare has forever
played its part in anchoring political sense between and within our
social structures. These are scenes of consecration for humanity conceived as civic pugnacity: 'at the bottom-line of national ideology, we'll
find that the subject who *is* is man as male, and is a male male, a manly
man. And that's what he *should* be'.[40] The Iliadic myth of the warrior's
ἀριστεία as the proving-ground of real existence pulls us (men?) back
still into the regressive fantasy that we live in some individual-scale,
directly co-operative, self-bounded tribal culture, where the localism
essential to the heroic champion can pass as a plausible reading of our
lives, our only text-to-be (chapter 5). Of course we 'know', like those
imperial Romans, like those democratic Athenians, like even those
social configurations which produced their 'Homeric' recitations in the
first place, that this bears no real relation to any world we inhabit. It is
the flame of ideological atavism that draws us, moths in the glare of
its beacon. We, all of us, know our selves, the order of our being, in
and through (the denial of) our very distance / our 'lapse'? / from this
the nostalgia of Europe's origins: the positioning of the 'Man-at-Arms'
as his City's Shield and Spear. Nothing could be so simple. No condensation, no image-repertoire so massively reinforced by centuries of
inculcation with charismatic text and educational scene of training in
militarist machismo, with or without the balm of pathos / the chauvinism of conquest. Yet, the ordeal of 'Thebes' may show, nothing is so
reliant on carefully elaborated articulation and on insistently patrolled
shepherding of the psyches it would condition.

The *Iliad*'s modelling round a transcendental design – the 'Plan of
Zeus' – contributes to its narration a drive towards totalization that
fetishizes 'The Duel' as the orgasmic finale, the Warrior binding the
corselet of Power and Knowledge tight round his Self as he drives
home the metal in his hand through the body of his partner. The narration constrains this paradigmatic primal scene to converge with the
story that bears it in a teleology where we can know that Everything is
all along directed toward the ending that is the fight 'to the end'. The
point of the storytelling is to arrive at the conviction that human agency
crystallizes when the Warrior decisively and conclusively drives home
the point of his blade. Yet the scene depends on choreography for a
Duet, for the victor needs his victim's co-operation for their *pas de*

[40] *After* Henderson (1989A) 97.

de ... ath. The absolute difference between life and death which is the stake and productivity of Combat is founded on an initial parity, the opponents must interlock in a blur of proximate interchangeability, we and they must find each other's values from a mutuality in the 'fairness' of fight. The hero 'knows himself' through the foe he merits. There is even necessarily a bond between the participants that tends toward the homoerotic, for the show-down functions as show-case, for 'manliness'. They and we must find what we admire, or / Why not say it? / *love*, in the reflected ideal gleaming and dinning from the flashing weapons and thundering armour of that best of beetles, the hard-case *HuMan*. This way the thorax will fill with the spirit of prowess and ... we'll – join the marines.

The *Aeneid* forces such a reading upon the *Iliad*, mightily establishes this as the epic tradition, classical tradition, Tradition *tout court*, how fathers-who-were-sons re-make sons-who-will-be-fathers in their own form. Homer's text runs on from its dénouement dance of Achilles with Hector to shape its meaning through reception in and of the poem by way of memorializing scenes of negotiation and burial. / These feature and constitute 'commentary' and so risk side-tracking readers from finality. They court a discursive, dialogical, suspended reaction from readers, on out of the text and into their lives.[41] / The immeasurably abrup– terminat– of the *Aen*–, in the very departure of Turnus' life from the body at Aeneas' fee–, insists, to the contrary, on running us through (with) the charismatic moment of slaughter, without compunction or softening. We are obliged, with the suggestive shadow of the *Iliad* in our minds and the promptings of the myriad variations, and discourses, on the paradigm of *arma uirumque* that have been pressed into making up the entire duration of the Roman national epic before us, to 're-make' our own final reckoning up of the sense. / The poignancy, the poin–

After Lucan's warped dejection of the ἀριστεία from his own, openended, epic – dislodged from the text, perhaps, to await some patriot's revenge on the Caesars, some more conclusive Cassius Chaerea, a final conspiracy of Roman warrior-heroism, possibly a re-make starring Annaeus Lucanus-'*Brutus*' (chapters 3, 5)? – the majesty of Roman

---

[41] Lynn-George (1988) esp. 230–76, 'The homeless journey', is the most sophisticated / heart-felt exploration of the tensions surrounding the ?closure? of the *Iliad*. Ahl (1989) shows how simplificatory the notions of narrativity that have generally been applied to the reading of ancient epic have been, how simplistic the claims for closure.

story-telling returns to the sanctified ways of Western war. Statius' pantheon of warriors stakes out a mighty terrain for *uirtus*, to be focussed, perfected and topped by the duel between the rival commandants, the sons of Oedipus. Then *Thebaid* continues its travail, with a full exploration of its signification through a panoply of aftermath scenes: struggles to memorialize the slain, fresh slaughter to that end, suffering on suffering, and the régime of mourning ... Statius takes the space to fix the dynamics of 'Cadmean Victory' into his own, '*Theban*', portrait of humanity; and the bard survives to carry through to completion and completeness the 'intent' of Virgil's narration. Statius shores up the sense of The Duel from the lability which its unpoliced termination risks at the hands of its readers / if he does not rather bring out the necessarily delicate poise of heroism above an abyss of our suspicion and mutiny, if he does not indeed even tarnish and topple the whole shooting-match. / The 're-make' –

7 COMBAT AT THEBES / THE BATHOS

The Western Way of War, conceived by the Greeks as trial by ordeal / leads [us] their descendants into the pit of the holocaust.[42]

At its simplest, martial epic was purpose-built to hammer home cumulative thrusts with the hand-held sword. The 'wrong' scene would be the killing of the wrong / unfairly matched / victim, as when Aeneas' sword pierces the body of the female commandant Dido. (Destinedly, Aeneas had his alibi: we witness his absence, away with his fleet. And there were no finger-prints.) The Italian *uir* Turnus is contrastively defined as the 'right' object of 'the right war in the right place'. 'Bad' slaughter, however, was elaborated in terms of its positioning / even its 'morality', as the belligerent interpreter will always insist on lying to us. / Thus Aeneas will become the *uir* fit to receive and bear his *arma* only when he has soldiered on through his ordeals to reach the site of the homeland he is readied to kill or die for. He journeys from Dido to occupy the *domus*, the *ara*, the *moenia* of the *Urbs*, the supreme, overriding, object of his desire. (Home. Stability. Spatial selfhood. Identity. All he lost with Troy.) Consecrated by his *aduentus* here, he can be embraced by Love, mother-love generating love of the fatherland / his

---

[42] Hanson (1989) 'Introduction' 13.

progeny, he can be wrapped henceforth in the divine *arma* that he has been forged to fit: *AMOR > ROMA*. We see, *uirtus* is the use of *arma* in 'Defence' / as we euphemize all warfare waged *pro patria* / after the archetype Hector.

Aeneas wields 'the sword of deathstiny' (*Aen*. 8.621, *fatiferum ... ensem*) once he has been positioned / joyful, rapt in wonder (vv. 617–25) / as his society's 'Human Shield', the shield he both wears and, in both senses of the word, 'becomes' (*clipei non enarrabile textum*, v. 625, 'the unsayable fabric of epic discourse, all that the sign "shield" shields from summation: the shield-ensign that signifies the warrior's worth, the mettle of his *uirtus*'). And just as we are to recognize in the 'bad' emblem of the trophy Aeneas makes of the 'bad' victim, who seizes the initiative, spoils the Duel, 'attacks Aeneas' sword-blade with his throat' (10.907f.), that the arms are the man / *Mezentius hic est*, taunts Aeneas over the emptied rig of armour (11.16, 'Introducing the great Mezentius, large-as-life!') / so we will see that the 'good' sword-thrust is powered by comradeship, the agent's adrenalin fired by soldierly *pietas*, when Aeneas slays Turnus at the sight of the despoiled sword-belt of Pallas round the 'wrong' torso: the arms signify and make present the whole force of the soldier's *uirtus*, as good as driving the warrior by remote control. Such 'fraternal' solidarity valorizes the warrior's valour: set alongside his like to make the paradigm of the patriot State, forbidden to 'fraternize' with the other side's brothers-in-arms ... / The alibi inside-out, as values must be, on the battle-field, where –

'Our' armies must forever massage themselves into making real for themselves the myth of Homeric epic and its re-makes, where family-units – phalanxes of brothers – regularly stand shoulder-to-shoulder in action, naturalizing 'national service' as a system of 'blood-ties'. (Classic scenes at *Il*. 11.426–55, *Aen*. 10.338–44, cf. e.g. 390–8, 575–601, esp. *morere et fratrem ne desere frater*, v. 600, 'Be brothers in brotherly death'.)[43] In this respect *Thebaid* more than runs true to form. (Cf. 8.448–55, where twin brothers regret killing twin brothers; 9.272–5, where a true brother dies sooner than desert his brother; v. 292, one twin is spared, one is speared; 10.654, brothers metaphorically as well as literally fight side-by-side; 12.744, triplet brothers are slain by Theseus.)

But '*Thebes*' tilts the whole epic apparatus toward negating this fun-

[43] Juhnke (1972) 74f.

damental feature of its design precisely by working up to its climax of protagonist brothers 'fighting together'. The story fixates on the dese-cration of war and its categories as its Theban 'theme', unveiled from the first in Statius' / disgustingly unforgettable / abusage *fraternas acies*.[44] Thus the curse on Thebes from (the dejected Cronian brother) Pluto, re-writing father Oedipus' mandate, takes the form: *fratres ... fratres alterna in uulnera ruant* (8.69–70, 'Brother after brother, brother upon brother, taking turns to deal out the wounds, to dive onto the wounds, let Theban alternation commence!'); Tisiphone, Oedipus' hellish double, orders: *non solitas acies ... sed fratrum* (11.97f., 'War gone strange – lines of brothers'); Polynices' bloodlust craves: *scelus et caedem et perfossi in sanguine fratris | exspirare* (11.153f., 'wickedness/slaughter/a chunnel dug through my brother before I breathe my last in the lake of his blood'); Piety must make her vain appeal to: *quis nati fratresque domi* (11.478, 'Calling all parents and brothers!') ...

Thebaid does present its readers with hallowed epic scenes of broth-ers-in-death / where the warriors love their death, it brings them closer than men can ever be / locks them together in what Statian jaundice, however, pictures as a sickeningly eternal 'hug', 'the kiss' of the sons of Ide (3.151, *complexus ... oscula*):

> procubuere pares fatis, miserabile uotum
> mortis, et alterna clauserunt lumina dextra.   (2.642–3)

> *Undivided they fall. Deathstiny deals them a shared end.*
> *Pray to die this way. We'll find, like them, a place in everyone*
>   *who has a heart.*
>   *Their hands closed each other's eyes,*
>   *they watched over each other's death,*
>   *a twosome alternation of soldierly righteousness.*
>   *The right hand, the sword hand,*
>   *the Man's pledge, hand of righteousness,*
>   droit, son dieu.

But this Man's Talk / we drool as brother watches brother die, closes the other's 'eyes swimming still in light' (v. 638, *oculos etiamnum in luce natantes*) / is, as we shall see, stained by Statian lamentation and in any case figures as but foil to the guilty 'alternation' of Theban brother-

---

[44] Cf. *consanguineas acies sulcosque nocentes*, 4.436, 'blood-link lines, ploughed Guilt'.

hood, along with all the other cues to 'think siblings' massed through the poem:[45] *fratri concurro, quid ultra est?* (11.185, 'I invade my brother: the absolute limit').

The potential for Thebes to breed cameos of *uirtus* is squandered, off the killing fields, in *Freitod*, defiant suicide – from Maeon, the bearer of bad news to a tyrant (3.91), then Menoeceus' devotion for the city, his *mortis amor* (10.804).[46] In the deathstined 'fall' of Amphiaraus into Hell's abyss (8.1, *incidit umbris*) / that 'one small step for epic originality' (8.101, *noua fata*). In the last-minute reprieve of Hippomedon from drowning, for ('Palinuran') overwhelming – still 'no chance for him to die a hero / not with Statius' limited poetic resources' (9.491, *nec magnae copia mortis*). In whatever Statius / and we / make of Capaneus' verbal theomachy, that thunder-struck display of 'infernal madness, was it? Or *uirtus egressa modum*? Headlong glory? Megadeathstiny? Pride before fall / supernal wrath smiling death?' (10.831–6).[47]

Unless we find *uirtus* / rather than its snuffing / displayed in that *tour de force* of romantic / tragic sentimentality, the exploits of mother Diana's ('Camilla'-esque) Arcadian-archer: *miserande puer* Parthenopaeus (9.716, 'Virgilian pathos of immature death' ~ *Aen.* 6.882 of Marcellus).

Unless it is to be found worked into / that parody of Patroclean comradeship / the blood-brotherhood-in-arms of Polynices and Tydeus, that grows into the chiefest martial sub-theme of the epic? In Tydeus we may find *Thebaid*'s own favourite foil of warrior idealism / fetishism, set to frame the ultimate scene of mutual fratricide with the contempt of perversion. In Tydean *uirtus* shall we find, even, 'Das *Hauptwerk* des Statius'?[48]

---

[45] Eteocles–Polynices, Menoeceus–Haemon, Euneos–Thoas, Jupiter–Neptune–Pluto, Mars–Apollo, Hercules–Bacchus–Apollo, Mars–Mercury, Sleep–Death, Castor–Pollux, Boreads, Belidae, Minos–Rhadamanthys, Ismenus–Asopus, Amphion–Zethus, Cadmus–Europa, Jupiter–Juno, Apollo–Diana, Athena–Hercules, Cydon+ sister, Argia–Deipyle, Antigone–Ismene, Furies, Fates, Muses, Nymphs. Cf. Feeney (1991) 350–2 on the rivalry of Jupiter–Dis.

[46] Cf. McGuire (1990) 28–33; Vessey (1973) 117–31.

[47] On the signal arms of Capaneus, cf. Harrison (1992).

[48] See esp. Bonds (1985). On 'The Death of Tydeus', see Vessey (1973) 283–94. On Tydeus' madness keying *Thebaid*'s poetic, Hershkowitz (1995A) 54–8: from 1.408, *rabiem . . . cruentam* through 9.1f., *rabies . . . cruenti* | *Tydeos*.

8 EPIC AT THEBES / THE BIAS

We are much less Greek than we believe.[49]

/

Let me eat off his head
so we can really see –[50]

This boarish Calydonian (2.469–75) / one-man plague and brother-killer (1.397, 402, *fraterni sanguinis*, 2.113, *fraterno sanguine*) / first enters the text outcast and refugee in need, to re-make 'beggar Irus *versus* beggar Odysseus' upon Argos' threshold.[51] From 'alternation' of verbal abuse (1.410, *alternis*), he proceeds to a 'duel' of feral clawing for brute needs, namely shelter from the storm, before he is taken up to play his opponent Polynices' 'Pylades' (1.473–7), the perfect brother-in-law, that brother we never had: *alius misero ac melior mihi frater ademptus* (9.53, 'the other and better brother it will hurt to lose'). Polynices' partner for a double royal wedding to the princess sisters becomes his diplomatic representative, his flyweight champion and pocket-general. He joins, teams up with, represents, stands for and stands in for, his 'mate', they are a couple as good as – married, their two hearts beat as one. (Eteocles treated Tydeus as if he were Poly-nices, cf. 7.540, *nec frater eram*, 'I wasn't even his brother!' And Tydeus' battle-cry calls just like an Oedipodionian for 'Anyone with menfolk I've slain – a father, perhaps? A brother or so, our other halves, our semblances?' – for slaying next (8.668f., *nulline patres, nul-line iacentum | unanimi fratres?*)

Tydeus is to be Statius' answer to the epic tradition of the sturdy (defensive) warrior. This one-man army (2.491, 8.701f.) figures the mobile wall and human shield, trusty stalwart of stability, the team-man's resistance 'for the good of the cause' (re-made decoction of *Iliad*'s Ajax, Ennius' Aelius, *Aeneid*'s Turnus, Lucan's Scaeva).[52] / But already in the introductory scrap with Polynices, the 'fighting' for

---

[49] Foucault (1979) 217, cf. Euben (1990) 298, 'Nor do we live in anything approaching a Greek polis.'
[50] After Dylan (1990) '10,000 Men'.
[51] Cf. Ahl (1986) 2876, Bonds (1985) 232 for the boars.
[52] Cf. chapter 5, Schetter (1960) 37–9, Zwierlein (1988) 68–70.

Thebes was pre-cultural, Oedipally regressive – homing in on the eye-sockets:

> ... scrutatur et intima uultus
> unca manus penitusque oculis cedentibus intrat.   (1.426–7)

> *Digging right inside the face*
> *some pre-human claw passes inside*
> *and the eyes give ground.*

We will find that this is typologically prefigured by and textually pre-figures the mythological song-within-the-song of Statius' 'Alcinous'/'Dido'/'Evander'/'Latinus'-precipitate, the King of Argos Adrastus' aetiological hymn to 'Poetry', to *Phoebe parens*, which shuts this book that (as we remarked) was opened by Oedipus' gouged eyes. Here the 'pre-human claw ... and ironclad rippers' (*unca manus ... ferratique ungues*) of Apollo's post-'Cacus' monster suffer when his 'Hercules',[53] Coroebus, comes to 'rummage in the dark' (*scrutatus latebras*) before the folk come to 'ogle the eyes bruising in death' (1.616f., *uisere ... liuentes in morte oculos*). In this myth (fixing *Aen.* VIII with the end of *Aen.* I) we will find, displaced and condensed, anticipated lineaments of *Thebaid*, seeded *Hauptmotiven* (headlines) of its paradigm: Python's 'hug' (v. 564, *amplexum*), the rabid pack's, and the monster's, 'blood-baby-munch' (vv. 589, 603f., *morsu depasta cruento* |, *morsu ... cruento* | *deuesci*).[54]

Supposing this 'Man', Tydeus', charisma has survived the ferocious savagery of his entrée, only a Polynices could swallow his last martial feat of *uirtus*. Recall first that Achilles was verbally smeared, by Hector's mother, uniquely smeared, as a bestial outsider, with ὠμηστής (*Il.* 24.207, 'Eater of the raw').[55] This was, then, once the worst that could be said on how people ought not to (tr)eat.[56] Well, let us just watch

---

[53] For Tydeus and the other six as Hercules *manqués*, cf. Vessey (1973) 198f. and n. 3, Brown (1994) esp. 35–8. They are, like him, like his bestial victims: ibid. 204.

[54] See Vessey (1970), Kytzler (1986), Brown (1994) 174f. for the reverberations of the 'Coroebus' myth through the poem. *Scrutari* and *rimari*, uncommon in Latin epic, are salient in *Thebaid*; *uncus, unguis, dentes*, get their claws–talons–hooks into Sphinx's territory: tragic fighting all over Thebes (see Appendix).

[55] Cf. Segal (1971) 61. Achilles *threatened* to eat Hector raw (22.347); Hecuba will *wish* to eat Achilles' liver (24.212f.).

[56] Cf. Segal (1971) 61.

Thebaid's dying 'Patroclus'/'Pallas'-deposit, Tydeus, as he has the head of his killer fetched and, as his admiring patron Athena comes to award him Herculean divinity, she and we / must / see him expire thus:

> ... illum effracti perfusum tabe cerebri
> aspicit et uiuo scelerantem sanguine fauces
> – nec comites auferre ualent.   (8.760–2)

> *Her eyes met Tydeus*
> *drowned in brain-pulp smithereens,*
> *pervert jaws wicked with lifeblood still alive.*
> *The comrades can't get it away from him.*

This is 'ultimate' social deconstruction to set alongside incest and fratricide, approaching the Platonic Tyrant's endocannibalistic fili-cide.[57] This ΥΨΚΚΗ | Tydeus' last memory and memorial / is the way 'Thebes' must see its feast of *uirtus*: eating into the brain. As it does in reading / ingestion through our eyes. Does *Thebaid* / not / vomit, revile, its own story-patterns here?

Manic vision had linked Tydeus to his killer in a gaze that has no ending: (*Tydeus*) *uultu ... occurrit, ... uidit | ora trahique oculos, ... spectat atrox ... gliscitque tepentis | lumina torua uidens et adhuc dubitantia figi* (8.751–6, 'met him face-on, saw his face, eyes a-trailing, grimly watched the sight ... grew expansive, seeing the eye-lights grim, not yet decided to get fixed'). The guardian angel, soldier Athena of the flashing eyes, had managed her fighter Tydeus' martial career so far. But finally, even she must 'turn away in aversion' and 'purge those luminous eyes, with mystic fire, with an epic river-flow of ablution': *fugit aversata iacentem, | nec prius astra subit quam mystica lampas et insons | Elisos multa purgauit lumina lympha* (vv. 764–6: this the book-end, two-thirds through the Virgilian twelve-book plan, instructs us just what to do once we leave our recitation, and turn for respite from the text).

We Oedipuses must burn out the sight / unless we blot Tydeus out with tears of derision. / *Statius!*[58]

---

[57] *Rep.* 571c, 619b. For the '*Odpl*' construction of Greek tyranny, see Vernant (1982). On the cultural atopia of cannibalism, see Detienne (1979) 53–67, 'Gnawing his parents' heads'. For Tydeus' head-munching, cf. Beazley (1947) 3–5, Dewar (1991) 57.

[58] *Thebaid* attacks its – our – eyes: decapitated 'wide eyes search for their trunk' (*hiantes | truncum oculi quaerunt*, 7.645f.); the trampling war-horse 'mashes helmet into face,

Athena's aversion from Tydeus points forward to the most authoritative moment in all readings of *Thebaid*, her (our) Almighty Father's
'imperative aversion' from the brothers' showdown, *auferte oculos*
(11.126): *ut ... uidit pater ... | 'uidimus ... licitas ... acies. ... lateant ...
Iouem: sat ... sontes ... uidisse. ... turbanda dies ... Ledaei uideant neu
talia fratres.' | Sic pater omnipotens uisusque nocentibus aruis | abstulit* (vv.
119-35, 'When the Father saw ... he said, "We have seen lines of regular war ... Let the brothers hide from Jupiter's sight; enough to have
seen the guilty ... I must smog the day ... And they mustn't see, those
twin-boys of Leda, those brothers!" Thus the Almighty One. And he
tore his gaze from the fields ploughed with guilt').

Tydeus' and Polynices' brawl already pre-patterned the brothers'
Duel:

>   ... coeunt sine more, sine arte,
> tantum animisque iraque, atque ignescentia cernunt   525
> per galeas odia et uultus rimantur acerbo
> lumine ...
>   ueluti ...   530
>   sues ...
> igne tremunt oculi, lunataque dentibus uncis
> ora sonant.   (11.524-33)

> *Come together, right now:*
>   *bare of skill, bare of style,*
>   *pure mental drive plus hate; ablaze, they eye*   525
>   *loathing through helm, through helm loathing;*
>   *faces rifle faces with acid*
>   *sight ...*
>   *... like*   530
>   *boars ... quivering optic fire,*
>   *and crescent, claw-toothed,*
>   *mouth-faces din.*

The scopic drive / all-consuming desire to watch the mirror-self of
brother / watch itself smashed to pieces – guides the duel to / as its

shield into chest' (*in uultus galeam ... calcat*, 8.541); one victim, 'shot by a self-burying
barb with triplet claws, pulls out the arrowful of left eye' (*luminis orbe sinistro ... callida
tergeminis acies se condidit uncis ... oculo plenam labente sagittam*, 9.751), before 'the re-
doubled wound fills out his darkness'; he hunts from memory before 'falling over a
corpse' (vv. 753-6); corpses show 'arrows sticking straight up, stuck straight into
eyeballs' (*mediis ... sagittae | luminibus stantes*, 12.30).

fetishized end: our readerly stand-in, within the simile of the 'boars', a blenched hunter, turns spectator and stills his hounds to listen, while the sibling Furies play admiring arena-crowd (11.533–8). Prematurely exultant Polynices tells dying Eteocles, 'You see, you've let yourself get out of shape!' (v. 548, *uides* ...); he proclaims his victory, 'I see the heavy eyes' (of a Dido), a face 'swimming in death' (v. 558, *cerno graues oculos atque ora natantia leto*, cf. *Aen.* 4.688). Let someone go fetch sceptre and crown, fast, 'while he can see!' (vv. 559f., ... | *dum uidet*). The bard prays that 'Just one day shall ever see this abomination, any-where, any age' (vv. 577f., ... *uiderit una dies*). Aggression as the hot light of brotherly hatred will outlast their lives past the ignition of their bodies' shared pyre: *ecce iterum fratres ... exundant diuiso uertice flam-mae | alternosque apices abrupta luce coruscant* (12.429–32, 'Brothers. Endlessly.... Flames stream up with halved head and flash one crest, then flash the other crest, torn-off chunks of light, that Theban alternation'). In all this scopic horror, we shall recognize the curse of Oedipus' Thebes. Pre-made / its law of the eternal return / the 'Re-make' –

The 'hooked teeth' in the similitude here further relay us through the horrors of Tydeus' last mouthful (9.13, *morsibus uncis*) and when Polynices 'fell and crushed brother with his panoply' (11.573, | *concidit et totis fratrem grauis obruit armis*), we are bound to recall that earlier he 'disarmed naked, and he fell on the now void corpse of his best of friends', to lament Tydeus (9. 47–9, *abiectis ... armis | nudus in ... corpus amici | procidit*). / Like another Nisus, transfixed upon the body of dear Euryalus (*Aen.* 9.444, *super exanimum sese proiecit amicum*). / The fratricidal duel acts out the curse that caused it, and in turn the grief it evokes re-makes the fighting:

> ut quaesita diu monstrauit corpora clamor
> uirginis, insternit totos frigentibus artus   (11.599f.)

> *When daughter's cry located the bodies Oedipus groped for, he*
> *spread his every limb over their every cold limb.*

The 'trick death-blow' of Eteocles (v. 565, *erigit occulte ferrum*) is re-made when father's suicidal grief has him 'hunt the dagger(s)' in the corpses, only to find quick-thinking daughter has already spoiled his trick (vv. 628f., *occulte telum ... quaerebat*). The gouging of Oedipus' sockets is both what his sons must try to 'emulate', to outdo *upon the body that faces them*, and it is what their Father must wish vainly to repeat, as his mimetic tribute to the bodies that the curse of Thebes will not allow to separate off from their origin / but insists on reclaiming to its parental clutches.

Enter, then, Father Oedipus to feel (for) what he has done to his sons, 'that face far-away inside, | its cheeks/sockets, slag-heap of filth tracing lights out' (*ora genaeque | intus et effossae squalent uestigia lucis*, 11.584f.).[59] The avatar of Theban Madness, Tisiphone-style ('Enthroned in eyes sunk deep in the skull: iron light', *sedet intus abactis | ferrea lux oculis*, 'venom-swollen skin, doubled gesticulation of Wrath', 1.104–12, *geminas quatit ira manus*), Oedipus 'feels his way round those helmets, searches out the hiding faces' (v. 603, *tractat galeas atque ora latentia quaerit*), wishes his 'sight would return for a second dig, so he could do his thing, blitz his face' (vv. 614f., *o si fodienda redirent | lumina et in uultus saeuire . . . potestas*).

He swears himself blind:

> *That curse. It wasn't my fault, it wasn't, it wasn't:*

> ... furor illa et mouit Erinys
> et pater et genetrix et regna oculique cadentes;
> nil ego ...   (vv. 619–21)

> *Put it down to:*
> *Madness | The Fury |*
> *Pa | Ma | Power-Mania | My eyes, falling; |*
> EVERYTHING
> EVERYTHING
> NOT ME.

Let us look well / if we dare. The gaze of Oedipus' guilt detaches itself, with inexorable logic, from the retina of his ('Agamemnon' / 'Turnus') *ego*. As 'Allecto'-re-make Oedipus doubles up to play the bereft parent he cursed himself to be, / 'Evander parent of Pallas'-revenant, / the 'duel'-focussed and 'duel'-predicated epic narrative turns away / we may feel / from the agency of warrior deeds, and toward their

---

[59] *genae*, 'cheek', can only be cordoned from *genae*, 'socket', by our dictionary. (E.g. *OLD*, *s.v.*: (i), (ii).) Statius fixates on the visage of war, 'helmet + face' (*uoltu-* + *galea*: 5.355, 8.541, 11.526; *casside uoltu-* | 9.541, 879, 11.408, cf. 8.449, 9.700–1, 11.172, from Luc. 7.586, cf. Val. Flacc. 6.760 (an echoing book-end), Sil. 10.648; *genis . . . cassis*, 2.716–17, etc.).

reception, the aftermath of grief. Does the scene shift altogether – toward woman?

9 WOMEN OF THEBES / THE BOSSES

> She was out in the darkness, out in some black waste strewn with corpses, and she was going from one to another, looking, peering, yet dreading to see; she was looking for Eliot. There were bodies lying on their faces, ... bodies on their backs with faces ghastly upturned, bodies twisted terribly. They were everywhere. She had to go to them all, with the other ghosts that wandered like herself in that black waste. Killed ... blown to pieces, a voice was saying in her head, but still she had to go on looking and searching and wandering.[60]

/

> It is impossible to be a woman here. One must be dead. ... There are no men here, so why should I be a woman? There are heads and knees and mangled testicles. There are chests with holes as big as your fist, and pulpy thighs, shapeless; and stumps where legs once were fastened. There are eyes – eyes of sick dogs, sick cats, blind eyes, eyes of delirium; and mouths that cannot articulate; and parts of faces – the nose gone, or the jaw. There are these things – but no men.[61]

Our Father Oedipus' newly-fatherly wish is to join his sons, his brothers, the re-makes of himself, / in what may amount to utterly implosive perversion, / the formula of woman's grief cumulated and patterned through the length of *Thebaid*'s lamentable lines:

> ei mihi, quos nexus fratrum, quae uulnera tracto!
> soluite quaeso manus infestaque uincula tandem
> diuidite, et medium nunc saltem admittite patrem.   (11.624–6)

> *A   A   A   A   A   A   G   H*
> *Brothers wound tight together round their wounds. My fingers feel all.*
> *Unfasten, all I ask, hand from hand, these bonds of hate at last*
> *undo, and let me in, between you, finally: Dad. /*

---

60 Holland (1932) 171, *cit.* Tylee (1990) 230f.
61 M. Borden, 'The Forbidden Zone', *cit.* Marcus (1989) 128.

Statius earlier had his Mother (Ide) emerge from among the herd of matres who:

> scrutantur galeas frigentum inuentaque monstrant
> corpora, prociduae ...
>   ... lumina signant
>   ... ceruicibus ora reponunt.   (3.127–32)

> *They ferret through helmets of the cold ones,*
>   *they identify the bodies,*
>   *they label corpses,*
>   *they fall on the dead,*
>   *they close the eyes,*
>   *they stick the faces back*
>   *on their necks.*

Double-death bound, Ide rummages for those sons (whose last kiss we met already) through the cannon-fodder casualties (*quaerit ... natos*), clawing her face (*ora | ungue premens*) as she mourns the lot of them (3.134–9). She is come to bless Her Thespiad Boys with the pain of her lamentation:

> quin ego non dextras miseris complexibus ausim
> diuidere et tanti consortia rumpere leti:
> ite diu fratres indiscretique supremis
> ignibus et caros urna confundite manes.   (3.165–8, cf. 2.629–43)

> *I, only I, can speak this truth. This mother would interfere*
>   *if she undid from their piteous embrace these right arms,*
>   *the true Man's pledge to be true, to fight for right.*
>   *This epic death celebrates a sacred togetherness*
>   *that must not be broken. Claim the future,*
>   *brother-to-brother; merge once for all*
>   *in joint cremation. Fuse in the love*
>   *you bear your spirits after death:*
>   *one urn, one pair.*[62]

Statius will re-make this set-piece of set-pieces / in 'parapotamian',

---

[62] For the (traditional) 'con-fusion' of *una* in *urna*, cf. 3.148f., *felices quos una dies, manus abstulit una, | peruia uulneribus media trabe pectora nexi* ('Lucky sons! Lost to one day, one foe, and joined for ever – by a dirty great pole stuck right through your medals, a highway for wounds'), Ov. *Met.* 4.166, Luc. 9.1003. Cf. Brown (1994) 74f.

underwater transmogrification. / His 'Thetis'-figure, Ismenis, 're-
doubles' Crenaeus', Crenaeus', name (9.356, *ingeminat*). His last gulp
had been: 'Mother!' (v. 350). 'In grief she seeks her dead "water-baby"
in the murky depths' of River Daddy's bed (vv. 363–7, *penitus ...
occulta ... funera nati | uestigat plangitque tamen*). 'She rummages
through the helmets and rolls back the bodies face-down' (vv. 369f.,
scrutatur ... manu galeas et prona reclinat | corpora), hugs him to the
bank (v. 373, *amplexa*) and mourns 'his face that reflects back her own,
the eyes that looked back with papa's grim look' (v. 381, *hine mei uultus?
haec torui lumina patris?*). Another variant on Thebes' archetype, Ino
with drowned infant Palaemon (vv. 401–3). '*Thebes*', this is to say, even
threatens to *become* a Mother's lament:

> (i) Ino was last but not least in the poem's augural opening-cata-
> logue of preterite topics, *socio casura Palaemone mater*. | (1. 14,
> 'child Palaemon with her for keeps, she is ready to take the
> plunge to death: Mother's *Mutterliebe*', cf. 1.122, 2.381, 4.59,
> 562, 6.10, 7.421, 9.331, 402).
>
> (ii) Jocasta, mother/sister of Thebes – with 'grim eyes, bloodless
> cheeks/sockets' (7.474f., *truces oculos ... exsangues Iocasta
> genas*), she has Polynices chant 'Mother, Mother' (vv. 494f.),
> bids him 'overcome his aversion from brother' (v. 508, *fra-
> tremque – quid aufers lumina? – fratrem*); later she must try to
> halt the 'Coriolanus' within, Eteocles: she is compared with
> 'Mother Agave', son's head-in-hand! (11.318–20).[63]
>
> (iii-iv) Ide and Ismenis (see above).
>
> (v) Eurydice (5.632, 6.35, 136, see below).
>
> (vi) Atalanta. Her Parthenopaeus, the super-'Camilla/Pallas/Lau-
> sus'-in-one-bundle of gorgeousness, sexy gold-tunic from
> mum's needle (9.691f.), lengthily talks his book out to cur-
> tains, with his 'Poor Mama' refrain (9.885–907).
>
> (vii) Atalanta's mortal equivalent, the clawed cheeks/sockets of
> Menoeceus' mother (10.818, *ungue genas*) – her lament the re-
> make of *Aen.* IX's Euryalus' mother's (vv. 792–814) ...[64]

---

[63] See Hershkowitz (1994) 130–3 on the *impia belli | mater* (7.483f.).

[64] The night-attack in *Thebaid* X is to recover Tydeus' body. This re-makes *Il.* X, where
Tydeus' son is abroad. Statius meshes fighting with mourning: the squires 'rummage,
locate, (fail to) retrieve' the corpses of Tydeus and Parthenopaeus (v. 359, *scrutari
campum*, v. 370, *quaeritur*). Floodlighting from the Moon/Diana helped (v. 371, *mon-*

With the women, pick up the pieces. Statian epic haunts the dying fields of battle, makes of us 'the tourists flock[ing] in before the corpses are cold'.[65] Can our reader-sockets, our 'I', feel this Man's curse / war / un-make persons into the warrior male's crustacean *uirtus*? 'Helmet'-hide the 'face'? 'Hug' those sons tight in these Suppliant Women's 'mother's arms'?

Does *Thebaid* re-make epic – into Euripidean tragedy: 'With this ... shift from the rhetoric of eulogy to the ugly facts of blood, wounds, and bodily decay, the pathos of loss resurges unabated, and remains un-assuaged by the physical contact for which the mothers have longed'?[66] Can the case be made that the poem shows this meaning? Short of saying so / makes this its (bid for) tru –

10 NARRATION OF THEBES / THE BASIS

> Masculinity and individuality will only be reassembled and spoken if epos becomes epic through narrative closure and through the delivery of the story.[67]

/

> The ancients have passed down to us examples of epic poems in which the heroes furnish the whole interest of the story, and to this day we are unable to accustom our minds to the idea that history of that kind is meaningless for our epoch.[68]

Much of any epic must consist in delay, obstruction, deferral: anach-ronic time for hermeneutic thickening, for atmospheric amplification. Much of *Thebaid* spatially constricts itself to little Nemea, as against the worldwide dashes of Lucan's Caesar, the Odyssean charts of Virgil: cool Nemea's 'Herculean ... thickets' (4.646f.), 'too small to deploy/ catalogue (*euoluere*) an epic host' (5.43f.). Into its poetic wood, a

---

strauit funera), but Hopleus dies 'hugging' Tydeus (v. 403, *tenens*), and then, like a cornered mother lioness (vv. 414–19), Dymas invokes the Theban paradigm of Ino and Palaemon for pity (v. 425) before 'falling upon' Hopleus' body by way of 'burial' (vv. 439f., *pectus | iniecit puero*). Re-doubled horrorshow from *Aen.* IX's Nisus and Euryalus, as the foursome 'hug' death (v. 442, *complexibus*).

65 Masters (1996) 28, cf. 25–9.
66 Burian (1985) 149, *q.v.*
67 Pointon (1990) 134.
68 Tolstoy (1957) Book 3 part 1.19, vol. 2, 987.

(Callimachean) place for poetics, for juggling perspectives on epic 'greatness', on heroic might.[69]

Here, the Horatian poet of the *Siluae* could scarcely forget, the Pharaoh's master-poet had once played off Hercules with Adrastus, Molorchus with Archemorus/Opheltes, to make a Victory-Elegy fit for his sophisticated Queen-'Muse': Callimachus' ludibund *Aitia* originated the Nemean Games, courtesy of Euripidean Romance, from the incineration of an infant and the invention of mouse-trap technology in a hovel, via the lesson of humble theoxeny, to put Theban Hercules' immortalizing Labour of ἀνδρεία, his strong-arm strangling of the Nemean Lion, truly in the shade.[70] The passage was basic to Roman poesy, its sense well-understood.[71] The turn away from the grand ('Pindaric'/'Homeric') victor, toward the 'domesticity' of the woman's world, will mark this epic's mid-way stage, as Berenice's va(r)nished epinician in the *Aitia* heralded a mid-point turn in the form of their narration.

At Nemea, Statius offers, as if aside, a remarkable knot of 'combinatorial imitation':[72] a pathetic horror-show tale is told by its victim; thereby an innocent perishes senselessly; elaborate burial demands the 'heroic mockery' of funeral games. We recognize tableaux from the epic tradition – and an insistence on / and in / their re-making, / their re-conceptualization. With the Argive warriors-to-be, we meet the persecuted former princess, now enslaved child-nurse, Hypsipyle. And we return her two sons, Euneos and Thoas, found among our company. Model brothers, these: 'Identical twins. Totally' (6.343, *geminis eadem omnia*, cf. vv. 345, 434f., 477).[73] Retrieved, they 'tear mother in half with greedy hugs taken turn by turn. No Theban alternation, this!' (5.721f., *complexibus ambo | diripiunt ... alterna ... pectora mutant*). We are treated to, and created as readers by, *Thebaid*'s demolition of the happiness of this family re-integration, for the positioning and framing of the moment serves, like Odysseus' performance before Arete and

---

[69] See Brown (1994) *passim*, 4–8 on *mora* = narration; Nugent (1996).

[70] Cf. Colace (1982), Rosenmeyer (1982), Brown (1994) 43–56.

[71] See Thomas (1983) esp. 103–5.

[72] See Hardie (1990A) for this. Lesueur (1990) xviii–xxv lists the chief, paraded, intertextual episodes, Juhnke (1972) 315–70 tabulates 'Homerparallelen zu Statius' *Thebais*' in full.

[73] Cf. Hershkowitz (1994) 134 and n. 22 for other harmonious siblings.

Aeneas' before Dido, as the epic's reflexivity upon the dynamics of its own voicing and reception.[74] In this epic, it is the post-Phaeacian 'Nausicaa'-figure Hypsipyle who will take the chance of hospitality-niceties to operate, know and bespeak, narrative, taking over the post-war scarred warrior's privilege and charisma. This promotion of the woman's voice to tell the underside of *uirtus* displaces the site of epic from within: it is as if Virgil's Andromache were to step out of her narrated inclusion within Aeneas' perspective and take over the telling of *Aeneid* II + III for a '*Troades*'-style *narrative*.

We watch to see what narration does to the narrator and to the other 'readers in the text', what relations may obtain between the narrated and the narration, and what currents of textual electricity are generated from this laboratory of storytelling – how it may power the text that hosts the emblematic 'digression', what it might suggest to be the stake of the enfolding performance of narrative. / 'Why, how terribly self-conscious we are.'[75]

This, / we may recognize its patterning from the re-makes we have encountered, / is what becomes of Hypsipyle *as and because* she plays narrator: Nurse Hypsipyle put down her droopy child, / ominously / 'heavy-eyed and tired-faced' (5.502, *graues oculos languentiaque ora*). Along crept Snake, 'bruise-torched glare, swollen venom, claw-teeth and all' (vv. 508f., *liuida fax oculis, tumidi ... ueneni, adunci | dentis*). And then? The boy's 'eyes opened only for death' (v. 540, *in solam patuerunt lumina mortem*). Nurse comes 'a-hunting, runs through his little vocabulary, then runs through it again, in duplicate' (v. 546f., *ingeminans ... uisu ... quaerens*). She 'leans down' (*incumbens*), 'doubles' her kisses (*ingeminat*), 'searches' limbs for warm life (*quaerit*), to find 'sinew-bindings' awash with blood (vv. 565–95, *nexus*): 'No body. All. All is wound' (vv. 596–8, *totum ... in uulnere corpus*). She grieves 'for his lovely face' (v. 613, *heu ubi siderei uultus?*). Mother – Eurydice – burns 'to throw herself on the remains' (6.35f., *super prorumpere nati | reliquias*), her women 're-double' their keening (*congeminant*). Mother screams she is ready to die, to share a pyre with Hypsipyle – so long as she can first 'feast her eyes' (*exsaturata oculos*) on the revenge (vv. 175f.). At the epic funeral ceremonies, the soldiers stage their military-

---

[74] Cf. Götting (1969) 50–62, Hardie (1993A) 65f. for comparison with Homer and Virgil.
[75] After Handke (1971) 27.

style rite of 'aversion from the polluting sight of evil' (vv. 205f. *prospectu uisus interclusere nefasto*).

What Hypsipyle tells us, while she and we dump 'her' infant in the way of the passing Snake's fatally clumsy tail-swish so that Nanny can serve us Argives, is her '*Iliupersis*'-with-a-difference / the tale of inter-necine massacre on Lemnos. This is Myth's show-place of anti-*uirtus*, where gender turns turtle:[76] the island was stocked of old with *armisque uirisque* (5.305); but the men left their women/home/re-productivity/ploughing's furrow-line, *non arua uiri* (v. 309), until the women dared to take up *arma . . . uirum* (v. 353). Eventually these 'un-women are re-made': | *arma aliena cadunt, rediit in pectora sexus* (v. 397), when Venus and Amor insinuate into their minds the Argonauts' | *arma habitusque uirum* (v. 447). Soon the isle is full of baby noises (v. 462).

But before that, Lemnian upset in gender-/power-relations has seen the poem's first condensation of the patterns of 'killing' with those of 'mourning': one Lemniad 'probes where to wound her man' (v. 210, *uulnera . . . rimatur*). One 'keeps eyes wide, gets her foe first with a quick hug – as he becomes aroused for his knifing, he feels for her' (vv. 212–17, *oculis uigilantibus hostem | occupat amplexu, . . . oculis . . . tremens .. murmure Gorgen | quaerit*). A mother forces a sister 'to see herself in the face of fratricide: she falls on sibling's corpse' (vv. 227–34, *heu similes . . . uultus | aspiciens . . . iacenti | incidit*). The scene is 'floodlit' by Bacchus (vv. 285f.) and Sun 'averts light' from Lemnos (v. 297). Most markedly '*Theban*' of all Lemnian pre-echoes, Polyxo, 'cheeks/sockets erect and eyesight suffused with pulsating blood' (5.95f., *erecta genas aciemque offusa trementi | sanguine*), sets her stakes at 'four sons; + father': *uulnera fratrum | miscebo patremque simul spirantibus addam* (5.127f., 'My recipe calls for brothers – with a dash of Dad; add before all the ingredients go flat'). She models for all *Thebaid*'s Oedipal con-fusions of 'Brother + Brother – Add: Father' to follow. Tisiphone, for one, *fratrem huic, fratrem ingerit illi, | aut utrique patrem* (7.467f., 'She piles Brother on x, Brother on y, or Daddy z on x + y').

Put 'warrior wives hugging their "men" onto their blades in bed' together with 'epic funeral games for a "patriarch-Anchises"-re-make-as-cot-death' and feel the shift within narration through Hypsipyle. /

---

[76] Vessey (1970A) esp. 46f., Brown (1994) 113–23; Götting (1969) 63–79, 81–6: Lemnos figures Thebes *and Argos*, so every polity. Bloch (1970) on epic playing off *arma uirumque*.

Infanticide, 'the killing of children', always spells, or threatens to spell, the suicide of narration, 'the killing of story-telling'.[77]

II LAMENTATION AT THEBES / THE ABYSS

The narrative concerning Niobe, with its story of slain children buried finally only after a delay, reflects something of the situation within the *Iliad*. But the telling of the tale does not end in burial ... The story passes into an indefinite structure of openness beyond burial, ... in which it closes by suspending its statement of any final determinate meaning ... The text does not stage a final, full revelation of meaning but rather achieves a certain suspended position of 'meaningfulness': that indefinitely open indication of a certainty of sense in the absence of any single, specific determinate meaning.[78]

/

Every family history is an abyss.[79]

With the Funeral extravagance for Hypsipyle's / Eurydice's dead baby, the special service as previously used, a dozen times, by Niobe (6.517: *the* 'Theban mother', 1.711; cf. 3.193, 4.576, 9.682), we glamorize all *Thebaid*'s Innocents, those Babes-in-Arms: Argia's 'Astyanax'-re-make Thessander (3.683). Ino/Leucothea's Palaemon/Melicertes (cued in at 6.10–14). And Linus, who features at Opheltes'/Archemorus' funeral as ... embroidery (6.64–6: His mother 'abominated it to aversion', *oculos flectebat ab omine*). And we may feel primed to find Statius' epic militarism collapsing around its 'weakness' for the memorializing voice of the warriors' bereaved womenfolk:

> ... unius ingens
> bellum uteri, coeuntque pares sub casside uultus   (11.407f.)

One huge
   war. One huge
     womb. Come together,
       face, in your helmet, and face, in yours. You are
        The Same.[80]

---

[77] Simon (1987).
[78] Lynn-George (1988) 250, 252.
[79] Federspiel (1984) 137.
[80] Smolenaars (1994) 225 *ad loc.* compares Manil. 5.463f., *Thebana ... bella* | *uteri*. Cf. Henderson (1994); Brown (1994) 79–93, 'The gendering of grief'.

The annihilation that is the Father's curse / that Father who is also his children's brother / can cry for the Mother–Sister's womb: *Thebaid*'s 'primal scene' may supplement, / more than comment upon and amplify; rather, substitute and displace, / its staged paradigms of 'martial' *uirtus*. The climax it / maybe / delivers as the 'marital' narrative of sisterhood forged in defence of human rights between bride and sister / the (Callimachean) alliance between Argia and Antigone. / An 'alternat(iv)e' 'battle-line' to defy Creon, 'fraternize' with the Enemy, bury Polynices. (Cf. the simile of the sisters who bury Phaethon, 12.413–15; anticipated at 3.173.)

A 'sexually-charged picture of grief',[81] this comradely sorority: 'they drop together (*lapsae*) for an embrace à trois (*amplexu*), split the limbs 50/50, and with a groan from her, then a groan from her, go back to his face (*ad uoltum*), take turns for (*alterna*) possession of their favourite neck (12.385–88). These sisters of mercy will compete manically / manfully for Creon's punishment, in a 'Me, choose me!' verbal 'duel', a mock-'*Thebaid*' (*alternis . . . uerbis*, 461) / 'You'd have thought it was the familiar Theban wrath and hatred!' (v. 462). /

Is this what Thebes is (worth) fightin' for? / '20 km of corpses, burning like dead leaves, does rather put one out of focus, I dare say.'[82]

Woman, / this time, the bride, / wades through Statius' killing fields:

> dum funus putat omne suum, uisuque sagaci
> rimatur positos et corpora prona supinat
> incumbens, queriturque parum lucentibus astris.   (12.288–90)

> *She comes upon the dead – each one she assumes is hers.*
> *Eagle-eyed she rummages through the fallen,*
> *rolls over corpses face-down, leans down, wails:*
> *'The stars won't shine.'*

Argos' wife of wives, Juno, floods those fields with light (v. 312, *infuso lumine*), until Argia:

> . . . uidet ipsum in puluere paene
> calcatum. fugere animus uisusque sonusque,
> inclusitque dolor lacrimas; tum corpore toto
> sternitur in uultus animamque per oscula quaerit
> absentem . . .   (vv. 316–20)

---

[81] Hershkowitz (1994) 143.   [82] Hamilton (1916) 309.

She sees her man. In the dust. About flattened.
  Mind, sight, sound. All left her.
    Pain imprisoned epic tears.
      Every fibre of her body.
        She spreads her self on his face.
          She hunts his life. His breath.
            Kiss upon kiss. It is gone.

She, *Aarghia*, wails:

huc adtolle genas defectaque lumina ...
sed bene habet, superi, gratum est, Fortuna ...
      ... totos inuenimus artus.
ei mihi ...
hoc frater?   (vv. 325–40)

Here. Lift your cheeks.
  Those sockets. Dead, dead eyes ...
    Still. Praise be to Heaven! Thank you, Fortune! ...
      I have found him. All of him. His body checks out.
A   A   A   A   A   A   G   H
... This.
    This thing.
      This?
        A BROTHER –

Next, wife will be joined by sister, out combing the corpses too, for
the age-old unison of antiphonal lament (vv. 366, 375, their twin search
for dead menfolk, *quaeris ... quaesitura*) / 'Andromache'-and-'Juturna'
re-makes, joined in humanity's sisterhood. / But *Thebaid* can give us
only a semblance of the grief it must ultimately gesture to defer. The
pain of the women of Thebes / *and Argos,* / their lamentation, must lie
in the next, / impossible, / epic narration, way beyond Statius' powers
to realize.[83]

We must eternally imagine for ourselves widow Evadne's 'search'
(*quaesierit*) for a bolt in her breast, too (12.801f.). And widow Deipyle's

---

[83] *Thebaid* often gestures beyond its power to describe: 'Le maître des silences est Stace;
il en présente la gamme la plus variée, la plus riche' (Bardon (1943–4) 120, cf. 110–14,
e.g. 2.163, 3.102f., 4.145, 7.452, 10.273f., 815f. The speech 'broken-off' *in aposiopesi* is
a special colour of the poem, e.g. 1.465, 3.87, 291, 4.517f., 12.380). Cf. Rosaldo
(1989) esp. 177, for devastating critique of ethnography's coldness to the pain after
death, after the wake – as if rites *work*.

'lying on her corpse's kisses' (vv. 802f., *iacens super oscula saeui | corporis*). / All this for Capaneus, and for Tydeus.

Then conjure up 'the bloodless face' of the *genetrix Erymanthia* Atalanta's Parthenopaeus, every mother's son, 'lovely in death' (*consumpto seruantem sanguine uultus*). Statius can only treble the double mourning from its 'double armies' (*geminae pariter ... cohortes*) on both sides: *Arcada ... | Arcada ... | Arcada ...* (vv. 805–7). Epic came too soon for this lovely boy,[84] not yet nor ever a M –

12 POEM OF THEBES / EPIC OF STASIS

> The *Thebaid* ends with lamentation for the dead / not with paeans for Theseus' victory.[85]

We saw that *Thebaid* reels in the fighting for Thebes with successive gestures of closure; / but the *Epigoni* always wait, to re-make '*Thebes*' in the next generation, so survivor Adrastus can get to play Oedipus, lead *his* heir to oblivion at Thebes (7.219–21).[86] Theseus brings vengeance; / but his intervention imports fresh violence.[87] 'Lament, or rather ... the *praeteritio* of lament', formally consecrates, draws a line under, the killing; / but persists. The *Epilogue* brings poem to port; / but as a textbook which will inform future generations – and serve a 'lesson' to (whichever) Caesar. / Or rather, *Epilogue* offers readers-to-come an implied reading, through '*Caesar*', to take their own measure of the politics of '*Thebes*'.[88]

But *Thebaid* has not *not* mourned the death of *uirtus*. This has filled its plangent lines all along. The epic can only imagine what com-

---

[84] Hardie (1990A) 9–14, Hershkowitz (1994) 136 and *passim*.

[85] Ahl (1986) 2897.

[86] At 11.443–6, Adrastus gallops off to hide, to find darkness for living death as if an Amphiaraean Oedipus, as if down to Hell (cf. Ahl (1986) 2858).

[87] Against e.g. Vessey (1982) 575, 'The epic ends on a note of uplifting optimism', cf. Vessey (1986). Vessey (1973) 315 claimed 'It is through [Theseus] that evil and madness are finally eradicated when he slays first Haemon (747ff.) and then Creon (774ff.), last representatives of the *gens profana* of Thebes.' But the text only *says*: 'Theseus' spear stuck through two horses into Haemon's chariot-pole and ... he homed in on Creon alone' (12.747–53). Theseus is set up by Statius, ambushed by '*Thebes*', cf. Hershkowitz (1994) 147.

[88] Hardie (1993) 46–8; Malamud (1995) 190, 194f. on didaxis; cf. Braund (1996A).

memoration of Manhood could be like, / can only lament that it cannot lament:

> quis mortis, Thebane, locus, nisi dura negasset
> Tisiphone, quantum poteras dimittere bellum!
> te Thebe fraterque palam, te plangeret Argos,
> te Nemee, tibi Lerna comas Larissaque supplex
> poneret, Archemori maior colerere sepulcro.   (6.513–17)

> *Man of Thebes, what an occasion for your death,*
> */ how the poet could exploit the topos,*
> */ if the iron law of Theban madness had not forbidden it!*
> *Your city-nymph Thebe could show up for the funeral*
> *right next to your Brother, for all to see, and*
> *your other city Argos could join the mourning,*
> *with the neighbours:*
> *(heroic-victor-proclaiming) Nemea,*
> *(venomously seven-mouthed) Lerna,*
> *and (non-Achillean) Larissa,*
> *humbly offering ritual*
> *locks for your grave.*
> *Memorialized:*
> *bigger than*
> *infant*
> *Archemorus,*
> *a greater*
> *epic send-off.*

Thebaid 'ends', as we saw, by explicitly representing itself as a successor to Virgil's *Aeneid*. In this very gesture of filiation and affiliation to the Augustan epic, the Flavian poem marks out a challenging difference from / impassive / Virgilian epic's decorum. If we conclude that Statius stages his work as an emulation, a challenge, a re-making of the classical tradition, we / may / find that the reverential disciple has undone the master-text by taking over the original, re-directed it toward quite other ends.

Statius' text was doomed from the start to fall punily short of its quintessentially strong predecessor. Distended swell of hot air,[89] epic

---

[89] Tumid *Thebaid is,* / says hyperbole, / Tisiphone's skin, *suffusa ueneno | tenditur ac sanie gliscit* (1.106–7, suffused with venom, stretched and puffing putrid'). Here – as in

energy hyped to paroxysmic frenzy programmed to collapse in an over-weight faint,[90] *Thebaid* knows the great days of Rome, when the great books in Latin could be written, were long since past. / But full-bloodied *Thebaid* all the while infiltrates the structures of Virgilian epic with intently revisionary, even subversive, re-working of the traditional values.[91]

The very subject of the Theban saga may have always connoted, / perhaps, even, stood for, / a contestation of the 'Iliadic' values of the Homeric civilization(s) of classical Antiquity. Such a meaning may be lodged indelibly and unmistakably in the theme from the beginning, from the beginning, that is, of European Literature.[92] So Statius may display a lability always latent in the old vision of warrior reality, ex-posing an uncomfortable instability at the heart of those old city-state paradigms for civic existence which ordered Antiquity into a single temporality.

Thebaid's fealty to Virgil may figure a 'strong' re-reading of the *Aeneid*, as itself a text about to turn, for ever, toward a plaintive critique of the militarism of its narrative of action. The suggestion then would be that Statius' 're-reading' strengthens and emphasizes an incipient tendency in Virgilian narrative so that it may reappear, amplified and strengthened, to full view. / Not the warrior display of *Arma uirumque*, but its disfiguration and displacement before the pain of woman's bereavement.

Theban Sphinx always already condenses, / does she not? / the epic's Oedipal question for its readers. Is she, all along, in her Oedipodionian *domus*, the *Thebais*: 'cheeks/sockets erect and eyes suffused with old

---

'tumid' Antimachus (Catull. 95a.10) – 'swell' Polynices (1.299), Tydeus (2.114), Eteocles (2.346), Capaneus (3.600), Hippomedon (9.442), Parthenopaeus (9.781), 'swollenfoot' Oedipus (11.378, 676), Creon (12.174); Wrath (1.411–2), War-Horses (6.418) and armies (7.528), venom (5.508), Ganges and Ismenos (4.387, 9.459).

90 Cf. Hershkowitz (1995A), esp. 63, '[Thebaid's] frenzy-fuelled excessiveness cannot be sustained but instead diminishes and finally disappears. The epic plunged in madness, seemingly *sine limite*, will soon, like the waves raging *sine litore*, grow qu–.'

91 The tracks *Thebais* is to tread in recall Lucretius' devotions to Epicurus, 3.4: cf. Clay (1983) 40, 'On first impression it appears that he considered himself a follower, but it is also clear that in relation to his reader he regarded himself as a leader and that in terms of Roman poetry he viewed himself as taking a path taken by none before him.' See Malamud (1995) 194f.

92 See Hardie (1990) for Ovid's Thebes in *Metamorphoses* III, an important re-source for Statius.

blood' (*erecta genas suffusaque tabo | lumina*) ? She 'hugs' (*amplexa*) human remains, gnawed bones (*semesa . . . ossa premens*) clutched to her naked breast in hideous parody of woman's grief carrying out the dead. She dominates the visual-/battle-field (*uisu . . . frementi | conlustrat campos*), ready for all-comers with her 'cursed tongue, claws a-sharpening, bite drawn' (*dirae . . . linguae, . . . acuens . . . ungues |, . . . strictos . . . dentes*, 2.505–14).[93]

Not the paradigm of *uirtus* hung on its age-old narrative peg, but the poetic affirmation of G U I L T. If Theseus models all-too-distant a reader, sorting out Theban disaster all too firmly and cleanly, all too violently and vitiated a wind-up,[94] then / perhaps / we can use those Oedipal sockets of ours, feel what we cannot see? With Statius? Perhaps – but he could not possibly confirm this.

> I fought with my twin
> That enemy within
> Till both of us fell by the way –[95]

... And Argos? / And Argia?

> From my words you will have reached the conclusion that the real Berenice is a temporal succession of different cities, alternately just and unjust. But what I wanted to warn you about is something else: all the future Berenices are already present in this instant, wrapped one within the other, confined, crammed, inextricable.[96]

Appendix: Cutting Statius' eye teeth on Seneca, *Oedipus* 957–65

Statius drew for his 'Theban' vision on the blinding of *Oedipus* in Seneca's tragedy (Lucan's uncle; power behind his protégé Nero's first years as emperor; engulfed in 65 by the Pisonian conspiracy: chapters 5, 7):[97]

---

93 Sphinxes emblazon both Polynices' sword (4.87) and Haemon's helmet (7.251f.); cf. Moret (1984) 4 n. 8. Tragic Oedipus was, already, the Sphinx re-made in its image, cf. Mastronarde (1970) 321f. on Sen. *Oed.* v. 100, (her) *unguis* ~ v. 968, (his) *unguibus*.

94 Cf. Rabinowitz (1989) 120–31 for this phenomenon.

95 Dylan (1978), 'Where are you tonight? (Journey through dark heat)'.

96 Calvino (1979) 125, 'Hidden Cities 5': the ultimate cityscape.

97 Cf. Vessey (1973) 95, Hill (1990) 109.

'... fodiantur oculi' dixit atque ira furit;
ardent minaces igne truculento genae
oculique uix se sedibus retinent suis ...   959
... manus in ora torsit. at contra truces   962
oculi steterunt et suam intenti manum
ultro insecuntur, uulneri occurrunt suo.
scrutatur auidus manibus uncis lumina ...   (vv. 957–65)

In the end, the crazed voice of Wrath said:
  'Eyes. Must dig out my eyes.'
    Ablaze, menace, inferno. From cheeks glower sockets,
      Eyes. All but slip past the retina ...
        ... Yanked his hands into his face. Lowering back,
        Eyes. No recoil. Follow their hand. Ready, keen.
          Charge their wound. On the offensive.
            He rummages. Glutton.
              Human claws. Eyes ...

Our tragic Oedipus could see worse: *nunc manum cerebro indue* ('This time, dip
your hand right in your brain', Sen. *Phoen.* 180). Outdoing epic Hecuba's
attack on Polymestor: *digitos in ... lumina condit | expellitque genis oculos ... |
immergitque manus ... | non lumen ..., loca luminis haurit* ('She buries fingers in
eye-lights, pops eyes from sockets/cheeks, plunges hands in, wipes out, not the
light, but the place for the light', Ov. *Met.* 13.561–4).[98]

---

[98] See Poe (1983) esp. 154–6: our look into the dark madness of Senecan Oedipus is
mocked by the act of Oedipus' body.

PART IV

Histories of Rome

7 Tacitus: the world in pieces

> Power is the essential subject of political history.[1]

> Time will say nothing but I told you so
> Time only knows the price we have to pay
> If I could tell you I would let you know.[2]

Tacitus' *Annals* begin by describing the City of Rome in a double sequence. Successive power blocs are traced, from the kings to Augustus; and, shadowing them, writers of history degenerate from olden times' frankness, through Augustan lapse into flattery, and down the switchback of intimidated lies and posthumous vilification to Nero. He will himself, he writes, 'recount from the last days of Augustus through the rest of the dynasty without animus or bias: the reasons for both of those are a world away / he abhors' (1.1, ... *quorum causas procul habeo*). The historian (impossibly) exorcizes warped passions from his work; but Rome is headlined as the (affective) subject, and the politics of interpretation have been topicalized as frame for the interpretation of politics.[3] *Dis*passion does not last a sentence.[4]

The gesture does not simply seal Tacitus from implication in his narration, behind the impassive rhetoric of the annalistic genre and a double safety-door of assassination and end of dynasty. No, writing '*Rome*' opens wide the involvement of historian and reader in the narration. 'Tacitus is not merely recording some events of the past but confronting his readers with issues which are no less essential for the life of responsible citizens today than they were at his own time.'[5] The annalistic form of 'our *Annals*' (4.32) binds the work to the politics

---

[1] Syme (1958) 375.
[2] Auden (1968) 44, 'If I could tell you'.
[3] Mitchell (1982/3), Plass (1988) 12. At 4.53.3, Tacitus includes (the sort of) information left out, he notes, of 'annals' – for once?
[4] Cf. Williams (1990) esp. 146.
[5] Classen (1988) 116. Critique: Rubiés (1994).

of the *res publica*, consular figureheads leading a *yearly* change of the
guard to link human with solar time. *Annals* are the voice of the tribune, the censor, the consul, of *that* Rome, they can speak no other
language.[6] It was not possible to write *Annals* before (in the myth of
respublica libera) Brutus expelled the Tarquins. Had Augustan dictatorship ended that world, together with its sanctioned voice, ' "the
word" [as] the accepted truth, the official version of reality'?[7] At Tacitus' late stage (as he positions it), was the story of Rome to be autho-
rized as one of deformation and desecration of that heritage? What
Tacitus documents under the flag of dispassion (so: laments, protests,
contemns?) is collapsed into the reigns of emperors, as Livian history
of Rome *Ab urbe condita* is ousted by Tacitean history of the Caesars'
re-foundation *Ab excessu diui Augusti*. Rome kept consuls alongside
emperors, so (how) could post-Augustan history ever step out of the
shadow thrown over it by (un)nostalgic nostalgia for the Republic?
Annals were doomed to work their way away from their formative basis
(*causas*), from what was lost; and to trace that loss, demolish their own
raison d'être.

   Tacitus tells that and how the cumulative procession of reigns
through the first dynasty produced derealization, measuring the aliena-
tion of Roman discourse from its former meanings in an exponential
series of degradations from one tyrant to the next ... mockery of a
monster. The savage ironies of repetition and refraction arising from
Nero after Claudius (half lost from the MSS) after Gaius (completely
gone) after Tiberius – all of them *Caesar Augustus* re-makes – articulate

---

6 'The annalistic form was traditionally associated with the republican past, and Tacitus
   wanted to evoke that past, if only to deny its application to the present ... In rejecting
   traditional annalistic history, Tacitus rejects also an interpretation of history' (Ginsburg (1981) 100). 'The quality that sets him apart from other Roman historians is his
   ability, while living within, and actively serving, the Principate, to look at the history
   of the past hundred years with the eye of a Republican writer' (Martin (1981) 234).
   Tacitus is, however, not just out to 'deny': his work unpicks the story it painstakingly
   assembles and definitively weaves together. And Tacitus remains the 'Republican
   writer', *uellet nollet*, precisely because he memorializes what succeeded the Republic.
7 Hodge and Kress (1988) 147: this (tribal) 'word' is 'a statement which has the absolute
   modal power it has because it is deprived of its transformational history, of the process
   by which it came into existence, and the different versions which have been trimmed
   and reworked into their place in the "word" '. Tacitus' work next to obliviated his
   sources; his wishing away of proximity and over-investment lever him up to the status
   of speaker for the state of the world.

a Roman myth of power which may, like Statius' *'Thebes'* (chapter 6), never be un/tied from/to its particular referent – however distantiated and disavowed. The challenge for Rome's third dynasty, embedded in its library of eternal (eternally relevant) Augustan classics, was to elude or duck the role of repetition of its predecessors' descent into senseless entropy, and to resist positioning as a continuation of the slide.

Historians found their own solutions. Even Greek writers could be more or less 'far from' the writing traditions of the Republic – Alexandrian Appian chose the succession of conquests that assembled the world, his world, as a state; but Dio the double consular keeps his Greek *Roman history* close to traditional year-on narration of *his* Rome (chapter 1). In Latin, while Tacitus wrote resolutely on, Suetonius the palace private secretary chose biography for his account of imperial Rome, cutting through the panoply of court structure to feature the emperor as effectively the sole *locus* of power. Suetonius' *Lives of the Caesars* lustily embrace the consequences of this revisionary analysis. As in the book you are reading (chapter 2), *Julius* starts the autocracy; in Suetonius, personality makes a Caesar – more than his place within a dynasty, on a trajectory that falls away from the first Augustus' inauguration. Rome becomes an expression of imperatorial will, and whim – another new start with each . . . psychopath.[8]

Tacitus, by contrast, *annalyses* Rome, as an imperial system with a continuing repertoire and linear direction.[9] His work derives his present from the Flavians, their era from the Julio-Claudians, and – implicitly – the first Augustans from the rubble of the Republic. *Annals* must contest, but tell of their trouncing in, the fight for control of Rome in the language of politics. There is nowhere for Nervan *ciues* to

---

[8] Cf. Wallace-Hadrill (1983) 110, 'Suetonius has no place in a history of the political ideal of liberty. He avoids politics as a subject.' That is, a very recognizable politics – the politics of the disavowal of politics. Ammianus complains of the trivialization of emperor fetishism (26.1); cf. Fornara (1983) 73.

[9] For example, the *Histories* start from 1 Jan. 69 CE, not from the decease of (*non*-deified) Nero. Only 4.1, *C. Asinio C. Antistio coss. nonus Tiberio annus . . .* , points half-way to what might have been (Syme (1958) 90 and n. 2). Of the Nero books, only XIV begins with a consular year: the opportunity to ring XIV between matricide and the uxoricide it spawns (with rebellion in the Amazonian fens to fill the sandwich, cf. Roberts (1988)). Imperial figures are set off by annalistic form: Germanicus leads off in all the years he is alive; in XII, Agrippina dominates the starts of each of the six years. End-of-year obituaries chart the death of *libertas*, the end of a world (Gingras (1991/2) on *Ann.* III). See Ginsburg (1981) *passim*.

hide from the questions pressed by Tacitus' renewed politicization of that language. Nowhere in Rome – nowhere in the world.

This essay clings to the materiality of Tacitus' writing in eliminating person from narration; but explodes annalistic discreteness. A sarcastic lunge for the real: 'faire de l'annalyse une variante de son objet'.[10]

I FIXING THE WORD

Such is the problem. It is likely that opinions will continue to differ.[11]

Tacitus relentlessly documents the construction of an imperial world from a blend of detritus from the old order with icing from the new. But his writing resists the structures of dominance whose success inexorably imposes their perspective on his narrative. History is not *simply* bound to vindicate winners: as Tacitus himself remarked, dead tyrants have their panegyrics (p)re-written as invective. If the grip of the Caesars controls Everything, supplying doctored language, sea-sonably adjusted conceptual resources, and cultural traditions in re-tread, nevertheless Tacitus' retrospect processes this take-over and hi-jacking of the Roman world through a censorious frame that refuses to endorse a word of it.[12]

His first paragraph indissolubly associated the fraud and deception tooled into the control of post-Augustan society through violence done to language with the falsification and disfigurement of its historiog-raphy. He advertised the double-bind knotted in his own writing – no need to scan the *Annals* to find *the* editorial comment, emotional out-burst, or forced interpretation which will (finally) betray the historian's true/sincere/inner/underlying/deep 'view': he'll never be caught with his rhetorical trousers down, his work is ironized beyond anything so crude.[13] Instead, his text writes in 'anti-language', held always just beyond reach of secure reading, recuperative comprehension, not a

---

[10] After de Certeau (1990²) xxxvi.

[11] Goodyear (1972) 91 on *Urbem Romam* (1.1.1).

[12] Cf. Williams (1990) 161–3.

[13] Luce (1986) carefully works toward this view. History written under autocracy about autocracy hands readers a role in the poetics of suspicion: they should be too sophis-ticated to chase a hint, too alert to be content with any narration; and ready to jump to conclusions, to follow the author beyond what can be documented. And not to trust the narrator too far.

'story' but a deadly serious challenge to think out, re-think and be out-thought by 'the consular historian'.[14] The most he offers for 'key' is the foreword (more below).

Like this chapter, the *Annals* present, with scarcely an expostulation, a ludibrious slide from the entrée of Tiberius pussy-footing with the Senate, to Nero's extraction of 'just des(s)erts' from a feast of fun at the expense of his élite, when the consul victim Vestinus, who was left out of the Pisonian plot to kill the emperor, is actually *made* a con-spirator by Nero because he hates him, 'out of close friendship'. A cohort of guards held the party surrounded on into the small hours and nobody moved till the host was led out, a doctor fetched, veins opened and silent plunge in a hot bath. The night creature Nero revelled in their terror at (as they thought) their own impending deaths and quipped, 'A fair price for a ticket to a dinner fit for a consul' (15.68f., *pro epulis consularibus*). Tacitus' less-than-idealist and less-than-idealized plotters, Lucan and Seneca included or dragged in, foul up in the incompetence only to be expected from ham Neronian courtiers, outwitted by the royal *prima donna*, who switches effortlessly into 'generalissimo' vein to order immediate assault on Vestinus' party (15.69.1).[15]

Still Vestinus *Atticus* (*sounds* like an Athenophile ... democrat?) fea-tures as one excluded from the conspiracy for typically ignominious reasons – 'personal feuds, as well as anxiety that he was headstrong and a loner'; because – among the bizarre parade of others' motives – Ves-tinus 'might go for freedom – or else pick someone else for emperor'. Or at any rate, plenty of people believed that was why Vestinus was left out (52.5, *ne ad libertatem oreretur uel delecto imperatore alio*). In the tangle of discontents, Tacitus matches Lucan's 'hatred' (*uiuida odia*) with the consul elect Lateranus' 'love of Rome' (*amor rei publicae*, 49.2f.); the feeling that the end was nigh rallied others (*finem adesse imperio*, 50.1). Tacitus declares first of all that he can't get to the bottom of the plot (49.1), but he has shown that oppositional politics did include the dimension of some change from rule by emperor – if

---

[14] 'Anti-language': Hodge and Kress (1988) 86f. 'Consular historian': Syme (1958) e.g. 503, 'Contemporary events ought to have pulled a man back to the theme and manner of the c. h.' Cf. Williams (1990) 161–3, 'self-reflexivity'.

[15] 'Grasp the nettle (*praeuenire*) ... Storm Johnny's citadel ... Crush this crack outfit.' Cf. Woodman (1993) *passim*, esp. 123f. For the principate = civil war, cf. Keitel (1981).

only on the lunatic fringe (= a consul's prevalent image, his death-sentence ...).[16]

The Republic was not to be resuscitated by this bunch: but assassination of a Caesar *always* returned speculation to the Ides of March 44 and the twenty-three differently inspired daggers that went into Julius:[17] the bunglers planned for the ungentle giant Lateranus to fake a petition at Nero's knees, knock him down and flatten him; the soldiers among the crew would pile in for the slaughter. Everyone would (have) enjoy(ed) *that* year's Cerealia – and those ever after (53.2f.). This charade, as will appear, was already, momentarily, a behind-the-scenes factor in Tiberius' opening fumbles. But more important, the Pisonians' tyrannicidal impulse was not inherently any more or less likely to achieve their immediate objective than Cassius Chaerea's had been in 41 CE, when (another) C. Caesar (Gaius) was run through. That rather similar coup, which had prompted painfully protracted discussion about restoring the Republic before it collapsed in the face of the imperial guards, was for Tacitus the only 'peace-time' overthrow of an emperor.[18] Nero's deposition in 68 CE was, in a sense, the vindication of the Pisonians – successful in their failure.[19]

On the structural level, the organization of the Annals as hexadic book-units, ringing Tiberian tragedy (I–VI) with Neronian melodrama (XIII–?XVIII?) round their chiastic inferior doubles [Gaius and] Claudian clowning as if in a fated symmetry of return and a farcical descant of pre-destination, beggars mere annual organization of their contents.[20] The colour of the narrative changes to develop a cumulative vision of tyranny. But *Annals* document their own brainwashing *passim*, offering a debate on their own conditioning as imperial *adulatio*.

To take just one example, casual 'Newspeak' such as the phrase *segnis et dominationibus aliis fastiditus, adeo ut Gaius Caesar ... solitus sit* ('Mr Sloth who so "wearied" other reigns that Caligula ... regularly'), in the first sentence of XIII, poses an insidious reader-trap. It equivocates in the term *dominatio* between 'reign' and 'ruler', stamping a

[16] Cf. Bartsch (1997) ch. 3.
[17] Cf. Woodman (1993) 107.
[18] Cf. Jos. *Ant. Jud.* 19.70–95, Wiseman (1991), Woodman (1993) 107.
[19] Both Gaius' and Nero's Tacitean demises are lost.
[20] Cf. Williams (1990) 147. For the comic/satiric turn to Claudius' XI–XII, cf. Vessey (1971), Dickison (1977).

period of Roman time, a universe of life-spans, into the monological terms of imperial nomenclature. In short, in a word, a world: the 'wor(l)d' of imperial history.[21]

The formal polarity between this phrase and the opening words of the reign/hexad/book/sentence: *nouo principatu ... Nerone*, ('the new reign ... Nero') is a 'lead' for readers. Does the suggested synonymy between the approved euphemism *principatus* and the *Realpolitik* (ab)usage *dominatio*, in the acceptance of which the Roman world is implicitly downgraded to an Emperor's *familia*, (not) deconstruct imperial discourse? What is at stake in the narration of this history is precisely whether it can trace the archaeology of its own conceptual repertoire. The whole text swarms with naturalization and de-familiarization of the language it has available.[22] What ironies inhere in such an apparently non-committal, formal, purely *linguistic* categorization as (L&S entry *s.v.*) '*principatus* 2. Of the empire (*post-Aug.*), reign, empire, dominion, sovereignty'! Registration in regular parlance empowers the tyranny, translates it into a particular realization of power.

The question before the reader who reaches/starts book XIII, then, is: just where in the text did such usages dull into the norm, into the transparency of quotidian discourse? A question first proposed in that opening salvo cataloguing power-structures at Rome through history: *dictaturae ad tempus sumebantur; neque decemuiralis potestas ultra biennium, neque tribunorum militum consulare ius diu ualuit. non ... longa dominatio; et ... potentia cito ...* ((i) 'Dictatorships were taken up in emergency, on a temporary basis, to meet a crisis, from time to time; (ii) the Board of Ten held power short of two years; (iii) the pseudo-consular authority of the (so-called) "military tribunes" was ephemeral. A despotism, a trice; and power in an instant ..', 1.1.1–3). Second- or twentieth-century readers long habituated to such (ir)regularities are led back by the *Annals* to the wellhead, to inspect the processes of erasure and blot, emendation and corruption, which produce the

---

[21] *fastiditus*, a *hapax* in *Annals*, draws eyes to the phrase. In 1.4.2, *imminentis dominos* played a scary version with the same counter: 'the slave-drivers hulking over people' are 'the next ruler(s)'. *dominatio* was not domesticated, even by second-century CE 'moderates', cf. Benario (1975) 134f., Zaffagno (1981) 37.

[22] Cf. Wordsworth (1987), writing the history of historicity. Thus, not *SPQR*, but *senatus milesque et populus* swear the oath of allegiance to Tiberius (1.7.3), *populus et senatus et miles* witness Messalina's bigamy (11. 30.5).

smooth surface of a courtly propriety. Tacitus shows up the tragedy and farce of its formation. Such is the peaceful settlement left by Augustus for Rome to fight over as dynasties came and went.

The text also works to jam together the two ends of the spectrum of power in Rome of the Caesars, pouring out a stream of polarized hatchet-men to articulate tyranny in its characteristic form of murder. Thus 'centurions and a tribune on hand' are joined by *custos et exactor e libertis Euodus* ('Mr Despatch the freedman, to detain the prisoner and see to the punishment'); 'in came the tribune in silence and the freedman squawking lots of subhuman abuse' (in a word and a blow, the tribune's sword killed Messalina: 11.37.3–5–38.1). Later, Agrippina in her death-chamber 'sees the freedman Anicetus with the trierarch Herculeius and the admiralty centurion Obaritus in attendance . . . The trierarch first bashed her head in with his baton, then the centurion drew his sword . . . and finished her off – messily' (14.8.5f.). 'A centurion butchered' Rubellius Plautus 'for Pelago the eunuch to see: Nero had put the centurion and his squad under his command, as a royal servant over his minions' (14.59.3). Similarly with the pairing of the *eques Romanus* 'Celer' with the *libertus* 'Helius' (Messrs. Swift and Sunlight), as *ministri*, 'hitmen', to feast Silanus *proconsul Asiae* on poison and so start Nero's Reign (13.1.2f.).

This is also part of a 'chapter' of larger antitheses which match Silanus with his companion in death, Narcissus *Claudii libertus*. On the one hand, there is the jagged deformation of a Tacitean paragraph of labyrinthine syntactical machinations. He entwines the Machiavellian mentality of an anxious Empress with a *mot* from Nero's prequel the crazed Caligula – a tracer back to the beginning of the last book and the erasure of the last Silanus – inside a frame which cites 'the word round town'. Popular comparison weighs up the infant Macbeth Nero against his opposite, his stemmatically well-placed 'alternative', the slow-burning proconsul, whose pedigree is his death-warrant. On the other hand, all this complexity is jarred up against the note-form brevity that studs Narcissus' demise with Sallustian-censorious blocks of damnation.[23]

---

[23] Klingner (1955) in a classic paper shows the contrapuntal opposition between these deaths: esp. *ignaro Nerone* ∼ *inuito principe*; *mors paratur* ∼ *ad mortem agitur*; *per dolum Agrippinae* ∼ *iurgiis aduersus Agrippinam*; swift toxin in the limelight *inter epulas* ∼

Tacitus puts this paradigm polarity forward as telling analysis of the setting to one side of the trappings of the Republic. The real forces of power are now royal women[24] and imperial servants, in a scrap between pedigree and palace to pick over the carcass. Rome becomes the satirical stew of discourse mobilized, for example, by luscious Messalina on the counter-attack: the Showgirl launches her bimbo body at her old man's eyes, her little ones at Daddy's arms and the alliterative *Vibidia uirginum Vestalium uetustissima* at the High Priest's ears, legs it crosstown, hitches a lonely ride on the trash-wagon. Only for the freedman Narcissus ('*Narcissus*', that wor(l)d!) to drown her out, remove the lot of them, risk the priestess and turn his eyes away (11.32–4). All to make sure Claudius, just once in his life, would live up to his name, 'so his hearing could be "cloddish and claused" even if she owned up' (28.3: one of those multiple absurdities with the per-version of imperial 'Law'). This sort of schism / carnivalized mess in the representation of power in action traces back to the shift in the *locus* of power to the words of the tyrant, those special words that sound for all the world like Latin but which spell a grammar all their own: *libertus* not *centurio*, *Palatium* not *militia*, *diuus* not *deus*, *mater* or *uenenum*, not *SPQR* and *uictoria*, *epulae* not *curia*, *cubiculum* not *forum*, *seruitium* not *libertas* ...

This Rome cannot decide whether it has become Alexandria, it just feels that way temporarily, it manages to hide the fact from itself, or it must never think any such thing: 'doublethink is the general condition of knowing that a statement is both true and not true, both true to experience and true to "the word", to the social definition of reality'.[25] *Annals*, like Orwell, so frame their represented world with pejoration that the fragmentation of their 'socially validated truth' is very soon realized for any reader.

---

drawn-out unspecific presumed extinction *aspera custodia et necessitate extrema*; a con-trast with Nero ∼ a strong tally between their vices; the long-dismissed cipher ∼ the key-figure in the struggle with Messalina. (Cf. Martin (1981) 228.) For Tacitean techniques of '*Spannung*' (tension), to rip apart settled confirmation of expectations, monological reception, authoritative finality, see Vielberg (1987) 25–76, Plass (1988) 26–55, Williams (1990) 140–6.

[24] Gender and kin transgressions are the mytho-logical shop-window of the politics of tyranny.

[25] Hodge and Kress (1988) 151.

2 GOING TO PIECES

The prime quality of Cornelius Tacitus is distrust.[26]

I can doubt the reality of everything but the reality of my doubt.[27]

The *Annals* insist throughout that narrative, the structure of explanation, the category-system which bounds social thought, is founded on repetition and on feed-back pressures to repeat; while the very compulsion to repeat produces mutation, deviancy and perversion. Modelling of what lies before and ahead in history after the precedence of the past infects the formation and trajectory of the narrative with the fatalism of the 'always already'. Things lapse.

On the grand scale, the story is structured as a decomposition round the focal imperial figures. Reluctant Tiberius is another 'late Augustus', one deprived before he started of a prince's charismatic entrée, with only decline up ahead, from the moment of the coronation onwards. Presumably the *Wunderkind* Gaius hatched fully-grown, enthroned without Augustus' rise to power: a second emperor who was never meant for the throne. The third in a row of these, Claudius, is a Tiberius *manqué*, the senile tyrant but this time lacking the laurels of a *dux*. And Nero is a Tiberius *in reverse*: a second boy-king, and the ultimate limit to the family of Augustus (these Augustuses), the given telos informing 'their' narrative all through. The comedy of such repetition of history, the satirical defamation of history as such repetition, makes of every Domitian a 'Bald Nero' and every Napoleon le Petit the pettiness of the 'great' Napoleon.[28]

Tacitus' dramatic writing deploys a sceptical rhetoric of *ludibrium* (mockery) to engage readers in appreciating the absurdist illogic of imperial entropy. *Annals* bundle together physical abuse, verbal quip, mockery, absurdity, and scandal in their stream of outrages against the person, the Roman state, the Latin language.[29] When power-relations between ruler and the rest are rushing apart at great velocity, the emperor's joke becomes an essential component of his armature. When

---

[26] Syme (1958) 398.

[27] Gide *cit.* Kellman (1980) 5.

[28] Mehlman (1977) on Marx on ludicrous Napoleon III.

[29] See Plass (1988) esp. 15–25, '*ludibrium* and political wit'. The literary entertainments of post-Augustan *declamatio* and *recitatio* (Woodman (1988) 160–96, esp. 183–5) were key institutions in the production of (sophisticated) imperial subjects.

Tacitus quotes a rude remark from Gaius, 'Silanus the Golden Wether' (13.1.1), or when he says young Nero quipped (*non absurde*, 'more than passably'): 'The freedman is going to lay down his office' (13.14.2), can the world-soul be taken at his word? How is it to be imagined that a piece of civic flesh looks to a word-ruler?

Language and behaviour lose their comprehensibility in the force-field of a dictator. Regular personal relations cannot survive there. With the emperor's mission to abuse civility go the efforts of all Romans to communicate in all seriousness, their words emptied of purchase on their world. Vestinus' guests found they were the entertainment for a feast of imperial fun, however physically absent Nero may have been: how much of court life could prove to have been orchestrated from afar, *à leur insu*? In return, was an emperor ever in anyone's company? Nero may even have made it an ambition to achieve this contradiction (more below). Certainly every Neronian banquet was his – the wicked fairy of the tale.

The narration works 'poetically' with and on its repertoire of shading devices to jolt thought. Thus Tacitus fixes surprise-effects to conclude each of the Nero books: (i) XIII: the figgy life-tree of Rome's twin infancy withered, was at least taken to be a portent, 'until . . . it grew new shoots'; (ii) XIV: out of these shenanigans 'sprang the plot against Nero, that epic movement, world-shaking and . . . ill-starred / a flop / bringing fresh disaster' (*magna moles et . . . improspera*); (iii) XV: Nero refused the offer to become *diuus* just yet, thank you, in case some nasty pieces of work 'turned it into an omen of his exit from imperial history, because a *princeps* only holds divine honours *after* his dealings with mortals are over'; (iv) the *exitus* of XVI belongs in its place below. These – and all the other 'joke' structures, verbal, physical, or conceptual – open gaps in discourse that won't ever quite be patched over again. They leave a residue – both in the remainder that exceeds any attempt at interpretation; and as a benchmark for later emulation, the challenge of hyperbole to chase fresh hyperbole to outmatch its impact.

Annals XIII–XVI deploy and contest the stereotypicality of their Nero. He is the Julio-Claudian who came into the world 'during', and so was created 'by', the *Annals* (Gaius toddled into 14 CE, 1.40.2). Readers can hope to know their Nero from the cradle, know him definitively. On him and his reign, the plot of history enforces a completeness and closure: premature and violent death that spells the end of the dynasty. The writing also queries this drive toward mastery of its misbegotten creation, by satirizing the 'pre-judgementality' of its categories, its language, its precursors and its cast of players and play-makers. The narration fragments and dissipates its own authority, not least by directing its readers to notice its narratology, the fix of it all. Tacitus means to make each moment in every episode chime and clash with the others, in thematic inter-dependence; but he exposes how patterns that permit events to be construed are sure to miss their targets. If this is so for the 'readings' by the characters, what immunity can their narrator's readings of them and of Rome hope to claim?

Such an approach to reading the *Annals* was prompted from the first: *Urbem Romam a principio reges habuere* ('From the beginning kings held the city of Rome', 1.1.1). Here is a point of origin for the representation of political power in Latin: the self-replication of *regnum*, transcending the life and death of any individual, in successful perpetuation. The relations in force here remain inscrutable, in the transparency of *habuere*. At the same time, the echo from the start of the narration in Sallust's *Catiline*: *Urbem Romam, sicut accepi, condidere atque habuere initio Troiani* ..., ('At the start, as it has come down to me, Trojans founded and held the city of Rome', *Bell. Cat.* 6.1), refers readers beyond the unrepeatable model of pristine power from which *Roma* deviated, eternally: how far will the historian shadow and/or differ from his predecessor?[30] Nevertheless, *Annals* set in place the model of kingship, as unquestioned Nature, 'as it was in the beginning'. The next words institute the cultural system of Tacitus' Rome: *libertatem et consulatum L. Brutus instituit* ... ('L. Brutus set up liberty and the consulate').

Tacitus' Rome will be measured against the grid programmed here: Book 1 closes with the post-Augustan version of 'consular elections', a list cooked up by the emperor on principles unknown, unknowable and likely non-existent, from the documents, especially – in the nature of the case – the emperor's papers: Tacitus 'could not possibly confirm *anything*' (1.81.1). The opening paragraph shows the crucial longevity of Brutus' Rome – shrugging off the temporarinesses of interruption by legitimate dictatorships and the like, but in time exhausted by the illegitimate coups of first-century potentates – eventually taken under the *imperium* of Augustus: *nomine principis* ... ('under the name *princeps*':

---

[30] The opening of Sallust's *Histories*, *A principio* ... *urbis*, 1.8, re-doubles the intertextuality, cf. Zaffagno (1981) 44f.

henceforth to mean, always, 'in the name of the emperor – not *not dominus*'). While that tiny *et* between *libertatem* and *consulatum* proposed an unproblematic equivalence between this quadrisyllabic pairing, the outline has now descended to the 'real' world of faithless language – perhaps as durable as the Republic? The jury would have to be out for many a century yet. The reality of power henceforth begins from the recognition that the naming of the terms of power is what counts.[31] The *Annals* will not again retail 'things in the world', such as *libertas* and/or/= *consulatus*, faithfully delivered in language. For a veiling of the terms used for the 'interruptions' to the Republic – *potestas, ius, dominatio, potentia* as *imperium* – is achieved by the word *princeps*, through its power to mean *rex* while barely even saying *principium*.

In the shift from the Age of Kings to the Augustan 'Principate', is there a place left for *libertas* and for *consulatus* to bear meaning? Or are they henceforth verbal screens at the disposal of court protocol? The terms will be held up for scrutiny from Tiberius to Nero: what meanings can they be given, can Latin, that protocol of senatorial administration, give them, 'now', post-Augustus? What Latinity do they inaugurate? And was the epistemic shift instantaneous and entire, over between Actium and 14 CE; or does there survive the first Augustus (there does) the task of working through the implications of the revolution in all its ramifications through the Roman world? Not the primary terms of 'settlement'; but constant revision of the lexikon of imperial relations, like a permanently re-hashed proscription list.

3 THE ONCE AND FUTURE KING

What had the Caesars but their thrones?[32]

The *Annals* tell at every turn a very simple tale indeed, simple as primeval paternal Kingship (almost). The 'genogram' of dynasty, in all its crudity, its mystificatory ramifications: the Flavians of the *Histories* had produced their second father figure, correctly succeeded by his elder, legitimate, son, the suitably dashing and charismatic hussar Prince, without challenge from his artistic little brother, tied to apron-strings

---

[31] Cf. Plass (1988) 144 n. 29; 145 n. 33 for 'corrections' that replace words with glosses, 50–4 for 'unmasking' rhetorical figures that unsteady reading.

[32] Yeats (1962) 99, 'Demon and beast'.

and de-masculinized (chapter 6). Only for Domitian to go bad, naturally, when deathstiny removed Titus before he was much more than
potential and promise: once the *domus* passed to the anti-type brother,
the house was doomed ... This level of '*1066 and all that*' pop mytho-
logic *is* an important interpretative level in the organization of the
Annals – the bottom line that sophisticated reading must vainly struggle
to jettison.

Many forms of continuity with the previous Rome survived as if
intact. Among them, transmission within the aristocratic Roman *gens*
persisted, as a key coding of imperial power. Calibrated with this was a
familial nexus of kin and social relations, mothers, sisters, freedmen,
slaves, clients, friends; within a complex fabric of public, political,
institutions – Senate, lawcourts, state-cults, armies, provinces, embas-
sies ... The interlinking of *domus* within *urbs* within *orbis*, the divisions
between Rome, Italy, Empire, and barbarian Other; the inter-articulation of career-structures, ambitions, rewards ... All this Republican
business survived, ever more finely-tuned, geared up to incessant
administration of the world.[33] But this globally active system was, it
could be held, just a blur of activity, a proliferating confusion of activity, covering with a quasi-self-fabricating illusion of solidity a total subsumption and realignment of power-relations and intelligibility. For
the force-field of the 'palace' in practice ran Rome. Bedroom diplo-
macy and harem politics, the Greekling *libertus* in charge of Roman
legions, or thanked for waiving his royal pedigree for imperial service ...[34] The categories of the Republic must implode under the
st(r)ain of it all.

[33] Cf. Ginsburg (1993) for senatorial business anchored in the pre-Caesars past. All
Tacitus' parades of concern with the technicalities of Roman Law and administration,
the 'digressions' on Roman customs, localities, festivals, the lists of officials and their
careers, campaigns against the ring of tribes, records of offences to world-order
(*monstra* etc.) – all this traditional material feeds back Roman identity into the (form
of the) *Annales*; then on round the loop and back into reinforcement of Roman identity, its categories, its cultural formation.

[34] 14.39.3, 'Polyclitus', 'Mr Fame at last', in Britain: 'He made the aliens grin – in them
libertas still blazed away, they hadn't yet made the acquaintance of freedperson power.
What really phased them was this: a general, an army could murder a major war, then
kowtow to lumps of slavery' (*seruitiis*: the wor(l)d *confector* here obliges a reader to
take notice). And 12.53.3, Pallas – on the unsuccessful proposal of a Cornelius Scipio,
of all the degenerates; the incoming consul and future die-hard Barea Soranus (P.
Clodius Soranus Barea: just in time to die before the text does, 16.33.2) has just voted

To another view, the 'real' story of the Julio-Claudian dynasty, the *domus* of Augustus, reads this way: the self-originating King asserts the power to represent the state, as its ideal *uir – pater, ciuis, miles, dominus* and eventually one of the revered *maiores*. He is the One: he gives the orders, the words are his; he sees all and knows all; owns the property, determines the proprieties, distributes the proper names: *habere* is probably the only word wide enough to suggest it. Inside his house, he orders his family – marries a suitable, fertile, devoted wife; she is chosen by himself; her ties with her kin pose no threat. In his City, he rules wisely – public works, generous to the needy, a helping hand for the calamitous, sensible administration, law-giving, adjudication. In his realm, he bounds off the alien, looks after the soldiers, conquers when prudence dictates, shows personal dash and produces trophies, loot, memorials. He outlasts opposition, obliges with benefactions, wins loyalty by his exemplary life-style, and successfully arranges for his replacement in due succession. He judiciously melts his power and its sanctions of violence away from view, behind a diplomatic vocabulary of paternal respect, the panoply of disarming representations that stand-in for power. He binds the future to his plan, leaving a son, an undisputed and legitimate son, unambiguously marked out to fill his shoes, protected by the divine aura of the father. The son is mature, tried and tested, he would deserve his elevation even were it not bequeathed to him, he has already represented the King. To allow his ascension, the latter dies naturally, in bed, leaving a widow to lead universal mourning. *Vive le roi* ... Such is the myth of Augustus (as summarized at the end of 1.9.3–6, NB 6, *principis nomine*).

From the myth, the story of Augustus, which is told only as an exemplary ἀρχαιολογία in summary, must depart: Augustus began (again) as the Julian faction's *Caesar dux reliquus*, ('surviving generalissimo', 1.2.1), trading in the triumviral pseudo-title for that of consul (*posito triumuiri nomine consulem se ferens*). He took control without the opposition of the dead ferocious, and with the co-operation of the honoured complaisant (*quanto quis seruitio promptior*, 'the readier

him the mockery of 'praetorian insignia', signs of vacuity that evacuate sense from Roman Order, and the largest golden handshake from the Senate on record – for bringing to imperial attention the issue of female cohabitation with slaves. The 'servile' Pallas (named for the Arcadian Prince) is pre-cast as lover of the empress (Weaver (1972) 165).

to ditch *libertas*'). 'To consolidate autocracy' (*subsidia dominationi*, 1.3.1), he handed out 'back-to-back consulships'; had his (step-)sons hailed with the title '*imperator*', and 'his' (adoptive) boys called '*princeps Jr*' and '*princeps Jr*' – and, dead keen underneath the denials, had them 'pencilled in as *consules*'. His destined heir – left apparent as sole survivor – was paraded as 'son, colleague in high command, co-holder of power à la tribune'.[35] He removed from the scene one adopted then discarded seed of dispute, as such, but, as the clan went to pieces, stored another such up for the future by enforcing adoption on his heir, over and above the heir's own natural son and presumptive heir. Still, when he died all was calm, he had successfully carried off his world revolution (1.4.1) under the guise of peaceful continuity. With 'conservative words' (*eadem magistratuum uocabula*) – and barely anyone in the world still in one piece, who had seen the Republic (1.3.7, *reliquus*: ring back to 1.2.1, where this started).

Augustus, like most Roman emperors (barring Vespasian, and Marcus) had no natural son-and-heir. He had stolen his *already* 'happily married' wife. His own child (by earlier marriage) was undisputed, but *female*. The wife's sons were not theirs, no kin of his. Having no brothers, he tried first his sister's boy, with his daughter for pledge. He was obliged to turn second to his right-hand man, passing on said daughter and grafting his sons into the imperial family. This batch of heirs perished and the finger of fate indicated just one stepson – though as noticed above, there remained (i) a discarded grandson (son of right-hand man) for nuisance value; and (ii) big trouble brewing in one deceased stepson's son queering the nest of the elder stepson's, the heir's, own young son.

This story is already complex, a complex deflation of the myth. It

---

[35] *imperator*: not the general hailed in the moment of victory, but an exaggeration of the honorific; *principes*: pun on the traditional mock-title for prime ephebes, 'principal boys', and a cheapening of the chief title for imperial power itself, in mock-dissimulation of the wor(l)d 'principate'; *consul*: fixed years ahead, so *mock*-consular years ahead. Infantilization as the transgression that constitutes despotism; *filius, collega imperii, trib. pot.*: triple fiction of *adoptive* kinship, *fa ctitious pseudo*-consular honorific, and a fix abusing as if with technical precision the (long-worthless) wor(l)d of the Republic's watchdog. A triumphant paradigm for the work of equivocation in forging imperial discourse. Three phrases to be treated as mutually inter-translating synonyms, a knotted representation in language of Caesarian 'Everything'. *Trib. pot.*: '*uocabulum* for the Highest on High, to obviate the *nomen* "king" or "dictator", but outshine other shares in power by some *appellatio*' (3.56.1–5).

anticipates the stories to come, but not as they came about. Tiberius will lose his adopted son (his brother's son), then his natural son, then the eldest pair of his brother's sons. He leaves what he is left with, Gaius the next of his brother's sons, and the boy Tiberius Gemellus, co-heir and rubbed out soon after the succession. Gaius was enthroned in his twenties, liquidated before he was thirty. This time Claudius, another ageing intended discard (like Tiberius), is restored by a quirky whim of history 'to his rightful inheritance', as Tiberius' brother's son. Claudius, when his time came (shortly before, indeed) is succeeded by his son. To be more precise, by *his* wife's son, adopted over his own natural son (by earlier marriage). As can hardly be missed, this scene is like the *déluge* Augustus left behind, with the pattern of Britannicus as the 'Drusus' to Nero's 'Germanicus' superimposed on that of Britannicus as 'Agrippa Postumus' to Nero's 'Tiberius'.

These are tales about complexity: myth, and Augustus' bid to master history, teach that dynastic success clings for all it is worth to a simple formula of '*simplifiction*' – the production of spurious simplification, the enemy of history, negation of successiveness – and (free) debate. Simplification is the model of absolutism, because all proliferation of circumstantialities and of leading roles spells slippage, qualification and disruption to the transmission of power. For example, the *domus* was organized to annul difference between patriarchal generations: but any *atrium* would be likely to display a neater stemma than these Caesars'. And while the passing of time, the emperor's longevity, and his successful cultivation of subjects helped weed out untidy clutter, the accidents that befell and were contrived within the imperial family only dispersed ever more inventive claims to power, in ever more out-landish degrees of outlandish relatedness to father Augustus. The cal-culus of kin could lead, for instance, to the inauguration of what was to be the final reign of Rome's first dynasty with the liquidation – as such – of a series of *sons-of-a-great-grandchild-of*-Augustus.

Nero's reign is pre-destined to witness the end of the last male 'rela-tive' of Augustus. This coding now stretches to encompass the mass of families whose obliteration was in many ways this ultimate emperor's lifework. Now that both collateral and affinal relationships to the nth degree were to count, at least for the obsessional and paranoid players (i.e. all of them, for this is a contagious 'game'), the effort to suppress dynastic rivals took in a devastating cumulation of death. Leaving aside the male descendants already listed, plus the stocks of females so far left out of account, descent from Augustus' daughter Julia cursed the Aemilii Lepidi, the Iunii Silani, Cassius Longinus; marriage with Germanicus' daughters doomed an Aemilius Lepidus and a Cassius Longinus, too, along with a Vinicius. Descent from Octavia's daughter Antonia encompassed the Domitii, Messalla Barbatus, Faustus Cornelius Sulla Felix, Crispus Passienus; descent from Tiberius' son Drusus and Livia Julia was Rubellius Plautus' death-warrant. To play the dynastic game of the *Annals*, it must be known what a *diui Augusti abnepos* is and who were the *progeneri Caesaris* (see 13.1.2 and 6.45.3), the *nepotes pronepotesque* in Augustus' will (1.8.2), the *communes nepotes* of Augustus and Livia (5.1.4) . . . To understand the dynasty, it must be evident, very simply, that Augustus is *abauus Neronis* (13.34.1).

Imperial power re-conceives the world in its terms, it inhabits and dominates (an ever-widening circle of) persons as pawns in its game, functions of its plot. The imperial history of stemmatics. Desire, ambition, beauty, cunning are caught unsettling the claims of birth, marriage, adoption. Swept up into the jealousy of simplifiction are those, too, who 'coulda been king', the *capaces imperii* assortment: anyone that anyone important, or that 'everyone', ever thought twice about (1.13.2f.). This doubles up to include women, the carriers of purple futures, *capaces matrimonii* (12.1.2–3.1). In the Pharaonic world of the Palace, the chances of fertility (male or female), the risks of parturition and the accidents of gender begin paragraphs, but physical proximity and sexual desire often write the chapters: the anti-logic of 'die-nasty' was Fortune's funfair, the paranoid dooming of candidates by their very selection, promotion, exposure. The best bet could be the one nobody in the world had thought of: Claudius (3.18.4) – the one who just happened to have the best claim in terms of pedigree. If Tiberius was universally set aside, Claudius was universally uncanvassed – playing 'sole survivor' and clownish clone, in a ludibrious 'ten little Indians' tale that was still running in the second century CE.

A simplified version comes from the horse's mouth, when Tiberius tells all: *Cuncta mortalium incerta, quantoque plus adeptus foret, tanto se magis in lubrico dictitans* ('We all have to die, that's for sure – nothing else is. The more you got, the slipperier your pole. That was his line and he was sticking to it', 1.72.2). But, it must be remembered, this is imperial jabber – it cut no ice then, at any rate: 'all the same, he didn't make anyone believe he thought like one of us' (72.3, *ciuilis animi*).

Tiberius, like any potentate, must have been out to even up the odds he saw stacked against him: 'for he brought back impeachment for treason (*legem maiestatis*), the same erstwhile name, but a different issue in court – for those who had dragged the Roman People into disrepute. What they did was tried, what they said didn't count.' For its second 'leg' this mind-twister has the worst smears against the emperor the informer can imagine to smear the victim with (having smeared the emperor with): 'they were believed to have been said because they were true' (72.3, 74.4).

The specifics of the reversal of signification in the term *maiestas*, once named for the lessening of the greatness *of Rome*, now became, not a way to redress deeds by a debated decision, but a way to use words to use words (words that were recited as having been spoken, committing the crime they cite) to perform deeds, in the service of imperial history. It will not be the mere performance – the score – of Tiberian and Neronian treason trials that registers; it is the (anti-)logic in its re-oriented functioning around the person of the emperor that is highlighted, from its inception. In the new Order, there is no trial, it is a matter of the tyrant's (however benign) perception of how threatened he feels, where he feels like waving his power. 'Should it be generosity, liquidation or menace this time?' This is power as power *over meaning*: 'Wor(l)d-Power'. The misnomer *maiestas* de-stabilizes Roman discourse. Systematically. Into pieces.[36]

Tacitus' proem smuggles into his refusal to narrate the Augustan period the stakes, the principles and the *jeux* of dynastic 'politics'. The sketch offers a model of over-simplification; and proceeds to discredit its own authority, opening up the space for full presentation of the specific complexities of the main, proper, subject in question. In what follows, where the text hovers between prologue and narrative, a complex sequence of contributions to the senatorial 'sucksession' debate frames a series of revisionary accounts of Augustus that contest the author's preliminary version(s). The carefully constructed bridge blurs the scene of the burial (virtually cut from view, pageantry and all) and

---

[36] Arbitrary (so constitutively 'ambiguous') violence publicly negotiated as the power to name 'treason' *defines* despotism. Law is where language is on trial and public boundaries of 'normality' marked: *maiestas* is a mockery of law and so a pathology of language (cf. Plass (1988) 65–8).

its concomitant summary of views for and against Augustus, into that
of the senatorial debate. Instead of prayers to the new deity *Diuus
Augustus*, an effusion of strictly non-celestial histrionics, senatorial
prayers to Tiberius to take control. These prayers soon turn to a grov-
elling plea to Tiberius for mercy, which works only when it turns into
prayers to the Augusta. So to further senatorial adulation, this time
in Livia's direction, something else for Tiberius to disallow (1.14.3 ∼
1.8.1).

While it may be possible to re-write 1.8–14 into a chronologically
discrete and successive account, this would obviously, from the few
traces of welded continuity I have just highlighted, be to un-write
Tacitus, who wishes to enframe *sermo* about Augustus and the succession with senatorial *adulatio* in a reciprocal smear of malice and
hypocrisy. The smear is not just a record of the mentality, the atmosphere, the *Zeitgeist* which permits this first succession charade. It is
not only a rhetorical device through which the declaimer can touch
up the histrionics of his scene; not simply the consular historian's
insinuation of his own considered interpretation of the significance
of Augustanism, its legacy of meaning for power at Rome. It is before
all the annunciation of a quest to problematize the forms of its own
knowledge. Readers are forced to attend, and make their intervention
in the (senatorial) debate which invented succession.[37] In hallowing
Augustus, to build retrospective legitimation into the programme for
easing in the next Augustus, whoever that must be.

Through the improvisation of this inaugural scene readers are initiated into the ceremonial circus of fawning for Rome. Tacitus makes
sure there is an edge to it all: genuflection in the House (1.11.5, *ad
genua ipsius manus tendere*) progresses to prostration by the House (12.1,
ad infimas obtestationes procumbente): then a senator's private attempt to
supplicate Tiberius proves near-fatal (13.7, *Tiberii genua aduolueretur*).
When the rugby-tackled emperor took a dive, the guard thought it
must be either the Ides of March again, or the Pisonian conspiracy
already, and nearly topped the senator.

---

[37] 'Not so much a debate as a ceremony' (Syme (1974) 486): no one knows their lines,
everyone fluffs, dries, freezes, blurts, blows it – they're very willing but haven't seen
the script. The ritualization of the Senate is the *Annals'* first political scenario.
Already, 'speaking out' is incorporated within the game of servile adulation, e.g. 1.8.5
(cf. Plass (1988) 118–20).

4 THE KING IS (NEARLY) DEAD

> However this may be, he writes like a descendant of a dozen consuls.[38]

The *Annals'* opening tableau subtends Tacitus' Nero. The simplicity of dynasty, its economic rationing of 'moves' and 'pieces', re-plays its moves. The emperor in his dotage adopts a step-son, dispossessing a closer heir; when he looks ready to backtrack, he is snuffed by the Queen Mother, who hushes up the death until the transfer of power is secure. The new reign is inaugurated with liquidation of a threat: the rival heir's days are numbered. There will be a charade in the Senate – fair words of 'civility', while the army is taken in hand and presented with its new *signum*, 'watchword' – that enactment of power to order meaning. The routine of 'changing the guard' unrolls unstoppably, as the kingmaker *Augusta* is snubbed by her protégé, pilots among *amici* and *liberti* are dropped, leading senatorial figures file past, to die hard, chiefs of police come and go from their praetorian prefectures, dream-boat military types seek olde-worlde adventure and victory, but eventually find the long arm of Big Brother stretching out to the ends of the earth to reel them in before they achieve too much. The King, meantime, degenerates into lust, mass mayhem, the world is 'managed' through letters to the Senate. The arbitrariness of that anti-*lex* of *maiestas* hots up,[39] and simplifiction runs its course. Through elimination of alternative rulers, placement of empresses to provide heirs, and finessing of the future in the succession-stakes. To put things more simply still, Tacitus compels his readers to find in Nero the repetition-in-difference of Tiberius.[40]

The ring in *Tiberii Gaique et Claudii ac Neronis* (1.1.5) is unmissable. Then come *Tiberium Neronem* (4.3) and, as Augustan successor, *Neronem* (5.6): both of these owe their thrones to adoption and a new name, but one is that Claudian cuckoo in the nest, Tiberius, the other the return to Augustus' descent in harmonious fusion with the Claudian alternative, Nero. The latter had the best stemma of all, ready for its termination, the ultimate simplification. He moved from *L. Domitius*, via *Tiberius Claudius Nero Caesar*, or *Nero Claudius Caesar*

---

[38] Goodyear – that annalistic name – (1982) 654.
[39] For 14.48.2 as (signalled) recall of 1.72.3, cf. Ginsburg (1986) esp. 533, Bradley (1973).
[40] Cf. Goodyear (1972) 125f., Walker (1952) 70 and n. 1.

Drusus Germanicus, to *Nero Claudius Caesar Augustus Germanicus*. The parallelisms proliferate: first Livia Augusta, then Agrippina Augusta – mothers, stepmothers, Tanaquils, and worse;[41] both viricides, but the second a 'Clytemnestra' who will meet her 'Orestes'. Agrippa Postumus, then Britannicus. Agrippa Postumus,[42] then M. Iunius Silanus. Germanicus > Britannicus, with Martina > Locusta. Agrippa > Sejanus. Sejanus > Seneca. Sejanus > (Macro, see 6.50.9)[43] > Burrus > Tigellinus. The fall of Sejanus > the Pisonian aftermath. Tiberian treason-trials > Thrasea Paetus' 'intransigence'. Germanicus > Corbulo. Germanicus and Piso > Corbulo and Ummidius Quadratus / Caesennius Paetus ... A simple tale of caliphate, Rome's estrangement from Rome. 'Agrippa, named for foot-first birth – the only lucky one of those on record, if gout, a rotten life and death and (through his descendants the Agrippinae) Gaius and Nero are not, rather, the worst luck for the world – Agrippa, the self-begotten *nouus*, won the Empire but not its throne, reserved for his genes. All so that the last of his progeny could ape his feet-first birth and then wage world war on the human race' (Plin. *Nat. hist.* 7.45f.). This Nero was shaped by the dynastics of a century.

This narrative is fabricated, put in place as the bottom line of the *Annals*, reinforced by its stereotypical familiarity within Roman culture, as a core of fiction, melodrama, and rhetoric. At this level, of doxa, no surprises can catch anyone out – as noticed, that most unClaudian, and final, Claudius just goes to show that not everything runs in the blood. Even as similarities register, then differences are protested, the hold of the stereotypes is confirmed. One Piso or Poppaea is not another Piso or Poppaea, Messalina hardly returns in Statilia Messalina, Tigellinus is but a shadow of Sejanus, Agrippina Maior was renowned for fertility, *castitas* and *uniuiratus*; her daughter was not: 'all' they had in common was *muliebris inpotentia* ('women, so out of control', 1.4.5, 12.57.5).

---

[41] Livia *nouerca*, 1.3.3, 1.10.5, 1.33.5; *nouercalibus odiis*, 1.6.4, 12.2.1. Cf. Livy 1.41, Charlesworth (1927), Martin (1955).

[42] Like Nero, *Postumus* ('last-born' after father's death; 'first killed' after grandfather's death, 1.6.1) cannot *simply* die: his pretender is seen to by the same Crispus again (2.39.4, cf. Allen (1947)).

[43] A reminder that the simplicity/complexity of Tacitus' patterning of 'succession' is lost with the starts of Gaius and Claudius. For the contrast of Claudius' and Tiberius' deaths, cf. Keitel (1981) 206f.

The 'stuff' of imperial history is distributed and pressed into 'topical' patterns, routines, sequences, clichés. These are the 'themes' of the *Annals* (e.g. decline of the emperor's character), its tableaux (poisoning – with discussion of time and place, kind of poison, the expert, the party, the marks, the stingy funeral, rumours of *stuprum*), its traffic signs (a 'domino-theory' that 'X is safe while Y survives' – *sc.* 'both are doomed'),[44] its 'B'-movie SFX (the crowd buoyant at false upturn), and atmospherics (empress engorges pleasure-gardens). Patterns grand and small, echoes in congeries and in solitary, the whole performance a kaleidoscope of 'annalistic' recurrence, of 'subverted-annalistic' difference. The writing features a perpetual work, not a set-piece or purple-patch episodic speciality, for it is made out of (exposing) ideologically naturalized structures and sets which over-assign forms and roles to 'events' and to temporality.

Readers come to XIII more than primed. *prima nouo principatu mors* ('First things first: change the emperor and someone dies') at once clinches the tip-off at the end of XII, which already pointed back to where Tacitus came in:[45]

> ... caelestesque honores Claudio decernuntur et funeris sollemne perinde ac divo Augusto celebratur, aemulante Agrippina proauiae Liuiae magnificentiam. testamentum tamen haud recitatum, ne antepositus filio priuignus iniuria et inuidia animos uulgi turbaret.

> ... *and heavenly honours for Claudius were voted and funeral-rites conducted much as for Augustus the Divine, Agrippina rivalling her great-granny Livia's epic production. No reading of the will, though: putting stepson before son can put people's tiny minds in a spin of maleficence/malevolence.*

primum facinus noui principatus ('First things first: the new emperor gets to work', 1.6.1) serves now as prequel, Tiberius as Nero's avatar, building on all the Julio-Claudian history Tacitus has taught through three reigns. If '*Tiberius*' acted out the poetics of suspicion,[46]

---

[44] *incolumis* is the constant formula for the *Annals*' programme: e.g. 3.56.5, 4.7.2, 5.3.1, 6.51.6. The plot of XIV is strung between 14.1.1, *incolumi Agrippina* and 64.2, *Agrippinae nomen ... qua incolumi.*

[45] Cf. 1.10.8, *et caelestes religiones decernuntur*; 1.8.1–4, *testamentum ... honoribus*; 1.3.1, 3, *filium ... priuignos, priuignis ... filius*, etc., Williams (1990) 149. The repression of the 'magnificence of Livia' in the funeral pageant is re-marked sardonically by this second act of repression.

[46] Cf. Gilmartin (1973–4).

if sceptical scrutiny of his scepticism showed how despotism makes its despot and its subjects rotten, the pedagogy is now set for renovation. Repetition has charted the coordinates for succession as a routine, starting with the (all-important) rapid visit to the praetorian camp and promised donatives, followed by (ceremonial) ratification in the Senate and missives round the provinces, etc. (12.69–13.5: sarcastically abbreviated by Tacitus as if too well-worn for words). So '*Nero*''s mock-*Bildungsroman*[47] can be tracked by a text that 'knows', always, more than the boy can know. The ephebe grows into a given role, hedged round by a legacy of preconditions from which he will cut loose. This prince will outplay 'Pentheus-*cum*-Orestes'. Through total transgression, the child destroys Everything to make his name, make his 'Age' and become himself. Cancels his mundane origins, the past, then conquers mortality by suicidal self-cancellation in *déluge*. The *Übermensch* ends the drama by destroying the theatre. He was born to the plot – tearing the plot of the Good King's *uita* to pieces.

5 UNEASY LIES THE HEAD ...

We need more room
build an extension
a colourful palace
spare no expense!

Welcome to this house
be one of us.
Come into this house
be one of us.[48]

Nero took his first bow (extant)[49] at *ludi saeculares*, the re-start to Roman temporality that beds *Annales* into their heritage of Republican history: 'L. Domitius' still, but a nine-year old (in Virgilian Ascanius/

---

[47] For maturation as symbolic entrée into the cognition of a new social convolution, cf. Moretti (1987) esp. 3–5. Hodge and Kress (1988) 240–60 discuss 'Entering semiosis: training for culture' powerfully.

[48] P. Townshend, 'Welcome' on The Who (1969).

[49] 6.22.6 promises to tell later of the prophecy of Nero's coming reign – by the son of Tiberius' chief star-gazer. 'Son of Tiberius' is a perfect prediction. Prodigies (14.12.3f.) and prophecies (14.9.5) are Roman myth-intensifiers, colouring Nero with exotic monstrousness; and rubbishing simple story-tellings. Cf. Plass (1988) 74–8.

Julian/Caesar-shoes), riding in Claudius' *ludicrum Troiae* (the Troy game of Julian myth) with flash-forward to his forthcoming adoption and re-labelling as '*Nero*' (11.11.5). 'The plebs were more his fans than Britannicus' – *loco praesagii* ('a sort-of forecast') – and word went round that Herculean serpents had guarded his cradle.' 'Pure myth, adjusted to fit foreign silliness', Tacitus observes, then 'argues' against the likelihood of all this that 'Nero later used to tell it with just *one* snake, singular – and *he* would not take anything away from him self' (11.11.6). Here are two ways to frame first ideas about Nero: Roman state-pageant and Greek hero-tale. A (crucial) third comes from dynastic history: 'Nero was Germanicus' sole (male) survivor ...' The début marks Rome's 800th birthday, just sixty-four years since Augustus formally delivered the new era of the principate. Ludicrous, stage-struck Nero hatches in the 'pure myth' of imperial history's arena, the circus deathstiny of Rome.

Nero next appears as Pallas' argument in favour of Agrippina for empress: Germanicus' grandson and a proof of her fertility (12.2.3). The instant that his mother was sure to marry Claudius, she had Octavia's fiancé ruined so that marriage with her son could go ahead (3.2). Once married, she rehabilitated Seneca – to be praetor in the *res publica*, her boy's tutor in the palace, and her pet adviser in his rise to the top in the psychodrama (8.3) – and had Octavia betrothed afresh (9.2). Nero's adoption followed, his coming of age and a second, contrasting, scene at public games (*ludicro circensium*) showed Nero outstripping Britannicus. Enter mother-in-law, and the boy Britannicus gets guards for tutors (25–6 ~ 41–2: see Appendix). Sweet-sixteen Nero just has time to marry Octavia and inaugurate his career of public service, showing off his oratory: to save Troy (from tax), as a true Julian should, he re-tells the dynasty back to Aeneas 'and the rest of the mythology back before the ark'; he wins a grant of aid for burnt-out Bologna; delivers Rhodes into freedom; gets quake-flattened Apamea a tax-free quinquennium (12.58). Irony drips from each item: Nero's eloquence was Seneca's; his tangled pedigree (Domitian, Claudian, Iulian; from Germanicus ...) and sense of self were indeed 'mythical'; he will be the Roman incendiary who flattened the City; *libertas* and tax-remission are (in retrospect) odd gifts from 'a' Nero (cf. 15.45). Then comes the show-down: Nero's ('Caieta', nurse-figure) Aunt Domitia Lepida is destroyed by Mum because she was coaxing and

spoiling him into her pocket. This coup alerted Narcissus to Agrippina's strategy, broke his health and thus enabled the plot to remove
Claudius. So to the succession-sequence (12.64–9).

Tacitus repressed the machinations leading up to Augustus' ascension. This time, the antecedents have been supplied. The twist in that
opening shot *prima nouo principatu mors ...*, that it denies agency to the
emperor, has been fully motivated. A telling summary of summary
execution follows: ... *Iunii Silani proconsulis Asiae ignaro Nerone per
dolum Agrippinae paratur* ('To start the reign, death: Junius Silanus',
holder of the highest post in the Republican career of state service.
Nero knew nothing, it was Agrippina's wily doing ...', 13.1.1). Here
is the inside story of power clinging to mother's skirts, silent and
deadly.[50] The public rituals will follow, sham *laudatio funebris*, then
coronation-speech, amnesty, a new deal and empty promises in the
Senate (13.3–4). The senile fool Claudius had made *ignarus* ('knowing
nothing') his own epithet (esp. 11.2.5, *adeo ignaro Caesare ut ...*), now
a bright young spark fights in the dark: Nero has 'scarcely passed his
boyhood', so mother looks after his interests. The other coronation
victim, the *libertus* Narcissus, is next even eliminated *inuito principe*
('against the not-yet-omnipotent will of the one-day-almighty emperor',
13.1.4). This Nero is still wet behind the years, under tutor Seneca's
thumb – a princeling whose incipient sex-life is massaged to keep him
docile, dosed by his handlers on *uoluptatibus concessis* (2.2).[51] The sign
of the times is Mumma's Boy's first watchword for 'his' epoch – commanded by his first active verb: *signum .. more militiae petenti tribuno
dedit Optimae Matris* ('to the officer who requested the watchword
according to the military traditions of Rome, he gave the signal: "To
my dear mother, on Mothers' Day"', 2.5). No Tiberius, this! And so,
'all honours were publicly heaped on her'.

It might look as though emperor buries emperor, but Claudius'
exsequies are written into euphonious secondariness: *decreti et a senatu
duo lictores, flamonium Claudiale, simul Claudio censorium funus et mox*

[50] But the textual trigger *apertius quam ut fallerent* (13.1.3) underscores deviation from the
crisp 'Tiberian' snuffing of Agrippa Postumus, hushed up enough to elude inspection,
cf. Kehoe (1985).

[51] Again, Nero is to be read as 'son of Tiberius', cf. Drusus at 3.37.3, *neque luxus in
iuuene adeo displicebat: huc potius intenderet ... quam solus et nullis u o l u p t a t i b u s
a u o c a t u s maestam uigilantiam et malas curas exerceret.*

consecratio ('the Senate decreed the widow two guards of honour[52] and the Claudian priesthood; as for Claudius, meanwhile, bury the censor and then declare him in heaven', 13.2.6). Prince *Wunderkind* has no ... voice. Last time, derision was for the need to guard Augustus' cortège, as survivors of March 44 recalled the mob cremating the forum to give Julius a decent send-off (1.8.7); this time, everyone giggles through Seneca's state-of-the-art oratory while old stagers tut that this was the first ghost-written Emperor.[53] Nero 'right away in his boyhood years diverted his lively mind elsewhere, to artinesses, verse-composition even – good basics there' (13.3.7). The coronation niceties mark Agrippina's total ascendancy over *res publica* and *princeps*. But they also mark the first moment of her slide. The naïf novice promises his Senate (13.4.2f.):

> non enim se negotiorum omnium iudicem fore, ut clausis unam intra domum accusatoribus et reis paucorum potentia grassaretur; nihil in penatibus suis uenale aut ambitioni peruium; discretam domum et rem publicam. teneret antiqua munia senatus, consulum tribunalibus Italia et publicae prouinciae adsisterent: illi patrum aditum praeberent, se mandatis exercitibus consulturum.

> *We shall not be judge of all matters, so that the power of a few may bush-whack people by closing the doors behind prosecutors and defendants in one cosy home. Nothing in the bosom of my house will be knocked down for a price, dead-end for anyone on the make. Here is my house. There is the state. They are poles apart. Senate, hold fast your ancient duties. Italy and State Provinces, attend the consuls' assizes, so they can grant access to the Senate, while I consult the interests of the armies delegated to me.*

'He meant it and they believed him!' – the complete opposite of Tiberius (1.11.4, *plus in oratione tali dignitatis quam fidei erat*). This talk rings hollow to us: Agrippina acted as 'judge' of whatever 'matters' she chose (13.1), and before that she played her 'Tanaquil' role precisely as warden of the palace gates. She had detained Claudius' children inside with her, plus the imperial corpse under wraps, *et cunctos aditus custodiis clauserat* ('and had all entrances sealed with security men, oc*clauded*',

---

[52] Contrast 1.14.3: 'Tiberius allowed Livia not one lictor'.

[53] The *tristitiae imitamenta* of 13.4.1 recall Tiberius' *doloris imitamenta* at Germanicus' funeral, 3.5.6.

12.68.3 ~ *acribus namque custodiis domum et uias saepserat Liuia*, 'You see Livia had barred the house and streets with tight security', 1.5.6).

The same power-ratio, at the very heart of imperial history, had the Senate take one sentence-step toward fulfilment of Nero's promises, and no more: *multaque arbitrio senatus constituta sunt* ('plenty of resolutions were established by the authority of the Senate') adds up to just *one* move against selling advocacy; plus *one* move against self-promotion. Even this pair of ultra-traditional chestnuts from the old Republican repertoire barely got past the widow of Claudius (13.5.2):

> quod quidem aduersante Agrippina, tamquam acta Claudii subuerterentur, obtinuere patres, qui in Palatium ob id uocabantur ut adstaret additis a tergo foribus uelo discreta, quod uisum arceret, auditus non adimeret.

> *But Agrippina opposed that, on the basis that the decisions of Claudius were being overthrown. The Senate got it through, though they were summoned for it to the Palatine where a back-door was tacked on so she could attend, not poles apart but a curtain's thickness, to bar vision but not deny a hearing.*

Here the 'ancient duties' of the Senate clash with 'imperial *acta*'. Instead of Nero's *teneret*, *obtinuere*. Far from corruption 'in one cosy home', the Senate had to meet 'on the Palatine' – not so that imperial subjects/citizens could 'attend' (*adsisterent*) the consuls, but so that the Queen Mother could 'attend' (*adstaret*) the Senate. Rather than a question of public 'access to the Senate' (*aditum patrum*), the Senate was itself 'summoned to the Palatine' for one private individual's benefit; where doors were no longer to be 'closed', now an extra 'door' was tacked on to the Palatium: *discretam domum et rem publicam* turns out to spell, exactly, *uelo discreta*, enough to mean that the *de facto* petticoat emperor could 'not be seen' but could 'hear all they all said'. This check to Agrippina's invasion of the public domain makes its own, opposite, point.

From the inside of 'her' imperial house to the margins of the Senate-chamber, *Annals* lurches to the other pole, the international publicity of foreign policy in the open air (13.5.3):

> quin et legatis Armeniorum causam gentis apud Neronem orantibus escendere suggestum imperatoris et praesidere simul parabat, nisi

ceteris pauore defixis Seneca admonuisset uenienti matri occurreret.
ita specie pietatis obuiam itum dedecori.

*Why she also made to climb the emperor's dais and co-preside when Arme-
nia's ambassadors pleaded their nation's case before Nero – but for Seneca's
warning to go meet mother-trouble half-way, while the rest were nailed to
the spot in terror . . . So it was that the scandal was confronted on its way,
with a show of devotion.*

Far from granting others the right to judge cases, Nero must baulk
his mother from hearing this 'case'. Instead of provincials approaching
the consuls' 'tribunals', his nearest and dearest climbed Nero's 'dais'.
Not, then, the *patres* and their ancient (= Republican) *munia*, but
imperial history's twisted mock-*pietas*[54] from son to *matri*. A world
where the Emperor means to look after his legions, but can only
'(counter-)attack' a single female's coup on his own citadel, to seize
half his throne. In this tightly-written sequence of symbolic moments,
Tacitus concentrates the implosion of private with public, personal
with corporate and national, dynastic with governmental, post-Augustan history with consular, senatorial, international decorum. Where
people had feared 'enslavement to a woman' with Livia (1.4.5), where
'Everything had been subject to a freedman' (11.35.1), now 'All things
were subject to a female' (12.7.5). This was made possible by the
emperor being a stripling, whom people saw as 'ruled by a female'
(13.6.2). Even his counter to Agrippina satirically replaced the 'blueprint and manual for running an empire' of his (*sc.* Seneca's) maiden
speech from the throne (*consilia . . et exempla capessendi imperii*, 13.4.1)
with a practical lesson in (Senecan) elementary life-skills, 'Meet trouble half-way, grasp that nettle' (*uenienti . . . occurrere, obuiam ire*, 5.3).[55]
Still at the stage where 'his vices were still under wraps', this is no
Tiberius – just a boy having his toys taken away by Mom (1.4). Child's
play.

When the novice does perform imperial duties, it is to appoint the
right general – a Domitius big enough to fill the shoes of a Trajan:

---

[54] With 13.5.3, *ita specie pietatis*, cf. 14.3.7, *et cetera ostentandae pietati*, Tacitus' only uses
of the (cancelled) wor(l)d – used twice to ensnare the best of mothers.

[55] Cf. Kenney (1979) 6: 'Was he perhaps in the habit of exhorting his imperial pupil to
grasp the nettle?'

Domitius Corbulo – to face the crisis of Parthian invasion (instead of his purple self). One of those ironically true rumours scared Rome, shy of its puny *princeps*: 'he is just-turned seventeen, under a woman's thumb, a war can't be run by schoolteachers, dammit, – battles, sieges, all that stuff'. Optimists did their best to cheer up: 'He beats dim old Claudius, under his slaves' control, Seneca *et al.* do have tons of experience (Of battles, of sieges, of war? Hardly!), an *imperator* at seventeen's not that different from Pompey and Octavian in their civil campaigns' (13.6.2 *versus* 3f.).[56] This is Tacitus, doing his worst – looking forward to pointing up one more cosmic imbecility of imperial history. Here is mastery: *Nero ... iubet ... mandat*, in a streamlined chapter of efficient military response to invasion: levies, redeployment; the regal names Agrippa (!) and Antiochus bossed, clients alphabetically installed – *A*ristobulus in *A*rmenia, *S*ohaemus in *S*ophene (13.7). For this, Nero got the *uestis triumphalis*, an *ouatio*, and a Mars *Ultor*-lookalike-statue out of the senators, who were pleased – *really* pleased, no *really* pleased – about Corbulo's appointment. A big man and a big talker, experienced and wise, all that: but ham-strung by a rival governor and reeled in by Nero, who ordered a laurel to be added to his own *fasces* as Roman C.-in-C., 'in honour of' *their* successes (8–9).

Annals glimpsed a campaign and produced a *dux* (13.9.6), but just when 'it seemed a page was opening up for epic tales of gallantry' (*uidebaturque locus uirtutibus patefactus*, 8.1), the writer is denied annalistic adventure (for the umpteenth time). As Nero's Rome shaped up for a stirring fight, the devious Parthians went and ... withdrew, 'as if adjourning war', 7.2. After this flash in the pan, Nero plays note-form Caesar in that annalistic end-of-the-year zig-zag of petty state-business: *Caesar ... petiuit ... prohibuit ... Nero ... retinuit ... prohibuit ... reddidit* (10f.). The lurid boy back in his bedroom-jungle now lionizes his father, making a start at self-invention in a re-re-birth, after the consecration of his 'father' Claudius (who has now ceased to seem to live), with a statue for Domitius *père*.[57] Mock-consular insignia for ... his guardian spell more self-assertion, first planks for a personality. Nero's first birthday as emperor almost re-structured the *Annals* for ever: but

---

[56] Nero just declared *neque iuuentam armis ciuilibus aut domesticis discordiis inbutam* (13.4.1).

[57] 'Domitian' Nero re-fabricates a second nature for himself (cf. Griffin (1984) 22).

he declined to accept the senate's offer to re-start the year in December as a present. Later, Nero will tie time to his pantocratic coat-tails, switching day and night, merging years. But next year, Nero is beginner consul, and plays at a collegial consulate, too, forbidding the other consul to submit to the oath of allegiance to imperial acts if they were his. A smart Senate showed its appreciation for this – 'to help his boyish mind carry over into where it matters its elation at the glory he was getting from trivialities' (11.1). It started to work, perhaps, as 'kindness followed' and Nero 'restored a senator to the House'. If only so that Tacitus can deflate this (and with it the whole performance) as a recital of Senecan speechification, *uoce principis* ('His Master's Voice', 11.2).[58]

The political diary, the annalistic timetable, may be presumed to continue, but officialese yields to sensation behind the scenes. This same princely figure is in love, at war in the family. Like any *adulescens*. Parent power is getting chipped away, the boy is sliding into love of a freedwoman, Acte: Nero thought the world of her. As in any comedy, a gang of 'teenage smoothies' (*adulescentuli decori*) is in cahoots with the amator, the traditional conspiracy against parental veto. But with a difference, for there were two of them, surrounding their impressionable leader with a world stripped of difference, 'one from a consular family' ↔ 'one the son of an imperial freedman'.[59] Nero grows beyond rank, status, and the like. At the start, the vandalism of these rowdy youths is only – only! – different because one is the emperor in disguise (13.25). All the lads out on the town of a Saturday night, orgying down by the Mulvian Bridge, could have been adapted to stage an ambush on his life: the graphic imagination of old Graptus, one of the palace freedmen, implanted the fear into Nero's mind. And *his* memory was, like Tacitus' and his readers', *Annals*-long (47.2, *Tiberio abusque*). Emperors needed other ways to express themselves – they could never allow themselves out. Unless a controlled event could be found . . .

---

[58] These notes bear fruit: the consular colleague here will die (with a back-reference to the shared consulate), in a family suicide-pact through Nero's hatred/fear, 16.10.5; the restored senator here, rescued by Senecan eloquence *de clementia*, will be killed as consul elect in the aftermath of the Pisonian plot, 15.60 (with 15.61.1, *sequitur caedes Annaei Senecae* . . . : no *non sequitur*, this).

[59] Cf. Bartsch (1994) 19. One is Otho, pimp and future emperor; the other, (stupidly named) Senecio, dies as consul elect, just after Lucan, in the post-Pisonian bloodbath, 15.70.2.

Meantime, this first example of that policy of running Nero's sex-life diverts from annalistic history, and from the purchase of verifiable factuality. Instead, a lip-smacking drool of sensationalist melodrama. Written in a bizarre Tacitean excrescence of multiple ablative absolute after multiple ablative absolute, 'explaining' why 'mother was in the dark till she fought back, but by then the sex-object piece of goods had crept in too far, the elder statesmen were blocking as best they could, the girl harmed no one and filled the emperor's needs, because he couldn't stand his wife Octavia, after all she was suitably well-born and she was a good girl through and through, and maybe it was all in their stars or maybe, who knows?, naughty's always nicest' (not a whisper about her age: barely in her teens by Tacitus' under-estimate, 14.64.1). To 'burst out' in the frenzied finale: '... couldn't stand wife, and made them afraid he'd burst out and outrage women of distinction, if he were blocked from lust with *her*' (13.12.2).

This is the making of Nero, growing up in the murky world of women, wiles, webs (*artes, blandimenta, insidiae*, 13.13). Sex sets up death, scandal crime, *amor uenenum, cubiculum epulae*, Acte/Agrippina Britannicus.[60] Just skirting, i.e. flirting with, incest, *Annals* have Agrippina 'approach[] the youth with the offer of her apartment, her bosom', to hush up 'hmm ... what starting to *live* plus being no. 1 call for' (*prima aetas et summa fortuna*, 13.3). She is *falsa* but 'doesn't fool' Nero (*neque ... fefellit*), the offer of 'her assets' (*suarum opum*) is at once unmasked when she complains about the crown-jewels, 'her son was splitting up the Everything he owed her'. The stripling is pushed into self-assertion, de-thrones his first 'co-regent', Pallas (the fantasy 'King of Arcadia' who 'behaved like an absolute monarch', 14.1). The sequence amplifies Agrippina's outbursts, from invective against the freedwoman facility, through complaints about her son's gratitude, to 'terror-threats' dinned direct into Nero's ears: 'Britannicus is now a man.' She forces son to act in his own right, to look out for himself: he begins to 'think' (*uolutare secum* ..., 15.1).

Children's games are still the scenario. The colouring of this story must not get lost for a single paragraph. For this is the infancy of Nero's reign. Time for a young royals' Christmas party game of for-feits: 'in one of the bits of play-acting by the peer-group, where they

---

[60] Acte sets up Poppaea to set up Agrippina, cf. 13.12.1, *infracta paulatim potentia matris* ~ 14.1.5, *infringi potentiam matris*.

tossed for who should be King, the lucky lad was Nero'. In this game-that-was-no-game, Nero for a hoot ordered Britannicus to sing everybody a song, to role-play as Nero. Instead of derision, Britannicus sang covertly of his own hero-tale role as the dispossessed princeling, sang of himself. This Nero understood, and the understanding matured him on the instant: spine, command, guile – all in a rush (13.15.4):

> quia nullum crimen erat neque iubere caedem fratris palam audebat, occulta molitur pararique uenenum iubet, ministro Pollione Iulio praetorio cohortis tribuno, cuius cura attinebatur damnata ueneficii nomine Locusta, multa scelerum fama.

> *Because no charge was on and he didn't dare order his brother's execution openly, he worked at it under cover and ordered a preparation of poison, with the assistance of Julius Pollio who saw to it that a poisoner with a record was brought in on the job, Locust, Underworld Megastar.*

Here *Annals* imprint Nero's completion of the inaugural execution of his reign, as another Agrippa Postumus. Agrippina began the job by sinking the 'surrogate' Silanus and then knocking out Narcissus. By himself disposing of the second rival 'heir', the emperor takes over the engine-room of power; and Nero replaces mother with mother's witch.[61] The poisoning of Britannicus by Nero repeats, in *Kindergarten* form, Agrippina's poisoning of Claudius – and, besides, ensures that Nero's disposal of Agrippina, when it comes, will have to be innovative! (So 14.3.3.) The toxic trainee characteristically has his rival poisoned 'by his schoolteachers'. But 'the runs' run in the Claudius family. So an 'instant poison' is rustled up – once more. The same code of conduct applies: a food-taster in the way; secrecy needed.[62]

The scene of scenes in Nero's maturation is next.[63] The banquet of death for Britannicus his *alter ego*, the self he must kill first, or never

---

[61] 13.15 ~ 13.1: *occulta ~ per dolum Agrippinae, molitur ~ molita, parari ~ paratur, uenenum ~ uenenum, ministro ~ ministri*; 13.15 ~ 12.66.4: *damnata ueneficii nomine Locusta multa scelerum fama ~ nuper ueneficii damnata et diu* [= cue] *inter instrumenta regni habita.*

[62] 13.15.6 ~ 12.67.1: *exoluta aluo ~ soluta aluus*; 15.6 ~ 67.3: *uirus cognitis antea uenenis rapidum ~ rapido ueneno*; *praegustator:* 16.2 ~ 66.5; secrecy, in case: 16.2 ~ 66.2: *ne ... proderetur scelus ~ ne .. facinus proderetur*). Cf. Drusus' eventually confirmed poisoning, 4.8, and Agrippina's suspicions, 4.54.

[63] Cf. Havelange, Henne, Delvaux and Pirlot (1982) for a feast of ideas; Bartsch (1994) 12f., 81f. On 13.15 ↔ 12.66, cf. Townend (1960) 109f.

become Nero – the monster. The emperor presides over a fantasy-sketch from some novel of Persia, a '*Cyropaedia*' come to Rome: *mos habebatur* ('It was / was regarded as Custom ...', 13.16.1), it begins – sardonically enough. 'The imperial children would sit with the other élite youngsters and eat under the eyes of their nearest and dearest, on a table reserved for them – frugal too, compared with the grown-ups.' Britannicus was there, where he belonged, but this is also a glimpse of a future that Nero must abort before it is too late: was Lucan along-side Nero, under uncle Seneca's eye? We know Britannicus' friend, young Titus, was, and 'was really sick from the poison he tasted'. He never forgot the moment, and made it last until Suetonius' day ... (Suet. *Tit.* 2).

Nero's rival heads the younger generation, watched over by the pro-tective, murderous, gaze of relatives. How to keep the routines un-ruffled but pull off murder, in the broad daylight of hospitality? In a world where the 'food-taster' was himself part of normality? Hot punch is cooled with deathly cold poison and instantaneous death silences the victim, snatching away his voice along with his (last) breath. Those who understood the making of imperial history maintained the deco-rum of still silence and made Nero the centre of attention. Tacitus' gaze joins theirs, as he acts unconcern (*reclinis*, 'laid back') and speaks his li(n)es: 'Don't worry, he's been a sickly child from a toddler ...' This is all 'perfectly normal behaviour' (*solitum ita*).

Nero eases into his role of Man of the World, a Tiberius-in-the-making, *nescio similis* ('Faking ignorance'). All around him, a swirl of amateur conturbation, physical or mental. Barely a clue from the narrator, but everything offered to the imagination. The derisory 'ex-planation' finds a roomful to collude in it. Anything to bridge to a return to calm, for those with *altior intellectus* (i.e. they knew this is the way of it, they knew profoundly how superficial it is? Or did they expertly piece together the situation? – But did that require 'deep sen-sitivity/understanding'? An equivocation and a half?). Double-died experts will find no difficulty in seeing a flicker of inner alarm in Agrippina 'despite her facial suppression', seeing that this shows she is no longer *ignara*, like schoolgirl Octavia and unlike the fast-growing Nero. Agrippina's terror is for her own look-out. *No-one* worries on Britannicus' account. She would know that she now had something in common with Octavia – innocence, so helplessness, and exposure to killing of next of kin. How much of this Octavia understood is unknowable. For she was a perfectly-drilled student of imperial etiquette: 'though she was not old enough for finishing-school, she had internalized the lesson of burying pain, affection and the gamut of emotions'.[64]

Good manners saw everyone through the show: ... *ita post breue silentium repetita conuiuii laetitia* ('So it was that a short interval was succeeded by a resumption of the jollities'). The pregnant moment of silence has been explored, fissured and fragmented, so that the feast can finish up, in the correct spirit of passive complaisance. 'Happiness' has become a norm of self-suppressed pretence, letting the world wag.[65] Silence, holding one's peace, is an imperial wor(l)d – here taken to pieces.[66]

The episode extends, with 'burial the night of the murder' and 'report to the people'. The service was already booked: disgusting? The rain poured down: who credits divine displeasure? At fratricide? But Nero's Rome knew that thrones don't share. They 'knew' that 'of old': who does not? According to the dominant tradition, a few days before, Nero had taken advantage of the boy (i.e. buggery). So, the killing should have come sooner? Was it in fact a kindness? Still, it was at table – and that is (supposed to be) sacred. He didn't even have time for a last hug of his sisters – does that strike home, or is it a bit wooden?[67] It was a rush-job, his enemy gloating the while, this was the last of the Claudii, he'd been defiled sexually before the poison could contaminate him ... Such, at any rate, is what available accounts other than Tacitus' offer at this point. Is their rather strident, lip-smacking ghoulishness what is wanted?[68] Nero's view is left to consider: appeal to traditional practice from him, he had timed Britannicus' demise to precede his adulthood, so only a child's funeral could be sanctioned; second, appeal for commiserations, he had lost his brother, and so had

---

[64] Cf. Tiberius' senators, 1.7.1: *Annals'* first lesson at court; cf. Zwierlein (1990) for tears inside.

[65] Cf. Vielberg (1987) 90f.

[66] 13.15 consists of a deformed string of unpredictable phrases, with thirteen passive verbs and only the poison and Nero for active agents, *peruasit, ait,* deeds + imperial words. On Tacitus' use of the pregnancy of silence, see Plass (1988) 144f. n. 30.

[67] 13.17.3, *ne tempore quidem ad complexum sororum dato,* cf. Agrippina's various hugs, above, and Britannicus and Octavia's mission *in complexum patris* to save Mum (11.32.4), with Betensky (1978).

[68] 'Source-critical' moments in Tacitus are modal signals to the reader (= 'Don't be so passive') and rhetorical devices of *praeteritio,* cf. 4.10 (eunuch-buggery etc.), 14.2 (incest), 14.9 (necroscopophily).

simplified the imperial family to just himself, last survivor now of the Julio-Claudians.[69]

Of course, Nero will stay a 'boy', to the end. His story takes its cue from Cupid's bow, love-sick tribune of the plebs Octavius *Sagitta* (now there's a name!). Then, 'you know how it is when passion implodes' (13.44.6), a miniature novelette brings on Tacitus' transmogrified tale of Gyges and Candaules' wife, from Herodotus' preliminaries. Poppaea transfers from Otho to Nero, 'the beginning of great evils for the Republic' (45.1). Before Nero stretch the insults of his 'Electra', Poppaea, ready to give him a piece of her mind: 'Are you still a *pupillus*, taking orders like a Claudius ?' (14.1.1).[70] Later, too, the challenges of evil whispers: 'Your boyhood is over, your youth is strong and healthy: slough nanny Seneca, your own pedigree lines up enough teachers' (14.52.6). School is out, for ever. So Nero plays Agrippina to Agrippina's Claudius.[71] He turns for help to Mr Indefatigable, *'Anicetus'*, who may look to the Nation like 'Prefect of the Fleet HQ, Misenum', but is in imperial history a 'schoolteacher' (14.3.5, *pueritiae Neronis educator*).

But this is when/where *Annals* goes to Hollywood. Melodramatic denunciations from the panto-mime 'Paris'' 'script' started it (13.21.5, *quasi scaenae fabulas componit*).[72] On his début as megastar, Thespian Nero (over-)acts his way through his 'last goodbyes' to Mother (14.4.8), 'directs his first scene' to frame Agrippina's messenger (*ipse .. scaenam ultro criminis parat*, 7.7), and goes on to work up through motor-racing ('a regal pursuit') and guitar-concerts ('a divine glory and glorification'), dress up in Apollo-costume in Greek cities and Roman temples, and 'produce' aristocratic companies.[73] As he says for himself,

---

[69] Return of the sequence from 4.7–9, where Sejanus eliminated Drusus, with choice of poison, *stuprum* (Sejanus' with Lygdus), insincerity at the funeral, the parade of the legendary Julian and Claudian antiquity, and the Emperor's turn to the state (4.8.4, *solacia e complexu rei publicae petiuisse* ∼ 13.17.5, *reliquas spes in re publica sitas*).

[70] *obnoxius*, cf. 12.1.1; by 16.6.1, Nero is *amori uxoris obnoxius*, that's why this 'Periander' tyrant fatally kicked her in the pregnancy. Because of mytho-logic (cf. Mayer (1982).

[71] 14.1.1, 3.2 ∼ 12.66.2, *diu meditatum scelus non ultra Nero distulit .. hactenus consultans, ueneno an ferro uel qua alia ui* ∼ *tum Agrippina sceleris olim certa et oblatae occasionis propera .. de genere ueneni consultauit.* Half-way stage at 13.20.5, *Nero trepidus et interficiendae matris auidus non prius differri potuit quam ....*

[72] The theatre falls upon the narrative like a dagger: 13.24.1, *theatrali licentiae* > 25.4, *theatro rursum* > 28.1, *fautores histrionum*, 31.1, *amphitheatri*, 52, *Pompei theatrum ...*

[73] 'An actor living in his own unreal world' (Scott (1974) 106), sc. '*his own* world', the Neronian world he made real, the only real thing in Nero's world was acting. Cf. Plass

Mother's death was his real *dies imperii* – the day his egg hatched (7.6).

Tacitus' third hexad is at last ready to roll. All has been build-up, so far, paving the way for his own performance before the people, 'last but not least' (*postremus ipse scaenam incedit*, 15.6). Only, at first, with the guitar, his coaches in attendance, and still in private. His own invented wor(l)d of the 'Neronia', the festival he designed to promulgate his self, brings Greek games to Rome, obliges *Annals* to chronicle Roman stage-history in a review from the foundation. This registers another new low for the ... Republic. Nero is next awarded the prize for eloquence without being a competitor (20f.): Seneca still writes all his material (11.4). The First Night of acting in public, a dry-run out in the sticks (Greek Naples), makes the theatre collapse, 'luckily' (15.33f.).[74] In 'the most famous rumour in ancient history',[75] Nero plays 'private dancer during the Fire of Rome' (an *Iliupersis*: 15.39.3, *inisse eum domesticam scaenam*), he went walk-about among his subjects kitted out as Racing-Driver, driving the latest model – to the public games to 'celebrate' the Fire (45.7). Yet, even after all this, Nero is still busy clearing out his school desk: as Seneca says, 'He's run out of relatives, so he'll have to see to his schoolteacher now' (62.3).

The stage-struck emperor survives the plot which would have handed star billing to his under-study Piso. A popular 'joke' muttered that 'if one Actor King sings with his lyre, but the next "sings" in tragic gear – it's all just as bad, Nero or Piso' (15.65.2). One idea for getting rid of this strutting king was to 'stage' it, work it into a performance from *ille scaenicus* (50.6, cf. 59.3). By the time that Nero finally milks applause from the *SPQR* (16.4.2, *primo carmen in scaena recitat; mox .. ingreditur theatrum*), Nero has 'come out', to act his own script on the world stage.[76] This Pharaoh disposes of his chance of heirs, Poppaea, with a cross-kick, turns her into an Egyptian-style mummy, and delivers, all by himself this time, an inimitably eloquent *epitaphion*: 'Beauty! Mother of a baby-goddess! Not Fortune's Favourite but Excellence Itself' (16.6).

(1988) 11, 'Real make-believe ... could lend events a fictional quality'; Manning (1975), Edwards (1994) 91, 'Rome itself under Nero's rule became nothing but a stage-set'; Bartsch (1994) 3f.

[74] Another para-Tiberian touch: cf. 4.62f., collapse of amphitheatre, and 4.64, fire in Rome.

[75] Develin (1983) 90.

[76] Cf. Bartsch (1994) 22.

Such is Tacitus' ludibrious tale of the one-man show of absolute power that is written for the tyrant by his acting it. This is the destruction of the res publica along with his domus. By now, the victims lined up by the narrative in advance, the royal women Agrippina and Octavia, the fallen freedman Pallas, the potential dynastic rival-claimants Rubellius Plautus and Cornelius Sulla (13.18–23), have all passed on, a row of three of their heads on platters displayed to Nero and Poppaea to end XIV (57–64), and swathes have been cut through the many establishment families of the Pisonian plotters . . .

No skulking on Capri,[77] minimal Tiberian occultatio (secretiveness) for the extrovert Boy Wonder. All he managed, it could be concluded, was to turn the naughtiness of the traditional adulescens, his flexing of ego against the norms of adulthood, into a spectacular, the pantomimic solo-performance he devises to play to the assembled citizens of Rome, in and out of their arenas. The year 67 CE would see him hit the specially synchronized Greek festival-circuit, to do homage at the home of world drama – and bring down the Annals! For the MSS will peter out before the self-inventing tyrant, now the 'Nero' of legend, can crown his artistic career, some way short of bowing-out with that final line: 'Qualis artifex pereo' ('I am the Last Movie', Suet. Ner. 49.1).[78] By then 'Nero''s play with identity as transgression – the Absolutely Free – has engrossed the narrative of superbrat adolescence into the maximally autotelic role of emperor[79] until, what wor(l)d is there?, Agrippina's toy has become the melodramatic metonymy for ultimate dominatio, cataclysm for Roman mos and biblioclasm for their textual representation, Annales.

6 BLOTTING OUT HISTORY

For him writing was not a substitute for politics . . . but an extension of it.[80]

---

[77] Nero's momentary 'skulking' in Campania (14.13.1) is supposed to recall Tiberius (4.57, etc.).

[78] Last words in Dio 63.29.2. Suetonius' Nero does half a dozen takes after this.

[79] The logic which obliges despotism to express itself in an ever-staling fashion-parade of displays of transgressive behaviour fought a constant winning/losing battle with the Roman ideology of the princeps ciuilis and its rhetoric of 'refusal'. Imperial bio(hagio)graphy feeds on readerly desire for the satisfactions of imagining the ingenuity of the transgressions.

[80] Martin (1969) 141.

From the first, *Annals* harnessed old and new worlds as *res publica* and (imperial) *domus*. The dam bursts in Tiberius' ninth year of 'public peace and domestic bloom' (4.1.1, *compositae rei publicae, florentis domus*). *Annals* turn the image-repertoire of the emperor's *domus* inside-out, and back again, between Tiberius and Nero.

(i) Tiberius, the former absentee and virtual exile on Rhodes (1.4.4, *secessus*, 4.57.3, *secretum*), was forever secretive (3.37.2, *secreta*); eventually he quit Rome (6.38.2, *abscessu*), letting Sejanus quake his home (4.52.1, *commota principis domo*) and choosing 'to live far from Rome' (4.57.2, *abscessus*), leaving for good as if in exile, or in death (4.58.2, *excessisse ... exitii*): on his new island fastness, 'the house menaced the rocks below' (6.21.2, *saxis domus imminet*). If home meant Rome, Tiberius was for shutting up shop, and hid away.

[(ii) Gaius' house has gone up in smoke.]

(iii) Claudius' house took a beating (11.28.1, *domus principis inhorruerat*; 12.1.1, *conuolsa principis domus*).

(iv) When Seneca–Nero proclaimed the 'palace and state separate' (13.4.2, *discretam domum et rem publicam*), this was honeymoon hogwash. As was recounted, Nero splashed himself, his hooligans and his parties, all over Rome: 'treating Rome as his home' (15.37.1, *totaque urbe quasi domo uti*). When Rome was torched, so was his home; but still, rumour said, 'he sang the sack of Troy on a domestic stage at a time of public disaster' (39.1, 3: *flagrantis urbis ... domesticam scaenam*). But Nero had plans for Rome: 'he exploited the fall of his country to build a palace for himself – the *Domus Aurea*, a modern miracle' (42.1, *usus est patriae ruinis exstruxitque domum*).[81] 'What was left of the city that was surplus to palace requirements' (43.1, *urbis quae domui supererant*) became *Neronian* Rome. As people felt all along, 'he seemed to be after the glory of re-founding the city and giving it his name' (40.3). But Rome could not hold him. The world was his playground – bringing out that private acting to Greece, touring Alexandria for banquets *not* 'fit for a consul', but up to the requirements of a ... Pharaoh/Alexander/Antony.[82]

---

[81] Cf. Elsner (1994); Tacitus is inverting Livy 5.55.2 (end of first pentad), Kraus (1994) 285–7.

[82] Cf. Woodman (1992) esp. 176, 182.

Readers should have walked out on all this, arm-in-arm with Thrasea
Paetus, that brave and bold consular squint askance at imperial history.
Out of the House. 'Breaking his habit of silence, or else laconic "OK",
when up against flattery of the emperor, he quit the Senate and for
himself created high risk, for everyone else the seeds from which Freedom springs – he did *not* manage to plant' (14.12.2, *sibi causam periculi
fecit, ceteris libertatis initium non praebuit*). What may citizens make of
this protest, and its deflation? Does Tacitus say – or mean – 'Which, as
Tacitus observes, was dangerous to himself, and *could* not lead to independent behaviour on the part of others'?[83] This *has* to be more than
a pun on the wor(l)ds *exiit/initium* ('going out / coming in'). But what?
How 'could' an *ex*-it like Thrasea's 'beg-*in*' anything in the fighting
against Neronian Rome? When senatorial discourse could be no more
than indifferent alternation between jabber and silence, a voiceless
scream of important impotence, at the call of *dominatio*.

All an emperor can do, as Tiberius taught, is muddy the water a little
– and so worry the mice to pieces. To be honest, to be '*Nero*', a despot
can only *enjoy* his monopoly of meaning, by turning to a 'private' sense
of humour, 'poetic' irony, a taste or aesthetic of behaviour in a one-
man show: 'I might not have told you that "my Mum's corpse sure
looked purty" [14.9.1], but I *will* have Sulla's grey head on a plate for
one, all the way from the Western world's end [Marseilles], so I can say
"Yukkh! At his age. He should have used Grecian 2,000" [57.6]. For
symmetry 's sake, I'll have Plautus' head on a plate, too, fetched all the
way from the East [Asia], all so I can say to myself [59.4] "Why, Nero,
upon my word *** –

At which point, the MSS, not being able to face this quip, walk out
in protest with the eloquent silence of a lacuna. Nero–Henderson's
joke, anyhow, was: 'Why, let me tell myself – I'm the only one who can
appreciate it – was this the conk that launched a thousand ships?'[84]
Both these jokes just so Nero can bring the house down again, for
encore, and give Octavia some splendid 'divorce-presents': 'Burrus'
house' (Did Nero kill this aide? Was he one that got away? Nero forgets
now), 'Plautus' estates' (no comment) plus *infausta dona*, the memory
between the lines of that other dear departed skull conjuring up that

---

83 Syme (1958) 556: that 'could' – is, or was, it in *praebuit*? Could it be in a politics of
    interpretation?
84 Dio–Nero's joke for here is 'I didn't know he had a big nose' (62.14.1).

'lucky' name that runs in the house of the Sullas (Sulla Felix
Sulla *Faustus*). What better joke in Neronian Rome than the dictator
pathetic descendant in traditional exile in Massilia, home of the free?
What fun when he was destroyed in a snap of Tigellinus' fingers for his
nomen dictatorium, whereas Plautus, his partner in imperial history's
dance of death, was a dynastic victim of 'his grandfather Drusus' popularity' (57.3). But Octavia will top the lot. Once Nero has her head to
complete the set, 'I'll give it to my Salome to eyeball and keep' (64.4).
Tacitus rates 'these jokes a kill' (59.6, *grauioribus iam ludibriis quam
malis*). Specifically, this 'joke' is prompted by the ?joke? that Sulla 'n'
Plautus are solemnly removed from the senatorial roll. When death has
already done this.

But Tacitus–Nero can hold too many of these jokers in the pack. He
may merely revolt, fascinate with disgust, miss the chance to re-double
the double-think. Except in annalysing the exquisite paroxysms of Nero
come of age, wise-cracking Roman skulls into pieces, *Annals* ration
their rich vein of comic cuts. Tacitus trains citizens, to find terms on
which to join his debate.[85] *Annals* check out credentials: does the
reader rise above the tide of *seruitium*? Read hyper-power any better
than these senators and princes? Where did s/he buy easy options,
skim, switch off – and buy the 'rumour' or the 'hero', embrace the
stereotype, the automaton doxa? How to apprehend a 'pattern', for real?
And pierce Agrippina's curtain, that veil between knowledge and
desire?

When the historian Cremutius Cordus burns for praising Brutus and
calling Cassius 'last of the Romans' in *his annales* (4.34.1), *Annals* put
the conspicuous absence of the tyrannicides from post-Augustan Rome
where it cannot be missed. The last words of III, before the crash of
Sejanus pushes Tiberian Rome over the cliff, had the *populus Romanus*
feeling their presence through the physical repression of their images

---

[85] The Tacitean '(loaded) alternative', tension between markers of appearance and
reality, diffraction through rumour, and suspension of authority from the narration,
don't invite readers to share their viewpoint. They tempt, oblige them to confront
their values. They open a debate (cf. Sullivan (1976), Whitehead (1979); Walker
(1952) 241f., Köhnken (1973); McCulloch (1984), Shatzman (1974); Ryberg (1942),
Develin (1983)). The ultimate question is, what view to take of (views of) Thrasea
Paetus (Walker (1952) 229f., 'the subject of some of Tacitus' most taunting criti-
cisms', *versus* Syme (1958) 561 n. 8)? The political martyr refutes any prescription or
proscription of freedom. (On the 'passion' of Thrasea, Saumagne (1955).)

from public procession. Now their *Annals* repeat the message: Cremutius could protest that Livy, Pollio, Messalla and other writers had not been punished for respecting Brutus and Cassius, and ridicule the idea that he was fighting for Rome: ' "Am I inflaming the people at a rally while Cassius and Brutus are under arms and in control of the fields of Philippi bent on civil war? No – I'm seventy years too late to see them alive" . . . But when the historian's exit was recorded, and his books "cremated", the work simply went underground. How thick *are* the powers-that-be, thinking that future memory can be snuffed out? Punishment authenticates critique. Greeks or Romans, all tyrants who have burned writers and writings have only generated shame for themselves and glory for them' (35.3–7). As was observed, for example, the triumviral proscribed left living and in many cases walking memories for post-Augustan Rome. Almost all on the list in chapter 1 are mentioned, or their descendants appear, in 'our *Annals*': say thirty-three out of forty: Tacitus' obit for Tiberius brands him, and his Rome, to the end: *Nero . . . proscriptum patrem exul secutus* (6.51.1: no. (x) in chapter 1).[86] Similarly, Tacitus knew, 'descendants of Tiberius' atrocities were still around', to look over *his* shoulder (33.4, *multorum . . . posteri manent*). Had he put tyrannicide in the frame (1.2.1, 1.10.2, 2.43.3) with this very moment of self-declaration in mind?[87] If the cap (of liberty) fits . . .

7 MAKING A SPLASH

Somebody said dignity was the first to leave.[88]

Imperial history ~ *Annales*. A discursive clash between language and desire, meaning and power, challenging any civic mentality to suffer, probe and resist the draining away of Rome from itself that unwinds from first to last. With their last gasp, the MSS bring on a small sideshow of *libertas*, the best simulacrum it can muster, and reel the film in early, with a traditional (Theramenes-style) toast from the victim Thrasea Paetus, *the* reflection of Nero (13.49.3). This is another repeat, degraded by latecomer repetition, but the best available. For all that,

---

[86] Nero's great-grandfather Domitius Ahenobarbus was no. (xiii), Galba's great-grandfather no. (xxxiii).

[87] Cassius' image was still getting a Cassius into danger in 65 CE (16.7.3).

[88] Dylan (1995), 'Dignity'.

Thrasea steps right out of the farcical shadow of Tacitus–Seneca's 'Socratic-suicide' number: no hemlock here, no neat conclusion to *this Phaedo*.[89]

Yes, here Roman veins spray their page of imperial history with an 'Absolutely Free' Cynic matinée, a sardonic splash for *Iuppiter Liberator*, showpiece for posterity. *Specta, iuuenis* (16.35.3, 'Catch this, young man'). Make it work! It will! Here is the ultimate *simplifiction*, the finale, 'exit', finis of *Annalysis*, wor(l)d without ***:

> post lentitudine exitus grauis cruciatus adferente, obuersis in Demetrium * * *
>
> *as the slashes in both arms work s-l-o-w-l-y,*
> *crushingpaincomesonagainandagainpainafterpaincrushing . . .*

```
              m        i
                             .
   – t o     e      e     r      . u . . s
        D         t             . w .
                                       .
                                       .


                                    . e
                                    t .
                                   .
                                   .
                                      . .
                                      . . u . . . .
                                             .
                                             . .
                                                . r
```

Appendix: Responsion between *Annals* 12.25 and 12.41

These episodes, like most of the 'court intrigue' sequences, are very closely dove-tailed. Tacitus cannot always be so clear: 12.41.7, *sperni quoque adoptionem*, cues 25.4, *adoptionem*.

---

[89] Seneca sprayed his attendants with (bloodied) bath-water, 15.64.4 (cf. Dyson (1970) 78f., Woodman (1993) 118 and n. 53, for the *symbolic* failure). Octavia's remarkable veins simply refused to work (14.64.3: fantasy of pathos, cf. Bastomsky (1992)). Petronius coolly chatted, warbled and scribbled, chopping into and binding up his veins for fun – and nuts to philosophy (16.19.2).

The scenes, 12.25 ~ 12.41:[90]

follow new years' consuls: *C. Antistio M. Suillio consulibus* ~ *Ti. Claudio quintum Seruio Cornelio Orfito consulibus*;

begin with 'Domitius/Nero' in a passive construction of haste: *festinatur* ~ *maturata*;

show Claudius worked upon: *stimulabat Claudium . . . his euictus* ~ *Caesar . . . cessit*;

with the argument of national interest: *consuleret rei publicae . . . partem curarum capessituro* ~ *capessendae rei publicae habilis uideretur*;

to grant new status to Nero: *in familiam Claudiam et nomen Neronis transiret* ~ *consulatum Nero iniret atque interim designatus . . . atque princeps iuuentutis appellaretur*;

whose precocious age is spelled out: *triennio maiorem natu* ~ *uicesimo aetatis anno*;

the Senate grovels: *quaesitiore in Domitium adulatione* ~ *adulationibus senatus*;

tout le monde sees what it means for Britannicus: *nemo adeo expers misericordiae fuit quem non Britannici fortuna maerore adficeret* ~ *spectaret populus hunc . . . illum . . . ac perinde fortunam utriusque praesumeret. . . . qui . . . sortem Britannici miserabantur*;

as the victim's retinue and staff are stripped away: *desolatus paulatim etiam seruilibus ministeriis* ~ *simul qui centurionum tribunorumque sortem Britannici miserabantur remoti . . . etiam libertorum si quis incorrupta fide depellitur*;

and he is stitched up with 'protection' from stepmother: *perintempestiua nouercae officia* ~ *datosque a nouerca custodiae eius imponit*;

who herself climbs – through a pun – to higher honours: *augetur et Agrippina cognomento Augustae* ~ *suum quoque fastigium Agrippina extollere altius: carpento Capitolium ingredi, qui honos . . . uenerationem augebat feminae*;

and flexes her muscles: *sed Agrippina quo uim suam . . . ostentaret* ~ *nondum tamen summa moliri Agrippina audebat ni . . .*

Similar linguistic and conceptual motifs trace back to 12.8–9, then 11.11, then 6.48 . . . As was claimed, the *Aeneid* takes similar pains with *its* monumental construction.

[90] Cf. Devillers (1994) 153f.

8   Livy and the invention of history

... donec ad haec tempora quibus nec uitia nostra nec remedia pati possumus peruentum est.[1]

For the times they are a-changin'.[2]

This book ends with a final essay that summarizes a thesis arguing for attention, in reading narrative history, to the scene of writing, even at the expense of the narrated. More mimetic still, to the shifting relations between these two faces of history-writing. This issue has run through all that has preceded.

Writing Rome into a history-book required sympathetically monumental determination. 'Limits suspended, the thousandth page takes off, every time – all that expensive paper used up. As prescribed by the vast list of contents, the law of the genre.'[3] Rome is 'a huge topic, demanding immense labour to match'.[4]

Martial's marvellous miniature Livy (*Titus Liuius in membranis*) relays the impossible challenge of representing the spatio-temporally boundless *imperium* at the level of material production of text. It encapsulates the same immensity:

> pellibus exiguis artatur Liuius ingens
> quem mea non totum bibliotheca capit.   (14.190)
>
> *Tiny parchment pages shrink vast Livy*
> *when my library can't fit all of him in.*

---

[1] Liv. *Praef.* 9, '... till it's got so in these times we can't stand our corruption or the treatment for it'.

[2] Dylan (1964), 'The times they are a-changin'.'

[3] Juv. 7.100–2, *nullo quippe modo millesima pagina surgit | omnibus et crescit multa damnosa papyro: | sic ingens rerum numerus iubet atque operum lex.*

[4] *Praef.* 4, *res est praeterea et immensi operis,* cf. ibid, ... *ut iam magnitudine laboret sua,* 4.4.4, *in aeternum urbe condita, in immensum crescente,* 5.7.10, 6.23.7, 28.28.11, *in aeternum conditam.*

Writers who tell the story of their culture from the origin, as Livy wrote *ab urbe condita* (= *AUC*), raise the expectation that they will tell the whole tale, to the end. And Roman history, by the reckoning of Romans, had come to encompass (virtually) *omnia*, by the first century (chapters 4, 5). Therefore, to say the least: 'the scale on which Livy chose to narrate the history of Rome undoubtedly proved to be as important a determinant in his selection of sources as any other'.[5] It is traditional to remark that 'the sheer scope ... is formidable'.[6]

How to imagine the historian facing up to the investment that would be required? Livy was known in no less than 142 books to the tradition that produced the *Periochae* (summaries). If the *explicit* in the majority of their MSS *omnium librorum* is accurate.[7] Books CXXXVI–CXXXVII have entirely lapsed from the *Periochae*, except (in most) for the marks in the numeration of their omission; many of the later efforts only just exist. We have nothing of Livy's own narrative beyond XLV except a handful of short quotations. Very few come from Livy writing on the fighting for Rome. Those that do are, with one exception, of little scope or significance: 'From the Rubicon Caesar attacked the world with five cohorts' (from CIX); 'C. Crastinus struck the enemy with the first spear' (from CXI); 'The eunuch who killed Achillas in Egypt was led in Caesar's triumph' and 'Forty thousand books burned with the Alexandrian library' (from CXIV); 'No one helped Cato's fame with eulogy, and no one harmed it by abuse' (from CXIV) ... Not much more. Information about Livy on his life-time must come from tantalizing hints at the margins, and from the weighty *Preface* that heads the *AUC*.

I THE INTERVENTION OF HISTORY

The only thing he knew how to do was to keep on keepin' on.[8]

We must wonder (the prefixing of the *Praefatio* insists on it) what the author thought he was about, when he was about to begin. And it is

---

[5] Luce (1977) 173.

[6] Ogilvie (1982A) 458; cf. Ogilvie (1965) 26 (with *Addenda ad loc.*).

[7] E.g. Kraus (1994A) 284 is too sure where we stand: '... *though by an accident of history, the Ab urbe condita is now actually an endless text, even as the Rome it represents was to be without end*'.

[8] Dylan (1984), 'Tangled up in blue'. Dylan has been the index of temporality for this book as writing.

easy to elide our distance and blur this into reckoning what the author thought his *reader* was about to begin. Books that mean to be gargantuan must calculate their chances of coming to fruition. It is all very well for historians to position their work as continuation of their predecessors'. Pollio took up *roughly* where Sallust's fifth book lapsed in the writer's death – Sallust himself having continued the account of Sullan campaigns both civil and otherwise by Sisenna, continuator of Sempronius Asellio.[9] We do not know where Pollio aimed to stop; but have no reason to suppose he did not realize his aim – he lived on long enough (chapter 4). Under Augustus, the great geographer Strabo also wrote a historical continuation of Polybius' *Historiae*, 'Πολύ-βιος – that is – the perfectly named "Long-Lived"' (11.9.3). Monumental composers could – should, even – always look after themselves. The more carefully, the more their edifice matters to the community, and the closer they get to delivering it perfect. An abortive first instalment needs special circumstances to become poignant. Otherwise, the suspicion is: 'just not up to it'. On the other hand, nothing quite so evocative as the lack of Virgil's *ultima manus* to polish his masterwork, those eerily echoing half-lines, the *maestro* defeated – by ... (all readers must supply their own answer).[10]

Finish and finishing (in both senses: cf. chapter 4) are the great question marks hanging over every would-be textual colossus. How many great writers in the making have not been half selfish enough? Another compiler of a huge 'History', Pliny the Elder, chews over his authority-figure Livy in *his Preface*. 'Professes himself lost in wonder that this classic should have remarked at the start of a (lost) book, that he had aimed for fame enough, and could have stopped – but his restless mind fed on the work. Really', he tells his 'Vespasian' (Titus), 'he should have written for the fame of the world-conquerors, word-conquering Rome, not his own; it would have been a greater merit to have kept going through love of the work, not for his own state of mind, and done it for the people of Rome, not for self' (*Nat. hist. Praef.* 16).[11] As this bid to topicalize self-promotion indicates, 'we know that

---

[9] 'The series of Latin historians commencing in Gracchan times and extending into the empire gives every appearance of a relay race', Fornara (1983) 67.

[10] Cf. Broch (1983).

[11] Cf. Howe (1985) 563. Pliny's own (lost) history was a continuation, in 31 books, *a fine Aufidi Bassi*.

it is available to writers to refresh from time to time their readers' efforts by repeat prefaces' (Serv. *ad* Virg. *Georg. Praef.*).

To contemplate this is to see Livy adjusting his own sense of the project, 'from time to time'. The very effort to persevere – as Livy briskly remarks in an extant *prooemium*, he saw himself wading out into a sea getting ever deeper (31.1.5) – presumes intermittent occasions for taking stock and so for re-affirming or adjusting the conception of the whole;[12] more, the practice of periodic or rare editorial communiqués would, once the writer saw himself able, likely or bound to adopt and develop it, allow him to wrestle with the task at hand without needing to be entirely sure quite how it would chime with what would in time come to succeed it. Fresh policy could take care of fresh thinking. And further thoughts on the way there must be, since the enterprise was so enormous. No 'wonder' this 'restless' author is having the time of his life: the time *AUC* took to write became its author's life-time, his way of life.

Composers of epic and history all stared down the barrel of mortality. As observed before, grand themes called for authority. Youth would ruin the monument. Yet seniority risks involuntary cessation. A rule proved by the exception of Lucan, whose *BC* was as prematurely silenced as … Caesar's *BC*, for very different reasons (chapters 2, 5). Readers speculate ever after on the end that Lucan had in his sights, if indeed he had any. Cato's suicide? Munda, that 'last battle, for the mundus'? The Ides of March? Philippi? Actium?[13] If his work was banned by Nero soon after its inception, did that thrust before him the possibility of premature termination? Did the thought change the poem, and the poem change the writer, until he made certain that some undead Caesar–Scaeva would appear at his back, to take him off for execution, made certain his guillotined text would unendingly press its abbreviation upon us (chapter 5)?

For his part, loyal lieutenant Hirtius fired his plodding pen at the objective of extending Caesar's lines from *Gallic wars* VII, to join forces with *BC* I–III, and press on *usque ad exitum non quidem ciuilis belli, cuius finem nullum uidemus, sed uitae Caesaris* (*BG* 8.1.2, 'right up to the end, not of civil war, whose finish we do not see, but of Caesar's life'; chapter 2). Even Hirtius' fellow-officers responsible for covering

---

[12] Cf. Luce (1977) 8.

[13] For these rival views, cf. Ahl (1976) 306–26, Häussler (1978) 257f., O'Higgins (1988) 208 n. 1, and chapter 5.

Caesar's further civil campaigns did not prolong the agony beyond Munda, as far as the tyrannicide; as for Hirtius, whenever his labours began, after March 44, he had only months to draw up his columns of *Commentarii*, before he was killed as consul successfully leading the Republic against Antony, months before the Second Triumvirate and Rome's second proscriptions (chapters 1–2).

Lucan's fight against Caesar, however, trains readers to project the time-frame for themselves – until they too will see that the Republic itself was 'only a temporary pause in *regnum* at Rome' (*BC* 7.438–41), just as Tacitus' first chapter in the *Annals* proposes (chapter 7). If Lucan had wished, ended up by wishing, that the end would be the end of Nero, his '*Caesar*' made it the Pisonian fiasco. As Julius is penned in that palace at Alexandria by his own *bellum ciuile*, it burns down the largest library in the world: all those books lost *to* the world. To be joined a century later by the end of *Lucan*, the making of *his* book (chapter 5).

Other epics had greater odds stacked against their successful conclusion. Statius started in his thirties, finished in his fifties, *Thebaid*, for Vespasian who finished the civil wars of 69 CE, and (in time) for Titus and Domitian, sons finished by an Oedipal curse. He found it took layer on layer of ending to bring it on in, until the poem *scrutinizes* how the *sense* of ending is produced rather than *performing* this (chapter 6). Baby *Achilleid*, however, was halted in book II, cut short by Titus' early demise, by the assassination of Domitian, by Statius' own decease: Achilles would never grow up, and go to war (chapter 6). Silius brought his wars to a triumphal conclusion, contracted an incurable disease, and starved himself to death: as Cremutius Cordus argued, 'it doesn't signify if you italicize the silly Carthaginians or the Romans' (Tac. *Ann.* 4.33.4). Valerius Flaccus' ship never comes in, his *Argonautica* sail on endlessly. Earlier, Lucretius' atomic *elementa*, in flux in the dance of his exemplary scriptural *elementa*, could *ex hypothesi* never escape the pulsation of genesis/mutation. Ovid's *Metamorphoses* constantly mutate form, metamorphosed, under revision. Virgil's attempt to capture history's *longue durée* with aetiology did not stop his epic finishing him off. 'Virgil [is] describing the progress of Aeneas from the broken city of Troy to a Rome standing for empire without end (*imperium sine fine*) ... And in the journey of Aeneas the episodes are related internally; they all exist under the shadow of the end.'[14] *Aeneid*

---

[14] Kermode (1966) 5.

is unfinished, whether or not unfinishable; but it scarcely lacks its end, whether in the sense of those last lines in linear order , which finish off Turnus (and many hopes for humane mercy / fears of Caesarian clemency), or in the sense that its structuring on the *archē/telos* (beginning/end) of post-Actian revision is inconclusive. Though and because Virgil did not live to see Augustus' secular games, his poem's renovations of the Roman past were firmly tied to the ordering of the Roman present through the new imperial order.[15]

Time caught up on the poet schooled for the ultimate dare of laureate Homeric epic by protracted graduation from young pastoral through median didactic (cf. chapters 3–4). Long before time got *his*, Virgil's, Caesar, that survivor Augustus (chapter 7). Whereas Lucan began writing with (to all appearances) his whole adult life stretching out before him, as before *his* Caesar; but five years of writing, another five of reigning, and they both came to a full stop. Foreseeable, foreseen? Who could say?

Rome's first epic poet, Ennius, is closest poet analogue for Livy, or so it is agreed.[16] His hexameter *Annales* appear to have been written in the 170s, in five triads of books up to xv. 'The original conclusion to the *Annals*' was the fall of Ambracia, the triumphal return of Fulvius Nobilior, the foundation of the Temple of the Muses and the 'tired old horse' simile for *sphragis* (authorial seal, or signature). PerEnnius was thus completing *Annals* down to 185/4 around 161 (Varro has Ennius say that in Book XII it was our 172).[17] Pliny suggests in his phrase *sextum decimum adiecit annalem* an appendix, a revised 'plan' and (?) a supplement in the form of a sixth triad of books: on the Histrian war to 171, getting written to ... the end of Ennius' days, traditionally fixed at 169.[18] Two points leap out.

(i) The effect of re-vision is to deplete any finitude. No longer 'where to stop', but 'what could justify stopping'? How can *any Annals* achieve closure? Dio would have one answer – bringing *Roman history*

---

[15] Kermode (1966) 11. Cf. Rajan (1985) for the 'unfinished' *versus* the 'incomplete' poem. Proust and Joyce played well-documented games of writing against/with time.

[16] Cf. Skutsch (1968) 18f., Jocelyn (1972) 1020f.; Gratwick (1982) 60f., Sheets (1983) 22.

[17] Varro *ap*. Gell. 17.21.43.

[18] Plin. *Nat. hist.* 7.101, *Q. Ennius T. Caecilium Teucrum fratremque eius praecipue miratus propter eos sextum decimum adiecit annalem* ...

all the way down to his own 'goodbye, cruel world' exit, retiring back
to Greece away from court and politics. Tacitus had another – stopping
with the twin finales of imperial history in history. *Histories*; then
Annals. The second writing of (the first) dynasty trained on the start of
the first writing, of the second (dynasty). But how can the march of the
Republic ever halt?

(ii) Ennius reached his own lifetime around half way through his original plan – if that *was* to finish up dedicated to that temple to music,
where poetry belongs, for good. Devoted to the cause / his task, the
annalist writes on, as and if he lives on. The poem's trajectory crosses
its *archē* before it reaches its *telos*. It *could* scarcely be the case that the
vision of Ennius in the mid 170s incorporated in its dream the annals
of 169, 170, 171, etc. By comparison with Ennius, the Livian 'loop' is
accepted by most scholars as operating on a far more extravagant scale.
From some point well before his narration ceased, 'he has now to deal
with events that had occurred since he began his work'.[19] For Ennius,
writing pages that sported himself and his contemporaries changed the
tempo, the attitude, and the poetic of his song. The political dimension
turned toward a heroizing journalism.[20] The paradigm stayed before
readers of epic throughout Antiquity – *the* model rejected by Virgil's
damning of the flow of *Annales populi Romani* in favour of dynastic
myth-making with his (virtually) achronic *Aeneid*.

We saw how Tacitus both places the epistemic shift that informs his
work as the ascension of Augustus, and plays back and forth across that
line to relativize it within the eternal history of the City of Rome. The
question presses, for Livy: how will he position his 'Augustan' viewpoint? As a strong terminus, or just a phase of the (on-going) foundation of the City? If Livy reached Actium, would his work change its
nature, willy-nilly? And what would it do to (the) History if life, or
rather death, intervened – at and in whichever consular/Caesarian
year?

Among historians in prose, Livy would find cause to spend most
time in the company of Polybius, and Polybius' writing history most
closely pre-figures his own. Where Polybius was available, for the late
third and at least early second century, Livy quite rightly made his

[19] Syme (1959) 62.   [20] Cf. Goldberg (1995) 111–34.

(Greek) narrative the core for his own, quite likely with more devotion than he gave any other precursor, still shaping *AUC* when our MSS give up the ghost (XXI–XLV). For Polybius, the 'end' of history was the moment when his world, in Greece, ended. The Romans put an end to independence, and independent history, of most of the Mediterranean domain brought together by Alexander: Polybius was deported as a prisoner/hostage in 168, became an honoured house-guest of the Scipio–Fabius–Aemilius complex of families, and settled to write an account of how Rome had conquered the known world so swiftly between 217 and 167 – with 264–220 for ἀρχαιολογία to originate the struggle against Carthage that would finally be over when Scipio (with Polybius in attendance) finally wiped the city from the face of the earth in 146. As Polybius wrote on, his own standing changed; and so did his understanding. He was in a position to see how Rome administered the universe interwoven by conquest.[21] Returning to (Roman) Achaea in Greece in 150, perhaps half way through his narrative, he was brought to see 146 as the proper point to end history (3.4.13, 'as if making a new start at writing').[22] Polybius played a high-profile mediator role in the aftermath of the Roman destruction of Corinth in that year, marking the end of formidable resistance to Roman rule in mainland Greece. As he wrote on, Polybius, too, passed the date when, in his early thirties, he had begun to write. He successfully completed the 40 books of his 'pragmatic history' (39 plus an authorial résumé), re-conceived, and the early books re-written, as he lived and wrote through the realization of the epistemic shift whose arrival had provided his (cataclysmic) point of departure (3.4.7). The bulk of his trailblazing history bringing the politics of world empire to the new subjects, from the inside, is now lost apart from excerpts and partial summaries (after the first five or six books), but he did indeed live up to his name – until some time after 118 he fell off a horse.

Polybius is one model for the writer who, above all, survived. His and his country's fall handed him the best base there could be from which to write Rome; and write with Rome – to prescribe a new order of existence for Greeks. Even if history did leave him with the impossible culmination of devastation at Carthage and Corinth (empire as universal terror?). A century later, Pollio, Caesar's officer, and Horace,

---

[21] Cf. Walbank (1975) on Polybius' συμπλοκή.

[22] Cf. Walbank (1972) 181–3. In a paper in progress, I re-examine this *communis opinio*.

Brutus' officer, also survived to write (with) Rome. But they survived fighting 'for' Rome, then wrote and lived through the Caesarian aftermath. Virgil and Livy survived the civil wars, too, to write the most ambitious efforts to comprehend Rome from their post-*bellum* perspective. All of them went through the trauma of re-thinking the story of their lives, and their country; and found anything they wrote before Augustus taking on never suspected significance before their very eyes (chapters 3–4).

2 BEGIN AT THE BEGINNING

L'historicité est invention.[23]

In Livy's case, most scholars want him to start writing soon after Actium, and publish (whatever this may have entailed) his first five books, as a pentad, in around 27–25. Then he *need* not have put *anything* into pre-Augustan words.[24] At any rate, he had a chance to vet what he had written in the knowledge that Octavian was now history. Livy's career somehow brought him from periphery to metropolitan centre, as it became a court. In his boyhood, his home town had strongly resisted the Caesarian invasion of 49, though Caesar brought the area full Roman citizenship and so partnership in a new 'Italy': Livy insisted that an augur really *did* read Caesar's victory at Pharsalus in the sky over Patavium (CXI: Plut. *Caes.* 47). Loud rumblings from a distant shore? No, even for a provincial youth, Pompey and Caesar were obviously fighting for Everything, not least Italy.

Somehow Livy managed to get to the right spot at the right time, young enough to aspire to writing Rome *AUC* with some prospect of success. Aged about thirty, with no other career we know of. Needing to seize a worthy *archē* for his history of Rome (or Italy, or *imperium*), perhaps the new order of autocracy – however long that might endure.[25] But where was he bound – what was the *telos* whose conception allowed Livy to begin?

---

[23] Veyne (1983) 195: 'Les historiens ... n'expliquent pas les événements, quoi qu'ils pensent; ils les explicitent, ils les interprétent: l'historicité est invention.'

[24] Following Woodman (1988) 128–38, Kraus (1994A) 5 holds: 'It is likely that L. started writing before Actium (31 BC)'; Moles (1993) counter-argues for a post-'Augustus' date. They stay outside the slippage in temporality intrinsic to long-term composition.

[25] Cf. Fornara (1983) 73.

First, a fantastic possibility: 'Livy's original plan may have been to carry his History down to the death of Augustus.'[26] In one version of the rage for order, Livy is allowed a plan for 150 books, in five triads of decades: I–XXX, XXXI–LX, LXI–XC on Marius and Sulla, XCI–CXX on Pompey and Caesar, plus a projected 30 books on Augustus.[27] An obsolescent view, next: 'In Livy's original plan the goal was evident: Actium, the end of the Civil Wars, and the Triumph of the young Caesar.... Reaching that limit in the composition of his histories, he decided to go further (one may conjecture). He added the supplement of nine books (i.e. books CXXXIV–CXLII).'[28] The consensus is that Livy's plan was to write *AUC* to the death of Cicero in the triumviral pogrom of 43 (chapter 1): 'the last book in Livy's original plan seems to have been book CXX, which included an epitaphion for Cicero'.[29]

An attractive notion, the birth of the historian as the death of the orator; the birth of Republican history in the death of the theorist of its writing.[30] And this may transmute, through time, into Livy starting off as the imperial history of the *Caesares Augusti* meant to go on, by nailing that martyr's head and writing-hand to the rostra of the Republican forum (no. (xli), chapter 1). (As if) to prove Cremutius Cordus right (chapter 7), for no despotic mutilation silenced that tongue, and Cicero always retained legendary status, not least as voice of *libertas*. Like the rest of the cast from the Rubicon to Philippi, the last generation of the Republic, Cicero lived on in every Latin reader's cultural *and political* repertoire. As we have seen, Rome could never securely escape such primal scenes: every moment was but a step away from another Ides of March, the return of '*Brutus*' (chapters 3, 5, 7). Yet post-Augustan Rome retained for the duration that other narrative, from Philippi to Actium, the conversion of civil war into the settlement that must end history, with the new order of eternal autocracy. Revolution or settlement, this dialectic became the formative base for all Livy's post-*bellum* thinking. His continuing existence and interpretative role made Livy one of post-Augustan Rome's greatest cultural role models.

The Elder Seneca, writing up and publishing probably soon after

[26] Laistner (1963) 80.
[27] Wille (1973) 117. The same tidy-mindedness in an old MS reported by Giovanni Colonna: 'Livy wrote 150 books' (Reeve (1991) 463). Nicholas Trevet's 'rumour that Livy wrote 300 books' presumably means 'far too many to read' (ibid.).
[28] Syme (1959) 38.
[29] Woodman (1977) 34.
[30] Livy is 'flesh of Cicero's theory of historiography' (Walsh (1966) 119).

the assassination of C. Caesar (Gaius), rightly showcases the death of Cicero – the last moment in history re-invented, constantly, by the declaimers in their imperial funhouse of closet oratory. Indeed, the most dramatic fragment that we have of Livy writing as primary historian, on his own lifetime, belongs to Seneca's compilation of *mots* produced on this very topic (*Suas.* 6). Livy's reported version ends neatly enough, with: *si quis tamen uirtutibus uitia pensarit, uir magnus, acer, memorabilis fuit, et in cuius laudes persequendas Cicerone laudatore opus fuerit* (6.22, from cxx, 'If at the end of the day, though, some writer such as myself produces an evaluation of his overall significance, he was an epic hero, incisive and deserving a full historical account of his life and times: Cicero – who must call for a Cicero for eulogist, if his write-up is to be pursued at the requisite length').[31] This memory (or impression – or take-off) is indeed the biggest single incentive to establish the *communis opinio* on Livy's 'original plan'. Since the same collection of memories showcases the finest early imperial historians on the same topic, apologetically forced on his declamation-struck triumvirate of young sons, Seneca at a stroke supplies us – in reverse order – with all we can now read of Bruttedius Niger (*Suas.* 6.20f.),[32] Cremutius Cordus (19; 23, cf. chapter 7) and Aufidius Bassus (18; 23); most of our Pollio (14f.; 24, cf. chapter 4); and that solitary sizeable chunk of late Livy (16f., 22). In each case, Seneca re-tells the grisly end of Cicero; then the historian's effort at *elogium* (summary assessment after death). Given the otherwise completely blank void where our knowledge of these crucial works ought to be, it is not surprising that so much importance has been trusted to this little review. Though Seneca does have his debating society remind us that 'one let his father get proscribed, another his uncle', and so put a perspective on Pollio's 'lasting and unsurpassed hostility to Cicero's fame', Seneca does *not* remark that either Pollio or Livy's histories homed on 7 December 43 (in Julian time).[33]

But there is some evidence to explain why it is held that: 'Books

---

[31] In the contrast with cxvi, 'it's unclear whether Julius were better born or not born for the Republic/state', is almost all our *direct* evidence for Livy's position on the fighting for Rome.

[32] Cf. Woodman and Martin (1996) on Tac. *Ann.* 3.66.1.

[33] *Suas.* 6.7, 14: broker of the Caesarian triumvirate, Pollio had let his father-in-law L. Quinctius get on the list in 43 (chapters 1, 4). Survival brought many a complication – and pegged entertainment to politics, to political history, fed into the middle of Julio-Claudian Rome by Senecan longevity.

CXXI–CXLII, composed toward the end of the reign of Augustus, were held back for some reason or other and not given to the world till later.'[34] And: 'These books were written as a supplement to Livy's great work, somewhat in the manner of books XVI–XVIII of Ennius' *Annals*.'[35] 'An afterthought to the original plan and may have been too politically controversial to be published in Augustus' lifetime, ... An "appendix".'[36] It has been an axiom that Livy's narrative from 42 to 9 in books CXXI–CXLII represents a second phase of writing.[37] The evidence for this is the (striking and unparalleled) note in *Periocha* CXXI: *(liber) qui editus post excessum Augusti dicitur* ('[this book] is said to have been published after the ascension of Augustus').

Part of the text of the summary is in our oldest MS (N); presented as sub-title in the next oldest MS (P, and relatives).[38] Speculation has ensued. The 'susp[icion]' that Livy left CXXI–CXLII for after Augustus' decease with 'prudence' ... because of the 'resolute independence in his writing'.[39] Less romantic caution: might speeches *by* Augustus in Livy, in Livian style, have to wait for deification – the price of immortality (as Nero reminded us, chapter 7) sticking at death *first*?[40] The sub-titles to *Periochae* CIX–CXVI (in most (collated) MSS) stoke up the argument: *qui est ciuilis belli primus/secundus/tertius/et c.* Some accept CIX–CXVI as a Livian unit, and dare detect another *Preface* in *Periocha* CIX–CXVI's opening shots: *causae ciuilium armorum et initia referuntur contentionesque de successore C. Caesari mittendo, cum se dimissurum exercitus negaret, nisi a Pompeio dimitterentur* (chapter 2, Appendix). Resisted

---

[34] Syme (1959) 39.

[35] Stadter (1972) 299.

[36] Ogilvie (1982A) 458. Ogilvie's last formulation (1984) 119: 'On the whole, I am now convinced that Livy's final plan was 150 books, which, as Luce has argued, were structured in units of 15 and written in units of 5.'

[37] Luce (1977), Wille (1973), Crosby (1978), etc.

[38] Reeve (1991) 481 and n. 107. Jal (1984) cxx found the sub-title in (I think) four out of twenty-four of his collated MSS (one of them now lost); he prints the 'sub-title', but doubts its 'authenticity': Reeve (1988) shows this is loose talk: the questions of 'truth', and of meaning, remain.

[39] Walsh (1966) 120.

[40] Syme (1959) 72; cf. Kraus (1994A) 7f. Note that Syme (ibid. 38) warns that Klotz improbably read *dicitur* as *dicitur a Liuio*. And Walsh naughtily writes (1961) 8: '*We are told that* 121–42 were not published until after Augustus' death' (with n. 1, 'The oldest MSS of the *Periochae state that* CXXI was published after Augustus' death'). Contrast (1974) 9, '... which *he is said* to have held back ...').

by others – not least in the name of symmetries – those pentads, decades, and multiples thereof that are written so firmly into the 'law' of
survival for extant Livy (I–X; XXI–XLV; and – *secunda decade* – attested
as the familiar reference unit by Pope Gelasius in 496, *Epistula aduersus
Andromachum* 35).[41]

These *Periochae* are themselves 'text'. An unfamiliar and tricky genre
– summaries? résumés? abridgements? précis? indices ...?[42] Can we
learn to read sub-titles (superscriptions? glosses? *subtleties* ...?) of *Periochae*, themselves *made* (as is often argued) from 'Epitomes' *made*
from Livy's narrative? Our sense of the impact of the fighting for Rome
on Livy's writing for Rome hangs on this challenge. Over a very big
drop, then.

Similarly, *if* the *Periochae* heroically followed Livy to the very last
book he wrote, or published, and *if* they are fully preserved *in that sense*,
the end was in 9, when Drusus, Tiberius' brother and Claudius' father,
broke a leg, and finished off both Livy and himself. The finale would
climax in an *elogium* by the second emperor, on the throne when Livy
died, if not when he penned CXLII, followed by another from Augustus,
already a god or soon to become one. Was this *the* place to stop? 'This
was the culmination of the grandiose Augustan plan of conquest in
central Europe ... He *had* to stop. The year 9 BC was the ideal date ...
Melancholy but proud commemoration of the Emperor, dynasty,
Claudia uirtus ... The year 9 BC therefore appears to be both a necessary and an attractive terminal date.' Then Livy *cannot* have died 'pen
in hand' at his desk. Rather, he ekes out his final years with (i) CXXI–
CXLII safely stashed away – released on an unsuspecting world after 14
CE, perhaps not until Livy's own expiry-date (17 CE – or earlier?); (ii) I–
CXX the living monument of this living legend at court; and (iii) nothing
after 9 given the Livian treatment.[43]

The picture draws on layer upon layer of mediation. And on strong
desire for powerful structure, whether in planned symmetry or in

---

[41] Syme (1959) 32 *versus* Stadter (1972), Wille (1973), Luce (1977), Crosby (1978),
Walsh (1961) etc. The Scholia to Lucan 10.471 and 521 show that *a* gathering of Livy
could carry the rubric: ... *ut meminit Liuius in libro quarto [belli ciuilis]*, ... *ut meminit
Liuius in libro quarto belli ciuilis*, on civil war events that belong to CXII (but cf. Stadter
(1972) 298 for cold water).

[42] Cf. Jal (1984) lxvii, 'Le travail de l'épitomateur', lxxix, 'Nature et style des *Periochae*';
cf. Fornara (1983) 19f., Luce (1977) 11.

[43] Syme (1959) 67, 70f.

grasped periodization, or (preferably) in both. To repeat, Petrarch, Boccaccio and everyone since report 142 volumes for Livy; but this is a dreadfully insecure factoid, no more (and no less) than the observation that the *Periochae* break a leg here.[44]

3 GO ON TO THE END

> History is . . . a provider of significance to mere chronicity. Everything is relevant, if its relevance can be invented.[45]

If the end was important – even determinative and constitutive – to *AUC*, then, we are left in a precarious position from which to tap into Livy's strategic thinking. Endlessness might have been, or become, the point, – that eternal Rome demands nothing less than every last drop of ink a patriotic narrator can squeeze out of life, and then some. But no one is in a position to argue it. Or, rather, no one can be sure of the rhetorical status of such a notion, as guide and protreptic to reading. Most especially, we have virtually no idea whether Livy thought, when he gazed from his window at the transfiguration of Augustan Rome, and found himself starting by burying the Republic / keeping memories of the Republic alive, then found himself deciding which campaigns, policies, and 'achievements' to write up, that the story could fit into the annalistic format he had developed as secondary historian. Now he had a new Rome/post-Rome to write around its dictator.

Tantalizing traces of Livy's own revisionary activity intervening on earlier thinking are found in the first decade, where Livy reports Augustus' word for it that the version he has been following has erred, and led him into an unacceptable construal of the traditions of legitimate power at Rome (4.20.5–11). All the same, Livy has not re-written the discountenanced narrative; nor does he abide by the directive when he continues.[46] The curious (post-'publication') insert dramatizes the

---

[44] Cf. Reeve (1991) esp. 484: the omission of CXXXVI–CXXXVII (naturally enough) confused scribes – as well as their modern editor. Summaries such as Ogilvie (1982A) 858, '*Periochae* of whole work preserved in MSS' promulgate a firm terminus, whether they mean to or not. Did the epitomators or *Periochae*-writers tire at CXLII – perhaps (well) before the end – as 'the editors' industry flagged and failed' towards the tailing-off end of our MSS (Syme (1959) 52)? Did *any* readers get this far? Only two tiny quotes are preserved from CXXXIV–CXLII.

[45] Kermode (1966) 56.

[46] Cf. Miles (1995) 40–7.

beginning of post-Augustan imperial history as the re-writing of the *res publica*. This has repercussions for our reading of the crucial *Praefatio*.

Attention to the *historicality* of Livy's writing must inform our reading of this overture with the same dynamic as chapter 4 explored for Horace's evocation of (the preface to) Pollio's *Historiae* (and chapters 3–4 explored for the situatedness of Horace's own thinking). If Livy wrote his preface before Actium (as some suppose) he would find it *changing* its meaning, *isdem litteris* (without changing a word). For *just what* still meant the same, what meanings had changed, what mattered less, or counted more, were exactly the questions faced by the Roman world.[47]

When Livy introduced late insertions into the text of the otherwise 'finished' first pentad, he was deciding, too, whether that *Preface* now looked antediluvian, or embarrassingly wrong; whether to alter it, or let it stand as the record of the view he had 'begun' his work with. In the process, he was necessarily revising his view, *whether he changed a word or not*; and as his work went on, he *must* be including within its writing the view he now took of his own change of view, namely the change which his writing was making, which his living through his writing made, and which his living through the changes he was writing about would make, as he reached the triumviral period and the date when he started to write *AUC*.

There is no possibility of deciding in what degree Livy chose to alter/ re-write/re-think/write the *Preface* we have, at what point in the composition, and supplementation with insertions, of I–V. Rather, the temporality of the pentad is set before us in Livy's decision to let his text stand, as preface to a work whose meaning he *cannot* have comprehended in the way its later sections would come to understand it.[48]

Livy may not (ever) have had (much of) a plan; or the *Praefatio* may map out the project of (say) I–CXX; or a battery of prefatory editorials may have adapted or moved the goalposts.[49] For sure, Livy *cannot* have

[47] Cf. Miles (1995) 92 n. 49.
[48] Moles (1993) offers cogent exegesis of the *Preface* – except that he puts 'Henderson['s] legitimate fun' straight with a naughty equivocation of his own (150f.): 'we can surely say that a particular piece of text *has more meaning* at a particular time'. This –
[49] 'Rhetorical training allowed Livy to cope with the great undifferentiated mass of Roman historical happenings, and, philosophically speaking, to make sense of it.' Or: 'his rhetorical power does not take control of the whole with the authority of a pan-optic vision', Ogilvie (1982A) 462; Walsh (1966) 117. Cf. Luce (1971) 265, 'The great

known what he was to write, when (however improbably) he one day
came to set down for posterity what had 'happened' on that day he sat
down to start writing. The same goes for the twenty more years he
managed to cover before retiring/expiring. Yet that *Praefatio* stayed at
the head of *AUC* however long it got, however long he went on / lasted.
As he knew it would.

An author who begins a book in their thirties and is still writing it
into their sixties if not seventies *must* be supposed to revise the conception of the work.[50] Pollio's book was a life-work in exactly the sense
that in it the writer set himself to make sense of a true story in which he
was a character, as the story ran on to change that character's view of it,
to change his sense of his own role in it, his sense of the view of it with
which he had started out, and his comprehension of the sense of the
changes his views and re-views had gone through. And that is precisely
what was on view in his *Histories*, what you would have wanted to
know, whenever Horace wrote and re-wrote his Pollio Ode, or in 23
when Horace published *Odes* I–III. What we want to try to comprehend
now. By comparison, '*Livy*' (somewhere between 'life' and 'love') tells
his life-story of Rome in a stupendously vast form of the 'organicist
fallacy'. The writer is born with his city; grows, flourishes, declines
along with his subject.[51] In the end, the race is on – will Rome's historian live to see his tale die with Rome? Or will his version of the
Tristram Shandy paradox – 'the more I write the more I shall have to
write' – slow the progress of history as the pressure on the enunciation increases after events of his own time loom up?[52] Short of extinc-

bulk of the history, as well as the huge time-span covered, militate against any easy
conception of the whole.' *Praef.* 9 ∼ I–cxx, cf. esp. Crosby (1978). Does 31.*Praef.* 2,
... *perscripturum res omnes Romanas*, announce a new open-endedness, 'writing eternity'?

50 Cf. Shattuck (1974) 12f., 'Proust often treated writing as a continuation of life by
other means ... As in life itself, the scope of action and reflection in the *Search*
exceeds the capacity of one mind to hold it all together at one time.'

51 See Kraus (1994) 268, [Livy] 'draws attention to the overlap of the content of his city
(the *Urbs* he is writing about) and its form (the *Urbs* he is writing)'.

52 Waugh (1984) 71, cf. 142f., 'The subject of the novel becomes the battle between the
chronological duration of the "writing" and that of the events in "history", and the
battle between these and the real and implied duration of the reading.' Livy's rate was:
166–91 = 25 books @ 3 years per book; 91–43 = 72 books @ one and a bit books per
year; 43 itself = 3 books (cxviii–cxx): see Stadter (1972) 304–6. But cf. Derrida's
derision (1993) 50, for Ariès 'describ[ing] what he dares to call "the slowness of his
progression", namely the fact that he devoted "fifteen years" to this task. Fifteen

tion, Seneca's *Historiae* fully embraced the politics of this fallacy, *Romanae urbis tempora distribuit in aetates* ... (*ap*. Lactant. *Inst. diu.* 7.15.14, '[Seneca] assigned the eras of Rome into "ages"'): thus infancy required strong parental guidance (= kings); now in infirm 'second childhood' (*altera infantia*), Rome again needs strong support (= autocracy).[53]

Or did Livy's Rome die already with Cicero, with Octavian, to be re-born with Livy and Augustus? Once CXXI–CXLII on 42–9 are positioned as the 'supplement' to I–CXX on 753–43, they complete but undo the story, for supplements are revisionary ratios, and this supplement alters the end of history along with the end of the *History*.[54] The 'here-now-us' of Livy's *Preface* (9, *haec tempora ... nostra .. sunt*) orients readers directly toward this shifting target between text and life.[55] As time and text pass, terms such as *Caesar, augustus, princeps*, and *res publica, consul, imperator, tribunus* are hollowed out and re-filled with a different sense, as the past defers to the returning view. Names, too – *Brutus, Horatius, Domitius, Liuius* – acquire and shed significances, under the shadow of the cancelled and re-negotiated end to history. In particular, the Livian 'loop' creates a slip-knot of signification along which all the signifiers run; its revisionary supplementarity is that of the 'extra piece in the jigsaw' (to use the old historiographical cliché), which in making us repeat the synoptic checking of fit across the whole set problematizes the whole notion of wholeness, of fit, and set, into the volatility of process.[56]

Readers of *any stretch whatever* of *AUC* are engaged with the histor-icality of the narration. Every word of every episode addresses the story of Rome from the position of the retrospect. It questions as it informs – is Book I a preface to Rome as *res publica*, Rome only *becoming* Rome with the *res publica libera* and its consuls in II? Is the end that of the

years! Fifteen years seem enormous to the historian for writing a history of death in the West from the Middle Ages to the present; according to him, ... "the field of my research moved backward when I thought I was reaching its limits, and I was each time pushed further, both upstream and downstream in relation to my starting point".' (Ariès incautiously labelled this 'the *metaphysical* nature of death'.)

53 Which Seneca? See Woodman and Martin (1996) on Tac. *Ann.* 3.27.1.
54 Stadter (1972) 299, Syme (1959) 38; cf. Derrida (1976) esp. 269f., cf. 6–26, 'The end of the book and the beginning of writing'.
55 Cf. Barthes (1981) 6f. on history's 'shifters', Miles (1995) 20; 'for a different sort of argument for narrative indeterminacy in Livy', see Miles (1995) 178.
56 See Henderson (1990) for visual presentation of this idea.

second Brutus in 42 (chapter 3) – or the Second Triumvirate (chapter 1), the end of duly elected consuls? Or did history continue through Actium, to the 'restoration' of consular elections in 23 (chapter 4)? Did Book I then become a part of the story of Rome – in which case the 'restitution' of the free Republic exposes the original foundation as a power-play from the first Brutus (who was, after all, legitimate heir of the Tarquins) – which ironizes the Augustan ceremonies? Weakening the shift from kings to consuls will paradoxically weaken the sense of continuity desiderated by Augustan restoration, for history will become a narrative of 'power', *dominatio*, whether by *reges*, by *consules*, or by *princeps* (as in Tacitus' Rome, chapter 7). Had Rome always consisted in eras dominated by particular strong men – from Pompey/Caesar back through Marius/Sulla, to Coriolanus and 'second founder', 'august' Camillus,[57] to Papirius Cursor and the rest? Not so *very* different from what now followed (the royal *Caesares Augusti*) and what preceded – the legendary kings?

Larger, more imponderable questions loom: was I–V a mythical preface to the history 'proper' of VI–CXX? Were I–CXX an annalistic ἀρχαιολογία prefatory to the history of Livy's primary research into *haec tempora . . . nostra*? There is no call to abandon these issues, merely because all Livy's work to construct his times is lost to us. That would simply be to miss the *writing* of *AUC*. Everything Livy writes speaks to his on-going perception of his relation to 'the word' of his society as it mutates through time, Roman time, Livy's time (chapter 7).[58] Conceivably the *best* (as well as the only) way to read Livy on (his ideas of) Rome since Augustus is, in any case, to read what we have – Livy on the antecedents to all the fighting for Rome and its aftermath.

'The real history' (after 27) 'is secret history'. Henceforth, what can be written in history will depend on the see-saw of flattery and vituperation, as courtiers flatter present emperors at the expense of dead ones (chapter 7).[59] We cannot know if that *Periocha* sub-title (CXXI), *(liber) qui editus post excessum Augusti dicitur*, attests *any* major *diuisio* in Livy's narrative. Nor whether it belongs anywhere near anecdotes such as the Elder Seneca's about Labienus, fiery victim of book-burning:

---

[57] Cf. Hellegouarc'h (1970), Miles (1995) 88–98.
[58] Livy forms Roman time textually, with units of gatherings and of books (e.g. Suits (1974) on XXXII).
[59] Syme (1959) 69; cf. Dio 53.19.3, with Fornara (1983) 89.

'we remember once when he was reciting a story / some history, he rolled up a good chunk of it and said, "What I'm skipping will be read after I'm dead and gone"' (*Contr.* 10, *Praef.* 7). The sub-title *may* itself attest understanding of the passing of the unpoliced right to write, like Labienus, like Seneca? Maybe something in a Livian preface to CXXI *does* lie behind the sub-title, but if so we have our work cut out to imagine what – Labienus precisely did *not* write down in his book-roll: 'This is not to be read until after my death or the emperor's, whichever comes first.'

But as Livy stamps his work on Rome, stylish and entertaining at all costs, as rhetorical *inuentio* (creative writing) works over the material his sources offer him, he involves readers in a sustained drive toward mastering Rome. All his work, whether leading or following standard practice around him, parades specific preferred forms and terms of explanation in accordance with contemporary likelihood, with rationalization in post-Actian terms, with post-Augustan re-ordering of Roman identity.[60] Always, writing Roman history is itself the history of that writing. There is no more over-riding need to look for masterful ordering to the – withheld–lost–unwritable–unimaginable–... end than there was with Tacitus (chapter 7). Which is not to say that all historicality does not operate under the aegis of the en–

> This is the end
> (my friend). The end.[61]

---

[60] Cf. Feichtinger (1992) on the ideological form of Roman exemplarity; Woodman (1988) 136–8 for Augustus fitting the ideal already generated by Livy; Santoro L'hoir (1990) 232–41 on the *unus uir* patterning, *after* Augustus, of heroism in Livy.

[61] J. Morrison on The Doors (1967), 'The end'.

Date chart

43   Death of consul Hirtius fighting against Antony.
      Second Triumvirate of Antony, Lepidus and **Octavian.** Caesar:
      proscriptions.
      7 December: **Death of Cicero.**
      Horace in Athens joins Brutus' forces.

42   **Antony and Octavian** defeat tyrannicides in double battle of
      Philippi: suicides of Brutus and Cassius.

40   Consulate of **Pollio**: Antony and Octavian reconciled by Treaty of
      Tarentum.
39–5   **Sallust** writes *Historiae* I–V.
c. 39/38 Virgil publishes *Eclogues.*
39/38 Virgil introduces Horace to Maecenas.
c. 35 **Horace publishes *Sermones* I.**
35   Death of Sallust. **Pollio begins *Historiae.***

31   **Octavian defeats Antony and Cleopatra at Actium.**
30   Their suicides in Alexandria.
c. 30 Horace publishes *Sermones* II.
29   Octavian's triple triumph. Virgil publishes *Georgics*, Horace publishes
      Epodes.
c. 29 (Or late 30s?) Livy begins *Ab urbe condita.*
27   Octavian re-styled **Caesar Augustus.**
c. 27–5 **Livy publishes (amended) *Ab urbe condita* I–V.**
24   Augustus returns from Gaul and Spain.
23   'Second settlement' formalizes life-dictatorship, restores **consular
      elections. Horace publishes *Odes* I–III.**
19   **Death of Virgil: *Aeneid* bequeathed.**

CE

5   **Death of Pollio.** *Historiae* I–XVII published/bequeathed.
14   **Death of Augustus.**
14–37 **Reign of Tiberius.**
15   End of consular elections.
17   (Or shortly before?) **Death of Livy.** *Ab urbe condita* **bequeathed**.
      Death of **Ovid**: (revised) *Metamorphoses* bequeathed/published.
25   **Suicide of Cremutius Cordus.**
37–41 Reign of **Gaius** (Caligula).
      (Under Gaius?) **Seneca the Elder** publishes rhetorical works.
41–54 Reign of **Claudius.**
50   Adoption of Nero.

54–68   Reign of **Nero**. Death of Britannicus.

c. 60   Lucan begins *BC*.

65   **Pisonian Conspiracy**. Seneca and **Lucan liquidated.** *BC* **bequeathed**.

67   Nero's tour of Greece.

68   **Suicide of Nero.**

69   **Year of the Four Emperors**: civil wars between Galba, Otho, Vitellius, the Flavians.

69–79   Reign of **Vespasian**.

79–81   Reign of **Titus**.

c. 79   Statius begins *Thebaid*.

81–96   Reign of **Domitian**.

c. 88   Silius Italicus begins *Punica*.

c. 91/92   **Statius publishes** *Thebaid*.

c. 92/3   Death of **Valerius Flaccus**: *Argonautica* bequeathed.

93/94   Statius publishes *Siluae* I–III.

95   Statius publishes *Siluae* IV.

96   **Death of Statius. Domitian liquidated.**

96–8   Reign of **Nerva**.

98–117   Reign of **Trajan**.

101   Suicide of **Silius Italicus**. *Punica* published by then.

c. 110   Tacitus publishes *Histories*.

117–38   Reign of **Hadrian**.

c. 120   (Or somewhat earlier?) **Tacitus publishes/bequeaths** *Annals*.

c. 161/2   **Appian publishes** *Romaika*.

c. 201   Dio Cassius begins research for *Roman history*.

229   **Dio Cassius publishes** *Roman history*.

Bibliography

Adcock, F. E. (1956) *Caesar as a man of letters*, Cambridge.

Ahl, F. M. (1974) 'The pivot of the *Pharsalia*', *Hermes* 102: 305–20.

(1974A) 'The shadows of a divine presence in the *Pharsalia*', *Hermes* 102: 567–90.

(1976) *Lucan. An introduction*, Ithaca, NY.

(1984) 'The art of safe criticism in Greece and Rome', *AJPh* 105: 174–208.

(1984A) 'The Rider and the horse: politics and power in Roman poetry from Horace to Statius', *ANRW* II.32.1: 40–110.

(1985) *Metaformations*, Ithaca, NY.

(1986) 'Statius' "*Thebaid*": A reconsideration', *ANRW* II.32.5: 2803–2912.

(1988) '*Ars est caelare artem* (Art in puns and anagrams engraved)', in Culler (1988A): 17–43.

(1989) 'Homer, Vergil, and complex narrative structures in Latin epic: an essay', in Marcovich (1989): 1–31.

(1993) 'Form empowered: Lucan's *Pharsalia*', in Boyle (1993): 125–42.

von Albrecht, M. and W. Schubert eds. (1990) *Musik und Dichtung: neue Forschungsbeiträge, Viktor Pöschl zum 80. Geburtstag gewidmet*, Frankfurt.

Allen, Jr, W. (1947) 'The death of Agrippa Postumus', *TAPhA* 78: 131–9.

Althusser, L. (1971) *'Lenin and philosophy' and other essays*, New York.

Anderson, L. (1982) *Big science*, Warner Bros.

Anderson, W. S. (1982) *Essays on Roman satire*, Princeton.

André, J.-M. (1949) *La vie et l'œuvre d'Asinius Pollion*, Paris.

(1967) *Mécène. Essai de biographie spirituelle*, Paris.

Armstrong, D. (1986) '*Horatius eques et scriba: Satires* 1.6 and 2.7', *TAPhA* 116: 255–88.

Armstrong, N. and L. Tennenhouse eds. (1989) *The violence of representation*, London.

Attridge, D., G. Bennington and R. Young eds. (1987) *Post-structuralism and the question of history*, Cambridge.

Auden, W. H. (1968) *Selected poems*, London.

Avery, H. C. (1993) 'A lost episode in Caesar's *Civil War*', *Hermes* 121: 452–69.

Bardon, H. (1943–4) 'Le silence, moyen d'expression', *REL* 21: 102–20.

(1956) *La littérature Latine inconnue*, Paris.

Barthes, R. (1975) *S/Z*, London.

(1977) *On Racine*, New York.

(1981) 'The discourse of history', *Comparative Criticism* 3: 5–14.

Barton, C. (1993) *The sorrows of the ancient Romans. The gladiator and the monster*, Princeton, NJ.

Bartsch, S. (1994) *Actors in the audience. Theatricality and doublespeak from Nero to Hadrian*, Cambridge, MA.

(1997) *Ideology in cold blood. A reading of Lucan's* Civil War, Cambridge, MA.

Barwick, K. (1951) *Cæsars Bellum Civile: Tendenz, Aufbau, Abfassungszeit und Stil*, Berlin.

Baslez, M.-F., P. Hoffmann and L. Pernot eds. (1993) *L'invention de l'autobiographie d'Hésiode à Saint Augustin*, Paris. (= *Études de Littérature Ancienne* 5).

Bastomsky, S. J. (1992) 'Tacitus, *Annals* 14, 64, 1. Octavia's pathetic plea', *Latomus* 51: 606–10.

Batinski, E. E. (1990–1) 'Horace's rehabilitation of Bacchus', *CW* 84: 361–78.

(1992–3) 'Lucan's Catalogue of Caesar's troops: paradox and convention', *CJ* 88: 19–24.

Batstone, W. W. (1990) '*Etsi*: a tendentious hypotaxis in Caesar's plain style', *AJPh* 111: 348–60.

(1991) 'A narrative Gestalt and the force of Caesar's style', *Mnemosyne* 44: 126–36.

Battaglia, D. ed. (1995) 'Problematizing the self: a thematic introduction', in *Rhetorics of self-making*, Berkeley, CA: 1–15.

Beazley, J. D. (1947) 'The Rosi Krater', *JHS* 67: 1–9.

Benardete, S. (1968) 'The aristeia of Diomedes and the plot of the *Iliad*', *Agon* 2: 10–38.

Benario, H. W. (1975) *An introduction to Tacitus*, Athens, Georgia.

Bengtson, H. (1972) *Zu den Proskriptionen des Triumvirn*, SBAW München. Heft 3.

Bérard, F. (1993) 'Les *Commentaires* de César: autobiographie, mémoires ou histoire?' in Baslez, Hoffmann and Pernot (1993): 85–95.

Betensky, A. (1978) 'Neronian style, Tacitean content: the use of ambiguous confrontations in the *Annals*', *Latomus* 37: 419–35.

Bleicken, J. (1990) *Zwischen Republik und Prinzipat. Zum Charakter des Zweiten Triumvirats*, Abh. Göttingen 185.

Bloch, A. (1970) '*Arma uirumque* als heroisches Leitmotiv', *MH* 27: 206–11.

Boes, J. (1981) 'A propos du *De Divinatione*. Ironie de Cicéron sur le *nomen* et l'*omen* de Brutus', *REL* 59: 164–76.

Bonds, W. S. (1985) 'Two combats in the *Thebaid*', *TAPhA* 115: 225–35.

Borges, J. L. (1970) *Labyrinths*, Harmondsworth.

Bosworth, A. B. (1972) 'Asinius Pollio and Augustus', *Historia* 21: 441–73.

Botteri, P. (1989) '*Stasis*: le mot grec, la chose romaine', *Métis* 4.1: 87–100.

Boyle, A. J. ed. (1983) *Seneca Tragicus. Ramus essays on Senecan drama*, Berwick, Victoria.

ed. (1990) *The imperial Muse*, Vol. 2: *Flavian epicist to Claudian*, Bendigo, Victoria.

ed. (1993) *Roman epic*, London.

ed. (1995) *Roman literature and ideology. Essays for J. P. Sullivan*, Bendigo, Victoria.

Bradley, K. R. (1973) '*Tum primum reuocata ea lex*', *AJPh* 94:172–81.

Bramble, J. (1982) 'Lucan', in Kenney and Clausen (1982): 533–57, 872–4.

Braund, S. H. (Morton) ed. (1989) *Satire and society in ancient Rome*, Exeter.

(1996) *Juvenal Satires book* I, Cambridge.

(1996A) 'Ending epic: Statius, Theseus and a merciful release', *PCPhS* 42: 1–23.

Bremmer, J. and N. M. Horsfall (1987) *Roman myth and mythography*, *BICS Supplement* 52.

Brennan, D. B. (1969) 'Cordus and the burial of Pompey', *CPh* 64: 103–4.

Brisson, J.-P. ed. (1969) *Problèmes de la guerre à Rome*, Paris.

Broch, H. (1983) *The death of Virgil*, Harmondsworth.

Brown, J. (1994) 'Into the woods: narrative studies in the *Thebaid* of Statius with special reference to books IV–VI', PhD Thesis, Cambridge. (= forthcoming (1998) *Narrative studies in Statius' Thebaid*, Oxford).

Brown, P. M. (1993) *Horace Satires I*, Warminster.

Brown, P. and S. Levinson (1987) *Politeness. Some universals in language usage*, Cambridge.

Brummet, B. (1980) 'Towards a theory of silence as a political strategy', *The Quarterly Journal of Speech* 66: 289–303.

Brunt, P. A. (1986) 'Cicero's *officium* in the civil war', *JRS* 76: 12–32.

Budick, S. and W. Iser eds. (1989) *Languages of the unsayable. The play of negativity in literature and literary theory*, New York.

Buffiére, F. (1956) *Les mythes d'Homère et la pensée grecque*, Paris.

Bullock, A. (1962) *Hitler. A study in tyranny*, Harmondsworth.

Burian, P. (1985) 'Logos and pathos: the politics of the *Suppliant Women*', in Burian (1985A): 129–55.

ed. (1985A) *Directions in Euripidean criticism. A collection of essays*, Durham, NC.

Calvino, I. (1979) *Invisible cities*, London.

Cameron, A. ed. (1989) *History as text. The writing of ancient history*, London.

Canfora, L. (1980) 'Proscrizioni e dissesto sociale nella repubblica Romana', *Klio* 62: 425–37.

(1996) 'Fonti Latine e uso del Latino in Appiano', *Atti dei Convegni Lincei* 125, *Filellenismo e tradizionalismo a Roma nei primi due secoli dell'impero (Roma, 27–28 aprile 1995)*: 85–95.

Carlson, G. I. (1977–8) 'From Numantia to necking: Horace *Ode* 2.12', *CW* 71: 441–8.

Carter, J. M. (1982) *Suetonius, Diuus Augustus*, Bristol.

(1991) *Julius Cæsar, The Civil War Books I & II*, Warminster.

(1993) *Julius Caesar, The Civil War Book III*, Warminster.

Cavell, S. (1987) '*Coriolanus* and interpretations of politics ("Who does the wolf love?")', in *Disowning knowledge: in six plays of Shakespeare*, Cambridge: 143–77.

Certeau, M. de (1990[2]) *L'invention du quotidien*, 1: *Arts de faire*, Paris.

Charlesworth, M. P. (1927) 'Livia and Tanaquil', *CR* 41: 55–7.

Chevallier, R. (1976) *Roman roads*, London.

Chiaro, D. (1992) *The language of jokes. Analysing verbal play*, London.

Citroni, M. (1983) 'Occasioni e piani di destinazione nella lirica di Orazio', *MD* 10–11: 154–6.

Clarke, M. L. (1981) *The noblest Roman. Marcus Brutus and his reputation*, London.

Classen, C. J. (1988) 'Tacitus – historian between Republic and Principate', *Mnemosyne* 41: 93–116.

Clavel-Lévêque, M. (1984) *L'empire en jeux. Espace symbolique et pratique sociale dans le monde romain*, Paris.

Clay, D. (1983) *Lucretius and Epicurus*, Ithaca, NY.

Coffey, M. (1976) *Roman satire*, London.

Colace, P. R. (1982) 'Il nuovo Callimaco di Lille, Ovidio e Stazio', *RFIC* 110: 140–9.

Collins, J. H. (1959) 'On the date and interpretation of the *Bellum Civile*', *AJPh* 60: 113–32.

(1972) 'Caesar as political propagandist', *ANRW* I.1: 922–66.

Connor, P. (1987) *Horace's lyric poetry: the force of humour*, Victoria.

Conrad, P. (1984) *The art of the city*, Oxford.

Conte, G. B. (1968) 'La guerra civile nella rievocazione del popolo: Lucano 2.67–233', *Maia* 20: 224–53.

(1970) 'Ennio e Lucano', *Maia* 22: 132–8. (= Conte (1988): 25–32)

(1974) *Saggio di commento a Lucano Pharsalia 6, 118–260. L'aristia di Sceva*, Pisa. (= Conte (1988): 43–112)

(1988) *La 'Guerra Civile' di Lucano. Studi e prove di commento*, Urbino.

Cooke, H. P. (1925) *In the days of our youth*, London.

Cooper, H. M., A. Auslander Munich and S. Merrill Squier eds. (1989) *Arms and the woman. War, gender, and literary representation*, Chapel Hill, NC.

Costa, C. D. N. ed. (1973) *Horace*, London.

Croisille, J.-M. and Fauchère, P.-M. eds. (1982) *Neronia 1977*, Clermont-Ferrand.

Crosby, T. (1978) 'The structure of Livy's history', *LCM* 3: 113–19.

Crowley, T. (1987) 'Language and hegemony: principles, morals and pronun-
    ciation', *Textual Practice* 1: 278–96.
    (1989) 'Bakhtin and the history of the language', in Hirschkop and Shepherd
    (1989): 68–90.
Culler, J. (1988) 'The call of the phoneme: introduction', in Culler (1988A): 1–
    16.
    ed. (1988A) *On puns. The foundation of letters*, Oxford.
Currie, H. McLennan (1985) 'Horace, *Carmina* II, 1.29–36 and Virgil, *Aen.* I,
    459–60', *LCM* 10: 110–11.
Curtius, E. R. (1953) *European literature and the Latin Middle Ages*, London.
Dahlmann, H. (1965) 'Zu Horaz, *C.* 2, 1, 25–8', *RhM* 108: 142–6.
Davies, M. (1989) *The epic cycle*, Bristol.
Davis, L. J. (1985) *Resisting novels*, London.
Derrida, J. (1976) *Of grammatology*, Baltimore, MD.
    (1978) 'The retrait of metaphor', *Enclitic* 2: 5–33.
    (1989) 'How to avoid speaking' in Budick and Iser (1989): 3–70.
    (1995) 'Dialanguages', in *Points*, Stanford, CA: 132–55.
    (1993) 'Awaiting (at) the arrival', in *Aporias*, Stanford, CA: 43–81.
Detienne, M. (1979) *Dionysos slain*, Baltimore, MD.
Dettmer, H. (1983) *Horace: a study in structure*, Hildesheim.
Develin, R. (1983) 'Tacitus and techniques of insidious suggestion', *Antichthon*
    17: 64–95.
Devillers, O. (1994) *L'art de la persuasion dans les Annales de Tacite*, Collection
    Latomus 223.
Dewar, M. (1991) *Statius' Thebaid IX*, Oxford.
Dick, B. (1963) 'The technique of prophecy in Lucan', *TAPhA* 94: 37–49.
    (1967) '*Fatum* and *fortuna* in Lucan's *Bellum Ciuile*', *CPh* 62: 235–42.
Dickinson, E. (1975) *The complete poems of Emily Dickinson*, London.
Dickison, S. K. (1977) 'Claudius: *Saturnalicius princeps*', *Latomus* 36: 634–47.
Dollimore, J. and A. Sinfield eds. (1985) *Political Shakespeare. New essays in
    cultural materialism*, Manchester.
Dominik, W. J. (1993) 'From Greece to Rome: Ennius' *Annales*', in Boyle
    (1995): 37–58.
    (1994) *The mythic voice of Statius: power and politics in the Thebaid*, Leiden.
Doors, The (1967) *The Doors*, Elektra.
Dorey, T. A. ed. (1966) *Latin historians*, London.
    ed. (1969) *Tacitus*, London.
Drakakis, J. ed. (1985) *Alternative Shakespeares*, London.
Drew, P. and A. Wootton eds. (1988) *Erving Goffman. Exploring the interaction
    order*, Cambridge.
Drummond, A. (1978) 'Some observations on the order of consuls' names',
    Athenaeum 56: 80–108.

Dryden, J. (1970) 'Discourse on satire' in *Selected criticism*, Oxford: 208–78.

Due, O. S. (1962) 'An essay on Lucan', *C&M* 23: 68–132.

Dunkle, J. (1967) 'The Greek tyrant and Roman political invective in the Late Republic', *TAPhA* 98: 151–71.

DuQuesnay, I. M. Le M. (1976) 'Vergil's Fourth *Eclogue*', *PLLS* 1: 25–99.

(1984) 'Horace and Maecenas: the propaganda value of *Sermones* 1', in Woodman and West (1984): 19–58.

Dyer, R. R. (1990) 'Rhetoric and intention in Cicero's *Pro Marcello*', *JRS* 80: 17–30.

Dylan, B. (1963) *The freewheelin' Bob Dylan*, CBS.

(1964) *The times they are a-changin'*, CBS.

(1964A) *Another side of Bob Dylan*, CBS.

(1974) *Blood on the tracks*, CBS.

(1978) *Street legal*, CBS.

(1984) *Real live*, CBS.

(1990) *Under the red sky*, CBS.

(1993) *World gone wrong*, CBS.

(1995) *Unplugged*, CBS.

Dyson, S. L. (1970) 'The portrait of Seneca in Tacitus', *Arethusa* 3: 71–83.

Eden, P. T. (1962) 'Caesar's style: inheritance versus intelligence', *Glotta* 40: 74–117.

Edwards, C. (1994) 'Beware of imitations: theatre and the subversion of imperial identity', in Elsner and Masters (1994): 83–97.

Eisenberger, W. (1980) 'Bilden die horazischen *Oden* 2, 1–12 einen Zyklus?', *Gymnasium* 87: 262–74.

Elsner, J. (1994) 'Constructing decadence: the representation of Nero as imperial builder', in Elsner and Masters (1994): 112–27.

Elsner, J. and J. Masters eds. (1994) *Reflections of Nero. Culture, history, and representation*, London.

Euben, J. P. ed. (1986) *Greek tragedy and political theory*, Berkeley, CA.

(1990) *The tragedy of political theory. The road not taken*, Princeton, NJ.

Evans, J. de Rose (1992) *The art of persuasion. Political propaganda from Aeneas to Brutus*, Michigan.

Federspiel, J. F. (1984) *The ballad of Typhoid Mary*, London.

Feeney, D. C. (1984) 'The reconciliations of Juno', *CQ* 34: 179–94.

(1986) 'History and revelation in Vergil's underworld', *PCPhS* 32: 1–24.

(1986A) '*Stat magni nominis umbra*. Lucan on the greatness of Pompeius Magnus', *CQ* 36: 239–43.

(1991) *The gods in epic: poets and critics of the classical tradition*, Oxford.

(1992) '*Si licet et fas est*: Ovid's *Fasti* and the problem of free speech under the Principate', in Powell (1992): 1–25.

Feichtinger, B. (1992) '*Ad maiorem gloriam Romae.* Ideologie und Fiktion in der Historiographie des Livius', *Latomus* 51: 3–33.

Fornara, C. W. (1983) *The nature of history in ancient Greece and Rome*, California.

Foucault, M. (1979) *Discipline and punish*, New York.

   (1981) 'The order of discourse', in Young (1981): 51–78. (= Shapiro (1984): 108–38)

Fraenkel, E. (1957) *Horace*, Oxford.

Fränkel, H. (1967) 'Über philologische Interpretation am Beispiel von Caesars Gallischem Krieg', in Rasmussen (1967): 165–88.

Frieden, K. (1985) *Genius and monologue*, Ithaca, NY.

Frow, J. (1989) 'Discourse and power', in Gane (1989): 198–217.

Fugier, H. (1968) 'Un thème de la propagande Césarienne dans le *De Bello Ciuili*: César, maître du temps', *Bulletin de la Faculté de Lettres à Strasbourg* 47: 127–33.

Fuhrmann, M. (1959) *proscriptio*, *RE* XXIII²: 2440–4.

Gabba, E. (1956) *Appiano e la storia delle guerre civili*, Florence.

   (1984) 'The historians and Augustus', in Millar and Segal (1984): 61–88.

Gane, M. ed. (1989) *Ideological representation and power in social relations*, London.

Gärtner, H. A. (1975) *Beobachtungen zu Bauelementen in der antiken Historiographie, besonders bei Livius und Cæsar*, *Historia Einzelschriften* 25.

Gelzer, M. (1969) *Caesar. Politician and statesman*, Oxford.

George, D. B. (1988) 'Lucan's Caesar and Stoic οἰκείωσις theory: the Stoic fool', *TAPhA* 118: 331–41.

   (1991) 'Lucan's Cato and Stoic attitudes to the Republic', *CA* 10: 237–58.

Giglioli, P. P. ed. (1972) *Language and social context*, Harmondsworth.

Gilmartin, K. (1973–4) 'Tacitean evidence for Tacitean style', *CJ* 69: 216–22.

Gingras, M. T. (1991/2) 'Annalistic format, Tacitean themes, and the obituaries of *Annals* 3', *CJ* 87: 241–56.

Ginsburg, J. (1981) *Tradition and theme in the Annals of Tacitus*, New York.

   (1986) 'Speech and allusion in Tacitus, *Annals* 3.49–51 and 14.48–49', *AJPh* 107: 525–41.

   (1993) '*In maiores certamina*: past and present in the *Annals*', in Luce and Woodman (1993): 86–103.

Goffman, E. (1972) 'The neglected situation', in Giglioli (1972): 61–6.

Goldberg, S. M. (1989) 'Poetry, politics, and Ennius', *TAPhA* 119: 247–61.

   (1995) *Epic in Republican Rome*, Oxford.

Goodyear, F. R. D. (1972) *The Annals of Tacitus*, Vol. 1: *Annals 1. 1–54*, Cambridge.

(1982) 'History and biography', in Kenney and Clausen (1982): 639–66, 890–5.

Gordon, R. (1987) 'Lucan's Erictho', in Whitby, Hardie and Whitby (1987): 231–41.

Gotoff, H. C. (1984) 'Towards a practical criticism of Caesar's prose style', *ICS* 9: 1–18.

Götting, M. (1969) *Hypsipyle in der Thebais des Statius*, Wiesbaden.

Gowers, E. J. (1993) *The loaded table. Representations of food in Roman literature*, Oxford.

Gowing, A. M. (1992) *The triumviral narratives of Appian and Cassius Dio*, Michigan.

Graham, J. F. ed. (1985) *Difference in translation*, Ithaca, NY.

Gransden, K. W. (1984) *Virgil's Iliad. An essay on epic narrative*, Cambridge.

Gratwick, A. S. (1982) 'Ennius' *Annales*' in Kenney and Clausen (1982): 60–76, 804–7.

Green, C. M. C. (1991) '*Stimulos dedit aemula uirtus*: Lucan and Homer reconsidered', *Phoenix* 45: 234–49.

(1994) 'The necessary murder – myth, ritual, and civil war in Lucan, Book 3', *CA* 13: 203–33.

Greenblatt, S. (1985) 'Invisible bullets: renaissance authority and its subversion, *Henry IV* and *Henry V*', in Dollimore and Sinfield (1985): 18–47.

Griffin, M. T. (1984) *Nero. The end of a dynasty*, London.

Grimal, P. (1943) *Les jardins romains à la fin de la République et aux deux premiers siècles de l'Empire*, Paris.

(1980) 'En attendant Pharsale, Lucain poète de l'attente', *VL* 77: 2–11.

(1990) 'L'*Ode* à Pollion, au sécond livre des *Carmina* d'Horace', in von Albrecht and Schubert (1990): 165–71.

Gruen, E. S. (1966) 'Cicero and Licinius Calvus', *HSPh* 71: 222–5.

Haffter, H. (1957) 'Dem schwanken Zünglein lauschend wachte Cäsar dort', *MH* 14: 118–26. (= Rutz (1970): 264–76)

Haller, B. (1967) *C. Asinius Pollio als Politiker und zeitkritischer Historiker*, diss., Münster.

Hamilton, M. (1916) *Dead yesterday*, London.

Hampton, T. (1990) 'Shakespeare (Corneille): writing after history', in *Writing after history: the rhetoric of exemplarity in Renaissance literature*, Ithaca, NY: 198–236.

Handke, P. (1971) *Offending the audience and self-accusation*, Methuen, London.

Hanson, V. D. (1989) *The Western way of war. Infantry battle in classical Greece*, London.

Hardie, A. (1983) *Statius and the Silvae. Poets, patrons and epideixis in the Graeco-Roman world*, Liverpool.

Hardie, P. (1990) 'Ovid's Theban history: the first "Anti-Aeneid"?', *CQ* 40: 224-35.

(1990A) 'Flavian epicists on Virgil's epic technique', in Boyle (1990): 3-20.

(1993) *The epic successors of Virgil. A study in the dynamics of a tradition*, Cambridge.

(1993A) 'Tales of unity and division in imperial Latin epic', in Molyneux (1993): 57-71.

Harland, R. (1987) *Superstructuralism*, London.

Harries, B. (1993) '"Strange meeting": Diomedes and Glaucus in *Iliad* 6', *G&R* 40: 133-46.

Harrison, S. J. (1992) 'The arms of Capaneus. Statius, *Thebaid* 4.165-77', *CQ* 42: 247-52.

Haury, A. (1966) 'Ce brave Varron ... (César, *Ciu.*, II, 17-21)', in *Mélanges d'archéologie, d'épigraphie et d'histoire offerts à Jérome Carcopino*, Paris: 507-13.

Häussler, R. (1978) *Das historische Epos von Lucan bis Silius und seine Theorie*, Heidelberg.

Havelange, M., N. Henne, H. and P. P. Delvaux and J. N. Pirlot (1982) 'Lecture plurielle de Tacite *Annales*, XIII, 16', *LEC* 50: 141-59, 237-56.

Heaney, S. and T. Hughes eds. (1982) *The rattle bag*, London.

Heath, S. (1972) *The nouveau roman, a study in the practice of writing*, London.

Heinemann, M. (1985) 'How Brecht read Shakespeare', in Dollimore and Sinfield (1985): 202-30.

Hellegouarc'h, J. (170) 'Le principat de Camille', *REL* 48: 112-32.

Henderson, J. (1986) 'Becoming a heroine (IST): Penelope's Ovid', *LCM* 11: 7-10, 21-4, 37-40, 67-70, 81-5, 114-20.

(1987) 'Suck it and see (Horace, *Epode* 8)', in Whitby, Hardie and Whitby (1987): 105-18.

(1989) 'Satire writes woman: *Gendersong*', *PCPhS* 215: 50-80.

(1989A) 'Not "Women in Roman satire" but "When satire writes 'Woman'"', in Braund (1989): 89-125, 139-49.

(1990) 'Livy and the inventory of history', *LCM* 15: 120-1.

(1993) 'Be alert (your country needs lerts): Horace, *Satires* 1.9', *PCPhS* 39: 67-93.

(1994) 'To recognize Bosnia/Statius, *Thebaid* 11.407-8', *LCM* 19: 25-7.

Hendrickson, G. L. (1906) 'The *De Analogia* of Julius Caesar: its occasion, nature, and date, with additional fragments', *CPh* 1: 97-120.

Herbert, F. (1969) *Dune Messiah*, London.

Hernadi, P. ed. (1989) *The rhetoric of interpretation and the interpretation of rhetoric*, Durham, NC.

Hershkowitz, D. (1994) 'Sexuality and madness in Statius' *Thebaid*', *MD* 33: 123-47.

(1995) 'Madness in Greek and Latin epic', DPhil. thesis, Oxford. (= forth-coming (1998) *The madness of epic: reading insanity from Homer to Statius*, Oxford)

(1995A) 'Patterns of madness in Statius' *Thebaid*', *JRS* 85: 52–64.

Hexter, R. and D. Selden eds. (1992) *Innovations of Antiquity*, New Haven.

Hill, D. E. (1990) 'Statius' *Thebaid*: a glimmer of light in a sea of darkness', in Boyle (1990): 98–118.

Hinard, F. (1985) *Les proscriptions de la Rome républicaine*, Paris and Rome.

Hirschkop, K. and D. Shepherd eds. (1989) *Bakhtin and cultural theory*, Manchester.

Hodge, R. and G. Kress (1988) *Social semiotics*, Cambridge.

(1993²) *Language as ideology*, London.

Holland, R. (1932) *The lost generation*, London.

Homeyer, H. (1977) 'Die Quellen zu Ciceros Tod', *Helikon* 17: 56–96.

Howe, N. P. (1985) 'In defense of the encyclopedic mode: on Pliny's *Preface* to *Natural History*', *Latomus* 44: 561–76.

Hübner, U. (1972) 'Hypallage in Lucans *Pharsalia*', *Hermes* 100: 577–600.

(1974) 'Eine übersehene Metonymie in Lucans *Pharsalia*', *RhM* 119: 350–7.

(1975) 'Studien zur Pointentechnik in Lucans *Pharsalia*', *Hermes* 103: 200–11.

(1976) 'Der Sonnenaufgang vor Pharsalus. Zu Lucan 7, 1–3', *Philologus* 120: 107–16.

(1984) 'Episches und elegisches am Anfang des dritten Buches der *Pharsalia*', *Hermes* 112: 227–39.

Huff, D. (1964) *Score. The strategy of taking tests*, Harmondsworth.

Hunink, V. (1992) *M. Annaeus Lucanus, Bellum Civile, Book III*, Amsterdam.

(1992A) 'Lucan's last words', *Collection Latomus* 217: 390–407.

Irwin, J. T. (1975) *Doubling & incest/Repetition & revenge. A speculative reading of Faulkner*, Baltimore MD.

(1980) *American hieroglyphics*, New Haven, CT.

Isager, J. (1991) *Pliny on art and society. Pliny the Elder's chapters on the history of art*, London.

Jal, P. (1963) *La guerre civile à Rome. Etude littéraire et morale*, Paris.

(1984) *Abrégés des Livius, de l'histoire romaine. Tite-Live, tome XXXIV¹⁻²*, Paris.

Jaworski, A. (1992) *The power of silence. Social and pragmatic perspectives*, London.

Jed, S. (1989) 'The scene of tyranny: violence and the humanistic tradition', in Armstrong and Tennenhouse (1989): 29–44.

Jocelyn, H. D. (1972) 'The poems of Quintus Ennius', *ANRW* II.2: 987–1026.

Johnson, W. R. (1987) *Momentary monsters. Lucan and his heroes*, Ithaca, NY.

Joly, D. (1983) 'A propos de mosaïque. Quelques réflexions des poètes', *Caesarodunum* XVII: 231–7. (= *Mosaïque. Recueil d'Hommages à H. Stern*, Paris)

Juhnke, H. (1972) *Homerisches in römischer Epik flavischer Zeit. Untersuchungen zu Szenennachbildungen und Strukturentsprechungen in Statius' Thebais und Achilleis und in Silius' Punica*, Munich. (= *Zetemata* 53)

Keegan, J. (1976) *The face of battle*, London.

Kehoe, D. (1985) 'Tacitus and Sallustius Crispus', *CJ* 80: 247–54.

Keitel, E. (1981) 'Tacitus on the deaths of Tiberius and Claudius', *Hermes* 109: 206–14.

(1984) 'Principate and civil war in the *Annals* of Tacitus', *AJPh* 105: 306–25.

Keller, O. E. (1891) *Lateinische Volksetymologie und verwandtes*, Berlin and Leipzig.

Kellman, S. G. (1980) *The self-begetting novel*, London.

Kenney, E. J. (1979) '*Incertum an et ante gnarum*', *Farrago* Michaelmas 1: 5–8.

Kenney, E. J. and Clausen, W. V. eds. (1982) *The Cambridge history of classical literature*, Vol. 2: *Latin literature*, Cambridge.

Kermode, F. (1966) *The sense of an ending. Studies in the theory of fiction*, Oxford.

Klingner, F. (1955) 'Beobachtungen über Sprache und Stil des Tacitus am Anfang des 13. Annalenbuches', *Hermes* 83: 187–200.

Köhnken, A. (1973) 'Das Problem der Ironie bei Tacitus', *MH* 30: 32–50.

Korzeniewski, D. ed. (1970) *Die römische Satire*, Darmstadt.

Kraggerud, E. (1979) 'Die *Satire* 1.7 des Horaz', *SO* 54: 91–109.

Kraner, F., F. Hofmann, H. Meusel and H. Oppermann (1959¹²) *C. Iulii Caesaris Commentarii De Bello Ciuili*, Berlin.

Kraus, C. S. (1991) '*Initium turbandi omnia a femina ortum est*: Fabia Minor and the election of 367 B.C.', *Phoenix* 45: 314–25.

(1994) '"No second Troy": topoi and refoundation in Livy, Book V', *TAPhA* 124: 267–89.

(1994A) *Livy, Ab urbe condita book VI*, Cambridge.

Kytzler, B. (1986) 'Zum Aufbau der statianischen "*Thebais*". Pius Coroebus, *Theb.* 1.557–692', *ANRW* II.32.5: 2913–24.

Laistner, M. L. W. (1963) *The greater Roman historians*, Berkeley, CA.

Lakoff, R. T. (1990) 'Winning hearts and minds: pragmatic homonymy and beyond', in *Talking power. The politics of language*, New York: 239–53.

LaPenna, A. (1952) 'Tendenze e arte del *Bellum civile* di Cesare', *Maia* 5: 191–233.

Lapidge, M. (1979) 'Lucan's imagery of cosmic dissolution', *Hermes* 107: 344–70.

Lausberg, G. (1985) 'Lucan und Homer', *ANRW* II.32.3: 1565–622.

Leach, E. W. (1988) *The rhetoric of space. Literary and artistic representations of landscape in Republican and Augustan Rome*, Princeton.

(1993) 'Horace's Sabine topography in lyric and hexameter verse', *AJPh* 114: 271–302.

Lecercle, J.-J. (1990) *The violence of language*, London.

Le Clair, T. (1989) *The art of excess. Mastery in contemporary American fiction*, Illinois.

Lee, A. (1990) *Realism and power. Postmodern British fiction*, London.

Leith, D. and G. Myerson (1989) *The power of address. Explorations in rhetoric*, London.

Lesueur, R. (1990) *Stace, Thébaïde Livres I–IV*, Paris.

Levin, H. (1953) *Christopher Marlowe the overreacher*, London.

Lewis, P. E. (1985) 'The measure of translation effects', in Graham (1985): 31–62.

Lloyd-Jones, H. and P. Parsons (1983) *Supplementum Hellenisticum*, Berlin.

Lounsbury, R. C. (1975) 'The death of Domitius in the *Pharsalia*', *TAPhA* 105: 209–12.

(1976) 'History and motive in book 7 of Lucan's *Pharsalia*', *Hermes* 104: 210–39.

Luce, T. J. (1971) 'Design and structure in Livy: 5.32–55', *TAPhA* 102: 265–302.

(1977) *Livy: the composition of his history*, Princeton, NJ.

(1986) 'Tacitus' conception of historical change: the problem of discovering the historian's opinions', in Moxon, Smart and Woodman (1986): 143–57.

Luce, T. J. and A. J. Woodman eds. (1993) *Tacitus and the Tacitean tradition*, Princeton.

Ludwig, W. (1957) 'Zu Horaz, C.2, 1–12', *Hermes* 85: 336–45.

Lyne, R. O. A. M. (1978) *Ciris. A poem attributed to Vergil*, Cambridge.

Lynn-George, M. (1988) *Epos: word, narrative and the Iliad*, London.

Maclean, M. (1988) *Narrative as performance. The Baudelairean experiment*, London.

Maftei, M. (1976) *Antike Diskussionen über die Episode von Glaukos und Diomedes im VI. Buch der Ilias*, Meisenheim am Glan.

Mahood, M. (1970) 'Words and names', in Ure (1970): 76–8.

Malamud, M. A. (1995) 'Happy birthday, dead Lucan: (P)raising the dead in *Silvae* 2.7', in Boyle (1995): 169–98.

Manea, N. (1992) *On clowns. The dictator and the artist*, London.

Manhire, E. B. (1985) *Zoetropes*, Manchester.

Manning, C. E. (1975) 'Acting and Nero's conception of the Principate', *G&R* 22: 164–75.

Marcovich, M. ed. (1989) *Silver and late Latin poetry*, Illinois. (= *ICS* 14.1–2)

Marcus, J. (1989) 'Corpus/corps/corpse: writing the body in/at war', in Cooper, Auslander Munich and Merrill Squier (1989): 124–67.

Marin, L. (1978) *Le récit est un piège*, Paris.

(1988) *Portrait of the king*, Basingstoke.

Marquez, G. C. (1983) *Chronicle of a death foretold*, Picador, London.

Marshall, B. ed. (1980) *Vindex humanitatis. Essays in honour of J. H. Bishop*, Armidale, New England.

Marti, B. M. (1966) 'Cassius Scaeva and Lucan's *inuentio*', in Wallach (1966): 239–57.

(1975) 'Lucan's narrative techniques', *Parola del Passato* 30: 74–90.

Martin, R. H. (1955) 'Tacitus and the death of Augustus', *CQ* 5: 123–8.

(1969) 'Tacitus and his predecessors', in Dorey (1969): 117–47.

(1981) *Tacitus*, London.

Martindale, C. A. (1976) 'Paradox, hyperbole and literary novelty in Lucan's *De Bello Ciuili*', *BICS* 23: 45–54.

(1980) 'Lucan's nekuia', *Collection Latomus* 168: 367–77.

(1981) 'The epic of ideas: Lucan's *De Bello Ciuili* and *Paradise Lost*', *Comparative Criticism* 3: 133–56.

(1984) 'The politician Lucan', *G&R* 31: 64–79.

(1993) *Redeeming the text. Latin poetry and the hermeneutics of reception*, Cambridge.

Masters, H. V. (1996) 'After the battle. A comparison of Lucan and Statius with regard to battlefields, bodies and burial', unpublished MPhil. thesis, Cambridge.

Masters, J. (1992) *Poetry and civil war in Lucan's Bellum Civile*, Cambridge.

(1994) 'Deceiving the reader. The political mission of Lucan, *Bellum Ciuile*', in Elsner and Masters (1994): 151–77.

Mastronarde, D. J. (1970) 'Seneca's *Oedipus*: The drama in the word', *TAPhA* 101: 291–315.

Matthews, V. J. (1973) 'Some puns on Roman *cognomina*', *G&R* 20: 19–24.

Mayer , R. (1982) 'What caused Poppaea's death?', *Historia* 31: 248–9.

(1986) 'Geography and Roman poets', *G&R* 33: 47–54.

McCulloch, G. (1989) *The game of the name*, Oxford.

McCulloch, H. Y. (1984) *Narrative cause in the Annals of Tacitus*, Beiträge zur klassischen Philologie 160, Königstein.

McDermott, E. A. (1992) 'Horace, Maecenas, and *Odes* 2, 17', *Hermes* 110: 211–28.

McDonnell, M. (1990) 'Borrowing to bribe soldiers: Caesar's *De Bello Civili* 1.39', *Hermes* 118: 55–66.

McGuire, D. T. (1990) 'Textual strategies and political suicide in Flavian epic', in Boyle (1990): 21–45.

McGushin, P. (1980) *Sallust. Bellum Catilinae*, Bristol.

Mehlman, J. (1977) *Revolution and repetition. Marx/Hugo/Balzac*, Berkeley, CA.

Miles, G. B. (1995) *Livy. Reconstructing early Rome*, Ithaca, NY.

Millar, F. (1973) 'Triumvirate and Principate', *JRS* 63: 50–67.

Millar, F. and E. Segal eds. (1984) *Caesar Augustus. Seven aspects*, Oxford.

Miller, P. A. (1991) 'Horace, Mercury, and Augustus, or the poetic ego of *Odes* 1–3', *AJPh* 112: 365–88.

Minadeo, R. (1982) *The golden plectrum. Sexual symbolism in Horace's Odes*, Amsterdam.

Mitchell, W. J. T. ed. (1982/3) *The politics of interpretation*, Chicago.

Miura, Y. (1981) 'Zur Funktion der Gleichnisse im 1 und 7 Buch von Lucans *Pharsalia*', *GB* 10: 217–32.

Moles, J. L. (1983) 'Virgil, Pompey and the *Histories* of Asinius Pollio', *CW* 76: 287–8.

(1987) 'Politics, philosophy, and friendship in Horace *Odes* 2, 7', *QUCC* 27: 59–72.

(1993) 'Livy's preface', *PCPhS* 39: 141–68.

Molyneux, J. H. ed. (1993) *Nottingham Classical Literature Studies* Vol. 1, Nottingham.

Montefiore, S. Sebag (1992) *King's Parade*, Harmondsworth.

Moret, J.-M. (1984) *Oedipe, la Sphinx et les Thébains. Essai de mythologie iconographique*, Paris.

Moretti, F. (1987) *The way of the world. The Bildungsroman in European culture*, London.

Morgan, J. D. (1990) 'The death of Cinna the poet', *CQ* 40: 558–9.

Morgan, M. G. (1971) 'Lucius Cotta and Metellus. Roman campaigns in Illyria during the second century', *Athenaeum* 49: 271–301.

Most, G. W. (1992) '*Disiecti membra poetae*: the rhetoric of dismemberment in Neronian poetry', in Hexter and Selden (1992): 391–419.

Moxon, I. S., J. D. Smart and A. J. Woodman eds. (1986) *Past perspectives. Studies in Greek and Roman historical writing*, Cambridge.

Mutschler, F.-H. (1975) *Erzählstil und Propaganda in Cæsars Kommentarien*, Heidelberg.

Nadeau, Y. (1980) 'Speaking structures. Horace *Odes*, 2.1 to 2.19', *Collection Latomus* 168: 177–222.

Narducci, E. (1973) 'Il tronco di Pompeo (Troia e Roma nella *Pharsalia*)', *Maia* 25: 317–25.

(1979) *La provvidenza crudele. Lucano e la distruzione dei miti augustei*, Pisa.

(1980) 'Cesare e la patria (Ipotesi su *Phars*. 1.185–192)', *Maia* 32: 175–8.

(1985) 'Ideologia e tecnica allusiva nella *Pharsalia*', *ANRW* II.32.3: 1538–64.

Nash, W. (1985) *The language of humour. Style and technique in comic discourse*, London.

Néraudau, J.-P. (1983) 'Asinius Pollion et la poésie', *ANRW* II.30.3: 1732–50.

Newmyer, S. (1983) 'Imagery as a means of character portrayal in Lucan', *Collection Latomus* 180: 226–52.

Nippel, W (1995) *Public order in ancient Rome*, Cambridge.

Nisbet, R. G. M. and M. Hubbard (1978) *A commentary on Horace Odes Book II*, Oxford.

Nugent, S. G. (1966) 'Statius' Hypsipyle: following in the footsteps of the *Aeneid*', *Scholia* 5: 46–71.

Nussbaum, G. (1981) 'Sympathy and empathy in Horace', *ANRW* II.31.3: 2093–158.

O'Donnell, J. J. (1978) 'The prologue to Lucan', *CW* 72: 235–7.

Ogilvie, R. M. (1965) *A commentary on Livy, Books 1–5*, Oxford.

(1982) 'Caesar', in Kenney and Clausen (1982): 281–5, 841–2.

(1982A) 'Livy', in Kenney and Clausen (1982): 458–66, 857–9.

(1984) '*Titi Livi Lib*. XCI', *PCPhS* 210: 116–25.

O'Higgins, D. (1988) 'Lucan as *uates*', *CA* 7: 208–26.

Oldfather, W. A. and G. Bloom (1926–7) 'Caesar's grammatical theories and his own practise', *CJ* 22: 584–602.

Oliensis, E. (1991) 'Canidia, Canicula, and the decorum of Horace's *Epodes*', *Arethusa* 24: 107–38.

Opelt, I. (1957) 'Die Seeschlacht vor Massilia bei Lucan', *Hermes* 85: 435–45.

(1980) 'Töten' und "Sterben" in Caesars Sprache', *Glotta* 58: 103–19.

Oppermann, H. (1967) 'Aufbau. Anfang des *Bellum Civile*', in Rasmussen (1967): 138–64.

(1977) 'Curio – *Miles Caesaris*? (Caesars Urteil über Curio in *B.C.* 2.42)', *Hermes* 105: 351–68.

Ormand, K. (1994) 'Lucan's *auctor vix fidelis*', *CA* 13: 38–55.

Orwell, G. (1954) *Nineteen eighty-four*, Harmondsworth.

Otto, A. (1971²) *Die Sprichwörter und sprichwörtlichen Redensarten der Römer*, Hildesheim.

Owen, E. (1935–6) 'Caesar in American schools prior to 1860', *CJ* 31: 212–22.

Palmeri, F. (1990) *Satire in narrative. Petronius, Swift, Gibbon, Melville, and Pynchon*, Austin, TX.

Pascucci, G. (1973) 'Interpretazione linguistica e stilistica del Cesare autentico', *ANRW* I.3: 488–522.

Pelling, C. B. R. (1979) 'Plutarch's method of work in the Roman Lives', *JHS* 99: 74–96.

(1986) 'Plutarch and Roman politics', in Moxon, Smart and Woodman (1986): 159–87.

(1988) *Plutarch, Life of Antony*, Cambridge.

Perrotta, G. (1948) 'Cesare scrittore', *Maia* 1: 5–32.

Petre, Z. (1971) 'Thèmes dominants et attitudes politiques dans les *Septs Contre Thèbes* d'Eschyle', *StudClass* 13: 15–28.

Petrey, S. (1990) *Speech acts and literary theory*, London.

Pfligersdorffer, G. (1959) 'Lucan als Dichter des geistigen Widerstandes', *Hermes* 87: 344–77.

Phelan, J. ed. (1989) *Reading narrative: form, ethics, ideology*, Columbus, OH.

Phillips, O. C. (1968) 'Lucan's grove', *CPh* 63: 296–300.

Pink Floyd (1987) *A momentary lapse of reason*, EMI.

Plass, P. (1988) *Wit and the writing of history. The rhetoric of historiography in imperial Rome*, Madison, WI.

  (1995) *The game of death in ancient Rome. Arena sport and political suicide*, Madison, WI.

Pocock, J. G. A. (1984) 'Verbalizing a political act: toward a politics of speech', in Shapiro (1984): 25–43.

Poe, J. P. (1983) 'The sinful nature of the protagonist of Seneca's *Oedipus*', in Boyle (1983): 140–8.

Pointon, M. (1990) *Naked authority. The body in Western painting 1830–1908*, Cambridge.

Poiss, T. (1992) '*Plenum opus aleae*. Zum Verhältnis von Dichtung und Geschichte in Horaz *carm.* 2, 1', *WS* 105: 129–53.

Pollitt, J. J. (1983) *The art of Rome c. 753 B.C.–A.D. 337*, Cambridge.

Pomeroy, A. J. (1988) 'Livy's death notices', *G&R* 35: 172–83.

Porter, D. H. (1987) *Horace's poetic journey. A reading of Odes 1–3*, Princeton, NJ.

Powell, A. ed. (1992) *Roman poetry and propaganda in the age of Augustus*, Bristol.

Pratt, F. (1952) *A short history of the Civil War (Ordeal by fire)*, New York.

Quint, D. (1993) *Epic and empire: politics and generic form from Virgil to Milton*, Princeton, NJ.

Rabinowitz, P. J. (1989) 'End sinister: closure as disruptive force', in Phelan (1989): 120–31.

Racine, J. (1982) *La Thébaïde, ou Les frères ennémis*, in *Théâtre complet* 1, Paris.

Radermacher, L. (1970) 'Horaz *Satire* 1, 7', in Korzeniewski (1970): 275–83.

Raditsa, L. (1973.) 'Julius Cæsar and his writings', *ANRW* 1.3: 417–56.

Rajan, B. (1985) *The form of the unfinished. English poetics from Spenser to Pound*, Princeton.

Rambaud, M. (1962) 'Essai sur le style du *Bellum Ciuile*', *IL* 14: 60–9, 108–13.

  (1966²) *L'art de la déformation historique dans les Commentaires de César*, Paris.

  (1985) 'L'aruspice Arruns chez Lucain au livre 1 de la *Pharsale* (vv. 584–638)', *Latomus* 44: 281–300.

Rasmussen, D. ed. (1967) *Caesar*, Darmstadt. (= *Wege der Forschung* 43)

Rawson, E. (1985) *Intellectual life in the late Roman Republic*, London.

Redfern, W. (1984) *Puns*, Oxford.

Reeve, M. D. (1988) 'The transmission of Florus' *Epitoma de Tito Livio* and the *Periochae*', *CQ* 38: 477–91.

  (1991) 'The transmission of Florus and the *Periochae* again', *CQ* 41: 453–83.

Reijgwart, E. J. (1993) 'Zur Erzählung in Caesars *Commentarii*, Der "unbekannte" Erzähler des *Bellum Gallicum*', *Philologus* 137: 18–37.

Rich, J. W. (1989) 'Dio on Augustus', in Cameron (1989): 86–110.

Richlin, A. (1992) 'Reading Ovid's rapes', in Richlin (1992A): 138–79.

ed. (1992A) *Pornography and representation in Greece and Rome*, Oxford.

Richter, W. (1977) *Caesar als Darsteller seiner Taten*, Heidelberg.

Rimmon-Kenan, S. ed. (1987) *Discourse in psychoanalysis and literature*, London.

Roberts, M. (1988) 'The revolt of Boudicca (Tacitus, *Annals* 14.29–39) and the assertion of *Libertas* in Neronian Rome', *AJPh* 109: 118–32.

Roller, M. B. (1996) 'Ethical contradiction and the fractured community in Lucan's *Bellum Civile*', *CA* 15: 319–47.

Rosaldo, R. (1989) 'Death in the ethnographic present', in Hernadi (1989): 173–82.

Rosenberger, V. (1992) *Bella et Expeditiones. Die antike Terminologie der Kriege Roms*, Stuttgart.

Rosenmeyer, P. A. (1982) 'The tradition of Kallimakhos as innovator: a reexamination in the light of the *Victoria Berenikes*', unpublished BA thesis, Cambridge.

Rosner-Siegel, J. A. (1983) 'The oak and the lightning. Lucan, *Bellum Civile* 1.135–57', *Athenaeum* 61: 165–77.

Ross, D. O. (1975) *Backgrounds to Augustan poetry. Gallus, elegy and Rome*, Cambridge.

Rowe, G. O. (1967) 'Dramatic structures in Cæsar's *Bellum Civile*', *TAPhA* 98: 399–414.

Rowland, R. J. (1969) 'The significance of Massilia in Lucan', *Hermes* 97: 204–8.

Rubiés, J.-P. (1994) 'Nero in Tacitus and Nero in Tacitism: the historian's craft', in Elsner and Masters (1994): 29–47.

Rudd, N. (1982) *The Satires of Horace*, Bristol.

Rushdie, S (1981) *Midnight's children*, London.

Russell, J. (1980) 'Caesar's last words. A reinterpretation', in Marshall (1980): 123–8.

Rutz, W. (1960) '*Amor mortis* bei Lucan', *Hermes* 88: 462–75.

ed. (1970) *Lucan*, Darmstadt. (= *Wege der Forschung* 235)

Ryberg, I. S. (1942) 'Tacitus' art of innuendo', *TAPhA* 73 (1942) 383–404.

Sallmann, K. (1987) 'Die Verschiebung der Genera in der Pollio Ode 2, 1 des Horaz', in *Filologia e forme letterarie, studie offerti a F. della Corte*, Urbino, Vol. III: 69–87.

Santirocco, M. S. (1980) 'Strategy and structure in Horace *C.* 2.12', *Collection Latomus* 168: 223–36.

(1984) 'The Maecenas *Odes*', *TAPhA* 114: 241–53.

(1986) *Unity and design in Horace's Odes*, Chapel Hill, NC.

Santoro L'Hoir, F. (1990) 'Heroic epithets and recurrent themes in *Ab Urbe Condita*', *TAPhA* 120: 221–41.

Saumagne, C. (1955) 'La "passion" de Thraséa', *REL* 33: 241–57.

Saylor, C. F. (1978) '*Belli spes improba*: the theme of walls in Lucan *Pharsalia* 6', *TAPhA* 108: 243–57.

(1982) 'Curio and Antaeus: the African episode of Lucan *Pharsalia* 4', *TAPhA* 112: 169–77.

(1986) 'Wine, blood, and water: the imagery of Lucan *Pharsalia* IV.148–401', *Eranos* 84: 149–56.

(1990) '*Lux extrema*: Lucan, *Pharsalia* 4.402–581', *TAPhA* 120: 291–300.

Scarry, E. (1985) *The body in pain. The making and unmaking of the world*, Oxford.

Schetter, W. (1960) *Untersuchungen zur epischen Kunst des Statius*, Wiesbaden.

(1962) 'Die Einheit des Prooemium zur *Thebais* des Statius', *MH* 19: 204–17.

Schlicher, J. J. (1936) 'The development of Caesar's narrative style', *CPh* 31: 212–24.

Scodel, R. (1987) 'Horace, Lucilius, and Callimachean polemic', *HSPh* 91: 199–215.

Scott, D. (1988) *Pictorialist poetics. Poetry and the visual arts in nineteenth-century France*, Cambridge.

Scott, R. D. (1974) 'The death of Nero's mother', *Latomus* 33: 105–15.

Segal, C. (1969) 'Horace, *Odes* 2.6', *Philologus* 113: 235–53.

(1971) *The theme of the mutilation of the corpse in the Iliad*, Mnemosyne Supplement 17.

Segal, E. ed. (1983) *Oxford readings in Greek tragedy*, Oxford.

Seitz, K. (1965) 'Der pathetische Erzählstil Lucans', *Hermes* 93: 204–32.

Sellar, W. C. and R. J. Yeatman (1960) *1066 and all that*, Harmondsworth.

Serpieri, A. (1985) 'Reading the signs: towards a semiotics of Shakespearean drama', in Drakakis (1985): 119–43.

Serres, M. (1991) *Rome. The book of foundations*, Stanford, CA.

Shackleton Bailey, D. R. (1982) *Profile of Horace*, London.

Shapiro, M. ed. (1984) *Language and politics*, Oxford.

Shattuck, R. (1974) *Proust*, London.

Shatzman, I. (1974) 'Tacitean rumours', *Latomus* 33: 549–78.

Sheets, G. (1983) 'Ennius lyricus', *ICS* 8: 22–32.

Shoaf, R. A. (1978) '"*Certius exemplar sapientis uiri*": rhetorical subversion and subversive rhetoric in *Pharsalia* 9', *Philological Quarterly* 57: 143–54.

Simon, B. (1987) 'Tragic drama and the family: the killing of children and the killing of story-telling', in Rimmon-Kenan (1987): 152–75.

Simon, C. (1969) *La bataille de Pharsale*, Paris.

Simpson, J. (1991) *From the house of war*, London.

Sinclair, P. (1995) 'Political declensions in Latin grammar and oratory, 55 BCE–CE 39', in Boyle (1995): 92–109.

Skutsch, O. (1968) *Studia Enniana*, London.

Smolenaars, J. J. L. (1994) *Statius Thebaid VII*, Leiden.

Spacks, P. M. (1986) *Gossip*, Chicago.

Spence, S. (1988) *Rhetorics of reason and desire. Vergil, Augustine, and the troubadors*, Ithaca, NY.

Stadter, P. A. (1972) 'The structure of Livy's history', *Historia* 21: 287–307.

Stahl, H.-P. (1985) *Propertius: 'love' and 'war'. Individual and state under Augustus*, Berkeley, CA.

Stray, C. (1994) 'The smell of Latin grammar: contrary imaginings in English classrooms', *Bulletin of the John Rylands Library of Manchester* 76: 201–20.

Suits, T. A. (1974) 'The structure of Livy's thirty-second book', *Philologus* 118: 257–65.

Sukenick, R. (1975) *98.6*, New York.

Sullivan, D. (1976) 'Innuendo and the "weighted alternative" in Tacitus', *CJ* 71: 312–26.

Syme, R. (1939) *The Roman revolution*, Oxford.

   (1958) *Tacitus*, Oxford.

   (1959) 'Livy and Augustus', *HSPh* 64: 27–87. (= (1979) *Roman papers* I, Oxford: 400–54)

   (1974) 'History or biography: the case of Tiberius Caesar', *Historia* 23: 481–96. (= (1984) *Roman papers* III, Oxford: 937–52)

   (1986) *The Augustan aristocracy*, Oxford.

Syndikus, H.-P. (1958) *Lucans Gedicht vom Bürgerkrieg*, diss., Munich.

   (1972) *Die Lyrik des Horaz*, Darmstadt.

Tannen, D. (1989) *Talking voices. Repetition, dialogue, and imagery in conversational discourse*, Cambridge.

Tannen, D. and M. Saville-Troike eds. (1985) *Perspectives on silence*, Norwood, NJ.

Tatum, J. (1989) *Xenophon's imperial fiction. On the education of Cyrus*, Princeton, NJ.

Taylor, L. R. (1925) 'Horace's equestrian career', *AJPh* 46: 161–70.

Teichmann, J. (1986) *Pacifism and the just war*, Oxford.

Thalmann, W. G. (1978) *Dramatic art in Aeschylus's Seven against Thebes*, New Haven, CT.

Thomas, R. F. (1983) 'Callimachus, the *Victoria Berenices*, and Roman poetry', *CQ* 33: 92–113.

   ed. (1988) *Virgil: Georgics I–II, III–IV*, Cambridge.

Tolstoy, L. N. (1957) *War and peace*, Harmondsworth.

Townend, G. B. (1960) 'The sources of the Greek in Suetonius', *Hermes* 88: 98–120.

Turney-High, H. H. (1949) *Primitive war, its practices and concepts*, Columbia, SC.

Tylee, C. M. (1990) *The great war and woman's consciousness. Images of militarism and womanhood in women's writings, 1914–64*, London.

Ullman, B. (1942) 'History and tragedy', *TAPhA* 73: 25–53.

Ure, P. ed. (1970) *Shakespeare, Julius Caesar, a selection of critical essays*, London.

Usher, S. (1969) *The historians of Greece and Rome*, London.

Van Dam, H. J. (1984) *P. Papinius Statius. Siluae book II*, Leiden.

Van Rooy, C. A. (1971) 'Arrangement and structure of Satires in Horace, *Sermones*, Book I: Satire 7 as related to Satires 10 and 8', *AClass* 14: 67–90.

Vernant, J.-P. (1982) 'From Oedipus to Periander: lameness, tyranny, incest in legend and history', *Arethusa* 15: 19–38.

Vernant, J.-P. and Vidal-Naquet, P. (1986) *Mythe et tragédie en Grèce ancienne*. T.II, Paris.

Vessey, D. W. T. C. (1970) 'The myth of Linus and Coroebus in Statius' *Thebaid* I, 557–672', *AJPh* 91: 315–31.

(1970A) 'Notes on the Hypsipyle episode in Statius, *Thebaid* 4–6', *BICS* 17: 44–54.

(1971) 'Thoughts on Tacitus' portrayal of Claudius', *AJPh* 92: 385–409.

(1973) *Statius and the Thebaid*, Cambridge.

(1982) 'Flavian epic', in Kenney and Clausen (1982): 558–96, 874–80.

(1986) '*Pierius menti calor incidit*: Statius' epic style', *ANRW* II.32.5: 2965–3019.

Veyne, P. (1983) *L'Elégie érotique romaine. L'amour, la poésie et l'occident*, Paris.

(1984) *Writing history*, Manchester.

Viarre, S. (1982) 'Caton en Libye: l'histoire et la métaphore (Lucan, *Pharsale*, 9, 294–949)', in Croisille and Fauchère (1982): 103–10.

Vidal-Naquet, P. (1986) 'Les boucliers des héros. Essai sur la scène centrale des *Sept contre Thèbes*', 'Oedipe entre deux cités. Essai sur *l'Oedipe à Colone*', in Vernant and Vidal-Naquet (1986): 115–47, 175–211.

Vielberg, M. (1987) *Pflichten, Werte, Ideale. Eine Untersuchung zu den Wertvorstellungen des Tacitus, Hermes Einzelschrift* 52.

Walbank, F. W. (1972) *Polybius*, Berkeley, CA.

(1975) ' "Symploke" in Polybius' Histories', *YCS* 24: 197–212.

Waldenburg, H. (1990) *The Berlin wall book*, London.

Walker, B. (1952) *The Annals of Tacitus. A study in the writing of history*, Manchester.

Wallace-Hadrill, A. (1983) *Suetonius*, London.

(1986) 'Image and authority in the coinage of Augustus', *JRS* 76: 66–87.

Wallach, L. ed. (1966) *The classical tradition, literary and historical studies in honor of Harry Caplan*, Ithaca, NY.

Wallmann, P. (1989) *Triumviri rei publicae constituendae. Untersuchungen zur politischen Propaganda im zweiten Triumvirat (43–30 v. Chr.)*, Frankfurt.

Walpole, H. (1969) *The castle of Otranto: a Gothic story*, Oxford.

Walsh, P. G. (1961) *Livy. His historical aims and methods*, Cambridge.

(1966) 'Livy', in Dorey (1966): 115–42.

(1974) *Livy*, *G&R* New Surveys 8, Oxford.

Waugh, P. (1984) *Metafiction. The theory and practice of self-conscious fiction*, London.

Weaver, P. R. C. (1972) *Familia Caesaris*, Cambridge.

Weigel, R. D. (1992) *Lepidus. The tarnished triumvir*, London and New York.

Wensler, A. F. (1989) 'Lucan und Livius zum Januar 49 v. Chr. Quellen-kundliche Beobachtungen', *Historia* 38: 250–4.

West, D. (1973) 'Horace's poetic technique in the "*Odes*"', in Costa (1973): 29–58.

Whitby, M., P. Hardie and M. Whitby eds. (1987) *Homo viator. Classical essays for John Bramble*, Bristol.

White, A. (1989) 'Hysteria and the end of carnival: festivity and bourgeois neurosis', in Armstrong and Tennenhouse (1989): 157–70.

Whitehead, D. (1979) 'Tacitus and the loaded alternative', *Latomus* 38: 474–95.

Who, The (1969) *Tommy*, Reaction.

Wilburys, The travelling (1988) *Volume 1*, Wilbury.

Wilkinson, L. P. (1963) *Golden Latin artistry*, Cambridge.

Will, E. L. (1982) 'Ambiguity in Horace *Odes* I, 4' *CPh* 77: 240–5.

Wille, G. (1973) *Der Aufbau des livianischen Geaschichtswerks*, Amsterdam.

Williams, B. (1990) 'Reading Tacitus' Tiberian Annals', in Boyle (1990): 140–66.

Williams, M. F. (1985) 'Caesar's Bibracte narrative and the aims of Caesarian style', *ICS* 10: 215–26.

Wills, C. (1989) 'Upsetting the public: carnival, hysteria and women's texts', in Hirschkop and Shepherd (1989): 130–51.

Wills, G. (1983) 'Critical inquiry (*Kritik*) in Clausewitz', in Mitchell (1982/3): 159–80.

Wilson, J. D. (1970) 'Ben Jonson and "*Julius Caesar*"', in Ure (1970): 241–52.

Winkler, J. J. and F. Zeitlin eds. (1990) *Nothing to do with Dionysos? Athenian drama in its social context*, Princeton, NJ.

Wiseman, T. P. (1974) 'The last of the Metelli', in *Cinna the poet and other Roman essays*, Leicester: 176–91.

(1991) *Death of an emperor. Flavius Josephus*, Exeter.

Wistrand, E. (1976) *The so-called Laudatio Turiae*, Lund.

Woodman, A. J. (1974) '*EXEGI MONUMENTUM*. Horace, *Odes* 3.30', in Woodman and West (1974): 115–28.

(1977) *Velleius Paterculus. The Tiberian narrative (2.94–131)*, Cambridge.

(1983) *Velleius Paterculus. The Caesarian and Augustan narrative (2.41–93)*, Cambridge.

(1988) *Rhetoric in classical historiography. Four studies*, Beckenham.

(1992) 'Nero's alien capital. Tacitus as paradoxographer (*Annals* 15.36–7)', in Woodman and Powell (1992): 173–88.

(1993) 'Amateur dramatics at the court of Nero: *Annals* 15.48–74', in Luce and Woodman (1993): 104–28.

Woodman, A. J. and R. H. Martin (1996) *The Annals of Tacitus, Book 3*, Cambridge.

Woodman, T. and J. Powell eds. (1992) *Author and audience in Latin literature*, Cambridge.

Woodman, T. and D. West eds. (1974) *Quality and pleasure in Latin poetry*, Cambridge.

eds. (1984) *Poetry and politics in the age of Augustus*, Cambridge.

Wordsworth, A. (1987) 'Derrida and Foucault: writing the history of historicity', in Attridge, Bennington and Young (1987): 116–25.

Wright, E. (1984) *Psychoanalytic criticism. Theory in practice*, London.

Wylie, G. J. (1993) 'P. Ventidius – from *nouus homo* to "military hero" ', *AClass* 36: 129–41.

Yeats, W. B. (1962) *Selected poetry*, London.

Young, R. ed. (1981) *Untying the text*, London.

Zaffagno, E. (1981) *Initiative semantiche di Tacito Annalista*, Genoa.

Zanker, P. (1988) *The power of images in the age of Augustus*, Michigan.

Zecchini, G. (1980) 'La morte di Catone e l'opposizione intellettuale a Cesare e ad Augusto', *Athenaeum* 58: 39–56.

(1982) 'Asinio Pollione: dall' attività politica alla riflessione storiografica', *ANRW* II.20.3: 1265–96.

Zeitlin, F. I. (1982) *Under the sign of the shield. Semiotics and Aeschylus' Seven against Thebes*, Rome.

(1986) 'Thebes: theater of self and society in Athenian drama', in Euben (1986): 101–41.

(1990) 'Thebes: theater of self and society in Athenian drama', in Winkler and Zeitlin (1990): 130–67.

Ziegler, K. (1966²) *Das hellenistische Epos*, Leipzig.

Zwierlein, O. (1986) 'Lucans Caesar in Troja', *Hermes* 114: 460–78.

(1988) 'Statius, Lucan, Curtius Rufus und das hellenistische *Epos*', *RhM* 131: 67–84.

(1990) 'Unterdrückte Klagen beim Tod des Pompeius (Lucan 7, 43) und des Cremutius Cordus (Sen. *Consol. Marc.* 1, 2)', *Hermes* 118: 184–91.

Index of passages discussed

General index